PHASES OF THOUGHT
IN ENGLAND

PHASES OF THOUGHT
IN ENGLAND

BY

MEYRICK H. CARRÉ

OXFORD
AT THE CLARENDON PRESS
1949

Oxford University Press, Amen House, London E.C. 4

GLASGOW NEW YORK TORONTO MELBOURNE WELLINGTON

BOMBAY CALCUTTA MADRAS CAPE TOWN

Geoffrey Cumberlege, Publisher to the University

PRINTED IN GREAT BRITAIN

PREFACE

THE design of the summary review of thought in England offered in this work is stated in the introductory chapter. Here I wish to record my obligation to a multitude of scholars whose writings have helped me to interpret the doctrines and arguments of the past. The acknowledgements in the notes represent a small proportion of my debt. And I desire to express my gratitude to Professor L. J. Russell, who generously read the typescript copy of the book and proposed a number of emendations.

M. H. C.

THE UNIVERSITY,
  BRISTOL

CONTENTS

INTRODUCTION

THE following chapters offer a brief survey of successive
moments in the life of philosophy in England from the first age
of Christian culture to the close of the nineteenth century. A
general inspection of so vast and complex a range of ideas must
acquiesce in a large measure of exclusion and suppression. It
must ignore at every stage a multitude of interesting details and
overlook many significant qualifications. But the attempt to
descry beyond the topographical particulars of this or that
mental district the wider expanses of the country is a justifiable
impulse. We desire to scan the broad motions of thought as
well as to examine the niceties of intellectual history. The study
of English speculation and criticism has suffered from concentration upon restricted tracts of the long record. Attention has
been especially confined to a few thinkers of the seventeenth
and eighteenth centuries whose investigations are peculiarly
interesting to the present tendencies of our inquiries. Yet these
thinkers are not wholly intelligible apart from the assumptions
of preceding generations, and for the proper understanding of
some of their problems and postulates we have to look far back
into the history of ideas. But there are large areas of earlier
reflection in England that call for recognition. If English
philosophy be defined in a narrow sense it is doubtless true that
'the real beginning of English philosophy is to be dated from
Bacon's break with Scholasticism'.[1] But it is not necessary to
define it in this exclusive sense. We are not compelled to limit
our view of fundamental discussion in England to recent explorations that have been written in the English tongue and
under the sway of physical science. By adopting a broader
perspective we bring into sight earlier reaches of native thought
that cannot be abruptly divided from later manifestations; and
we enlarge our vision in the process.

It is true that from the latter decades of the seventeenth
century much English discussion on first principles pursued a
line of its own markedly different from the movement of thought
in France and Germany. There emerged a distinctive British
method and doctrine that, apart from a brief interruption at

J. Seth, *English Philosophers and Schools of Philosophy*, London, 1912, p. 10.

the end of the nineteenth century, has coloured our outlook to the present day. In comparison with this special trend the older and far more extensive periods of philosophical inquiry in England appear to exhibit considerably less individual character. They appear even to vanish as separate forces. From the first era of ecclesiastical culture until the sixteenth century intellectual activity in England was a portion of the organic mental interests of Catholic Europe. Its problems and methods and language were those of the common mind of civilization. Scholars moved freely between the great centres of learning in England and on the Continent, and whether a treatise on metaphysics or cosmology was written in Soissons or Bath, Canterbury or Chartres was an irrelevant and accidental factor. Many philosophers of British birth taught at Paris, many learned men from France, Germany, and Italy became masters in the faculties of philosophy and theology at Oxford. The international commonwealth of thought was little affected by national differences, for thought in every quarter of the West was commanded by the inviolable system of theological truth. In fine the endeavour to trace a course of English inquiry distinct in identity from the universal culture of Christendom appears to be a perversely artificial proceeding.

But the objection is superficial. To say the least, the interfusion and uniformity of Catholic thought during these ages may be admitted and yet it may be interesting and valuable to observe the manifold developments of philosophical discussion as they unfolded in one locality. Even though Oxford or Cambridge or Durham were not the centres in which the fundamental and subtle controversies of the Middle Ages were most powerfully or most clearly debated, all the issues that agitated the schools were reflected in them and the history of our national culture demands a narration of this sequence of discussion. The deliberations over the principles of being, the conflict between Aristotelian and Neo-Platonic views of knowledge, the debate over theological and philosophical conceptions of causation, can be followed as they developed on English soil without denying the unity of ecclesiastical scholarship. Important accounts of medieval thought on these lines have been published in France and Germany, in Italy and Spain. Little has been done in relation to the earlier periods of thought in

England. Admirable studies of isolated portions of the story have been made and there have been detailed investigations of a few individual masters; but there has been little endeavour to view the course of inquiry as a continuous history. I hasten to add that the present survey professes to make a very limited contribution to such a history. It is concerned with the revolution of a few general notions; it passes lightly over some periods of discussion (the fifteenth century, for example); and it ignores the work of many thinkers who were influential in their day. It proposes, however, in the earlier chapters to observe aspects of the course of medieval hypotheses from the point of view of the schools in England; and, with due recognition of the constant interchange of notions throughout the European domain of thought, this is an investigation that could be fruitfully extended. But philosophical thought in England during the earlier stretches of our history has further claims to consideration. The inquiries of English thinkers concerning the general features of human experience possess, at many critical points of the debate, a sharper significance than that of a local mirror of the common development of ideas. It has become manifest that issues often developed in the English schools on lines that differed strikingly from developments elsewhere. 'Peut-être serait-il inexact de parler d'une école d'Oxford au moyen âge', observes M. Gilson, 'mais il y eut certainement un esprit d'Oxford au XIIIᵉ siècle.' And at other periods qualities of thought appeared that confer special interest on the intellectual scene in this country during the Middle Ages and the period of the Renaissance. We may venture to put forward more definite claims without presumption. At many junctures in the history of European thought English scholars made distinctive, even decisive, contributions to philosophical or theological theory; and several fresh departures in the principles of scholastic criticism and construction sprang from their arguments. Notable instances are the monastic culture of the Anglo-Saxons in the eighth century, the work of the Franciscan school of philosophers at Oxford in the thirteenth, and the critical nominalism of the English universities in the fourteenth. In the course even of our rapid sketch will be seen further grounds for maintaining that in the intellectual movement of Europe men of English race played valuable parts in the collective discussions of the schools, and that, while it cannot be held that English scholastic thought formed as a whole a distinct body of doctrine comparable to the utilitarian empiricism of later times, it manifested traits that influenced the rational explorations of the Middle Ages.

Bacon, Hobbes, Locke, Hume, Mill, and Bradley are not the only ornaments of philosophical speculation in our history. Anglo-Saxon England produced the greatest scholar of the Dark Ages in Bede. In the twelfth century this land gave birth to several of the pioneers of the earlier renaissance, such as Adelard of Bath, John of Salisbury, and Robert Grosseteste. During the culminating period of scholastic thought there appeared in the country a series of men who left their mark upon the philosophy of the West, Roger Bacon, Robert Kilwardby, John Peckham; and the first comprehensive synthesis of philosophy and theology in the schools was composed by Thomas of York. About the year 1270 there was born in the north of Great Britain one of the acutest minds of medieval inquiry, John Duns Scotus; and the age of criticism and disintegration that followed was dominated by the logic of William of Ockham. And there are many lesser thinkers worthy of commemoration in these ages, some of whom are mentioned in the earlier chapters of the present book.

There are two preliminary questions that require to be answered before we set out on our survey. It is necessary to explain what is included in 'thought'; and some definition must be given to the other term of our title, the term 'phases'.

I propose to describe certain facets of the schemes of ideas that have at different epochs determined the mental perspective in England. There are persistent bodies of belief that govern an epoch, guiding inquiry in many fields, directing intellectual interest, and shaping the methods of reflection. These enduring intellectual traditions are forms of intelligibility. They are expectations or demands that the world should be understood according to certain co-ordinated sets of principles. In the effort to explain the multifarious elements of experience, both in detail and as a whole, men have assumed at different eras different types of order in the light of which the variegated scene with which they are confronted has been perceived and interpreted. The nature of the order that provides the basis of the mode of explanation acceptable to a period is determined partly by the dominant interests of the period and partly by the range of knowledge generally available; and the former is the more fundamental factor. The broad philosophical outlook of a section of history is formulated within a context of values, of preferences, and of emotional propensities. The methods and interpretations that rule an epoch of speculation are intimately related to the prevailing moral and religious inclinations of the age, to the kind of hopes and dreads with which its experience is coloured. And the emotional currents that direct a fashion of thought serve to account for the tenacity with which the fashion is held in the face of new theoretical constructions.

Such persistent manners of thought can be distinguished at many levels of generality and in reference to various provinces. On a liberal view of mental history it is possible to descry three broad systems that have governed men's mode of understanding. These systems may be named Augustinianism, Aristotelianism, and Newtonianism; but the titles embrace far more than the doctrines of Augustine, Aristotle, and Newton. They include remote developments and applications of those doctrines. They comprise amalgamations of the original strains with new and even with opposing principles. Yet each of these outlooks on experience manifests a distinctive character, a discernible concatenation of tenets relating to knowledge and reality that can be traced through the changing conditions of thought. In the second chapter I describe the main features of the first of these schemes of principles in the form in which it was unfolded by Anselm in the eleventh century, and we shall observe the persistent vitality of important elements of this chain of ideas throughout later reflection. But already in the time of Anselm an extraordinary renaissance of thought had begun to sweep over Europe. Large sections of Greek science were rediscovered and a new system of logic was directed to the analysis of the fundamental problems of knowledge. I shall seek in the third chapter to view the first phase of this re-fashioning of beliefs through the eyes of two Englishmen, Adelard of Bath and John of Salisbury. The former reflects the revival of Greek naturalism and mathematics, the latter exhibits the changes in logic and metaphysics. The fruit of these remarkable developments appears in the thirteenth century.

In Chapter IV I portray the advance of the second great plan of thought, Aristotelianism, and delineate its distinguishing marks. But we shall perceive the continuing influence of the older tradition, now limiting and counterbalancing Aristotelian interpretations, now opposing them. Indeed the energy and variety of discussion during the golden age of metaphysics flowed from the acute tensions between the doctrines of contemporary Augustinianism or Neo-Platonism and the new knowledge and method derived from the study of Aristotle. A restatement of philosophical principles became an urgent task. The reshaping of conceptions at the end of the thirteenth century will be described, but we shall find that Augustinian ways of thought, largely in Arabic guises, were tenaciously repeated at Oxford and Cambridge in the following period.

Times of bold construction are succeeded by decades of criticism and sceptical analysis. This stocktaking occurred in the eighteenth and twentieth centuries after periods of comprehensive speculation. It occurred in the fourteenth. Strong currents flowed in England that pressed against the established positions. There appeared in the schools a line of radical critics who attacked not only the Augustinianism of the theologians but also the Aristotelian principles of the philosophers. We shall notice the lines of this great revolt in Chapter V; we shall catch some notes of the bitter disputes which turned Oxford into a field of battle. Points of difference included the relation between particulars and universals, between perception and thought, and the status of Platonic ideas. But the most disturbing effect of the advance of nominalism was the growing division between reason and faith.

Our narrative will move quickly over the long transitional age that precedes the rise of the next phase of thought. A great historian has remarked that the fifteenth century, if we exclude its last twenty years, was intellectually barren beyond any other epoch since the Norman Conquest. But it is also true that it has been least explored, and it is probable that further investigation into the conceptions of men such as Gascoine would qualify our judgement. Yet the revulsion from reason is patent and there begins a steady decline of speculative interest. We shall review in Chapter VI aspects of the eclectic and unorganized profusion of ideas that were thrown up by the revival of classical culture and the ecclesiastical revolution. The old framework of conceptions relating to the universe and to man's place in the scheme of things was shaken, but no acceptable substitute gained ground; and in the Elizabethan poets and dramatists the ancient forms were assumed. The scholastic landmarks reappeared: forms and acts, the hierarchy of perfections. Hooker expounded a metaphysic on which the Anglican Church could stand, but we shall find that this philosophy is substantially of the schools.

But revolutionary changes in ideas had been accumulating for generations. In the seventeenth century there arises a new theory of experience. Our third phase of thought enters with Francis Bacon, Robert Boyle, and the Royal Society, and already we can distinguish its characteristic marks and contrast them with those of the pre-scientific outlook. The wider applications of 'the new philosophy' by Descartes and Hobbes opened men's eyes to fearful dangers, and the latter portion of this decisive period brought a reaction to Augustinianism. The great scientific philosophers proposed compromises between the moral and religious principles of existence and the mechanism of nature. Now were shaped the distinctive principles and methods that prevailed in England for two hundred years. The chief architect of the system was Newton, its philosopher was Locke.

Here we shall visit familiar, too familiar scenes. But I hope to treat the theories of empiricism and naturalism from 1700 to 1900 as items in the single impulse of Newtonianism and to view the immaterialist, sceptical, and materialist developments of the eighteenth century as incidental consequences of the initial system of assumptions. The determined effort made by the Scottish school to meet the sceptical position did not succeed in subverting the classical positions; we shall discover the scientific tissue of principles, mental atomism, associationism, phenomenalism, relativism, and the rest, settled firmly in the minds of the teachers of the people in the reigns of George IV and Victoria; there are notable expressions of it in 1829, 1843, and 1855. The principles propounded by Locke and Newton continued to be associated with the wonderful developments of naturalist theory that arose in England at this time. And the great constructions of scientific philosophy put forward in the latter part of the nineteenth century rest upon the eighteenth-century conceptions of knowledge. Two magnificent generalizations provided the framework of the new vision of the universe, the law of the persistence of energy and the theory of evolution. But the Synthetic Philosophy of Herbert Spencer consummated the programme sketched at the outset of the latest phase of thought by Francis Bacon.

One further revolution of English speculation falls within the scope of our survey. Romantic aspirations and religious insights rose in rebellion against the aridity of the classic philosophy and against the positivism and agnosticism of its modern type. In the seventeenth century men had turned from the menace of 'the new philosophy' to Platonic idealism and Augustinianism. In the nineteenth they found salvation in a fresh idealism borrowed from German masters. Exploring knowledge and reality with the clues opened by Kant and Hegel they declared the total insufficiency of the historic English philosophy. They cut away the foundations of empiricism, they exposed the incoherence of the scientific system of ultimate truth, and they revealed a comprehensive spiritual reality that is manifested in all the processes of existence. There is little direct connexion between this idealism and the Augustinian Realism of the earlier phase of thought. But there are remarkable affinities, especially with the heterodox Arabian forms of Augustinianism. The close of our survey will awaken echoes of Anselm and of Roger Bacon.

Such, in bare outline, is the plan of this conspectus of phases of thought. It is necessary to add a few words concerning another aspect of the story.

I have referred to the moral predispositions that guide the effort of rational interpretation. Inquiries into the nature of existence have been directed throughout our history by religious and theological interests. And the theology that has animated reflection has postulated a design of principles that has profoundly influenced the course of speculation at all periods. The unquestioned chain of beliefs that formed the main dogmas of Christian monotheism controlled the categories of rational inquiry during the greater part of the history. The view of reality given by faith promoted conceptions of knowledge and experience, such as those of cause and substance and of the relation between the sensible and the intellectual order, that penetrated the philosophical search at every stage. Until the latest phase exploration and analysis is conducted within the orbit of revealed truth and the convictions that sprang from divine authority exercised constant and decisive force on metaphysical theory. In the earlier chapters I refer to some of the broader effects of theological assumptions upon thought in England. A principal and obvious demand upon experience was the interpretation of rational order in purposive terms, in terms of a will acting in relation to a consciously conceived end. The demand was expressed in manifold forms, from the naïve animism and symbolism of the eighth century to the mechanical teleology of the early nineteenth. The cruder tendencies of this outlook were balanced by deeper metaphysical notions that had descended from patristic theology. They became articulate in England in the eleventh century. The central idea in this more profound circle of beliefs is the doctrine of absolute self-sufficient being. The belief was an inheritance of Hebraic-Christian theology and of Neo-Platonic metaphysics and it inspires Augustinianism in all its many shapes, from the treatises of Anselm to the Gifford lectures. I shall refer to it in the second chapter and suggest the manner in which it influenced views of change, development, and causation; and I shall touch on the cardinal position of the idea of creation.

More special consequences of theological principles will be described in Chapter I. Without entering the domain of dogmatic theology we shall glance at certain preoccupations that have coursed through our history and imposed themselves upon intellectual understanding. These preconceptions have been due to the unique authority of the Christian scriptures. From the dawn of speculation in the land to the nineteenth century, the Bible was held to be divinely inspired and its assertions, whether they related to theology or history or natural philosophy, were accepted without criticism. The theory of inspiration underwent, indeed, important changes as the environment of thought progressed, but from the beginning to the end of our record the sacred position of the Bible exercised a powerful control upon secular inquiry, and no account of thought in England can overlook its influence. It was associated with a peculiar logic of investigation and this special method of thought will be briefly described in the first chapter. Throughout the medieval era the Scriptures, since they were the chief instruments of revelation, discharged a commanding function in philosophical inquiry. They lost their sovereign position gradually with the appearance in the sixteenth century of new conceptions of divine revelation.

The incessant clashes between the theological metaphysics and the conceptions of natural reason will come into prominence at all divisions of the story. There was an explosion in England in the thirteenth century, and thereafter there was a steady tendency towards separating the two spheres of thought, despite indefatigable efforts to unite them in one scheme. But in the seventeenth century the theory of secondary causes advanced to the front of the stage. The decisive change was the reassertion of Epicurean physics and its association with the new methods of the natural philosophers at Oxford and London. I shall take up the story of the adjustments that were attempted between Newtonianism and theology in Chapter VIII in describing the physico-theology of the apologists and the deism of their opponents. And in Chapter IX we shall observe the curious compromise with the historic religious predispositions of English thought offered by the scientific philosophers of the nineteenth century.

The phases of thought of our title indicate, therefore, modes of understanding that manifest in various provinces of inquiry common rational features, and these forms of intelligibility are sufficiently coherent to allow us to distinguish them from one another. The dangers of interpretation to which broad views of intellectual history are exposed will threaten us at every point. Thinkers are apt to be grouped together who would have been surprised to find themselves in company, and important differences between philosophers and the originality of individual contributions are likely to be ignored. The closer we get to the writings of thinkers in a period of searching activity, such as the thirteenth century or the seventeenth, the more we become conscious of the baffling cross-currents of ideas and the more difficult does the attempt to classify schools of thought appear. But an endeavour to discern large tendencies in the history of rational inquiry is natural and even indispensable, provided the limitations of the attempt are borne in mind. I have tried to survey certain complexes of thought relating to nature, man, and God that have been dominant at successive epochs of our history; and if I have succeeded in drawing a rough map of this immense tract of country, I hope that others may be encouraged to make more accurate explorations of the territory.

The amount of space devoted to the philosophy of Anselm in Chapter II appears to call for defence. Anselm was Archbishop of Canterbury from 1093 to 1109 and was well known to Saxon scholars before his consecration as archbishop. But he was born and bred in Italy, his philosophical works were composed at Bec, and his ideas produced immediately no striking effects in England. There is, however, evidence of a school of thought concerned with his methods in Kent during the twelfth century, and in the following centuries the development of Augustinianism in England owed much to his writings. He is frequently quoted by the Oxford masters of the thirteenth century and there was a vogue for his characteristic manner of reasoning in the fourteenth. More than any other treatises the *Proslogion* and *Cur Deus Homo?* introduced the dialectical mode of argument that became prominent in the schools in England, and we can observe the structure of thought relating to the bearing of Catholic belief upon reason, to the essential principles of things and the way of apprehending them, in short the structure of scholastic Augustinianism, nowhere more impressively than in the treatises of Anselm.

I

BIBLICAL PHILOSOPHY

I

ENGLAND, in common with the rest of Europe, owed her intellectual culture to the Catholic Church. And, throughout all but the most recent section of her history, the Christian theology has formed the matrix of reflection in every field of inquiry. This theology embraced a complex system of philosophical traditions drawn from Hebrew, Christian, and Greek principles; and, besides this composite body of belief, culture included from the earliest phase of Catholic civilization in the island fractions of Latin literature and science, conveying not only a body of lore in many spheres of knowledge but also methods and standards of investigation. Reflection on the great questions of experience was coloured by the curriculum of Roman rhetorical education. The association of the theological perspective with the intellectual aims of the late Roman schools shaped the foundations upon which the subsequent developments of thought were built.

An adequate description of this vast background of assumptions would halt us too long at the outset of our survey. But it is impossible to appreciate the earlier stretches of thought in England without glancing at the profound alteration in the quality and purpose of rational inquiry that had occurred since the classic age of Greek thought. The first stages in this radical change had fallen in the period before the advent of Christianity. The Christian religion entered a world that had recently undergone a profound transformation of philosophical interests. Serious reflection was still Greek but the quality and direction of Greek thought had altered. The previous centuries had seen unparalleled achievements in scientific and philosophical investigation. The moral life of man and of the natural world surrounding him had been persistently explored; and far-reaching discoveries in ethics, in mathematics, and in physics had been attained. The collection of notes named the *Problems* indicates the range and variety of the instruction given in the school of Aristotle; the *Problems* raise questions for research in medicine, physiology, mathematics, optics, mechanics, music, and philology. These advances in knowledge had been accompanied by progress in the logic of evidence and demonstration. At the Academy and the Lyceum in Athens, and later at the Museum in Alexandria, a volume of investigation in all branches of knowledge had been undertaken. In them and in other Greek cities there had worked generations of mathematicians, astronomers, biologists, physiologists, logicians, literary critics, and historians. But two centuries before the appearance of the Christian religious movement among the Jews, political and economic upheaval undermined the conditions that had nourished this activity. The old intellectual and moral confidence waned. The free self-contained communities that had nurtured the investigations of the schools were ruined by wars and by defeat. The city-states were engulfed in empires. Life grew commercial and cosmopolitan, and the sense of stability and continuity, without which no tradition of culture can be sustained, was destroyed. Men became detached from the responsibilities of citizenship; they felt themselves to be isolated and competing individuals whose only God was Fortune. Political and economic insecurity provokes disillusionment. It drives men on to themselves. The pursuit of knowledge gave way in this dissolving society to the search for personal salvation. Learning became divorced from scientific inquiries and turned to magic and to moralizing. A passionate interest in astrology sprang up, in the belief that the universe was relentlessly controlled by the path of the planets. Men sought rites that would bring individual regeneration; they longed after transcendental compensations for the hard chances of life; they eagerly clasped professions of supernatural authority. In the great cities, Rome, Alexandria, Antioch, Ephesus, there stirred profound spiritual unrest and confusion. Oriental cults that gave promise of salvation were readily embraced. The rituals and mythologies of Isis, Dionysus, the Great Mother, and the later cults of Mithra and Gnosticism, provided what philosophy had failed to provide; they provided gospels of redemption and of hope. The temples and groves of these religions multiplied on all sides, and with them there poured in a stream of credulity. Belief in demons and miracles, in dreams and portents, in divination and astrology, became rife not only among the masses in the towns, but also among the educated and among the political leaders. Many philosophical schools encouraged these superstitions. For Greek science, which had been the foundation of the older range of philosophic activity, had collapsed. The new leaders of opinion held that curiosity about the nature of the world is vanity. Any physical explanation is sufficient; it is a waste of time to discover which one is truer than another. Philosophy yielded to eclecticism, and remnants of Plato and of Aristotle were superficially amalgamated with one another and with Stoic doctrines. In the seats of learning, scholarship rather than speculation survived, and the energy of writers was diverted to the production of summaries, imitations, and commentaries on the thinkers of the past.

This transformation of the intellectual temper of western thought during the Macedonian and early Roman periods affected the interests and methods of thought for more than a thousand years. The mark of the era was its concern with moral and religious issues. The Hellenistic age produced indeed great scientific minds such as Aristarchus, Ptolemy, and Galen, and the Stoics explored logic and physics. But the drift of reflection flowed away from mathematics, natural science, and epistemology towards theology and practical ethics. During the centuries when Christian theology was being constructed, the lines of inquiry opened by the old Greek schools ceased to be pursued and the technique of thinking about the world and about man that had developed in them also declined. The mind of the Roman was essentially practical and the classical methods remained foreign to its genius. Cicero thanks the Gods that Romans were not like the Greeks; they knew how to limit the study of mathematics to useful purposes. The later compilations show an egregious lack of understanding of Greek mathematics and science. The type of science that was eagerly pursued by the Romans was astrology. The moralizing of the great Roman writers, especially that of Cicero and Seneca, greatly influenced medieval ideas, but none of these writers was deeply interested in logical and metaphysical inquiries. The intellectual tendencies of the age finally culminated in Neo-Platonism which satisfied the yearning for a religious philosophy and united the impulses flowing from Oriental mysticism with elements of the Greek tradition. The profound influence of this philosophy upon western thought will be referred to later. But Neo-Platonism quickly degenerated into a superstitious theosophy. Meanwhile there had been formed the characteristic ideas of Latin culture that were to persist through fifteen hundred years of western education. The ideals of this education were fashioned by the standards propounded by Cicero and Quintilian. These men are the masters of the fundamental methods and of much of the material of intellectual activity in the schools of the Middle Ages and of the Renaissance. The primary aim of this Roman culture was the production of statesmen and advocates. Learning was directed towards one purpose, the art of skilful and instructed eloquence. The seven liberal arts that provided the curriculum of western education, the *litterae humaniores* of Cicero, are drawn up in the *De Oratore* and the *Institutio Oratoria*; but the study of literature, mathematics, and philosophy are controlled by rhetoric. The liberal arts become adjuncts of *belles lettres* and of eloquence. By the fourth century intellectual culture had become a literary culture the guiding principles of which were derived from oratory. The formal rules of Quintilian, the *lectio, emendatio, enarratio, iudicium*, were applied to the reading of texts; the artificial classifications of the manuals of rhetoric were carried over into other fields; and the exposition of knowledge was regulated by the set parts of forensic speeches, such as the exordium, the thesis, the peroration. Literary freedom was constrained by laborious imitation and by exhaustive analysis of syntax and prosody. It had become infected with sterile philological erudition.

These methods had an important effect upon the formation of scholastic processes of thought. The tradition of classifying subjects under formal heads, of dividing and subdividing on a verbal basis, of collecting texts, descends to medieval writing. The penetrating influence of this educational tradition upon the thinking of the Middle Ages has not been sufficiently appreciated. Many of the problems of theology and philosophy were conceived by scholastic thought in accordance with the rules, forms, and definitions of rhetoric.[1] The methods of inquiry were influenced by the distinctions drawn by Cicero between the parts of rhetoric in *De Oratore* and *Orator*. The passion for

---

[1] R. McKeon, *Rhetoric in the Middle Ages, Speculum,* xvii, p. 1 ff.

etymology and for verbal associations that runs rife through the treatises and the *quaestiones* descends from the same source; and even the analogical method of interpreting Scripture owes much to rhetorical training. What is more important, the view of logical principles and of rational processes was deeply influenced by the discussions of Cicero and the rhetoricians. Much of the material of the logical text-books echoes the theories of demonstration propounded by the rhetoricians and in the *Topics* of Cicero. It was directed rather towards the modes of arguments than towards fundamental logical principles. Later phases of thought in England revived the intellectual precepts of Cicero and Quintilian and *De Oratore* and *Institutio Oratoria* became patterns of reflection in the fifteenth and sixteenth centuries. The later Roman culture maintained little contact with the older scientific interests. In the hands of men of letters, nurtured on rhetorical education, natural knowledge becomes a haphazard collection of quotations, anecdotes, and fables. For such writers as Varro and Pliny the study of nature meant a compendium of isolated curiosities and wonders culled from books and from rumour. The views of the older authors were accepted without question and their errors faithfully transmitted. No attempt was made to verify the facts. Greek had disappeared from the schools. St. Augustine, for example, received the best teaching available at his time, but he cites Plato, Aristotle, and Plotinus in Latin translations. The culture of the eastern empire was more fortunate; it had its Greek foundations, and there was a vigorous revival of Aristotle in the sixth century.

The oratorical standards of Roman culture passed into the intellect of the West. Their influence can be observed in the writings of the two great Latin Fathers whose ideas rule the early Middle Ages. All the thought of the time was assembled in the vast work of Augustine. Of his philosophical influence there will be more to say; we shall touch on the metamorphosis of Platonism into the Hebraic-Christian Platonism of Augustine and of Anselm in the next chapter. Beyond any other writer Augustine controlled the speculation of Christendom until the thirteenth century. But despite the pregnant suggestions derived from the study of Plotinus and his school that flowed from him into western thought, it is manifest that he is intent upon adapting Latin rhetorical culture to Christian principles. Many of his discussions on metaphysical themes are elementary and verbal. The argument lacks rigour. Key-words are used in several different senses. The course of the discussion wanders interminably, and the main point is often forgotten. The unsystematic and unverified collections of knowledge in the Roman encyclopaedias are applied to the elucidation of the Scriptures.[1] The further decline of the older culture is far more patent in the works of Gregory the Great, a hundred years later. He was not only ignorant of Greek, but he expressed strong disapproval of classical literature.[2] In the argumentative portions of his treatises his thought is extremely confused. He is totally uninterested in exploring the assumptions of the Faith; and in attempting to transmit the Neo-Platonic views of Augustine he misunderstands and distorts them. He displays no knowledge of mathematics nor of natural knowledge. And indeed by the time in which he wrote there was little to know about either. What Gregory does eagerly explore is a mass of crude popular belief concerning the visitations of angels and demons. The writer of the *Moralia* has lost touch with the canons of evidence; and in this respect he is representative of his age.

'The simplest and most fundamental objection to the rhetorical system is that it neglected the search for truth.'[3] We shall notice further elements in this culture in the next chapter when the educational basis of Latin thought in England is considered; for the ideals of the Roman grammar schools passed into the cathedral and monastic schools of the Church. But in the meantime the final stage of the decadence had been reached. The empire disintegrated and the civilized world descended into confusion. Art, literature, and the relics of philosophy passed into oblivion as the Huns, Alani, and Goths drove into the Roman provinces. At the beginning of the fifth century the hordes invaded Italy and in the year 410 Rome was sacked. The empire of the West collapsed in civil strife and barbarian

[1] For detailed examination of Augustine's methods see H. I. Marrou, *Saint Augustin et la fin de la culture antique*, Paris, 1938.

[2] Cf. his letter to Desidirius, Bishop of Vienne, on the occasion of the departure of the second band of missionaries for England. F. H. Dudden, *Gregory the Great*, London, 1905, i. 287.

[3] T. Haarhoff, *Schools of Gaul*, Oxford, 1920, p. 251.

violence. Large sections of the cultured classes were exterminated, libraries were destroyed, education ceased. Two centuries of disorder and Gothic rule reduced intellectual activity to a primitive level. A scanty tradition of learning, founded upon the curriculum of the Roman schools, was preserved by the Church; it was carried by the missionaries to Ireland, Britain, and Gaul. The apparatus of knowledge was directed more narrowly to the service of theology and to liturgical practice. The activities of the monastic and cathedral schools were principally concerned with preparation for the conduct of the Church offices, and this instruction concentrated attention on the study of the Bible. But the schemes of trivium and quadrivium were maintained and the rhetorical treatment of literature and of logic was preserved in an attenuated form in the schools. Yet despite these restricted interests and meagre standards there were revivals of scholarship in the West. Nowhere was there a more promising stir of ideas than in England.

We have glanced at the rhetorical element that served to shape the thinking of monastic scholars. Later sections of the narrative will indicate the effects of the Roman tradition on the intellectual processes of medieval periods. But meanwhile the dominating conceptions of western thought had been constructed; Christian theology had been formed. The essential dogmas of this theology provided subsequent thought with its most fundamental and enduring assumptions. In the period of the conversion of the barbarous peoples of the West the immediate task of intellectual culture was that of assimilating the mass of patristic theory without criticism or extension. Before we enter the English scene it will be necessary to observe certain characteristics of this governing chain of beliefs.

II

The rational aspects of the Faith that occupied the minds of monastic students embraced little of the metaphysics of the Fathers. Their outlook was coloured by three tendencies, the impulse to interpret reality in personal and dramatic terms, concentration upon the Judaic-Christian Scriptures, and distaste for independent inquiry. The central conceptions were the beliefs that supreme reality was a personal Being and that He had revealed His purpose in definite modes. The indefeasible

convictions that penetrated every mental activity in consequence of these beliefs distinguished Christian interpretations
of experience sharply from those of the ancient East and also
from the conceptions of the Greeks. The theology had, indeed,
been developed in terms of Greek metaphysical formulae, but
its animating notions must be sought among the phantom
records of Sumeria and Babylonia and in the desert monuments
of civilizations beside which the works of Pythagoras and Plato
are modern. We need not look farther into these distances than
the utterances of prophetic Judaism, whose visions were rooted
in corporate experience that stretch back at least to the ninth
century before Christ. Its basic monotheism had not been
reached by philosophical thinking; it was not an hypothesis that
sought to account for the order of the world or for the moral
beliefs of men. It was a practical discovery made by a number
of exceptional men among the half-savage Semitic tribes of the
Levant. The conceptions that governed the whole development
of western ideas were wrung from these men not by contemplation, but by bitter emotion, caused by the spectacle of the
idolatry and moral laxity of their people. In denouncing the
legalism and ritualism of the priests, the prophets asserted that
the National God, Yahweh, was moved to wrath not against
literal transgressions of the code, but against affronts to
humanity, such as injustice, cruelty, arrogance, and complacency. They appealed to the universal moral affections of
men, to their consciences. 'After those days, said the Lord,
I will put my law in their inward parts and write it in their
hearts.'[1] The universal and objective claim of moral intuitions
is now welded to the traditional tribal conceptions of deity.
The deity of Sinai and Carmel ceases to be the Yahweh of Israel;
He becomes the God of the earth and of all people. In the
magnificent vision of the second Isaiah the God is described as
the creator and ruler of the heavens and the earth. But He is
also the God who dwells with him that is of a contrite and
humble heart. Here cosmology and ethics are united in the
principle of a sovereign personal God. This monotheistic belief
provided an outlook that satisfied the demand of subsequent
thought for a coherent explanation of all that is in intimate
association with the highest practical ideals. The belief was not

[1] Jer. xxxi. 33.

the only possible inference from profound religious experience. Other creative religious intuitions of the East had led to different conceptions, to belief in a universal law or in an esoteric wisdom. And Greek religious insight never accepted the view that the ground of things was personal. For it spiritual reality was a region of timeless ideas or forms, or, in Stoic religion, a principle of reason. The Greek outlook remained polytheist, even at its most advanced development. The demiurge of Plato is the first among the gods, and Aristotle questions whether there may not be more than one unmoved mover. Western thought was controlled by the religious perceptions of Judaism and of Judaic-Christianity. The new form of the Jewish religion quickly coalesced with Hellenistic ideas, and the older impulses were modified and complicated in the process. But they remained, at the heart of the religious ideas of Europe, guiding speculation throughout its course.

In the Judaic-Christian faith a rational theory of things is involved. In the discoveries of the Prophets assertions of universal validity relating to the essential nature of things were implicit. Since they were Jews, these religious masters were utterly uninterested in the dialectical significance of their disclosures of reality. But as a result of them the Hebrews combined the belief in a single transcendent Deity with a passionate belief in His presence in the temporal events of human experience. He was concerned with the history and destiny of man and with the order of the world in which that destiny was set. The postulate of the essential transcendence of God coalesced, as we shall observe, with later theoretical construction. But the belief in the active relations of God with man was the source of Israel's moral strength. The inner unity of the nation had been preserved through disruption and defeat, not by political organization, for the Hebrews were deficient in political ability, but by religious faith. They believed that they enjoyed a special compact with the Kenite God, Yahweh; and trust in the God gave them a core of moral resistance against the disasters that befel them. *Multoque in rebus acerbis acrius advertunt animos ad religionem*; and the periods of religious revival in Israel occurred when the nation was threatened by a foreign power, or when it was held captive by the conqueror. Biblical philosophy assumes that the inner nature of things expresses the unfolding of a divine plan the purpose of which was the spiritual education and salvation of the human race. The first scene of the drama was the creation of the world out of nothing by God. In this world, man, the first Adam, was in perfect communion with the Creator. There followed man's disobedience to the divine will, and his banishment from the favour of God. This belief in the fall of man from spiritual innocence at some primeval point of time occupied a central place in the theological outlook. Next in the tremendous drama came the selection of the tribe of Abraham as the means by which the divine mercy was to be restored. There ensued God's revelation of Himself to Moses and the Covenant with Israel. This cardinal act of history was followed by the long story of the alternating apostasy and repentance of the nation. Finally, the divine plan culminated in the appearance of Jesus, through whom the division between God and man was once more bridged.

This theological picture influenced the logic of western thought in a general and in a special manner. In a wider sense it promoted the natural tendency of inquirers who had lost touch with Greek science to interpret phenomena according to moral and personal categories, such as instruction, disobedience, punishment, ransom. What is primarily intelligible is a will acting for an end. Reality becomes dramatic and the rationale of the play is the attitude of man to the will of God. Political and economic developments, poor and abundant harvests, pestilences and invasions, victories and defeats, are manifestations of the divine approval or displeasure. To the biblical philosophy nature also becomes dramatic. To it Greek scientific and philosophical thinking was wholly uncongenial. The Hebrews had manifested no interest in the physical and mathematical questions that had fascinated the Greeks. They had no conception of a physical order by which the Milesians had sought to explain all phenomena and events. Their views of natural connexions remained rudimentary, confusing accidental and relevant associations in the crude manner of primitive races. They continued to be dominated by the practical beliefs of animism. They did not learn to examine their moral or natural experience in systematic inquiry, or attempt to arrive at logical definitions of principles. In a word, much of their mental processes stayed at the level of an eastern

agricultural community. Even in the Graeco-Roman period
when Jewish thought had had opportunities of assimilating
Hellenistic culture the Jewish Rabbis displayed little knowledge of philosophy.[1] The primitive mode of thought contained
in the biblical narrative was applied to the understanding
of the natural order. The processes of nature are understood
animistically or at best teleologically. Thinkers of the Dark
Age adopted this dramatic theism. The methods of biblical
interpretation peculiar to western thought at the outset of
Catholic civilization in England will be referred to in the next
section; we must defer to that section further consideration of
the way in which the unsophisticated teleology of the biblical
record was applied to the understanding of human nature and
the material universe.

The more special consequence that followed from the belief
that God's purpose for man had been uniquely revealed in the
scriptural record has already been touched upon. Since all that
human reason can discover is nothing beside the truths revealed
by God Himself, scholarship becomes concentrated upon those
questions that arise from the Scriptures and from the great
dogmas of the Faith. The rest is vain curiosity.

'It is no hope to us in our hope of the life to come to discuss the
nature and position of the earth. It is sufficient to know what Scripture states, that He hung up the earth upon nothing. Why then
argue whether he hung it up in the air or upon the water and raise
a controversy as to how this air could sustain the earth, or why, if
He hung it upon the waters, the earth does not go crashing down to
the bottom?'[2]

There is only one source of perfect wisdom, the sacred Scriptures.
'If there is truth elsewhere, it is found here.'[3] This is one side
of Christian thinking, the propensity to confine attention to
revealed truth and to perceive all natural knowledge in its light.
Inquiry is coloured by an attitude of humble reverence towards
data assumed to be unquestionably true; intellectual pride and
inquisitiveness are deadly sins, and the implicit purpose of
scholarship is interpretation, not logical conviction. 'Holy
Scripture is incomparably superior to every form of knowledge

---

[1] Cf. W. L. Knox in *The Contact of Pharisaism with Other Cultures*, ed.
H. Loewe, London, 1937, p. 73.

[2] Ambrose, *Hexaemeron*, i. 6.   [3] Augustine, *De Vera Doctrina*, ii.

or science.' Such was the authoritative opinion of the apostle of England.

But during the centuries that had elapsed since the first formation of the Christian Church an elaborate philosophy of revealed truth had been constructed. The most sustained intellectual energy of the centuries that preceded the monastic culture of the northern lands had been poured into the theological controversies from the time of Irenaeus in the second century to that of Augustine in the fifth. In the enormous series of patristic treatises metaphysical problems springing from the doctrines of the Christian creed had been explored with indefatigable subtlety. The Christian theologians were led to wrestle with ultimate philosophical questions concerning the transcendence and immanence of the Deity in order to preserve the essential tradition of belief against acute criticism within the Church. In these discussions elements from the Greek schools, Platonic, Aristotelian, and Stoic, were employed. But the spirit and direction of inquiry were not that of the old Greek schools. Interest in knowledge was governed by the concern to establish the system of faith grounded upon the corporate experience of Christian community. And this preoccupation rendered irrelevant a large range of topics that had engaged the attention of the earlier generations of thinkers. From the first there were theologians who sharply rejected the learning and pursuits of the schools. In numerous passages they admit that Greek thought contains suggestions that contribute to the understanding of Christian truth, but they insist that Greek philosophy is wholly inferior to the assertions of the Faith. For its teaching is uncertain, while the truths of revelation are certain. Scripture and Apostolic authority is final. The unambiguous knowledge taught by the Scriptures is frequently contrasted with the vague surmises of Plato and of other philosophers.[1] Christians possess the only true demonstration, which is supplied by the Divine Scriptures and the heaven-taught wisdom. The demonstration of opinion ($\delta \acute{o} \xi a$) is human, and founded on rhetorical arguments and logical syllogisms. That from above is knowledge ($\grave{\epsilon} \pi \iota \sigma \tau \acute{\eta} \mu \eta$).[2] The great ecclesiastical statesman of the fourth century, Ambrose, declared

---

[1] See, for instance, Clement, *Protrepticus*, cc. v–viii.

[2] Ib. *Stromata*, ii. 2 and 4, Patrologia Graeca, 8. 942 and 944.

that the difference between Christians and pagans is that pagans
only guess, Christians know.[1] He echoed a common view when
he cried: 'Away with arguments where faith is required.' He
looked on philosophy as purely destructive and asserted that all
that was good in the Greeks had been borrowed from Scripture.[2]
This latter type of argument is frequent from the earliest period.
It was introduced by Philo and readily adopted by many later
writers who maintain that the Greeks stole their ideas from the
Jewish Scriptures. Some of the Christian writers descended to
ridicule and abuse of the Greek thinkers. Their motives were
impugned, their characters vilified; it is a favourite theme of
Tatian, Tertullian, and Arnobius that Plato, Aristotle, Zeno,
and other philosophers were actuated by craving for fame and
wealth. We may pass over these vagaries; they are mentioned
because it is this outlook that is echoed in the Saxon writers.
The important point is the contrast that was established
between the infallibility of revelation and the fallibility of
natural reason. The differences of opinion among philosophers
of the past is often given as a reason for disparaging or for
ignoring them. The only legitimate work of reason, of the
lumen naturale, is to assume the truths of revelation and to
supplement them. From the Hebrew and the Christian Scriptures is received a supernatural order of truths abruptly contrasted with the range of natural and human knowledge. It
would not be difficult to select sentences from the patristic
writings that assert the view that revelation had put an end, not
merely to controversy, but to all rational discussion. An
utterance of Lactantius, may suffice. 'Divine learning does not
need logic.' But though intransigent opposition to philosophy
remained a persistent force in western theology and found
voice, as we shall notice, at every period in England, yet from
the day of the great theologians of Alexandria Christian thought
drew upon Platonic, Aristotelian, and Stoic principles, and
through Augustine and Gregory Neo-Platonic conception passed
into the clerical schools. Nor did philosophical debate ever
disappear. Even during the period succeeding the Councils
when the dogmatic disputes of the earlier centuries had been

---

[1] F. Homes Dudden, *Ambrose*, i, pp. 14–15.
[2] In his reply to Symmachus. Roger Bacon repeats these opinions in the
thirteenth century, and Bishop Stillingfleet in the seventeenth.

authoritatively decided, even in the darkest days of intellectual culture, the right to criticize and to offer rational interpretations of beliefs was recognized; and in the primitive epoch of Catholic Europe toleration of unorthodox positions was more generous than in the middle ages.

Nevertheless all subsequent discussion on first principles was affected by the deliberate reconstruction at the dawn of ecclesiastical culture of the functions of thought. We shall observe more closely the relation of faith to reason in the next chapter. In the Merovingian age of Catholic Europe the role of intellectual pursuits was strictly confined. The task before them was defined by St. Augustine in *De Doctrina Christiana*. Since Christians possessed in the revelation of the immutable and eternal wisdom of God a sovereign source of knowledge that superseded all human inquiry, thought must be subordinated to the doctrines of the Faith. The faithful will not pursue natural and metaphysical philosophy for their own sakes, but for the sake of salvation. Many intellectual disciples, grammar (that is to say, Latin and other languages), chronology, natural history, dialectic or logic, and philosophy contribute to the grasp of theological truth. But the application of these disciplines was narrow and their range was severely restricted by the current tradition of the schools. And the principal paths to understanding were not to be sought among them, but in purification of the soul, penitence, the sacraments and, in general, life in the Church. For the goal is salvation.

We have seen that patristic culture repudiated empirical investigation. Augustine is again the architect of the later outlook.

'For besides that concupiscence of the flesh which consisteth in the delight of all senses and pleasures, wherein its slaves, who go far from thee, waste and perish, the soul hath, through the same senses of the body, a certain vain curious desire, veiled under the title of knowledge and learning, not of delighting in the flesh, but of making experiments through the flesh. The seat whereof being in the appetite of knowledge, and sight being the sense chiefly used for attaining knowledge, it is in divine language called, the lust of the eyes. . . . Hence men go on to search out the hidden powers of nature, (which is beside our end), which to know profits not, and wherein men desire nothing but to know.'[1]

---

[1] *Confessions*, x. 35 (54, 55), tr. Pusey.

Here is the perversion, to desire nothing but to know. Yet ecclesiastical learning recognized *scientia*, the investigation of temporal things. Knowledge of nature and of history was useful for inculcating the lessons of prudence and morality and for deciphering the evidences of divine guidance in the created world. But *scientia* and indeed all intellectual pursuits were subordinate to the paramount purpose of elucidating the Scriptures.

Accordingly it was upon the Latin Scriptures that ecclesiastical thought was chiefly concentrated. It was in association with the study of the Bible that philosophical exploration survived in the Mosaic schools. The Scriptures enshrined the Word of God to men. They possessed unique authority that elevated them above all other sources of knowledge. For monastic scholars of the sixth century the old and the new Scriptures constituted one continuous record of holy truth. The new Israel had inherited the inspired literature of the old. By A.D. 400 the canon of the sacred books had been settled and the two collections were approached with the same preconceptions. The special modes of interpretation that were devoted to the Jewish and Christian texts will be illustrated in the following section. These methods of studying the Scriptures withdrew monastic thinking from the classical forms of reasoning and investigation. But, as we shall find, the *curiositas* condemned by St. Augustine led scholarly monks to explore natural phenomena beyond the pages of Genesis or the Psalms, and the relics of metaphysics in the texts of the Fathers induced them to relate passages from Amos or St. Paul to Neo-Platonic principles. But ecclesiastical thought reflects in the manner of interpreting its central text and in the questions that it raised the cycle of themes and the rhetorical methods of the schools of the decadence. And this apparatus is directed to the service of the Faith. In sum, the assumptions that controlled monastic reflections divided them profoundly from ancient attitudes. This attenuated logic was not only concentrated upon theological issues; the theology that enveloped all ideas was unique. It was not a philosophy of religion, it was an assertion of revealed truths. Ecclesiastical thought guarded a precious legacy. Its task was to preserve and defend the system of truths disclosed to man in the Scriptures. In the previous centuries great intellectual energy had been spent in rebutting interpretations of the creed that sought to overcome its paradoxes or to explain its mysteries. But by the seventh century the need for a critical defence had shrunk and the intellectual movements that had formerly inspired the life of the Church had ceased to stir the minds of men.

III

On a spring day in the year 597 the priest Augustine and his band of lay monks from Rome set foot on shore near Richborough in Kent. Less than a hundred years later the final heathen group in the land was baptized into the Christian Faith. The Roman and Irish missionaries who worked during this primitive period introduced the Saxon tribes to the forms and elementary notions of Christianity; but the founder of ecclesiastical culture in England was Theodore of Tarsus who arrived at Canterbury to assume the direction of the Church in England as archbishop in 669. He was a renowned scholar as well as a great administrator, and with the help of the learned abbot Hadrian who had accompanied him from Rome, he imposed a coherent unity upon the local churches throughout the country and reformed their intellectual life. Bede describes in warm language the enthusiasm for learning that was kindled by the teaching of Theodore and Hadrian. He says that disciples flocked to hear their lectures on sacred and on pagan literature, and that rivers of knowledge flowed daily from them to refreshen the hearts of those who listened. He declares that there were still alive at the time when he was writing—about 730— some old men who had been pupils of these teachers and who knew not only Latin but Greek as thoroughly as their own tongue. 'Nor were there ever happier times since the English came into Britain; the Kings were a terror to the heathen, the minds of men were intent upon the joys of heaven, and all who desired to be instructed in sacred reading had masters at hand to teach them.'[1]

The principal scene of this activity in the days of Theodore was Canterbury where Augustine's school was reorganized under Hadrian. Here was revived the scheme of rhetorical culture in association with the Christian Scriptures. A wide range of the liberal arts was taught there including medical lore

---

[1] Bede, *Ecclesiastical History*, iv. 2, Everyman edition, p. 164.

and Roman jurisprudence. Later in Bede's day a greater school
of studies was founded at York by one of his own pupils,
Archbishop Egbert. As is well known, the reputation of this
school was so famous that Charlemagne invited its master,
Alcuin, to organize and preside over the school at his court; and
Alcuin's work there influenced literature and scholarship
throughout the Frankish Empire.[1] What attracted men to the
schools at Canterbury, York, Lichfield, and other episcopal
seats were the libraries as well as the teachers. The cultivation
of reading owed much to men such as Benedict Biscop who
made six journeys to Rome and 'brought back a quantity of
books of all kinds' from Italy and Gaul to form monastic
libraries. For with the multiplication of monasteries new
schools of study arose. The collections of books at Jarrow made
possible the work of Bede, who spending all his life in that
monastery, 'wholly applied myself', as he says, 'to the study of
Scripture, and amidst the observance of regular discipline and
the daily care of singing in the church, I always took delight in
learning, teaching, and writing'.[2] Besides the few schools that
provided more advanced work many elementary schools grew
up in connexion with the great churches and monasteries.

This sudden blossoming of culture among a people so recently
converted from rude paganism is remarkable in the history of
European letters. Aldhelm is the most notable instance of this
passion for knowledge. It drove him at the age of 30 to pursue
every available subject at the school at Canterbury and to
collect books for his monastery at Malmesbury. He is a product
of the restored literary culture of the Roman schools. Some forty
Latin authors are quoted by him in his writings. There were
many others who patiently explored the new collections of
manuscripts in the monasteries. The influence of this monastic
culture beyond England had been recognized in recent years.[3]
The extension of the Church in the Frankish dominions was
accomplished by Englishmen, and centres of learning were
established under English teachers. The leading names in the
intellectual life of western Europe during these centuries are

---

[1] On Alcuin and his work for culture see the moving tribute in E. Gilson,
Les idées et les lettres, Paris, 1932, p. 176.

[2] *Bede*, op. cit. v. 24. Everyman ed., p. 283.

[3] Cf. S. J. Crawford, *Anglo-Saxon Influence on Western Christendom*, London,
1933.

the names of English monks, Bede, Boniface, Willibrord, Alcuin, Dunstan. In the monasteries of the eighth century the theological conceptions and the literary equipment of the Dark Ages were rapidly assimilated; for a brief period there was a prospect that inquiry would burst beyond the bounds of the tradition. But the rich promise of the Saxon schools was not fulfilled. The primary condition for a development of original reflection is a tradition of knowledge. Searching questions can be raised only when a body of information has been accumulated and mastered, and when principles of interpretation have become customary. No tradition is possible in a society where the elements of life are insecure and the continuity of study is frequently severed. The monastic and episcopal foundations of education had scarcely been established when fighting between the rival dynasties of the North and South again flared up. Saxon scholarship, after a promising dawn, rapidly waned and in the tenth century it was overwhelmed by the Danish invasions. The general level of culture relapsed to a primitive level. Alfred's attempts to check the degradation of the monasteries failed and the reforms undertaken by Dunstan did not recover the ground lost by the destruction of the centres of learning by the heathen. To the Normans the English were a race of barbarians. The Saxon intellectual achievement has the appearance of a passing episode at the threshold of our history.

Yet there are many points of interest in the Old English period that bear upon the subsequent development of ideas. The country produced the greatest teacher of the Dark Ages. In the work of Bede there can be observed the character of thought at this preliminary stage of our culture, for the learning of the time is concentrated in him. But before we proceed to consider the biblical philosophy of which Bede is the greatest representative in the age, we may notice one or two circumstances that bear upon the intellectual life of the country.

It is interesting to observe the way in which Christian conceptions were closely mingled with indigenous popular ideas at the period of conversion. The chieftains and their followers embraced the new religion with remarkable complacency. Thousands among the clans in the south-east districts and soon large numbers of the people of Northumbria, East Anglia, and Wessex readily exchanged their gods for the worship of Christ.

A great part of the motives that induced the Anglo-Saxons to accept baptism with such facility was social. The kings, the ceorls, and their dependants were knit together by bonds of service and the decision of the leaders carried the people with them. The superficial nature of the first professions of faith is shown by the widely spread relapses into the older cults during the early generations of Saxon Christianity. Most of the Christian communities in Kent, Essex, and the North reverted to Paganism as soon as their Christian leaders were defeated by rival chiefs. But there is another circumstance to be recognized. By deliberate policy the new gospel made large concessions to habitual beliefs and practices. The missionaries were guided by instructions sent from Rome by their shrewd master, Gregory; and they were advised to adapt the new beliefs as far as possible to the old.[1] The new rites were grafted on to the cult of Thunor; the old temples were transformed into churches of the new religion; and the customary sacrifices were continued under the title of Christian festivals. The Teutonic gods, in fine, were baptized and passed into popular thought as heroes and saints. During the earlier generations of Christians men oscillated easily in their allegiance between the old and the fresh rites, and some of the great chiefs accorded equal dignity to the churches of Christ and to the temples of the tribal gods. The tolerant policy of the Italian missionaries towards the sylvan superstitions of the Saxons deeply influenced the general mind of the people. Ancient ideas and new became intermingled. A wealth of primitive conceptions and practices was poured into the spirit of English Christianity. The immemorial attachments to the gods of the trees and the springs flowed on in disguised forms. The tributes to the unseen powers of the sun and the corn, the rites of the sacred oak, the festivals of May Day and harvest, were translated into the Christian celebrations; and the incantations to Thunor and Frig were expressed in the mysterious language of Latin hymns. The animism of the Northern tribes lived on within Christian ecclesiastical culture, a luxuriant undergrowth of superstition and magic.[2]

The intellectual standards of the Church were infected by

[1] Gregory to Mellitus, Bede, *Ecclesiastical History*, i. 30.
[2] There are many accounts of the throngs of devils that besieged the bed and board of the medieval man. See, for instance, G. R. Owst, *Preaching in Medieval England*, Cambridge, 1926, p. 336 f.

these native habits of thought. And, on the other hand, the
prevailing conceptions of Christianity accorded with much in the
primitive outlook on the world. We have seen that Gregory's
Dialogues had given a powerful impetus to the confluence of
popular beliefs and Christian ideas. The most influential and
acceptable literature of the period was the literature of miraculous lives. These *acta sanctorum* are filled not only with wonders
wrought by holy men, but with demons who raise storms, set
fire to forests and houses, and plunge their forks into the bodies
of men. The labouring Saxon lived in constant terror of evil
spirits and would have little difficulty in assimilating tales of
the new Christian magic. He would appreciate the description
of Hell faithfully reported by the man of Cuningham.[1] And the
cures produced by sacred relics, the heavenly lights that floated
above the bones of the saints, and the power of religious men
over the elements, were modulations of familiar beliefs. Bede's
Life of St. Cuthbert is typical of this miraculous literature.
Many of the ordinary priests were as crude in their understanding of Christian practices as the thegns and villains of their
flocks. They uttered exorcisms to expel devils, blowing in the
faces of converts, placing salt in their mouths, and performing
many other ritual acts of initiation and invocation. A cloud of
magical beliefs were associated with the ceremonies of the
Church, especially with the consecration of the Host. But
though Christian ideas had a kinship with the old cults rooted
in the soil, the prevalence of primitive customs was a matter of
constant concern to the leaders of the Church. The serious
extent of the practices in the early period of Saxon Christianity
is shown by the penances ordained by Theodore for those who
sacrificed to devils and performed other heathen practices. At
the Council of Clovesho in 748 the Bishops were instructed to
discourage the pagan observances of the people, 'diviners,
sorcerers, auguries, omens, amulets, and charms'.[2] It was the
first of a long series of edicts on this issue.

The affinity between native mythology and Christian doctrine
was one that continued to affect the views of men in subtle

[1] Bede, op. cit., v. 12.
[2] Gee and Hardy, *Documents Illustrative of Church History*, London, 1910,
p. 19. The popular beliefs in spirits and magic were still rife, even among the
clergy, in the eighteenth century. Cf. G. M. Trevelyan, *English Social History*,
p. 318.

ways. A more explicit conflict of ideas with which the new church in England had to deal must be mentioned. As the Roman missionaries moved across the island they found their ideas sharply opposed by followers of the Celtic Christianity that had penetrated the country from the north and west. These districts had been visited by monks from Ireland and from the monastic settlements in the North; and the opinions of the Irish preachers differed in important points from the conceptions of the missionaries who derived their authority from Rome. The Celtic Church rejected the system of diocesan and episcopal rule which was an essential point of the Roman Church. And it departed in several usages from the practices of continental religion, the chief of which was the method of dating Easter. Behind these differences lay a vital conflict of principles. The perspective of the Celtic Church was strangely foreign to the spirit of the rest of Catholicism. There was a deep vein of asceticism, of detachment from the world in its outlook; tendencies that were most marked in the monastic centres in Wales. There are Manichaean elements in the religion of the Celts. Their prayers invoked the powers of nature and refer to a sovereign monster, 'the Dragon, great, most foul, terrible and old'.[1]

The celebrated conference held in the monastery at Whitby in 664 is the first critical point in the history of English thought, for by its decisions the Church in England was organically linked with the main body of Christian philosophy in Europe. It was a decision in favour of order, discipline, and authoritative doctrine. 'But as for you and your companions', declared Wilfred, the fiery abbot of Ripon, to the representatives of the Scots, 'you certainly sin, if, having heard the decrees of the Apostolic See, and of the universal Church and that these are confirmed by Holy Writ, you refuse to follow them; for though your fathers were holy, do you think that their small number, in a corner of the remotest island, is to be preferred before the universal Christ throughout the world?'[2] Thus spoke a man who had received instruction at the hands of a member of the Pope's Council in Rome, and who looked on doctrine with a European eye. Henceforth thought in the English Church was

[1] R. H. Hodgkin, *History of the Anglo-Saxons*, Oxford, 1939, i. 256-7.
[2] Bede, op. cit. iii. 25.

linked with the Catholic hierarchy and the Councils. But the
influence of Celtic Christianity had penetrated too widely to be
annulled by the decision at Whitby. It preserved in the
monasteries an ideal of severe self-discipline and of individual
salvation. And it must be added that at the time of the Council
the cultural resources of the Celtic Church were far richer than
those of the Roman section. Augustine and his forty monks
had been children of Gregory. There is no mention of education
in the Pope's correspondence with the Christian leaders. The
schools that had been set up were strictly concerned with the
service of the churches. The missionaries from Iona and
Lindisfarne diffused a wider culture. Until the coming of
Theodore almost all that the Saxon Church knew of Latin
thought was derived from Ireland. The monasteries in Ireland
had preserved a tradition of scholarship without parallel elsewhere, and numbers from the leading families of the Anglo-
Saxons crossed the seas in search of knowledge. But by the
great educational developments of the seventh century intellectual opportunities were provided at home. And these
developments were prepared for by the step taken at Whitby.

The scope and assumptions of inquiry in the Dark Ages can
be perceived nowhere better than in the works of Bede. His
writing is unusually clear in style, his interests comprehended
the intellectual pursuits of the time, and he does not disguise the
purposes that underlie his researches. He was well placed for
investigating ideas and history; for a library, ample for that
age, had been collected at Wearmouth and at Jarrow, and
these monasteries were visited by many scholars travelling between Canterbury and Gaul, and from Rome to Ireland. As we
have said, Bede's knowledge was obtained chiefly from Irish
connexions, and the Carolingian renaissance of education in
the ninth century descended through Bede and Alcuin from
the Irish Schools.

The bulk of Bede's work consists of commentaries on the
books of the Bible. In the list of writings that he gives at the
end of the *Ecclesiastical History* he recalls twenty-three exe-
getical works, ranging from a study of Genesis to a commentary
on the Book of Revelation. He stands at the head of a vast
river of mental preoccupation and activity that has coursed
through our thought up to recent times. More than any other

influence it has fashioned men's conceptions and formed their picture of the universe. The first intellectual culture in our land was predominantly a biblical culture, and this strain of ideas dominated thought until the seventeenth century. As we have noticed in the earlier period, the work of the monastic and cathedral schools was almost entirely directed to the study of the Bible, and the relics of the old rhetorical curriculum were transformed into preparation for the service of the Church. The ecclesiastical purpose that governed the training in the liberal arts of the trivium and the quadrivium restricted the scope of interest and of understanding, but it gave a utilitarian savour to studies that is absent from the artificial literary exercises and imitations of the old pagan schools. The work was necessary for the offices of the various minor orders in the Church, the readers, the psalmists, the clerks, and the copyists. Simple arithmetical skill, for example, was required in order to calculate the Church feasts.[1] In the higher levels the main intellectual industry for centuries was the compilation of extensive glosses upon the books of Scripture. These exegeses repeated endlessly the comments and views of the patristic writers, preserving their beliefs and methods of thought for generation after generation. For the legacy of ecclesiastical culture contained more than a religious cult and a moral tradition. It included beliefs relating to the structure of things, beliefs on the nature of causation and on the interconnexion of objects and events, beliefs concerning many provinces of natural information. And it included methods of investigation that were peculiar to the understanding of the sacred text. Our task is to distinguish these beliefs and methods.

The general character of this interpretation of experience has been delineated in the preceding section. Things and events were perceived and understood solely under the light of final causation. The embracing form of intelligibility is that of a supreme will that creates and disposes all life and nature in relation to moral ends. The outlook on reality was dominantly religious and ethical. It has been remarked that the Bible is the least metaphysical of all the great religious books of the world. And

---

[1] How simple it was may be gathered from the account that Aldhelm gives of his painful efforts to do sums, quoted in A. F. Leach, *Educational Charters*, Cambridge, 1911, p. 11.

it is true that the Jewish mind was devoid of logical and scientific curiosity. But the religious and ethical criteria that monastic teachers applied to the understanding of experience implied metaphysical principles; and we shall find that important philosophical conceptions were later associated with passages from the sacred text. The fundamental categories assumed in the Hebraic-Christian thinking of able monks at the dawn of our civilization are those of providence and creation. Aristotle had allowed a large place for chance and accident in natural events. In the biblical universe nothing happens without rational cause, for the moral purposes of God are everywhere present. For the implicit outlook of this age Boethius expressed the ruling principle. 'If any define chance to be an event produced by a confused motion and without connection of causes, I affirm that there is no such thing, and that chance is only an empty voice without any real signification. For what place can confusion have since God disposes all things in due order?'[1] The rational order of things is a moral order. The attitude towards the phenomena of the earth and the heavens was inherited from the meagre culture of the age, but the habit of interpreting physical events as symbols of moral instruction was ingrained in Judaic-Christian thought. Nature is a school for men. The world of animals and plants, of rivers and hills, is contemplated for the sake of the spiritual lessons it conveys. They comprise a panorama of hieroglyphics that signify to the eye of faith warnings relating to conduct or illustrations of the articles of Christian belief. Perceiving reality through the Scriptures and the commentaries, the Saxon scholar approached the scene of nature and history with naïve ethical standards of understanding. But the theological postulates that guided his ideas recognized in a primitive form the homogeneous and harmonious character of the natural universe. Though there is little notion of reciprocal reaction among natural events, the monotheism of biblical philosophy could absorb and inspire the later developments of natural philosophy. The theory of 'the wisdom of God in creation' defended in the seventeenth century is grounded upon the Hebraic inheritance of the first generation of English scholars.

The Bible and the commentators were the verbally inspired

[1] Boethius, *De consolatione philosophiae*, v, prosa 1.

text-books of natural knowledge, as well as of theology and conduct. Through the commentaries of the western Fathers the monks learnt most of their knowledge of physical fact. From the notes of Jerome and others on the sacred text they learnt of the habits of serpents, of the properties of precious stones, of the attributes of the olive and the hyssop; and of a hundred other details. But the beliefs of literate churchmen were drawn also from the Roman encyclopaedists. The most widely read source in which these ideas were transmitted was the *Etymologiae* of Isidore of Seville. It embraced almost the full compass of the knowledge of the age. The twenty books skim lightly over rhetoric, mathematics, music, medicine, theology, physiology, zoology, geography, architecture, agri-culture, and military science. The attenuated information compressed under these headings is compiled from old authors such as Jerome, Pliny, and Solinus. What must interest us here is not the matter but the quality of the thought displayed in such dictionaries. The leading principle upon which Isidore relies is philological; he explains the nature of things by attempt-ing to trace the origin of their names.[1] The method leads to quite superficial and erroneous conceptions, and it is not helped by the poverty of Isidore's scholarship. 'Corpus is so called because being corrupted it perishes', 'Homo is so named because he is made of humus, as Genesis says.' The method leads him into a mass of contradictions which he fails to notice because he lacks almost all sense of consecutive thinking. Passages are copied out in a haphazard way, from Cassiodorus or Lactantius or the Psalms, and there is no effort to relate the items to one another nor to seek any evidence for them beyond the fact that they are found in books.[2] Isidore turns for much of his information, not to the Roman secular writers, but to the Bible and the patristic commentaries. Bede in his early text-books for use in the cloister school copies from Isidore; but he also refers back to Pliny. Even in this field he raises the level of thought, displaying a cautious attitude to some of Isidore's reports, and correcting them by reference to earlier authorities.[3]

[1] The method descends from Plato, Cratylus, 435 *d*. Cf. E. Gilson, *Les idées et les lettres*, p. 164. It is widely used in the bestiaries and herbals of later times.

[2] E. Brehaut, *Isidore of Seville, An Encyclopaedist of the Dark Ages*, New York, 1912.

[3] C. W. Jones, *Bedae Opera de Temporibus*, Cambridge, Mass., 1943, p. 131 f.

And the universe of his *De Natura Rerum* is less capricious than that of Isidore. It transmits to early medieval reflection the cosmology of classical Rome, in which elements of Greek speculation survived. We need not refer to the details of his account of eclipses, comets, thunder, earthquakes, and other phenomena. The general scheme reveals the faint outlines of the universe of Hipparchus and of Ptolemy. The earth is the centre of a series of revolving spheres, and the fundamental constituents of the world are the four elements, earth, air, water, fire. There is a suggestion of natural order in this book that lifts it above the barren compilations of the age of decadence.

But the main scientific interest of Bede related to the computation of the dates of Church feasts. The calculation of the date of Easter was, as we have seen, a point of grave concern for the English Church; for the Roman practice differed from the custom of the Celtic Church and was the principal question at issue between the two bodies. It was inconvenient that one party of Christians should be rigorously fasting at the time when the other was rejoicing with feasts; and the discomfort became a source of acute friction when the two rules were followed simultaneously in the same household; as occurred at the court of Oswy, King of Northumbria.[1] It is unnecessary to enter into the details of the two systems of reckoning.[2] The incidence of the Paschal moon was calculated by the Roman Church according to a cycle introduced from Alexandrian sources in the sixth century; the British and Irish Churches had clung to the older and less accurate cycle. Into the Paschal controversy there had been poured for many centuries a large bulk of the scholarship and science of the age. In *De Temporum Ratione* Bede produced a treatise that displayed a power of systematic reasoning, grounded on a comprehensive study of the relevant literature, that places him far above his period. The interest in chronology led him to undertake his greatest achievement, the *Ecclesiastical History of the English People*.

From what has been said we may surmise that philosophy in the older sense had little honour among the Anglo-Saxons. The library at York contained a meagre group of works; Aristotle's *De Interpretatione*, a jejune treatise on the Categories falsely attributed to St. Augustine and Boethius' *De Consolatione*. Bede

---

[1] Bede, *Eccles. Hist.* iii. 25.   [2] See C. W. Jones, op. cit., p. 78 f.

displays no interest in philosophical topics. Indeed he dismisses
them with contempt. In a passage in the Commentary on the
Pentateuch he compares dialectic to the second plague of Egypt;
it surrounds the mind with deceptive cunning and produces
pride and loquacity.[1] These opinions are echoes of patristic
opinions and guided by the same preoccupation. All learning
is enclosed in the Scriptures. Aldhelm's studies at Canterbury
had taught him that the arguments of the Stoics or of Aristotle
are inane compared with heavenly philosophy. What value was
possessed by the ancient speculations had been terminated by
Christianity; such was the teaching of the monastery schools.
It is true that St. Augustine had recommended dialectic in his
De Doctrina Christiana, and that works of his containing philosophical matter, such as *De Musica* and *De Diversis Quaestionibus,* were favourite books among Saxon scholars. But the
monk's view of dialectic was derived from trivial examples of
the syllogism in such works as Isidore's *Etymologies.* Independent thinking was hampered for many centuries by the
meagre instruction in reasoning that had descended from the
rhetorical curriculum of the Roman schools. Bede moves
beyond these standards. He displays a critical sense of history
beyond that of any other writer of the age. He distinguishes
between witnesses who were present at the events reported and
those who heard them from others; he prefers primary literary
sources to derived ones; and he is at pains to correct errors in
the received texts. In his judgement he displays a moderation
and balance extraordinary in the period; as in the celebrated
instance of his tribute to Aidan, whose views on the Easter
question he considered 'detestable'.[2] These are qualities from
which English thought might have moved to a new level, in
spite of the assumptions by which it was confined.

IV

But the explorations of human reason were of secondary
value when compared with the reverent scrutiny of God's word.
We return to the Scriptures. The monastic mind was absorbed
in the record of God's dealings with His people and in His
revelation in the Church. The theory of things rested on the

---

[1] In *Pent. Exod.* vii, *Patrologia Latina,* xci. 302 *a*; 1 Sam. i. 4, ib., 510 *b*.
[2] *Ecclesiastical History,* iii. 17.

record; doctrine is proved from the pages of Holy Writ. Where questions arise the Saxon monk referred to the authority of the Church and to the mysteries of the Faith. 'All these matters we ought to revere by faith, not debate by reason, since where reason fails there faith is necessary.' These are the words of Alcuin, and express the sentiments of the school of York. He proceeds to say that we cannot explain the daily marvels of nature; God must be allowed to do that which is completely inexplicable to man, since He is omnipotent.[1] Mental effort moved narrowly within the commentaries of the Fathers, especially within those of the four chief Latin Fathers, Ambrose, Jerome, Augustine, and Gregory. It was presumption to criticize what was found written in the huge tomes of the Latin scholars. 'But I do not think that error ought to be attributed to me when, following the authority of great doctors I thought I ought to adopt without scruple what I found in their works.'[2] Bede is never tired of pointing out that he is only following in the footsteps of the Fathers. He felt it more important to transcribe the opinions of Gregory than to offer his own ideas. He was well aware that the time in which he was writing was ruder than the age of the Fathers. Independent discussion of the sacred text or criticism of the authoritative homilies upon it did not enter into his purpose in writing. An individual writer had the duty of conveying the truth accepted by the corporate Church, and even the modest Bede was accused of heresy for an opinion in an early work that was thought by certain brethren to depart from received doctrine. He was easily able to crush his accusers, whom he describes as loose-living rustics droning over their cups.

The main intellectual activity was directed towards the labour of communicating the existing tradition of sacred interpretation. Let us observe some of the methods of thought inculcated by this concentration on the Scriptures. For the Biblical philosophy of the seventh century history is the record of God's mighty acts. But more direct evidence of His providence is sought. His presence is proved by the witness of prophets, of miracles, and of marvels. He was believed to have revealed His mind through the ecstatic utterances of seers. The prophets of Israel anounced their messages as direct communications

---

[1] Alcuin, *Adversum Felicem*, iii. 2.   [2] Bede, *Commentary on Acts*, i. 13.

from Yahweh. They looked upon themselves as media whose privilege it was to transmit the Word to the people. Christian thought accepted this view of the functions of the prophets, and extended them to include the pronouncements of inspired men in later times. Supernatural gifts also embraced prediction of the future. A respect for oracles is indigenous in the eastern mind, and successful prophecy was held to demonstrate that the seer who proclaimed it was an instrument of the true God. When the doom or triumph that is foretold came to pass it was argued that it was the Lord who had brought it about. The argument from prophecy abounds in the patristic writings, from the treatises of the Apologists to those of the Latin Fathers; and the argument continued to be prominent throughout the Middle Ages. Ezekiel and Isaiah prophesied earthquakes, wars, and famines; these events occurred in later times, and it is concluded that the Jewish writings were divinely inspired and revealed God's purpose to men. It was a small step to claim infallible knowledge of the future course of history from a study of the sacred text. It had been believed, for instance, on the basis of cryptic passages in the prophetic books that the world would perish with the downfall of the Roman Empire. As that catastrophe became imminent Christians had pressing reasons for turning away from ephemeral intellectual inquiries. But naturally the most frequent class of evidence provided by prophecy were those references in the Jewish Scriptures that were taken to prove that Jesus was the divine Messiah.

Other proofs of God's presence in history were derived from the record of miraculous interventions in the usual course of events. He moved the shadow back ten degrees on the dial of Ahaz in order to bring conviction to Hezekiah. The godly walked unscathed in the midst of the furnace and the miracle converted Nebuchadnezzar. Proofs from signs and wonders pervade all primitive unsophisticated thought. There is little sense of interaction in things. Each striking event is qualitatively unique, the expression of a preternatural power. Some of the miracles may well have been cures springing from emotional faith. But many described complete reversal or suspension of the natural order of things. The leaders of the Church everywhere sought to strengthen the faithful and convince

unbelievers by pointing to the miracles of Christ and His
Apostles and to the supernatural wonders wrought by Christians
throughout the Empire. The rapid growth of miraculous
stories in the literature of the Church after the third century
marks the general decline in critical standards. In the fourth
century there began the cult of saints and martyrs, and with it
the main body of Christian writings for the instruction of
the age became stories of miracles of holy priests and hermits.
In this development the influence of Gregory the Great was
paramount.

The unique position occupied by Scripture required special
methods of interpreting it. For large sections of the vast collection of writings could not possibly be received in a literal way.
If we follow the letter of the Bible, 'what shall we find to correct
our sins, to console or instruct us, when we open the book of the
blessed Samuel and read that Elcana had two wives, we
especially, who are celibate ecclesiastics, if we do not know how
to draw out the allegorical meaning of sayings like these, which
revives us inwardly, correcting, teaching, consoling?'[1] This
method of interpreting Scripture inculcated a habit of inquiry
that is markedly different from other modes of rational discussion. Augustine had observed that the obscurity of Scripture
had been divinely arranged because men do not value what is
easily understood.[2] For the ecclesiastical ages the Scriptures
form a mass of symbolism. Since every section is directly
inspired the slightest words are susceptible of mystical meaning.
There was a threefold method of exegesis. The narrative could
first be interpreted in a literal sense. It could be taken to mean
what it said. For the medieval commentators this was the
least significant approach to the text. Convinced that they
were reading not a description, let us say, of the high-priest's
robes, but the oracles of God conveyed in human language, they
searched the narrative for secret meaning. This process of
decoding was guided by two rules; the narrative concealed a
moral and a spiritual meaning. The theologians of the epoch
expended a wealth of ingenuity in detecting figurative meaning
in the most trivial details of Holy Writ. The twelve bells on the

[1] Bede, *Samuelis Prophetae Allegorica Expositio*, *Prologa*, quoted B. Smalley,
The Study of the Bible in the Middle Ages, Oxford, 1941, p. 22.
[2] *De Doctrina Christiana*, ii. vi. 7.

Jewish priest's robes are symbols of the twelve apostles. The marriage of Jacob and Rachel is a sign of the union of Christ with the Church. 'They let him down by the wall in a basket.' The wall of Damascus, which means drinking blood, is the peril of the age; King Areta, which signifies descent, is the devil; and the basket, which is made of rushes and palms, means the union of faith and hope. Thus argues Bede on Acts ix. 25.[1] The mental disposition is one of casual association. Anything may signify any other thing if it conveys some theological or moral reference. The divine eloquence is a dense aggregation of substitutes and metaphors, in which the names of persons and places typify virtues and vices, the Church, Christ, the Saints. The name Jerusalem indicates the vision of peace, and the three names of Jerusalem point to the dogma of the Trinity. Passages are construed by comparison with others that have no connexion with them save a spiritual meaning imputed by the commentator. The coherence and logical plan of Scripture rests not upon natural reason but upon a primordial belief in its preternatural import. The sense resides in a region remote from the ordinary course of things and from literal meaning. The reasoning that pervades *divina lectio* is one facet of the reasoning that found in nature and history a cloak for spiritual lessons. But Scripture is the Word of God, and the long chains of citations that fill the pages of medieval thinkers conceal a peculiar form of logic. The concordance of texts relating to a question, such as the fallibility of the senses or the role of illumination, is taken to provide convincing proof of the point at issue.[2] One aspect of this lore that had a special fascination for Bede is the symbolism of numbers. Three recalls the Trinity, seven means universality, ten signifies the Law, eleven portrays sin, for it transgresses ten, fifty is a sign of penitence, and so on. And larger numbers can be shown to imply a chain of theological ideas, since they contain as factors several symbols. Bede notices that the Temple was built 480 years after the departure of the Israelites from Egypt. Now 480 is made up of 4 and 120, and 4 is the number of the Evangelists, while 120 is the age of Moses, the law-giver. Moreover, the number of the disciples in

---

[1] *Expositio Actuum Apostolorum*, edited by M. L. W. Laistner, p. 42.

[2] Cf. E. Gilson, 'De quelques raisonnements scripturaires', in *Les idées et les lettres*, p. 155 f.

Acts i. 15 is said to be about 120. The conclusion from these coincidences is that the building of the Temple at that date means that those who use the Law rightly are endowed with Grace as were the disciples.[1]

We have touched on the roots of these mental processes. They are not the outcome merely of ignorance and primitive notions. They reflect the implicit philosophy of the Church, that the God and Judge of the world has deliberately revealed Himself in the Hebrew Scriptures, and that the 'higher understanding' of piety could penetrate their mysteries. Time and space are veils concealing the supernatural purposes of God. This supernatural region is infinitely more impressive to the monastic scholar than the world of nature and of human history. The realm of divine purpose precedes the world of men and of nature and explains them. But God speaks in parables, and explanation of His message follows the way of allegory. Items that offer some point of resemblance are brought together from widely different contexts to support beliefs concerning the divine plan, and every circumstance is pressed to yield moral ideas. The method invited erratic leaps over the whole field of the sacred record, it fastened on superficial likenesses, and it evaded problems arising from contradictions and confusions in the text.

The subsequent development of biblical theory bears closely upon the history of general ideas in England. An adequate treatment of the phases of reflection would trace the vital influences that have been impressed upon thought by the varying methods of biblical interpretation. Not in doctrinal problems only, but in the whole range of intellectual inquiry scholars continued for a thousand years to decide issues by reference to the Scriptures. The complementary aspect of this movement is equally striking and more obvious; namely, the effect of intellectual changes upon the understanding of Scripture. For example, the broadening range of learning in the eleventh century altered the character of the commentaries, and the revival of logic and philosophy produced a new type of exposition which brought theological questions to the fore; exegesis passed into systematic doctrinal teaching. Discussions

---

[1] See C. Jenkins, in *Bede, His Life, Times and Writings*, edited by A. Hamilton Thompson, Oxford, 1933, pp. 173–80.

of another kind enter Biblical scholarship from the great cathedral schools of the following period; points of history, literary and linguistic interests, are adduced. The period of the great scholastic philosophies introduces a remarkable change in scriptural methods. The forms of the disputations in the schools are applied to the exposition of the Bible, and the main attention is given to the metaphysical implications of the passage in question. The Aristotelian view of knowledge had profoundly affected the attitude of scholars towards the sacred text. The main feature in such developments was the view taken at different stages of thought concerning the relationship between the literal and the spiritual meaning of Scripture. In the early period, the period of Bede, the literal meaning of the words is at a minimum. Under the authority of Augustine and Gregory the text is conceived as a divine message to men, written in cipher; and names, events, and places symbolize dogmatic and spiritual principles. When the narrative is trivial or unedifying, no literal meaning is allowed at all. At a later stage, while the allegorical meaning is still dwelt upon and deemed of most importance, the literal sense is recognized as possessing a certain value, in conveying moral lessons to the Christian reader. A further step is taken when, largely through the adoption of the methods of Jewish scholars, such as Maimonides, the literal sense is explained by reference to some knowledge of ancient Hebrew history and manners. Combined with the search for edification the new method approaches a history of religious and moral education. Often, too, the new information about the rituals or agricultural life of the Jews of the Old Testament suggests a rational explanation of the text. But, though the literal significance of the text acquires increasing importance the older allegorical and mystical modes of interpretation were maintained, and often dominated biblical study.[1] Through the centuries of allegorizing industry went on. We shall find Reginald Pecock protesting in the fourteenth century against the allegorical methods that were customary in his day. And in the crisis of the Reformation William Tindale complained that the literal sense had become nothing at all.

The authoritative literature of sacred doctrine, to the interpretation of which intellectual effort was eminently devoted

---

[1] B. Smalley, op. cit.

during the Saxon centuries of our history, constituted one element in the complex volume of indefeasible doctrine. The unquestioned body of truths that guided and inspired reflection in the monasteries rested also upon the credal pronouncements of the great Church Councils. In the Councils of Nicaea, of Ephesus, and of Chalcedon the dogmas of the faith had been solidified and defined; and heretical theories had been disallowed. Differences concerning points of faith were settled by reference to the decrees of the Councils. In addition, the inquiries of the cloister student were confronted with the ample manuscripts of the Fathers, containing in every section authoritative doctrine on theology and philosophy. Of these inspired teachers four dominated the minds of Saxon scholars, as we have seen; Jerome, Ambrose, Augustine, Gregory. Discussions on sin and grace, on predestination, redemption, and the sacraments, composed a fabric of citations from these authorities; and the beliefs of monks relating to the nature of the world and of man were principally derived from these sources. To these components of authoritative instruction must be added the *ex cathedra* utterances, the epistles and decretals, of the Popes. Abbots, bishops, and provincial Councils who failed to reach agreement on questions of doctrine were increasingly led to appeal to Rome.

This range of inviolable knowledge formed a unified system. Scripture, for example, was not held to add in any way to the content of Apostolic doctrine nor to the creeds. Intellectual discussion in the cloister schools reclined upon a corpus of belief enclosed in the oecumenical councils, in the writings of the Fathers, in the pronouncements of Popes, and, above all in the sacred pages of the Vulgate. In points of dispute and of suspected heresy scholars are found appealing to the Catholic faith, the Holy Scriptures, and the teaching of the Church.

When we compare the biblical commentaries of Bede with those of patristic times a change in the rational circumstances of inquiry is apparent. The Fathers were acutely aware of controversies stirred by heretical movements of thought, and such controversies compelled them to enter into large questions of theology and of metaphysics. None of these heresies were now living issues; a declaration of orthodoxy in the face of the Monothelite heresy was called for by the Pope in 679, but the meeting held at Hatfield on the matter occasioned no discussion of principles, and it is to be doubted whether anyone beside Theodore at that gathering understood the implications of the question. The task before thought in an age in which few could seize more than the simplest elements of Christian theory was to transmit the teaching of the Scriptures and the expositions of the great authorities of the Church upon them. England gave birth to the greatest scholar in this field. Before Bede's death in 735 the brief flowering of Saxon culture was already fading. To Alcuin England was decadent. Invasions and sectional strife had destroyed what laxity and corruption in the monasteries had undermined. But scriptural philosophy continued to control the attempt to understand experience. The Bible remained the principal source of truth. It became the chief pre-occupation of the university schools in the medieval period; and the reformers of the sixteenth century ascribed to it an authority no less absolute than that assigned to it by scholastic thinkers. At the opening of the scientific phase in the seven-teenth century men still clung to the figurative modes of inter-preting the Scriptures. It was not until the following century when natural religion governed theological discussion that the belief in allegorical communication began to recede. As the ancient theories of verbal or of plenary inspiration gave way, the moral character of the biblical message was increasingly emphasized. There occurred some notable clashes between scriptural truth and scientific knowledge in England during the nineteenth century, but the protests of clerical thinkers against the opinions of *Lux Mundi* were the last important manifesta-tions of the divided loyalty that had agitated philosophical reflection since the primitive period of English Christianity.

THE DEVELOPMENT OF AUGUSTINIANISM

I

DURING the later phases of Saxon history no signal development of ideas appeared. Alfred made strenuous efforts to revive the splendid memories of scholarship in the country and to educate himself and his people. He invited learned men to England, set in hand translations, and made far-reaching plans for the instruction of the young. In the translations and incidental notes of his later years we can observe his earnest attempts to cope with abstract ideas, particularly in the translation of the *De Consolatione Philosophiae* of Boethius. He speculates about the stars, the tides, thunder and lightning, and the growth of seeds. But his information is even less scientific than Bede's; and when he comes to discuss the philosophical notions of Boethius he is plainly out of his depth, struggling to grasp general ideas by visual metaphors.

Alfred's reforms failed to stem the decay of culture. The reorganization of the monasteries under Dunstan restored the healthy cross-fertilization that had stimulated the inquiries of the northern houses in the days of Benedict Biscop. In the tenth century learned monks from Fleury and Corbie gave instruction in English monasteries, and Englishmen went to study at the schools of Chartres, Fulda, and elsewhere. But the movement produced no departure in thought. Its most striking outcome was a series of writings in the English tongue such as the treatise of Byrhtferth on chronology. But there was no important development of Latin reflection. Philosophical discussion had been intermittently active since Alcuin, but the outlook of the monastic centres of study had remained conservative and there was little to distinguish the work that was done in them from the labours of Bede's time. Monks collated passages from Scripture and the Latin Fathers in support of doctrinal questions and pursued the allegorical significance of the sacred text. The scope of interest was severely restricted. Dialectic was discouraged; if supernatural revelation had made known all that was necessary for man to know, what need was there for rational demonstration? There was increasing emphasis upon conciliar and episcopal ruling. The new spirit in the monasteries that was organized under Dunstan demanded intellectual obedience and discipline. Secular reading was frowned upon and interest in philosophy was discouraged. But general rational inquiry had become little more than a gloss upon the dialectical text-books. It was confined to trivial exercises in the syllogism. Logical investigation in the monastic schools of England was hampered by the mechanical view of reason taught in the courses of the trivium. The lamp of thought among English monks at the time of the Conquest burned low. A far more enterprising and informed level of reflection existed in the Norman abbeys and when the Norman monks began to enter the country in larger numbers after the Conquest a fresh vigour of ideas was infused into the traditional occupations of English scholars.[1]

But meanwhile the authority of sacred doctrine had been asserted. The trend of opinion in the eleventh century may be illustrated from the pronouncements of the first great Norman Archbishop of Canterbury. Lanfranc, like Anselm who followed him, was an Italian. In his youth he had been trained in the law at the leading school of Pavia. After many wanderings he entered the small Benedictine house at Bec, in the vale of Brionne. He became Prior and the fame of his teaching spread through the West. Bec became the seminary from which the leading ecclesiastics of the time were promoted. Lanfranc assumed control of the Church in England in 1070 and his energies were necessarily absorbed in problems of organization and authority. But his reputation as a scholar attracted many students to his lectures at Canterbury. Monks from Norman abbeys followed him to England and a number of houses were soon governed by men who had been educated at Bec. But Lanfranc did not invite the schools to undertake philosophical inquiries. He had formerly been renowned for his dialectical skill, but in a letter written soon after his translation to Canterbury he observed that since he had become a bishop he had abandoned the use of dialectics. In the celebrated controversy with his old master, Berengar of Tours, concerning the nature of the Eucharist he not only defended the orthodox view but roundly condemned rational discussion of theological dogma.

[1] Cf. D. Knowles, *The Monastic Order in England*, Oxford, 1941, p. 94.

He reproached Berengar with preferring reason to sacred authority, and he called upon God and his conscience to witness that he had no desire to resort to a rational interpretation of Scripture. He could not resist exposing a flaw in Berengar's logic, but he views the function of reason in a negative manner; its value dwells less in the task of establishing the truth, for that is known, than in refuting heresy.[1]

Yet despite the authoritarian tendencies of the tenth and eleventh centuries a current of logical and metaphysical discussion gathered force. During these centuries there sprang up a series of acute doctrinal controversies in the course of which rational justification was offered on either side; and echoes of these debates were caught in the English monasteries. The disputants addressed themselves to principles. Conspicuous among these controversies were the debates over the nature of the Eucharistic Elements, over the worship of images, and over the method of interpreting Scripture. The treatises that were produced on these questions and the replies that they called forth from bishop *scholastici* and others reveal the existence of a strong tension between the spirit of tradition and of inquiry. The current investigation reached its boldest expression in the work of Berengar, *De Sacra Coena*, written in 1068. We have referred to Lanfranc's reply to this work. Berengar naturally did not criticize the authority of the Scriptures nor of the Fathers, but he drew a contrast between a rational and a traditional interpretation of the sacred writings, and he declared that a man would rather die than prefer tradition to reason. Few went so far as this; and such utterances strengthened the forces of authority. But it would be quite false to the mental life of this time to suppose that there was any sharp division between the rational and the conservative theologians. There was never a school of rational theologians in opposition to those who upheld authority. No writer ever disputed the basis of the tradition, which was revelation. Nor did the most critical scholar doubt that the Church was divinely instructed. A writer who criticizes accepted views on certain points, upholds implicit acceptance of ecclesiastical tradition on other points. There was no conceivable alternative scheme of beliefs concerning the rational principles of the universe. The main activity of

[1] A. J. Macdonald, *Lanfranc*, Oxford, 1926, p. 92.

lettered men was devoted to the pursuit of the spiritual and
symbolic sense of the venerated texts. It was an activity of
commentaries and of glosses on the commentaries, and the
method of interpretation was dominantly moral. Compassed
by such a world the scholar believed before he sought to understand, and his understanding assumed the indefeasible authority
of his sources. Authority and doctrine preceded inquiry. 'Do
not seek to understand in order that you may believe, but believe
in order that you may understand.'[1] Modern phases of thought
failed to grasp the meaning of such assertions, and what was
a truism became a scandal. The structure of belief by which
the monastic scholar was confronted did not comprise a chain
of philosophical formulae. The questions under examination
could not be approached in the detached impartial manner
which later phases demanded on all subjects, for it was impossible even to perceive what the questions were without
becoming emotionally implicated in them. In the later phase
of thought the criteria of inquiry were derived from a preoccupation with physical objects and their relations, and here
indifference is not difficult to attain; in the medieval phases the
standards of judgement were formed from a preoccupation with
religion. When Augustine said that understanding is the reward
of faith, he expressed the principle that the Faith of the Church
was not to be attained through the neutral intellect. In order to
understand it the intellect must be illumined by belief, in other
words, by religious practice. We begin with authority, embody-
ing the corporate experience and reflection of the Church.
Authority opens the door. If a man enters, leaves doubt behind,
and follows the rules of good living, he will become receptive to
teaching and will at length come to see how eminently reasonable those doctrines are that he obeyed before he understood
them.[2] Fruitful reasoning on points of faith requires a purification of the heart; truth is not to be grasped apart from charity.
Such sayings are common in Augustine; it is the perspective of
monastic thought. The Aristotelian principle that there is a
conformity between the thing which is and the understanding,
and that knowledge is perfected by the assimilation of the

---

[1] Augustine, In *Joan. Evang.* xxix. 6; Migne, *Patrologia Latina*, xxxv. 1630.
[2] Augustine, *De Ordine*, ix. 26; *Corpus Scriptorum Ecclesiasticorum Lati-
norum*, lxiii. 165.

knower to the thing known, accorded with this outlook. A 'natural' mode of argument, starting from non-religious meta-physical premisses, could never reach understanding. Unless the mind submits to the discipline commanded by the Reality that is presumed to exist in faith, thought will grasp not the sub-stance but a shadow.

On the other hand, the artificial and pedantic training in logic that was given in the monastery schools provided scholars with an inadequate instrument for thinking and, as we have seen, there was already a revolt against dialectics on the ground of its futility in the eighth century. The contempt of dialectics sprang not from its content but from the superficial manner in which it was applied in the schools; the tradition did not favour its application to serious problems of theology and of know-ledge. The chief metaphysical works of Aristotle, the *Physics* and the *Metaphysics*, were unknown; but there was available a corpus of Aristotelian doctrine in the versions and com-mentaries of Boethius. In the eleventh century this system of theory began to be studied more earnestly and to be carried into fields of doctrine. The syllogistic method of reasoning is based upon the belief in essences, the belief that everything possesses a ground of existence, and that this is a system of general relations, a universal. The field of inquiry is assumed to consist of essential general natures and of inessential pro-perties and accidents attached to the general essences; and the essential natures and their properties and accidents can be distinguished by thought. These Aristotelian principles appear in the doctrinal discussions of the time; for instance, Berengar relies upon the theory of accidents and metaphysical substance to explain the relation between the bread and wine and the spiritual Body in the Eucharist. Other Aristotelian conceptions that were tentatively applied to theological questions were the conceptions of form and matter, and of actuality and poten-tiality. But this Aristotelian apparatus was interwoven with Augustinian conceptions. And the first notable development in men's conceptions of knowledge and reality was essentially an enunciation of the vision of Augustine. The movement entered western thought at the end of the eleventh century. Its main channel was the genius of an Archbishop of Canterbury.

The blend of Neo-Platonic and Judaic-Christian principles

that emerged from the fragmentary metaphysics of the preceding centuries grew chiefly from the writings of St. Augustine. But numerous other channels contributed to Augustinianism. Plato, Aristotle, the Stoics, Plotinus, the theologians of Alexandria, the Hebrew Scriptures, and the Apostolic writings entered into the living structure of the design. And during the confusion of the centuries following the collapse of the Empire, other strains mingled with the Augustinian perspective. It is beyond our purpose to distinguish all these elements. But we cannot appreciate this characteristic scheme of rational principles without glancing at some of its sources in the past; for as the system became more articulate and was called upon to meet new situations, the ancient roots gave life to memorable developments in our mental history.

II

The Christian Platonic tradition was sustained by a very imperfect acquaintance with the text of Plato. By the masters of learning among the monks Plato was only known directly through scattered quotations in Cicero, Seneca, and late Latin writers, such as Macrobius.[1] A number of references to him were found in the Fathers, but there were few quotations from the *Dialogues*. The most widely read Platonic passage was the version of a small section of the *Timaeus* in Boethius' *Consolation of Philosophy* which was held to teach the Christian doctrine of creation. But the original Platonic modes of thought had been transformed by numerous developments many centuries before their remnants passed into the current of European reflection. Successive schools of Stoicism, Alexandrian mysticism, and Christian dogma, had changed it into shapes remote from the views of the ancient school. Yet some affinities had been preserved between the older and later manifestations. The conspicuous mark of the thought of the Academy was the exaltation of precise general thinking over sensory experience. The impulse that governs this direction of interest sprang from primary postulates concerning reality. A guiding postulate was that what is real must be sought in what is objective, permanent, and intellectually coherent. It was not to be sought in what is most immediately impressive

[1] R. Klibansky, *The Continuity of the Platonic Tradition*, London, 1939, p. 22.

or what appears to be most concrete and indefeasible, the world displayed to sense-perception. Guided by the search for the reality beyond appearance philosophy found that the world shown to our human senses was contaminated with illusion and change. The shifting coloured scene that naïve opinion takes for the real world was shown to be pervaded by indefiniteness and confusion. It is inextricably tied to our senses, to our eyes and ears and hands, and it varies with variations in them. The true key to reality had been forged by the physicists and especially by those who had applied mathematical calculations to the interpretation of nature. In this direction there were found entities that were certain, clearly defined, and logically interconnected. They were untouched by the contingency that belongs to the region of perception. The realm of mathematical relations is timeless, coherent, and precise; it bears the marks of reality, and it is in this direction that the ground of things must be sought. The clue was pursued in principle beyond the level of mathematics, for mathematics relies upon things that are perceived by the senses. The method indicated by mathematics was pressed forward into a level of pure logic, until highly general entities, similarity and difference, one and many, being, motion and rest, were reached. These entities were not logical abstractions, but realities beside which the world of material things is a pale reflection. The science that treated of these realities, their classification, their relation to one another, and to particular things, was Dialectic. Dialectic points to an intelligible sphere of εἴδη, forms, orderly, timeless, immaterial. The method of seeking truth followed from this view of reality. The method was one of scientific and metaphysical deduction by which the characteristics of the perceived world could be demonstrated from theoretical knowledge of their principles. In the *Timaeus* a partial deduction of this kind was attempted.[1] The chief properties of the material objects perceived by our senses were shown to be derived from ultimate geometrical shapes. Plato also attempted to trace sensations of heat and cold to primary shapes and motions. But these speculations were put forward as 'likely stories'.

The Forms are not abstractions drawn from particular

---

[1] *Timaeus*, 47c–69a. The Platonic method was not reaffirmed in English thought until the seventeenth century in Hobbes' *De Corpore*.

perceptions; such a view is summarily dismissed.[1] They are not in any way modes of thinking; they are fundamental realities. Here is the source of medieval realism, the doctrine that universals indicated by a common name are real objects, not merely convenient symbols. The way of truth is the systematic exploration of the scientific and logical objects revealed by thought. But beside the logical and mathematical Forms that explain in principle the grounds of the material universe, human practical experience apprehends moral standards and ideals. In seeking the essential nature of ordinary moral notions, courage or piety or justice, we reach general kinds of moral realities that are partially revealed in different individual actions. Pursuing our inquiries we attain in the end the notion of an absolute goodness, to which all other types of goodness are approximations. There is a sovereign Form of goodness in which the fragmentariness and impermanence of our temporal strivings are fulfilled. And there is, too, an absolute beauty, the shadow of which is perceived in works of art and poetry.

The emphasis is on thought and the objects attained by thought. Man's mind is enmeshed in the passing things of the world, but through reason it can descry the eternal principles. The rational element in us is immortal and divine. It is immortal because it is rational, for the apprehension of necessary principles is not dependent upon sensory temporal experience. Since the objects that reason contemplates are timeless, reason also must be untouched by mortality.[2]

The transformations that the spirit of inquiry underwent during the Hellenistic and Graeco-Roman period have been referred to in the preceding chapter. The scientific and mathematical investigations that developed under the inspiration of the Platonic Academy receded and moral quests occupied the attention of the schools. In the field of metaphysics Platonism became fused with Aristotelian and with Stoic conceptions, and as a result the distinctive mathematical clue to reality faded. The objects of inquiry became essences and qualitative forms. But Christian philosophy was most deeply affected by the direction given to Platonic views by Neo-Platonism. In the hands of Plotinus the Greek tradition was moulded into a transcendental absolutism in which leading elements from

[1] *Parmenides*, 132 b.   [2] *Phaedo*, 78 b.

Aristotle were blended with Platonic principles. The religious turn that was given to the tradition by Plotinus can be illustrated by taking our stand at the culminating point of his great structure. In the *Parmenides* Plato had unfolded a chain of subtle logical arguments which follow deductively from the assumption that there is or is not a One or Whole. Plotinus interprets these arguments in a theological sense. The One becomes God, beyond all being, unknowable and ineffable. We cannot say what the One is for it is beyond all distinctions; it contains, but is more than, life, consciousness, thought, activity, beauty. All we can say of it is to say what it is not. Yet all that exists, exists through the One, for the principle in anything, in virtue of which it is a thing, whether it be a ship, or a plant, or health, or a soul, is its principle of unity. Material things or unities are farthest removed from the supreme unity, and as we move from nature to mind and from mind to reason we draw nearer to the level where thought becomes one with its object. All multiplicity is a consequence or outgoing of unity, ultimately of the supreme One. The One is identical with the Good. Here Plotinus relies upon the celebrated passage in the *Republic* in which the Form of the Good is said to be 'beyond being'. The absolute Good and the absolute One, the source of all things, are the same. In his discussion of the Absolute Plotinus affirms its suprarational nature.

'He that would speak exactly must not name it by this name or that; we can circle, as it were, about its circumference, seeking to interpret in speech our experience of it, now shooting near the mark, and again disappointed of our aim by reason of the antinomies we find in it. The greatest antinomy arises in this, that our understanding of it is not by way of scientific knowledge nor of intellection, as our understanding of other intelligible objects, but by a presence higher than all knowing.'[1]

The One is not a mathematical or logical unity; it is the transcendental ground of existence. Plotinus adopts the language of worship and of mysticism rather than the older Greek way of intellectual contemplation when speaking of our apprehension of the Supreme Being. The devotional outlook which animates his thought is characteristic of the intense preoccupation with religion that coloured the age; but no one

---

[1] Plotinus, *Enneads*, vi. ix. 3–4, translated by E. R. Dodds.

before him had combined the theological tendencies of the Stoics, of Plato, and of Aristotle, with such metaphysical power.

From the ineffable One there appears by a kind of generation or emanation the Spirit, or νοῦς, which comprises the highest stage to which human knowledge can attain. It is the intelligible universe of Platonic Forms. Below the Spirit lies the soul or mind, intermediate between the material world and the Spirit. Soul (ψυχή) embraces the world-soul and individual souls immersed in bodies. The highest development of the human soul is independent of the body. Plotinus also enforced the belief in the superiority of contemplation or reason over practice and over empirical inquiry. Action is the shadow of meditation, and weaker minds crave to see the truth in material form. It is the dunces who take to crafts and manual employments because they are not fitted for learning and meditation.[1] At the bottom of the hierarchy of being lies matter. Plotinus is not consistent in his account of the material world; but certainly one side of his thought emphatically conceives of matter as a source of evil. It is contamination to the soul to concern itself closely with physical things. The basis of this view lies in the Aristotelian principle that matter is the source of multiplicity and division. It thus represents the farthest separation from the One, a state of darkness and anarchy. This position deeply influenced Christian ideas of nature. And with this recoil from the visible and tangible world we may associate the indifference of this philosophy to temporal events. The cardinal concern of the soul is with a timeless realm. It has little interest in the spectacle of change and contingency.

Such are some of the elements in Neo-Platonism that entered into the heart of Christian reflection. They flowed into the stream of early European thinking through the writings of Augustine whose speculations are stamped with close study of Neo-Platonism. He had scanty knowledge of Greek, but it was through reading a part of the *Enneads* in a Latin translation that he was able to free his mind from the materialist arguments of the Manichaeans and turn towards Christian doctrine. In *De Civitate Dei* he cites also Iamblichus, Porphyry, and Apuleius, among those to whom he owed intellectual salvation;

[1] Ibid. III. viii. 4.

and in the same treatise passages from the *Enneads* are copied
into the text. But Neo-Platonic principles were adapted by
Augustine to serve ends at variance with those of the school;
they were inserted into a Christian framework.

The principle that rational research is the path to truth is
formally maintained. The way of knowledge is the way that
leads from *corporea* to *incorporea*, from the world of sense-
perception to the realm of the invisible and eternal Ideas. A
representation of the Neo-Platonic ladder of truth and being
appears. The philosophic search starts from practical acquaintance with the world displayed to the senses. From this level
the mind is compelled to proceed to the systems or rules that
explain the bare appearances of things. It is led on from the
judgements of the 'internal sense' to the wider principles of
scientia or *ratio*, the rational understanding of temporal things.
But beyond the categories of *scientia* the mind descries the
realm of pure thought, the objects of which are the Platonic
Forms, the *rationes necessariae* that explain and support the
lower levels. The apprehension of the Forms is the work of
intellectus. Finally the mind at rare moments attains a point of
spiritual intuition, a *totus ictus cordis*. The psychological ascent
of the soul depends on the recognition in the universe of a
hierarchy of beings, each level receiving its nature and explanation from the level that is superior to it in degree. Accordingly
each grade of knowledge points beyond itself to a more stable
and more comprehensive form of knowledge, while the contingency and imperfection of the lower grade is corrected by the
higher, until the intellectual understanding grasps the system
of unchangeable truths.[1] Augustine does not spend much time
on investigating the lower steps of the ladder of being. He
presses on to the sphere of the Forms. Several classes of 'divine
Ideas' are recognized. There are mathematical principles, such
as the rule of multiplication, that are known not by the bodily
senses but by an inner light. The remnants of Platonism appear
here, but the mathematics adduced is exceedingly elementary.
More generally, there are the principles of order, rhythm, and
symmetry, to which material things owe their being. The moral

---

[1] There are many accounts of the ascent in Augustine; e.g., *Confessions*,
VII. xvii. 23, *De Diversis Quaestionibus*, xlv. 1, *De Quantitate Animae*, xxxiii.
70.

principles of conduct also rest ultimately on a system of moral Forms. A man becomes good by 'adjusting his soul to those immutable rules and beacons of the virtues, which reside incorruptibly in that truth and wisdom'.[1]

The intellectual journey is suffused with moral and religious feeling as it is for Plotinus. The ascent is not a scientific ascent from local to universal laws, but the path of the soul towards regeneration and purification. It is the way of salvation. A Christian turn is given to the scheme. Augustine's early struggles with Stoic materialism profoundly affected the tendency of thought in Europe. The quest for truth becomes a quest for the God of Christianity. Above the sphere of the Forms the soul seeks for a sovereign source of the ideal standards to which all things aspire, a nature that is independent, perfect, omniscient; the quest is also a proof of the existence of an absolute Being, God. It is impossible to distinguish clearly the philosophical from the theological aspect of the inquiry. The logical analysis is at the same time a spiritual discipline, and the end sought is not knowledge but wisdom, *sapientia*. And wisdom means religious vision. So the search leads back to faith, for it must wait on the illumination which comes from Christian belief.

Accordingly a step is taken that divides by a chasm Greek from Christian thought. 'But somewhat later, I confess, did I learn, how in that saying, The Word was made flesh, the Catholic truth is distinguished from the falsehood of Plotinus.'[2] The conversion to Christianity opened a series of perspectives which were denied to Neo-Platonism; perspectives that issued from the capital principles of Hebraic-Christian thought. From acceptance of the Incarnation there followed an interest in time. Mundane events, the history of societies, the life and death of men, become of absorbing interest because they exhibit God's purpose in creation. Plotinus, following some cryptic utterances of Plato, looked upon history as a cycle of recurring periods, and he scorned the Christian belief in creation. Augustine wrote an epitome of human history, the cardinal point of which is the revelation of God in an historical figure. We are considering Augustinianism in this book in its dominant philosophical

---

[1] *De Libero Arbitrio*, II. xix. 52.
[2] The classic passage is *Confessions*, VII. ix. 13 ff.

aspect. And in this aspect it accords with the Oriental features of Neo-Platonism and with the Hebraic belief in transcendent Being. But we must not forget that there is another side of the philosophy of the great African teacher that transmits the dynamic and social ethics of the Hebraic-Christian perspective to the medieval consciousness. The world is not an illusion nor a tomb, for the divine plan is manifested in history and in nature.

In this Christian Platonism, then, the geometrical and dialectical way of truth with which we began has become transformed into a religious inquiry that moves within the postulates of the Judaic-Christian theology. The ancient mathematical deductions, the inquiries into harmonics and the ultimate configurations of physical bodies, give place to the preparation of the soul for union with the divine. The Forms become Ideas in the mind of God, and the foundation of contingent things, 'their property of being and permanence and that by which even for their defects they are ranged in their due place in the complex whole of the universe, are all due to the goodness and omnipotence of Him who supremely is'.[1] The detail of the world is explained by reference to the divine purpose in creation; and this has been revealed. Augustine frequently refers to natural investigations but he has little interest in these pursuits and he warns Christians against the vain curiosity of the *physici* on the ground that it turns the mind away from the contemplation of the eternal realities.[2] Ignorance of the temporal order of the world is no disgrace. Philosophers only guess at such matters as the number of the elements, the form of the heavens, and the species of animals; they have no certain knowledge. 'It is enough for Christians to believe that the only cause of all created things, whether celestial or earthly, visible or invisible, is the goodness of the Creator.'[3] All knowledge of any value is contained in the scriptures. Yet such utterances must not be pressed too far. Medieval students could find texts in their master that appeared to deprecate natural inquiry and to rest upon revealed faith. But it must be recalled that this conception of knowledge is Neo-Platonic, and that what is often put aside in these passages is not physical knowledge as such, but the empirical method of inquiry.

[1] Augustine, *Ep.* cxviii. iii. 15.   [2] *De Musica*, vi. xii. 39.
[3] *Encheiridion*, ix.

Hebrew and Christian principles are blended with Neo-Platonic modes of reason. In the previous chapter it was remarked that philosophers throughout the Middle Ages drew upon utterances in the Hebrew Scriptures that lent consecrated force to metaphysical inquiries. We have now to call attention to a fundamental strain in the Jewish faith that concurred with the Neo-Platonic theology. The Jews combined a belief in the personal activity of God in the world with an overpowering sense of His transcendent majesty. In many passages the Scriptures assert the doctrine of absolute Being. The texts of Exodus iii, for instance, are frequently resorted to throughout the Middle Ages when the foundations of things are in question.

'How gloriously then and divinely did Our God say to His servant, "I am that I am",' and then "Say to the Children of Israel, He Who is has sent me to you. For He Himself most truly is because He is altogether immutable. For this, in fact, is always the result of change, that what once was, is now no more. That, therefore, can truly be said to be which is immutable, but as to other things which have been made by Him, it is from Him that each in its own way has received its being.'[1]

Gregory the Great, who presides with Augustine over the modes of reflection at the dawn of the Middle Ages, insists on the principle. He distinguishes between primary Being and secondary being, between immutable and essential Being, and changing, accidental being.[2] And, to select an example from the later period, the author of De Primo Principio opens his work by invoking the cardinal Judaic text from Exodus, and proceeds: 'Thou art true being, thou art all being; this, I believe; this, if it be possible for me I desire to understand. Help me, Lord, in the search, so far as our natural reason can attain, for the true being that Thou art, beginning with the being that Thou hast proclaimed of Thyself.'[3] This postulate readily blended with the Neo-Platonic exaltation of the One, and provided a fundamental feature of the philosophy of the West. Ultimate reality lies beyond the temporal universe, which is created by the ultimately real. The pre-condition of

---

[1] Augustine, De Natura Boni, cap. 19.
[2] Magna Moralia, xvi. 45, xviii. 82; F. Homes Dudden, Gregory the Great, London, 1905, ii, p. 130.
[3] Quoted E. Gilson, L'esprit de la philosophie médiévale, Paris, 1932, p. 55.

mundane existence is absolute Being, that which really is,
beyond all limitation and contingency, eternal and unchanging.
On the one hand there is the universe of time and space, filled
from the depths to the heights with change and with composite
and corruptible existences. On the other hand is plenitude of
Being; and all the contingency and imperfection of things are
explicable only in the light of this Fullness of reality. The
directing impulse of reason sought for the meaning of processes
whether mundane or celestial in a Ground that is the necessary
condition of the lower orders of existence; it looked towards the
more complete levels of being, never towards the lower levels.
The primary conception implicit in this perspective, translated
into metaphysical terms, is the conception of self-sufficient
Being, *ipsum esse subsistens*; and other cardinal ideas, such as
those of perfection, of final end, and of creation came to be
conceived, as the ancient tradition was more definitely stated,
as subordinate to that of Being.

The conception of causation that governed the central course
of subsequent thought follows naturally from this postulate.
That which becomes and changes must be derived from that
which is unchanging and eternal; that which is indeterminate is
dependent upon that which is determinate, that which is contingent upon the necessary, that which is imperfect, composite,
and multiple upon the perfect, the simple, and the one. All these
conceptions, which fused with the Greek principle that the cause
must contain eminently all the reality of the effect, are supported
by the sacred tradition. The radical difference between Being
and contingent being determines the careful distinction that was
always drawn between creation and all other types of becoming.
To create means to produce being, and this is the prerogative of
Absolute Being alone. The mark of creation is to bring into
existence that which did not before exist in any form. It is
production from nothing. The God of Genesis, since he is Being,
does not require matter in the act of making. The religious
prospect on the universe that determined this credal principle,
issued during the thirteenth and fourteenth centuries in a
critical difference between Aristotelianism and the Faith.
Aristotle maintained that the world was eternal and had no
beginning; the Church held that it had been created at a point of
time by God. The difference occasioned a volume of discussion

on ultimate principles. And it formed a reason for the inter-diction of the *Physics* and *Metaphysics* in the schools of Paris at the beginning of the century, and again towards its close in 1277. Many philosophers tried to interpret Aristotle as implying a temporal beginning to the world, and Grosseteste laughs at their efforts to make him into a good Catholic. But our present concern is rather with the significance of the idea of creation as such than with the special question of the creation of the world. Creation is the prerogative of Being, and the essential difference between creation and other types of becoming is that the former is production from nothing, the latter production from previous existence. All types of becoming in the universe other than crea-tion are *ab alio*. They require pre-existent elements and agents; more precisely, they require matter that possesses aptitude for appropriate forms. No created beings can create. *Generatio* and *compositio*, the generation of living beings from other living beings, and the formation of fresh types of matter by composi-tion from the elements, are not acts of creation. We may there-fore put the inherent tendency of this perspective in a negative way. A doctrine of an immanent creation of reality would be impossible to it; it could not enter its horizon to suppose that ultimate reality could develop. That which changes is not wholly real, but something less. And there is a correlative implication of this faith. The act of creation cannot involve any diminution of complete Being, any emanation or outflowing of His nature. The substance of the created universe is not drawn from His substance. For God is self-sufficient. Inspired by Hebraic-Christian beliefs western philosophy instinctively rejected the Stoic and Neo-Platonic doctrine, transmitted by the Arabian thinkers, that the universe is an emanation from the highest to the lowest grade, of the One. The Divine Being can neither add to nor subtract from Being by the act of creation. The doctrine that power descends from Being through the intelligences that move the spheres entered later into the theory of natural causation. But central theological beliefs forbade any doctrine of an emanation of the Divine Substance.

The patristic thinkers had been occupied with cardinal problems that sprang from Judaic and Neo-Platonic concep-tions. They were confronted with the problem of reconciling the transcendent and self-sufficient character of the Absolute

Being with His operations in Nature and Man. The problem
is explored in the elaborate discussions on the Trinity and on
the twofold nature of Christ that stretch from the time of
the Apostolic writers to the time of Gregory of Nyssa. Yet the
prophetic conviction that God is eminently real dominates the
debates, and the persistent efforts to combine this conviction
with Greek doctrines of immanent development transmitted the
problem of Being and Becoming to medieval thought. What
is noticeable in the great theological debates is the insistence on
the Hebraic principle of Being. In seeking to describe the nature
of deity the Fathers employ such terms as *essentia* and *sub-
stantia*; terms indicating personality are rarer and subordinate.

But we must move over the centuries and approach the period
of philosophical renaissance in England. A powerful influence
upon the rational consciousness of men appeared in the ninth
century, which promoted the metaphysical outlook that we
have been considering. The treatise *On the Divine Names* was
held to be the inspired work of Dionysius the Areopagite, the
disciple of St. Paul, and was consequently accorded special
veneration by medieval thinkers. No book more deeply determined the character of speculation than this work. That
remarkable philosopher of the Carolingian era, Scotus Erigena,
translated it into Latin, and further translations and commentaries continued to appear century after century. The treatise
was, in reality, a transcription into Christian terms of the
Elements of Theology of Proclus, made by a writer of the fifth
century. Proclus was the most important thinker of the Neo-
Platonic school after Plotinus, and through the pseudo-
Dionysius many ideas of late Neo-Platonism penetrated
Christian philosophy. From Dionysius there descended the
negative, mystical theology which has appeared frequently in
England, especially after periods of excessive analysis and
logical refinement. We shall notice the presence of the teaching
of the *Divine Names* in the fourteenth century following upon
the exhaustive criticisms and subtleties of the great period of
scholasticism. And a further revival occurred in the Elizabethan
age. For Dionysius, as for Plotinus, God is beyond all predicates: He is the nameless One, the supra-essential, transcendent
being. 'For it is a Monad that unifies every unity, a super-
essential essence, an unintelligible mind, an ineffable word, or

rather the negation of reason, intelligence, word, and every particular form of existence.' This trend of thought accorded with the tendencies that we have distinguished, and Dionysius finds his way of negation confirmed by the Holy Scriptures. In many passages this fundamental text-book of the Middle Ages strengthened the metaphysical conceptions that had been assimilated from Augustine. The ascent of mind by way of sensation, judgement, understanding, and intellectual intuition, an ascent that is a spiritual as well as a logical quest, is unfolded by Dionysius. So also is the doctrine of exemplarism, which maintains that the archetypes or Ideas of all existing things dwell in the mind of God, a doctrine that underlies much of medieval realism. And the Augustinian method of reasoning from contingent and imperfect beings to the perfect and necessary Being is enforced by the argument of Proclus, speaking in the guise of the Areopagite. In addition, there passed into the mental vision of the ages of faith an imposing picture of a celestial hierarchy of divine beings which has its counterpart on earth in the orders and sacraments of the Church.

Such are the outlines of the system of rational sentiments that guided methods of investigation and determined logical ideals during the formative centuries of Christian Europe. Many centuries elapsed before they came to fruition. The disruption of society and the decay of scholarship permitted them to appear only in fragmentary shapes in the theological debates of the sixth and seventh centuries. And these fragments were mixed, as we have seen, with portions of Aristotelian logic drawn from the text-books of Boethius. In the writings of Gregory Augustinianism is diminished to the standards of popular religious beliefs; the metaphysical doctrines are presented in a summary and superficial fashion; and the forefront of interest is occupied by marvels and prophecies. Of all the Latin Fathers the works of Gregory were most studied in England in the first phase of our culture, and it is principally through them that the phantoms of Platonism passed into the heritage of English thought.

Soon after the invasion of Saxon England a large number of Norman theologians were appointed to prominent positions in the English Houses. Two distinguished scholars from Bec assumed in turn the control of the Church in England. We have touched on the influence of Lanfranc. The second, Anselm, was the pre-eminent philosopher of the age, and it was principally through him that the theses of Augustinianism became once more articulate.

III

It is not within our province to refer here to the troubled career of this extraordinary man. He was consecrated Archbishop of Canterbury in 1093 and died in 1109. In this interval he engaged in bitter conflicts with the governments of William II and of Henry I. He was an indomitable and far-sighted statesman, as well as an original thinker. And he was an inspiring teacher who won the devotion of men of all conditions.

The signal regeneration of thought accomplished by the works of Anselm owes nothing, it is clear, to intellectual circumstances in England. He was not even of Norman birth; he was an Italian from Aosta. No English influences can be ascribed to the formation of his ideas, for his distinctive treatises were written at Bec, before he came to England. The immediate effect in England of his remarkable vindication of rational theology was not considerable. His homiletic writings were widely known and copied, but his philosophy produced immediately no distinguished disciples in the country. But there is some evidence of a school of thought devoted to his ideas in the south-east of the land. His influence, and the influence of the Augustinian tradition which attains a fresh rigour and concentration in his writings are not to be looked for in an immediate circle, but in a living background of beliefs that endured for centuries in our thought. Great intellectual developments are not to be measured by the direct impressions that they produce. They are absorbed into the texture of beliefs and become the directing assumptions of later views of experience. The formulation by Anselm of the Augustinian traditions of the monastic schools contributed to the living mental perspective of later reflection. The characteristic design of his theological philosophy appears prominently at Oxford in the thirteenth century; there is a striking revival of interest in his writings among masters of the fourteenth century; his modes of thought are manifest in the works of Hooker and of Norris in the sixteenth and seventeenth centuries. It is impossible to understand the development of Augustinianism in this country without some account of the distinctive qualities stamped upon that enduring tradition by the *Proslogion* and the *Cur Deus Homo*.

The view of knowledge and reality in these and in other works is dominated by the Christian and Plotinian interpretation of the Platonic Ideas. The argument moves quickly to the sphere of absolutes, to absolute goodness and essential self-dependent being. These ideal absolutes are the fundamental realities, or rather aspects of the one Supreme Being, God. The degrees of knowledge are degrees of spiritual development, and the norms of truth confirm the beliefs of religion and of revelation. The restraints that were imposed on thought by the authoritarian monastic movement of the age have been noticed on a preceding page. The function of the rational discussion of theological truths lay rather in the task of refuting novel interpretations of doctrine than in seeking a philosophical basis for the contents of the Faith. We have seen that a movement of rational theology in a sense that was independent of the authority of the Faith and its appointed agencies of instruction was inconceivable. It was impossible for philosophical thinking to start from non-Catholic premises. And there were many leaders of opinion who argued that faith needed no philosophy. The distinctive achievement of Anselm is the enlargement of the scope of reason in relation to faith. He recalled monastic scholars to the capital Christian philosophy of St. Augustine. Faith does not rest upon a philosophical inquiry but it is aided by it. It is a mark of negligence, if after men have been confirmed in faith, they are not eager to understand what they believe.[1] Faith cannot stand on any foundation other than the revelation of God in Christ and in the Church. The creed provides the material of reflection and the task of the Christian thinker is to clarify its implications. He must start with faith and proceed to intelligible faith.

But Anselm in many passages gives the sense of moving beyond this position. He appears to set himself to demonstrate the logical necessity of the central tenets of the Catholic creed upon postulates to which all reasonable men would subscribe, whether they be Christians or not. The famous work on the Incarnation begins by claiming that the first part of the book proves by necessary reasoning the essential doctrine of the

[1] *Cur Deus Homo*, i. 2.

Christian Faith. That is to say, it claims to show that salvation for man must be attained through such a person as Christians believe Christ to have been, and to show this without assuming any knowledge whatsoever of the existence of Christ. And in the second part Anselm professes to demonstrate by equally clear reasoning that human nature was made for blessed immortality and that this end could only be attained by the intervention in history of a man who was also God. Therefore, he concludes, all things that we believe concerning Christ must have occurred.[1]

The nature of the reasoning which is used in such demonstrations must be considered in a moment. What concerns us here is that this procedure professes not to assume the doctrines of Faith, but to deduce them from principles of common human experience. But we must notice that these demonstrations are naturally concerned with theological ideas. They appeal to moral and religious conceptions not to scientific or metaphysical principles untouched by religious devotion. These ideas are not, ostensibly, the ideas of the Faith; they are hypotheses that a man, detaching himself by a philosophical effort from the familiar doctrines of the Faith, would be willing to entertain. The procedure is to argue, if a God such as religious faith requires, were to exist, then what follows? Anselm's rational theology, therefore, takes faith as prior, even when it renounces knowledge of the Faith. And this programme of necessary reasoning is carried out with many concessions to orthodox beliefs. The arguments largely proceed by inferring what course of actions are possible to God in virtue of His supreme goodness. And in these arguments the principal theses of Catholicism are assumed. In *Cur Deus Homo* it is assumed that God intended to make up from among men the number of the fallen angels, that the material world is destined to be renewed in a nobler form, and that this will not occur till the number of the elect is complete, that man would never have been subject to death if his original parents had never sinned, and that those who die will rise again with their former bodies. In all this there is little reference to authority; the argument is free from the usual excessive allusions to the pronouncements of the Fathers of the Church. But the discussion moves from strictly theological

[1] *Cur Deus Homo*, Preface.

postulates to strictly theological conclusions. Orthodox beliefs form the assumptions of its logic; and in this respect it is typical of the rational theology of the age. Rational inquiry rests on faith. 'If I say anything that is not put forward by a superior authority I desire that it be understood in the following manner. Although the conclusion be presented as a necessary one so far as my reason is concerned, it must not be taken as absolutely necessary but only as for the present having the appearance of necessity.'[1] For our reason is inadequate to compass Being; we can argue only by analogy within our limited experience, and by such demonstrations as are open to us. The philosophy of this age does not pretend to elaborate a system of truths in independence of the circle of supernatural truths revealed in Scripture. 'He who does not have faith has no experience; and he who has not experienced the truth does not understand it.'[2]

In the *Dialogue on Truth* Aristotelian formulae, current in the monastic schools, appear, such as the principles of *actus* and *potentia*. But the Augustinian concern with the absolute One, the source of being and truth occupies the forefront of the argument. Everything that exists is related to the supreme truth, to the one ultimate reality, and draws its being from the supreme reality, and this means that everything that is real is right. The supreme truth to which all truths are related is admittedly a fundamentally different type of rightness to all other types of rightness; it is the source of all these other types, and unlike them is itself derived from no further source. How is moral truth apprehended? It is not perceived by the senses; the 'rightness' even of bodies is grasped by thought operating beyond the sense-perception of physical objects. 'If there be a doubt whether the line of some body not present to the senses is straight, and if it can be demonstrated that it does not curve in any part, is it not proved by reason that it must necessarily be straight?'[3] The way to truth and rightness is by demonstration, that is to say, through the spiritual intellect. And since truth is rightness, if there were many really distinct kinds of truth there would be many distinct kinds of rightness, varying

---

[1] Anselm, *Monologium*, 1. The further title is *Exemplum meditandi de ratione fidei*. The sub-title of the *Proslogion* is *Fides quaerens intellectum*.

[2] Id., *De Fide Trinitatis*, 3.

[3] *Dialogus de veritate*, 11; Migne, *Patrologia Latina*, 158, 480.

according to the functional nature of things. But rightness is
not relative. It is one and immutable, and therefore the truth
is one and the same in all its manifestations. Truth is a fulfilment, a rightness; and every particular truth is related to the
supreme self-subsisting truth.

The features of Augustinianism, the conjunction of truth and
value, the assertion of the supremacy of *intellectus*, are evident.
The opening chapters of the *Monologium* enforce the teaching
of realism, applied to moral ideas.[1] We desire many kinds of
good. Among them we can distinguish those we seek for their
usefulness as leading to further good, and those we desire for
their own sake (*propter honestatem*). But all these goods differ
in degree; they are more good or less good. Now this means
that they are elements in a good which transcends them, a
perfect good by which they are measured. All good is good in
virtue of a supreme good. In the same way it is shown that
there must be an absolute greatness, in the sense of greatness in
worth. Examination of the nature of being reaches similar
conclusions. Whatever is must be either self-sufficient or
dependent on something other than itself. It must be *per se* or
per aliud. Existence *per aliud* must depend ultimately on
existence *per se*. There must be a self-existent Being, if we are
to avoid an infinite regress. Combining the three lines of argument, we have proved the necessity of an absolute goodness, an
absolute greatness, and an absolute Being. But the ultimate
Being must be one. It is impossible that there should be several
distinct ultimate beings. The ultimate Being must be supremely
good, great, and self-sufficient. Further this Sovereign Being
must be the source of all other things. It cannot derive its being
from any other form of existence, nor depend on any other
existence. It must exist through and by itself. A critical step
is now taken; the argument calls upon the doctrine of creation
that has been described. The Supreme Being must have created
the world of things out of nothing. It could not have created
the world from itself, for that would mean a process of change
in the Absolute Being, and the Absolute Being cannot change.
Anselm examines the idea of creation closely, and comes to the
characteristically Augustinian conclusion, that creation out of
nothing implies that the things to be created must have existed

[1] *De Divinitatis Essentia Monologium*; Migne, *Patrologia Latina*, 158, 142 f.

in the mind of the Creator as patterns or Forms. These divine Ideas, or interior words, are the *rationes*, the essential principles of things. The Supreme Being does not use pre-existent material in the manner of a human artificer. A further consequence is that since all things draw their existence from the Sovereign Being, they must be sustained from moment to moment through His activity. The world rests upon a continuous activity of creation. The argument now proceeds to show at length that an Absolute Being who is perfect and the source of all existence must necessarily be endowed with a chain of other attributes, life, justice, wisdom, power, almightiness, truth, righteousness, eternity, blessedness, and so on. All these qualities must be aspects of the one infinite Being in virtue of His supremacy in the universe. In the final chapters these abstract reasonings are brought to bear on religion. The supreme Being thus qualified is the Christian God.

The celebrated argument for the existence of God offered in the *Proslogion*[1] must be viewed in relation to the same general framework of ideas. The ontological argument is not prominent in theological discussion before the fourteenth century. During the striking revival of Augustinian notions in the thirteenth century by the great Franciscan and Dominican scholars at Oxford Anselm is frequently cited, but the references to the argument of the *Proslogion* are rare. Thomas of York relies on it, and Richard Fishacre quotes it in full. But the first important discussion of it occurs in the writings of Duns Scotus, who adapted it to his own purposes. It reappears in the seventeenth century, in the writings of Stillingfleet, for example. Later discussion of this argument detached it from its setting in Anselm's thought, and its import was consequently misconceived. Anselm was led to formulate it by the desire to find one simple rational proof of the existence of God, in contrast to the elaborate methods of the *Monologion*; but the proof presupposes the general positions of that work and becomes unreasonable apart from them. Anselm observes that even the foolish man of the Psalms who denies that there is a God must admit that the word God has a meaning for him. He must understand by God a Being than whom nothing greater can be

---

[1] *Proslogion seu Alloquium de Dei Existentia*, ii–iv; Migne, *Patrologia Latina*, 158, 227.

conceived, *id quo majus cogitari nequit*. But such a Being cannot
exist only in our thought, *in intellectu*, for in that case the Being
could be conceived to exist in reality, *in re*; and this is to be
greater than to exist only in thought. If the Being than which
no greater can be thought of were to exist only in thought, there
would still be a Being than which a greater *can* be thought of,
namely, a real Supreme Being. This is contradictory, and therefore the Supreme Being must exist not only in thought but in
reality. As is well known, this argument called forth a criticism
in Anselm's day from a monk of Marmoutier-les-Tours named
Gaunilo, and Anselm published the criticism and his reply to it.[1]
It is necessary to refer to this reply in order to bring out the
significance of the argument. After some discussion of Anselm's
use of terms, Gaunilo presses the point that the question
whether that than which no greater can be conceived exists or
not can only be proved by going beyond the thought of it to
experience. Someone might ask me whether I can doubt the
existence of the fabulous island of Atlantis which is said to be
more excellent than all other lands. I must admit the real
existence of the island, or else I must admit that some other land
is more excellent than that which I had already understood to
be more excellent than any. If any one argued in this way I
should either suppose him to be jesting, or I should not know
whether he or I would be the greater fool, I in agreeing with
him or he in supposing that he had proved the existence of the
island. The criticism anticipates Kant's point that in order to
prove that a hundred dollars exist independently of my thought
of them, I must look beyond the logical definition to perception,
to seeing and handling the coins.

Now, Anselm in his reply does not admit the relevance of this
criticism. His general position is clearly exposed in his answer.
He points out that the discussion concerns the Supreme Being,
not a particular object, and it must assume the standpoint of
Faith. It does not assume the standpoint of an unbeliever.
Gaunilo is a Catholic Christian, that is to say, a man who already
believes in the Supreme on the authority of revelation, and the
position of the fool of the Psalms is that he does not understand
how God can exist. He is not a sceptic. The terms of the dis-

---

[1] *Liber Pro Insipiente*; *Liber Apologeticus contra Respondentem pro insipiente*;
Migne, *Patrologia Latina*, 158, 242 f.

cussion must be understood within the frame of the Faith. The
meaning of the reality under discussion is therefore expounded
on the lines of the *Monologion*. The Being than which no greater
can be conceived must be eternal, and therefore cannot be
thought of as merely possible. And if it is eternal it is always
actual. It must also be wholly present in all time and place.
We may agree with Gaunilo that such an object cannot be
completely understood, but a man who cannot gaze directly on
the sun can see the light of day which is composed of sunlight.
The argument from the Lost Island does not meet the case.
For we are concerned not with some particular fact of experience
but with a unique object, namely Supreme Being. Anselm
agrees that he would himself have been a fool if he had attempted
to prove the existence of the Lost Island from the notion of it.
But he denies that he had done this. The argument refers to
id quo majus cogitari nequit and to nothing else. To paraphrase
his point; the Absolute is not to be sought for among the facts
of sensible experience, and arguments drawn from the relation
between the ideas of particular things and their existence are
beside the issue. He concludes by reiterating the point that if
when a man thinks of that than which nothing greater can be
conceived he is thinking of something which cannot exist, he is
not thinking of what he professes to be thinking. If he is thinking of such an object, he is thinking of an object that must
necessarily exist.

The argument presumes the Neo-Platonic doctrine of Being
to which we have referred. And it also presumes the Augustinian
doctrines of truth that have been outlined above. Demonstrative truths presuppose the existence of their objects. Truths
express things as they are, and what they are in their essences
are Ideas in the mind of God. It is God who is the source of the
objects of our thoughts. He is present both in our thoughts and
in the objects of our thoughts. Necessary truths imply reality.
It is impossible to deny logically the existence of something than
which nothing greater can be thought, and accordingly it must
exist in reality. The ontological proof rests upon the Augustinian
and Neo-Platonic view that necessary and eternal Ideas are the
principles of being. The ideal realities to which necessary propositions refer ultimately compose reality. There is no ultimate
distinction between the logical order and the ontological order.

The intelligible content of the *rationes necessariae* refers to a reality that transcends thought. The argument does not move from idea to existence, but points immediately to Being *per se*, and maintains that the non-being of Being is inconceivable. Once more we are met with the primary postulate of the Christian philosophy that descends from Augustine, the postulate that intelligible essence and existence are identical.[1]

One further side of this theological realism may be presented. It was confronted by an extraordinary challenge. And it is interesting to observe the response that this challenge provoked. The man who propounded the heresy was Roscelin, Abbot of Compiègne. We are largely dependent upon the remarks of his critics for our knowledge of the opinions of this thinker. It can be gathered that the thesis which he put forward was the unheard-of thesis of extreme Nominalism. Thought does not concern itself with reality. Concepts and propositions are signs and combinations of signs that are arbitrary in origin. Language cannot express things as they are; it obliterates the infinite complexity of reality. Universals are merely names, *nomina*, or even *flatus vocis*, noises. There are no common natures, no essences, in the real world; they are fictions fostered by language.

The repudiation of this Epicurean teaching in Anselm's *De Fide Trinitatis* is outspoken.

'Those dialecticians, [he wrote] or rather dialectical heretics of our time who think that universal substances are nothing but sounds and are unable to distinguish colour from bodies, or the wisdom of man from his soul, ought to be wholly excluded from the discussion of spiritual questions. For in their souls reason which ought to be the ruler and judge of all that is in man is so involved in corporeal images that it is not able to escape from them or to discriminate between them and the things that should be contemplated by reason and alone. For how can he who does not yet understand that many men are in species one man comprehend how in that most lofty and mysterious nature a plurality of persons, each of whom singly is perfect God, are one God?'[2]

The passage reveals the ground of the defence of Augustinian realism against the new nominalism. Realism is the rational

---

[1] Anselm's reply to Gaunilo was reproduced by Thomas of York in the thirteenth century.
[2] Anselm, *De Fide Trinitatis*, 3; *Pat. Lat.*, 158, 265.

correlative of the Faith. If a man is sceptical about the substantial reality of colour-in-general he is in danger of rejecting
belief in the Trinity. He turns away from the realm of intelligible essences to the region of particular and perishing things in
which the body and its senses are immersed. Nominalism meant
empiricism and empiricism rejected Christian philosophy.

IV

The lineaments of the philosophy that has guided much of the
searching spirit of the West have been sketched. Let us attempt
to comprise its features under seven heads. First, rational
exploration begins and ends within the orbit of the Faith.
Theological belief precedes understanding; the mind must
believe in order to understand. The embracing contours of the
truth have been revealed; divine authority is the preparation
for reason. Second, the form of reasoning that controls the
search for truth is the necessary, self-evident, intuition of the
rational mind. Truth is sought in the intellectual cognition of
principles, not through empirical and sensory inquiry. The
relativity and contingency of the sensible world leads, step by
step, to a realm of pure Reason. It follows, third, that the
objects of thought are the incorporeal, spiritual Ideas, eternal,
necessary, and immutable. The rule of thinking is to withdraw
from the uncertainty and instability of bodily things, and to fix
our minds upon the immutable principles. Fourth, these
principles are the essential foundations of the universe of things.
The basic principles of reason, of goodness, and of beauty, are
the basic principles of reality. They are not abstractions, they
are primordial forms of being. Intelligibility and ultimate
existence are identical. Accordingly, fifth, the outlook is
radically realist. The universals that pure thought apprehends
are objectively real, and are the source of the existence and
qualities of the particular items perceived by the senses.
Universals are *ante res*. And, sixth, these intelligible realities
are united in the mind of God, who in thinking them creates
and sustains the world. Lastly, this system of divine Ideas is a
system of fulfilments or realizations, expressing the purpose of
God for mankind.

It was observed above that there is some evidence that a
school of thought influenced by the writings of Anselm persisted

in the south-east of England.[1] Canterbury, Rochester, and Westminster had been closely associated since the period of the Conversion. At the beginning of the twelfth century the three sees contained men who had been companions of Anselm at Bec, such as Gundulph, Bishop of Rochester, Henry, Prior of Canterbury, and Crispin, Abbot of Westminster. Crispin was a close friend of Anselm and his writings display his association with the author of the *Proslogion*. The *Disputation of a Jew with a Christian*, which was widely read on the Continent as well as in England, was dedicated to Anselm and some of the argument echoes the discussion in *Cur Deus Homo*. The treatise *On the Holy Spirit* draws largely on Augustine but the manner is that of Anselm. The most interesting of Crispin's works is the *Disputation of a Christian with a Pagan*. The picture that it gives of philosophical discussion in the early years of the twelfth century in London will be described in the next chapter. Here mention must be made of features that recall the method of Anselm. Such are the way in which arguments taken from Scripture are put aside in favour of arguments drawn from reason, and the definition of the Deity as 'that than which there is nothing greater and which is above all things'. A work by a monk, Rodulfus, with the title *Sciens et Nesciens* shows the rational methods typical of Anselm. But monastic learning in England was confined mainly to the traditional modes of scriptural exegesis and to the compilation of lives of the saints. Meanwhile in the great schools on the Continent a renaissance of inquiry into the basic problems of experience was stirring, and early in the twelfth century thought in England began to respond to the fresh current of ideas. Yet Augustinianism grew and became deeply established in the rational consciousness. It mingled with the new Aristotelian logic and the new natural philosophy. Adapting itself to fresh developments of scientific knowledge, the way of understanding that had passed to the cloister schools from Plato, Plotinus, Augustine, and Anselm persisted into later thought. Its influence distinguished the inquiries of thinkers in England during the great period of scholastic reflection, it was powerfully affirmed in the sixteenth and seventeenth centuries, its characteristic tones were heard in the idealist movement of the nineteenth.

[1] R. W. Southern, in *Medieval and Renaissance Studies*, I, London, 1941.

III

THE NEW LOGIC AND THE NEW KNOWLEDGE

I

A SINGULAR glimpse of the intellectual scene in England at the beginning of the twelfth century is given in Gilbert Crispin's *Disputation between a Christian and a Gentile.*[1] The prologue to the work tells how two philosophers had arranged to hold a debate concerning the worship of the one God and the unity of the true religion. The place of this discussion is a London inn. A friend invites the writer, Gilbert, to attend the discussion but he hesitates at first, pleading in excuse the poor state of his health and the complexity of the streets through which he must find his way. At length he yields to his friend's pressure and allows himself to be led by the hand through the tortuous lanes of the city until he and his companion reach the hostelry at which the debate is to be held. The gathering comprises an inner and an outer circle; Gilbert's friend is a member of the inner group and enters the house while he himself takes a seat near the door. He finds a number of scholars sitting there earnestly discussing a text of Aristotle. The passage is from the *Categories* and maintains that if first substances, that is to say, particular things, did not exist none of the other substances, that is to say, universals, could possibly exist.[2] Other disputes on philosophical questions are proceeding near the spot where Gilbert is sitting. Two scholars are arguing whether grammar, or literature, should be included under logic. But before any solutions on these questions are reached an interruption occurs and the whole company turns its attention to a loftier theme. A member of the inner body, a person of dignified bearing, moves over to the group near the entrance and calls for silence, bidding all to listen with attention and respect to the discussion that was proceeding within. Two renowned philosophers belonging to different schools of thought were engaged in debate. One of them was an unbeliever and an adroit critic of the Christian Faith; the other was an orthodox thinker. At this point Gilbert begins his report of the dialogue.

[1] J. Armitage Robinson, *Gilbert Crispin*, Cambridge, 1911, p. 74.
[2] Aristotle, *Categoriae*, v., 2 b.

This prologue to the *Disputation between a Christian and a Gentile* may serve to introduce us to some aspects of intellectual life soon after the year 1100. In the first place this crowded meeting of philosophers, composed of an inner and an outer circle, is a symptom of the remarkable activity that was stirring the world of thought. The new mental vigour was partly due to improved conditions of social life. With greater security from civil strife and invasion towns became established, the machinery of justice grew, and trade and commerce moved with larger freedom. Men travelled in safety throughout Europe and ideas circulated with them. Manuscripts passed from one centre to another. From the rich stores of Italy books and learned men made their way to the north in the train of the Emperor. Multitudes assembled at the monastic and episcopal schools and listened to the lectures of celebrated masters on the problems of knowledge. It was the era of the wandering scholars. From all parts there moved bands of clerks, trudging along the wild roads towards some great centre of disputation, Chartres, Paris, Reichenau, Tours. As the twelfth century progressed the wayside hostels and the taverns of the cities became crowded with the *vagantes*. They begged their way with street sermons, they set up temporary schools of instruction in the rudiments of Latin, they earned their lodging with song and story. The *litterati homines* of Crispin's meeting may have been composed in part of clerks attached to local schools, Westminster or St. Paul's or Rochester, in part of scholars drawn from more distant cloisters by the fame of some teacher. But the main goals of the scholar-tramps lay across the Channel. It was the teaching of men such as Bernard Silvester, Gilbert de la Porrée, Adam du Petit-Pont, Bernard of Chartres, that drew them to France. At the beginning of the century Paris began to rival Chartres as the leading centre of thought. The discourses on logic of William of Champeaux attracted large numbers of scholars to the meetings in the school of Notre Dame. The courses of study in these cathedral schools still comprised the subjects of the trivium and the quadrivium; the old Roman rhetorical basis was still firm. But a new spirit was being infused into the tradition of grammar, rhetoric, and dialectic.

This wave of zeal for learning and thought resulted in a more definite organization of the higher centres of learning. The control of the cathedral school passed into the hands of the *scholasticus* who soon becomes the *cancellarius*, chancellor. The groups of students who gathered round a famous master acquired a common consciousness, an *esprit de corps*. The motley companies that gathered every morning in the cloister of Notre Dame, or under the shadow of St. Hilaire or St. Victor, began to develop a structure. There were titles of admission, rules of attendance, and licences to teach and to listen. In the year 1106 there appeared in Paris a challenging figure, Peter Abaelard. This young master soon became a magnet to itinerant scholars, and through him the movement towards the establishment of *studia generalia* was quickened throughout Europe. He became the foremost teacher of the age and from the concourse that gathered out of many lands to hear him there sprang the first and greatest of the medieval universities.

In England the cathedrals under the Normans had once more become intellectual centres. Libraries and schools had grown up round them and the leadership in thought was passing to such communities from the monasteries. Canterbury was the chief of these learned circles under the direction of Theobald, Archbishop from 1138 to 1161. Other important schools of study and teaching were attached to the cathedrals at Winchester, St. Paul's, Peterborough, and Durham. The library of the last-named contained 546 volumes and was celebrated in consequence. But during the twelfth century the copying of manuscripts rapidly increased. The principal philosophical texts were the versions by Boethius of portions of Aristotle's logical works, the same author's version of Porphyry's *Commentary on Aristotle*, and the *Topics of Cicero*. In the earlier part of the century the studies in dialectic show little advance upon the programme followed in the days of Alcuin, but the wind of the renaissance of ideas in France began soon to be felt in England. Crispin's philosophical club gives a glimpse of the new ardour for logical inquiries. We shall shortly observe further remarkable developments of the movement of ideas. One feature of the situation in England may here be mentioned. Crispin's writings suggest that there was a disposition to debate freely the rational bases of the Faith. The two dialogues with a Jew referred to in the preceding chapter and the dispute with the Gentile show a readiness to meet sceptical criticism. The

Conqueror had brought a number of Jews from Rouen and
settled them in London. The ruffianly William II received Jews
at his court and encouraged them to argue with his prelates.
He was accustomed to swear with a round oath that if they
defeated the Christians in argument he would transfer his
allegiance to them. Several other discussions with Jews besides
those of Crispin have survived. Theologians were led to offer
philosophical defences of the fundamental tenets of the Christian
position and they drew upon the resources of Augustinianism
in the process. The *Disputation* of Crispin states the objections
of the Gentile with striking frankness. He is made to point out
the unwarrantable glosses that Christians had introduced into
the plain words of Scripture.

But the discussions of the scholars' society in London
described by Gilbert Crispin hint at other currents of thought
that were now in motion. The ancient principles that had supported the dogmas of the Faith were being subjected to searching and disrupting criticism. Fresh information was available,
there was a wider curiosity among men, and a broader culture
appeared in the schools. And this influx of fresh ideas and
interests often aroused sharp conflict with the conservative
tradition of thought. The intellectual adventures of two
Englishmen of the period, Adelard of Bath and John of Salisbury, illustrate the coming of the new principles that were
transforming men's outlook. Little is known of the life of
Adelard. In his youth he left his native town of Bath and
crossed to France and became a student at the famous school at
Tours. Later he moved to Laon where he taught philosophy.
The treatise *On Permanence and Change* was composed in these
early years, but already he had travelled far abroad and mingled
with learned men of various regions. He became dissatisfied
with the traditional topics of inquiry and decided to broaden his
knowledge and to visit other teachers. Scholars were seeking
distant fields but few explored so far as Adelard; he is a prince
among wandering scholars. Many years were passed in arduous
journeys to Sicily, Greece, Asia Minor, and Syria. In the year
1126 he appeared again in his native city of Bath, occupied in
translating the works of Saracen natural scientists and mathematicians into Latin. Here, too, he composed his dialogue on
Natural Questions. He was a musician and records that he

played the cithara before the queen. There is evidence that during his later years he visited Spain. He became a celebrated teacher, and among those who received instruction from him was Henry Plantagenet, afterwards Henry II. There are indications that he was employed in the service of the king's government. He died soon after 1142.

The career of John of Salisbury is known in far greater detail. Scholarship was not his main concern. He was adviser to kings and archbishops and performed a leading part in the ecclesiastical politics of England and of Europe. He was born in the second decade of the twelfth century at Old Sarum. In 1136 he joined the throngs of scholars in Paris and attended the lectures of Abaelard and other famous masters. He presently moved to Chartres, the centre of new Platonic and literary developments. It throws an interesting light on the learning of the time that John was able to spend no less than twelve years in the schools of Paris and Chartres. Among the many renowned scholars whom he met were Thierry of Chartres, Gilbert de la Porrée, William of Conches, and Robert Pullen, men who were in the front of the new movements in thought. The last-named formed a school at Oxford. In 1148 John was present at the Council of Rheims where the great Bernard of Clervaux recommended him in warm terms to Theobald, Archbishop of Canterbury. He entered the archbishop's household in 1154 and lived for many years at Canterbury, though his duties took him frequently abroad. His active support of the ecclesiastical party led by the Chancellor, Thomas Becket, brought him the displeasure of Henry II, and when Becket succeeded Theobald as archbishop, John deemed it prudent to leave the country. He went to Paris and was engaged for some years in attempting to bring about a reconciliation between the king and the archbishop. In the meantime his principal works, the *Policraticus* and the *Metalogicon*, were written. The *Policraticus* includes a long invective against the idle pursuits of the nobility, among which is counted a devotion to magic and astrology. In the latter part of the work there are scathing attacks on ecclesiastical and monastic corruption. For the intellectual life of the period the *Metalogicon* is more instructive. Both works were dedicated to Becket. At length the two eminent antagonists composed their differences and John returned to England to make arrangements for the reception of the archbishop. He was by Becket's side on 29 December 1170, when the archbishop was slain in the cathedral at Canterbury. In 1176 John was appointed by Louis VII to the bishopric of Chartres. He played an influential role in affairs and was prominent in the third Lateran Council in 1179. He died in the following year at Chartres.[1]

Both Adelard and John are spirited writers and give caustic descriptions of the contemporary scene. Adelard in the dialogue with his nephew on Natural Questions observes that the present generation is possessed with an ingrained error. It thinks that no modern discovery ought to be accepted. Accordingly, when anyone wants to publish a new view of his own he attributes it to someone else. The remark reveals an environment in which novel ideas were being put forward, and it suggests that there was some risk in the process. There is evidence that a number of original works by Christian writers were published under the protection of Arab or Greek names.[2]

On the other hand authority and the established investigations were boldly questioned. Voices were heard to proclaim the rights of reason in unfettered language. Adelard contrasts what he has learnt from the Arabs under the guidance of reason with the teaching of authority which others are content to follow. Authority is nothing but a halter. The brutes are led by a halter and do not understand in what direction they are being led nor why they are going there. They only follow the rope that binds them. In the same way written authority leads many into danger because they are tied by animal credulity. Under the prestige of some authoritative name writers use such licence that they do not hesitate to recommend false doctrines to the dumb creatures that read them. Why do they not write on both sides of the paper since they can find readers to-day who expect no proof for any statement, but accept anything without question on the authority of some ancient name? If reason is not allowed to be first court of appeal it is given to each of us to no purpose at all. The very people who are called

---

[1] An enchanting picture of John of Salisbury is given by Helen Waddell in *Essays and Studies*, The English Association, vol. xiii, Oxford, 1928.

[2] L. Thorndike, *History of Magic and Experimental Science*, London, 1923, ii. 27.

authorities were accepted by their followers only because they
first pursued the way of reason. Reliance on mere authority is
contemptible, and the philosopher will reject it.[1] In another
passage he maintains that it is only when we have exhausted
the capabilities of human knowledge that we should have
recourse to explanation in terms of the Will of God.[2] These
utterances are symptomatic of the broadening scope of rational
activity and of impatience with the ancient occupations of
scholars. John also expresses this impatience. He scorns the
meticulous deference to authorities that prevails in the conservative schools. Students in these schools scrutinize every
syllable, almost every letter of the authorities, never ceasing
their criticisms and never reaching certainty on a single point.
They spend their time collecting opinions from every source
including those that are of no value whatsoever, and accumulate
such a mass of contradictory views that the original writer can
scarcely recognize his own ideas.[3] The philosophical outcome
of these vigorous demands for independent thought must be
considered in a moment. Let us first observe the account that
John gives of the expansion of culture in the schools, for this
expansion influenced the development of ideas.

In many of the great centres there was a revival of classical
and literary studies. John gives a valuable description of the
course of teaching followed by Bernard of Chartres, who was
master of the episcopal school and later chancellor in the early
years of the twelfth century.[4] The distinctive feature of this
instruction was its literary content. The scholars were invited
to follow the guidance of Quintilian, to pay close attention to
elegance of style and grammatical accuracy, to shun barbarisms,
and to weigh the niceties of scansion. They were advised that
nothing is more valuable for thought and life than daily exercises in verse and prose. 'Study Virgil and Lucan and whatever
philosophy you hold, you will find already expounded in their
pages.' But the study of logic and of mathematics was admitted, and all was crowned by ethics. John was himself a
disciple of this literary education and in the *Metalogicon* he

---

[1] *Quest. Nat.* 6.   [2] Ib. 11.
[3] *Metalogicon*, ii. 7, edited by C. C. J. Webb, Oxford, 1909, p. 72.
[4] Ib. i. 7, p. 13–25. Cf. J. A. Clerval, *Les Écoles de Chartres*, Chartres, 1895,
p. 158 f.

discusses it at length. And when he comes to treat of philosophy or logic the lessons of this humanist view of knowledge are still present. Dialectic must be applied to experience. When it revolves upon itself and is confined to academic abstractions it becomes wan and useless. It must enter the affairs of the home, of war, of the market-place, of the cloister, of the court, of the Church. The logic of the schools is all very well for the training of the young, but when a man reaches mature years he should put away not only word-play but even preoccupation with books. Every workman can discourse fluently about his craft, but it is not so easy to be skilful in practice. A physician may lecture at length about elements and humours and compounds and diseases, but anyone who is cured by treatment of this kind would rather be ill. A moralist may be rich in precepts so long as they are matters for talk; it is more difficult to demonstrate them in life. In a word, talking about an art is a good deal simpler than practising it.[1] A new spirit is here, pragmatic, humanist, progressive.

This spirit is intolerant of the formal exercises in logic that occupy students of philosophy. The *Metalogicon* professes to be a defence of the new logic against its detractors. The author is aware that his defence is rambling and excuses himself on the ground that he has scarcely been able to devote hours snatched from meals or sleep to its composition, for he has had to sustain the weight of the whole ecclesiastical affairs of England. But he prefaces his defence of logic by a lively attack on contemporary logicians. There is a lurid account of 'Cornificius',[2] a typical leader of the smart young men who bring learning into contempt with their sophistical arguments. They debate such problems as whether a pig that is being taken to market is held by the man or the rope, and whether a man who has bought a complete cloak has also purchased a hood. They make play with the import of double and repeated negatives and spin out discussions to interminable lengths. They scorn poets and historians or anyone who pays deference to the works of ancient writers. They are always forming new parties; new masters are hatched out as quickly as a chick puts on feathers. All kinds of novelties are introduced into the traditional subjects. This

---

[1] Op. cit. ii. 8.
[2] The name is derived from a critic of Virgil.

Moabite arrogance has even penetrated the cloister; there, too, you will find the wolf in sheep's clothing.[1]

There were no doubt pretentious, trifling, and mercenary types who frequented the lecture rooms and debating clubs, and those nurtured in the broader culture of humane studies detested the narrowness and utilitarian spirit of the new generation. But John is also attacking an important development, the work of certain circles in his own day that appeared to divide logical debate from living issues, even theological issues. These circles concentrated exclusively on dialectical discussion. Here John shows himself out of sympathy with an interesting movement. The persistent inquiries of Abaelard had founded a line of logicians who explored the meaning of words and the import of statements. They held that a theory of knowledge must be preceded by a critical examination of language. For these philosophers, logic was intimately associated with grammar, discussing not truth but meaning. This logic was destined to result in vital developments in English thought of which we shall later have to take notice. To practical minds it seemed futile. But there was another side to this movement, and here John's complaints were justified. The withdrawal of theological studies from philosophy which has been observed in the previous century persisted in many quarters. Philosophy was becoming detached from reality and occupying itself with formal inquiries. It is against this aspect of the new thought that John protests.

In the sphere of theology, however, there were signs of a new erudition. A literature of theological *Summa* had arisen, of which the most widely known was the four books of *Sentences* by Peter Lombard. We must pause at this title, for we have mentioned the most influential text of the Middle Ages. The theological trend of scholastic thought is due largely to the unremitting concentration on this work. In the following centuries the *Sentences* provided the main subject of study at Oxford and Cambridge, and every doctor of theology began his career with a course of lectures on the four books of Lombard. We shall find Roger Bacon complaining that the *Sentences* were read with greater zeal in the schools than the Bible; and it dominated the universities until the sixteenth century. Its

[1] *Metalogicon*, i. 3.

influence upon thought was pre-eminent. But this influence
was oblique. It dwelt less in the doctrines propounded than in
the manner in which they were set forth. The four books comprised a huge collection of opinions skilfully drawn from the
patristic texts, from conciliar pronouncements, and from more
recent writings, such as those of Bede, upon the principal dogmas
of the Church. From numerous authorities views on the
Trinity, divine providence, creation, the fall, the Incarnation,
the Sacraments, final judgement, heaven and hell, and many
other dogmas are copied with little comment. The varying
emphasis and the contradictory ideas of the Fathers on these
doctrines are left unreconciled. The work accordingly offered
unrivalled material for discussion and original thinking. It
provided ample scope for masters in the schools to develop
their own ideas, and in fact we shall find that many of the signal
contributions to the analysis of first principles that were produced by philosophers at Oxford during the thirteenth and
fourteenth centuries were made in the form of commentaries
on the *Sentences*. And there is a further characteristic of the
work that affected the speculation of the schools. The most
extensive quotations of views are drawn from the writings of
St. Augustine. Many of the elements of Augustinian Neo-
Platonism are exhibited in the course of the treatment of the
successive dogmas. The deep impression made upon philosophic
inquiry by Augustinianism owes much to the *Sentences*.

II

But we still have to describe another vitalizing wave of
thought that was passing over men's thinking and here we must
turn back to the pioneer labours of Adelard of Bath.

During the twelfth century a stream of Greek ideas flowed
into northern lands. The main channel of this revival of long
forgotten natural and logical philosophy was the Moslem
civilization of the Spanish peninsula. Spain had been conquered by the Saracens in the eighth century and had absorbed
the Hellenistic culture that the conquerors had borne with
them from the East. The caliphs were patrons of arts and
letters, and even in the ninth century Christians had been
attracted to Spain by Arabic learning. Gerbert of Aurillac,
afterwards Pope Sylvester II, had put himself to school in the

tenth century with Arab masters and acquired a reputation as a magician in consequence. In the year 1085 Toledo was regained for Christendom and was found to contain libraries of scientific and philosophical works and, what was even more fortunate, scholars acquainted with both the Arabic and the Latin tongues. The place became a factory of translation that drew the finest scholars of the age. Throughout the twelfth century the work of translation went on. The ferment of thought that was stirred by the circulation of the new knowledge in the schools of Europe can be appreciated if we mention a few of the leading translations that appeared during the century. Of fundamental influence on all forms of thinking were the translations of the main logical and scientific works of Aristotle. The *Prior Analytics*, the *Posterior Analytics*, the *Topics*, the *Sophistic Elenchi*, the *Physics*, the *De Caelo et Mundo*, the *De Generatione et Corruptione*, and the *Meteorologica* were translated from the Greek by Italian scholars between 1130 and 1180. Other Greek writings now made more fully known were the *Elements* and the *Data* of Euclid, the works of Galen and Hippocrates on medical science, and the *Almagest* of Ptolemy on astronomy. We have seen that before the twelfth century the only work of Plato known to Christian scholars was the version of the *Timaeus* by Chalcidius. Now the *Meno* and the *Phaedo* were translated from the original. In addition to this wealth of Greek thought a large number of philosophical and scientific writings by the great Arabian scholars were translated; works on algebra, arithmetic, astronomy, alchemy, and psychology; and metaphysical works by such philosophers as Avicenna, Alkindi and Alfarabi.

There were other routes by which Greek knowledge penetrated the West. Medical writings were carried back from Africa and wandering scholars discovered texts in Syria. But the principal source was Spain.

In this activity Englishmen took a distinguished share. Among the earlier translators was our citizen of Bath, Adelard. He translated the astronomical tables of al-Khwarizimi, an Arabian authority of the ninth century, and also a treatise in five books by the same writer on mathematics. He also translated an Arabic edition of Euclid's *Elements*. There were other notable translators and students of Arabic science in England, some of whom will be referred to on a later page. There was wide curiosity at the time concerning eclipses, and observers now began to use the Arabic astrolabe and Arabic mathematics in their calculations relating to these phenomena.[1]

It must be confessed that in spite of the preference that Adelard avows for Arabic philosophy to the blind reliance on authority, it is not easy to detect in the writings on physical phenomena of the twelfth century any striking advance beyond the methods of the ancient literary and theological compilers. Some scholars, indeed, transcribed at length Roman collections of natural wonders. Robert of Cricklade, prior of St. Frideswide's, Oxford, from 1141 to 1171, composed a *Defloratio* in nine books of Pliny's *Natural History*. Adelard's own *Questiones Naturales, Physical Problems*, was the most influential of these compilations, and if we look below the surface of the information conveyed, the work is an instructive illustration of the modes of thought still prevailing. The treatise is a dialogue in seventy-six sections. It begins at the bottom and moves upwards, treating in order plants, the habits of animals, human characteristics and physiology, the earth, the moon, and finally, the stars. The arrangement is significant. It follows the accepted system of the universe in which the celestial bodies occupy the most noble and most influential place. In the Preface the writer promises his hearer something new in the way of Arabic learning; but the method and content of the *Questiones* resemble the old rhetorical collections of natural knowledge referred to in the first chapter. The view of the physical world is still a tissue of unrelated curiosities obtained from ancient authorities. Trivial points are strung together with important problems. Adelard occasionally refers to an empirical test. Thus he observes that the localization of the functions of the brain is proved by the effect of injuries in different parts of the head, and he asserts that fresh water can be turned into salt by cooking over a fire. There is a notable utterance under Question LXIV where the master recommends his disciple to replace astonishment at the grand events of nature by a sober study of their causes. 'The mind imbued with wonder and a sense of unfamiliarity shudderingly contemplates from a distance effects without regard to causes

[1] L. Thorndike, *History of Magic and Experimental Science*, London, 1923, ii, pp. 83 and 171 f.

and so never shakes off its perplexity. Look more closely, take circumstances in their totality, set forth causes and then you will not be surprised at effects.' But the causes adduced in answer to the problems that are raised do not propose any new theories of natural processes. The principles that are stated or implied are the traditional principles transmitted by Boethius, Macrobius, and Capella. Most of the answers rely upon the old Greek physics, upon the four basic elements, earth, fire, water, air, and the four qualities that are contained in them, heat and cold, dryness and moisture. Why do plants sprout in the ground when no seed has been sown? Because the soil contains the four elements with their qualities. Air and fire cause the compound to rise, water causes it to expand, earth gives it solidity. Why do some animals chew the cud while others do not? Because the stomachs of some animals are cold, while others are warm, and animals with chilly stomachs are obliged to recall their food and masticate it a second time. Why do men of ability have poor memories while those of inferior ability have good memories? Because the force of the brain is derived from moisture, but retentiveness depends on dryness. Men who possess dry brains have strong memories but small minds.

Explanations in terms of the four elements are associated with arguments drawn from the notion of design. How is it that human beings cannot walk at birth, while animals can? Because the stronger limbs of animals are designed for fighting instead of for the practice of virtue. The weakness of human limbs consorts with man's rational powers. Also man's body is of the earth and is therefore drawn to the ground, but the limbs that support the seat of his rational activity are raised up so that he should not succumb to the earthward tendency of his body. Man is made for the activities that he pursues. To the surprising question, 'Why do human beings not have horns?', the answer is that man's warlike behaviour alternates with periods of peace, and if man were naturally provided with offensive weapons he would be unable when making treaties to lay them aside.

The fundamental principle that there is intimate relationship between the macrocosm and the microcosm, between the universe and man, enters. The matter of the stars is an harmonious compound of elements, and in this it resembles the mind of man. The outer sphere of the heavens contains the most spiritual beings. They have perfection of form, that is to say, they are circular; they are composed of a harmony of the elements; they occupy the loftiest position in the hierarchy of the universe; and they display an indefatigable vitality of movement.

So far there is little advance beyond the encyclopaedias of the decadent age. But in several sections there is evidence of the contemporary revival of Platonism. The Platonic references are drawn from the version of the *Timaeus* by Chalcidius. From this source comes the reference to the doctrine of reminiscence. The soul knew the real nature of things in the state before it was imprisoned in the body. It seeks the knowledge it has lost and, confused with the riot of the senses, is obliged to put its trust in opinion in place of knowledge. The account of dialectic is Platonic. Dialectic seizes the universal essences of things and strives to understand them as they have been conceived in the mind of the demiurge. The passage treating of the theory of perception again manifests the current influence of the *Timaeus*. The subject was attracting attention. The nephew of the dialogue propounds four theories of vision. The first is that the mind, situated in the brain, looks out through the windows of the eyes, perceiving things as they are without affecting them or being affected by them. The second is that the shapes of things pass from things to the eyes and thence to the mind, which then interprets them. The third theory holds that the mind puts forth a process that meets the influences coming from things and returns bringing back reports to the mind. The last theory is accepted by Adelard on the authority of Plato. The first theory is rejected on the ground that the mind is not a corporeal thing and does not require windows. Moreover, the eyes are opaque, not transparent. The causal or transmission theory is rejected on the ground that it falsely assumes that the mind is composed of soft material that can receive the impressions of things. The third view is considered to be unacceptable for the following reason. Supposing two men are gazing at the same objects in the distance. If one sees a white object and the other a black one, then according to the theory, the intervening air in which the form of the object is found will contain contrary qualities. The last theory is that of which philosophy approves. It holds that the brain generates a fiery current that passes from the mind along the nerves, producing vision of things outside. It travels along the optic nerves to the eye, and thence to the thing, where it receives the impress of the shape of the thing and returns with it to the mind. In support of this theory Adelard, as has been said, quotes Plato at length.[1] This is the theory of effluences that had descended from the early Greek physicists. We shall observe later developments of this theory in England.

Finally we may notice the postulate that the order of the universe is fixed and perfect. Any change is for the worse. 'Nothing can be better than it is, and if it changes it must be for the worse.'

There is a reference to the *Physics* of Aristotle that hints at the more recent discussions of the schools. And there are faint indications of the new learning in the sections on physiology. It is in the translations of the treatises on geometry and astronomy that occupied his later years that Adelard contributed to the movement of scientific thought. The details of this movement belong to the history of mathematics and astronomy. Our present knowledge does not allow us to trace the course of this development in the twelfth century with accuracy. But the names of several of those who were promoting the new technical methods in England have survived. Walcher, prior of the abbey of Malvern, had determined the time of the eclipse of 18 October 1092 by using the Arabic astrolabe, and had translated works on Arabic mathematics. The historian, John of Worcester, displays acquaintance with Adelard's translations in describing the eclipse of 1138. Robert of Chester broke fresh ground by translating treatises on mathematics and algebra by Arabic masters and by composing a work on alchemy in which he gives directions for chemical experiments couched in highly allegorical language. David of Morley brought back a valuable collection of books from Spain, but he did not find the state of learning in England encouraging. In his *Philosophia* or *Liber de naturis inferiorum et superiorum* he praises the Moslem philosophers and interpolates their theories into the Mosaic account of the creation of the world. The superior natures in the universe, the moon, the stars, and the eternal heavens, control the lower mundane order of things. Accordingly,

---

[1] Op. cit., Qu. XXIII. See *Timaeus* 45 *b* and the version of Chalcidius, ed. J. Wrobel, Leipzig, 1876, p. 280.

he is led to treat of astrology and the occult virtues of the plants. But the elements of the newly recovered Greek physics are mixed with magic and astrology. The continued interest in these studies in England is shown also in the work of Roger of Hereford whose *Compotus* or astronomical calculation was completed in 1176. There is evidence that Hereford was a centre of Arabic science in the latter part of the twelfth century. The guiding interest in astronomy was ecclesiastical. The motive was the desire to calculate the dates of the Church feasts as it had been in the days of Bede. One other interesting figure may be mentioned, Alexander Neckham. His mind reflects many sides of the movement of ideas in the latter decades of the eleventh century. He taught in Paris and afterwards at Dunstable and died Abbot of Cirencester in 1217. His writings manifest a keen interest in natural lore and, though his account of animals is largely derived from the traditional collections, he shows himself well abreast of the physics and astronomy of the age and cites frequently the recent translations of the natural world of Aristotle. And he displays extensive appreciation of the revived literary culture and the humanism of the period.[1]

III

But the more fundamental intellectual changes of the time issued from the introduction of the new logic into the higher studies of France and England. Here we may revert to John of Salisbury. His defence of logic in the *Metalogicon* takes the shape of a summary of the doctrine of Aristotle. The examination of the great questions of ethics or physics calls for a preliminary discipline by which what is false is distinguished from what is true. The rules of this science were discovered by Aristotle.[2] John gives a detailed account of the treatises that had recently come into the courses of the schools, putting particular stress on the *Topics*. The logic of demonstration which had been described in the *Post Analytics*, he finds perspicuous to few minds. This logic had almost disappeared in his day, being confined chiefly to geometrical reasoning. 'And

---

[1] For the work of the writers mentioned above see C. H. Haskins, *Studies in the History of Medieval Science*, Cambridge, Mass., 1924; L. Thorndike, *A History of Magic and Experimental Science*, vol. ii; and the *Dictionary of National Biography*.   [2] *Metalogicon*, ii. 2.

geometry is not widely studied among us except in Spain or on the African border.'[1] He concludes his analysis of the *Organon* by remarking that he does not assert that Aristotle expressed sound opinion on every point; his words are not sacred. He is not to be followed in theology, but in logic he is the master.

In most of this careful survey of the 'new logic' there is little application to the main problems of the age. And at the end of the work John deprecates inquiries into sacred matters and upholds faith. But in one passage he touches on important principles. The passage provides an opportunity for examining the transformations of thought that were now in progress. The discussions of the scholars' society in London at the beginning of the century hint at the issue that was beginning to absorb the attention of thinking men. It will be recalled that a group of logicians sitting near the entrance was discussing a saying of Aristotle that particulars are prior to universals. We have seen that the rational support of the system of general beliefs regarding the real nature of things was given by Augustinian Platonism. The system of general beliefs was the system of Christian theological faith, and the philosophical expression of the beliefs that afforded spiritual security and salvation was the ideal realism that had descended mainly from the great African father. Ideas at variance with this outlook were now entering from many quarters. Nominalism was condemned principally upon theological grounds, but the controversy over it excited a renewed examination of the problem of human knowledge. The incisive criticisms of Abaelard roused deep interest and opened many minds to the difficulties of the orthodox realism. But now the new logic was emerging in the schools. Masters were lecturing on passages from Aristotle that propounded disturbing views on the relation of universal to particulars. A number of theories were put forward in a general endeavour to reconcile the older Neo-Platonic doctrine with the new position. Adelard of Bath, in an early work on the *Unchanging and the Changing*, had attempted to combine the particular and universal factors of experience. By the middle of the twelfth century the problem was being discussed on all sides. In the second book of the *Metalogicon*,[2] John, without entering far into the problem, makes a valuable survey of the great debate so far as it had

[1] Ib. iv. 6.   [2] Ib. ii. 17.

developed in his day. Let us consider the significance of the question at issue.

According to Augustinian realism the path to that which is permanently real in the universe lies in the universals or general notions, such as colour, humanity, whiteness, that form the content of thought. These entities are not abstractions in the sense of convenient mental fictions. They are fundamental objects. They constitute the essences or principles of particular things that are perceived by the senses. Particular things appear to us in diverse shapes, in essence they are one. The particular items imperfectly reveal the universal essence; for example, particular men imperfectly reveal man; and particulars are related to these general essences as partially fulfilled purposes to an ideal. But it is the ideal that has genuine being. As ideal types of being the universals are Platonic forms interpreted in the Christian scheme as exemplars in the mind of God. The outlook, as we have seen, exalts the intellect over the senses. The human mind approaches the divine mind so far as it is freed from dependence on images and material things. The more it can think without admixture of sense the more it can seize reality, and the movement towards pure intellectual apprehension is also a movement towards spiritual enlightenment. The doctrine of Augustinian realism that the universal is *ante rem*, prior in being to particular things, men, stones, and trees, is woven at every point into religious conceptions. We have observed that Anselm constructs a proof of the being of God on realist grounds, on the basis that universals possess an existence independent of particular things.

A challenge to this view had come from the nominalism of Roscelin. On this view the real objects of our knowledge are not universal entities, but particular things, such as individual men. The unity, man, exists only in the term; there is no real unity, man. Concepts and universals do not express the real world but are symbols, mere names, *nomina*, arbitrarily applied. The common nature that they indicate is an invention of the mind. Universals are subjective. The contrast with the orthodox realism is complete; for Anselm it made rational theology impossible. But there are more detailed criticisms. The obvious retort to the view that concepts are mere words was that thought thereby became meaningless. We mean something when we utter words; they are not insignificant noises. The nominalist sought to describe meaning in terms of language. We use words to stand for general properties such as man or goodness, though there is nothing in reality but particulars. The answer to this is that it does not describe the facts of experience. We do not impose the common quality that is the content of meaning; we find it in things. Our concepts, and the words that express them, recognize an aspect of objects, namely, a general aspect. Man, colour, flower, are as genuine facts of experience as particular men, colours, and flowers. Moreover, the orthodox defenders went on to press the impossibility of the view of reality upon which the theory was based. They pointed out that it would be impossible to grasp even particulars apart from all reference to universals. This particular thing is an instance of a *kind* of thing. Otherwise we could have no knowledge of it at all. *This* rose is *a* rose, that is to say it is an instance of a common character that is manifested in countless instances. In the last resort a particular object of experience, however transient, is a thing, an entity with a definite nature, having essential characteristics that it universally possesses. It has an identity, and this identity makes reasoning possible. It makes possible discussion about trees, the Church, justice. And these, and all other topics on which we discourse, are things-in-general. We are back in realism.

But the new school of Aristotelian students was also exposing difficulties in the traditional realism. The main objection was that if universals are severed from particulars both become unreal abstractions. A universal means that which refers to a number of different particular items. Tree refers to many different particular trees, man to many different individual men. A particular means that which refers to a single item, such as *this* tree, *this* man. Now the traditional theory maintains that universals are superior kinds of things. They are the grounds of particular things, and they exist, or, in the language of this tradition, they subsist apart from particulars, immaterial, timeless, absolute. These realities can be known only by pure thought, *intellectus*. What is the status of particulars in this view? It holds that the universal essence of different particular things is one, and that the one takes on variety by becoming embodied in descending levels of particularity, genera, species, lower species, particular things. Now, if these particular embodiments were removed and the essential universal were to remain, there would be no differences between things. And the removal would not affect the universal essence. For these particular embodiments in virtue of which things are different from one another, are accidents, that is to say, external and inessential additions to the universal substance. The differences between two men that serve to distinguish one from the other do not affect the essence, man. When this doctrine is pressed it leads to a denial of all distinction between things, and if we cannot distinguish between things we cannot investigate them, nor think clearly about them. Things that possess contradictory qualities become fundamentally the same thing, because they belong to the same genus. Socrates and an ass, to quote a favourite example, must be really the same since they are both animal. Their differences, such as their rationality and irrationality, are accidental. Factors that must provide the basis for definition and inquiry are obliterated. The individual features that make one thing distinct from another become mere appearances. Moreover, the consequence of depriving the world of things of its variety can be pushed still farther. If variety is abolished in relation to one universal, it is abolished in relation to all the substantial universals also. For the many substantial universals derive their reality from the wider universals of which they are subordinate classes. In the end there is only one substantial universal. All others are appearances.

If universals are separated from particulars, the particulars become irrelevant additions to ideal reality, with fatal consequences to knowledge. But universals also become meaningless, devoid of content. For they are purely general and to be purely general is to have no features. If they are distinct from particulars they are wholly indeterminate.[1]

These criticisms of the prevailing tradition of thought are indications of the profound changes that were occurring in response to the renewed study of the text of Aristotle. In many quarters thought was moving away from its concern with transcendent forms and ideas to a concern with forms immanent

---

[1] The best source for current criticisms of extreme realism is Abaelard's treatise known from its opening words as '*Logica ingredientibus*'. It is printed in *Beiträge zur Geschichte der Philosophie des Mittelalters*, Band xxi, Heft i.

in the changing world of particular things. It was moving away
from concern with *intellectus*, pure thought, to concern with
ratio, the elaboration of the sensible elements of experience into
concepts. It was turning to recognize plurality, particularity,
individuality, as well as unity and universality. The movement
was bringing to light a fresh view of reality and a new view
of human knowledge. And this change of perspective deeply
affected the bearing of thought upon the over-arching system
of the Faith. For Anselm there had been no other alternative
between the high realism and the nominalism of Roscelin. The
former provided the only rational proofs of the Faith, the latter
was heresy. But in the eleventh century students were learning
from Boethius' edition of the *Categories* that the universal must
be secondary to the particular, the primary reality. This was
the text that the scholars of Crispin's club were debating. We
have seen that the Aristotelian position had been entertained
by writers long before the revival of Aristotelian studies in the
twelfth century. But now the Aristotelian view of dialectic
was being emphasized side by side with the Augustinian. In
the older tradition dialectic is the study of the ultimate principles of reason, the forms.[1] In the new, the province of dialectic is the sphere of probability and opinion, and embraces
the domains of physics, ethics, and non-demonstrative logic.[2]
The basis of this view of knowledge is the principle that knowledge is derived from perception. Human knowledge cannot
attain pure ideas; that is the privilege of the angels. Human
beings cannot hope to reach by their unaided powers beyond
'true opinion'.[3]

A vigorous discussion of these basic questions arose among
scholars in England, France, and Italy. John, in the passage to
which reference has been made, mentions four main schools of
thought, and the fourth is said to comprise many divisions.
After speaking of nominalism, which he declares had almost
disappeared with its author Roscelin, he mentions the doctrine
that was upheld by followers of the pre-eminent critic of the
older realism, Peter Abaelard, and says that he counts these
philosophers among his friends. The general line of this doctrine

---

[1] But Augustine is not consistent in his use of the word, and in *De Doctrina
Christiana* he recommends it as providing a training in practical logic.
[2] John of Salisbury, *Metalogicon*, ii. 13.   [3] Ib. iii. 33.

stood upon the teaching of Aristotle regarding the process
of forming concepts. We have noticed that the tradition of
Augustine, in its eagerness to vindicate the governing direction
of the Ideas, had paid scanty attention to the psychological
problem regarding the way in which the mind forms general
notions. The point is fundamental. Augustine had conceived
the mind as transcendent over the body and accordingly could
not admit that knowledge takes its rise from contact with
sensible things. It does not attain knowledge of universals by
means of abstraction from particulars, but by direct apprehension. Abaelard, on the contrary, taught that universals are the
outcome of the transmutation of the elements given in perception.
Thinking operates by isolating features that are common to
a number of particular objects and attends to these common
features apart from the individual things. These common
features, whiteness, humanity, red, are aspects of the world
perceived by the senses. But they are not forms of being distinct
from individual things. Discrete individual things provide the
starting-point of knowing; it begins with particulars and moves
to general objects. Thinking proceeds by breaking up the complex detail of the perceived world and refashioning it into objects
of thought. But this does not mean that it moves away from
individual things to a higher realm of being. The understanding knows ideas by abstracting them from things. But the
ideas are abstractions. Universals are the product of the mind's
activity in endeavouring to group sections of the world. The
sections are real, though they are abstract and partial views of
the world. Essential reality is beyond the reach of human
thought. In modern language the realm of human thinking is
the realm of phenomena.

This position supplied the elements of a psychology of thought
that had been lacking. But those versed in the older philosophy
were quick to point out its inadequacy as an account of reality.
They accused it of leaning too far towards nominalism. Before
the mind can abstract a common element from its perception
of different particulars it must judge that they possess the
common element. It does not invent the common element, the
universal; it discovers it already there. It is not imposed on
particulars. Our concepts, man, red, size, beauty, correspond
to independent facts. The realist school of thought insisted that

realism is required to account not merely for the relevance of thinking, but also of perceiving. A particular thing is an implicit universal, a unity in difference, and it could not be apprehended apart from the presence of a universal. It is the task of thought to disengage and to grasp by *ratio*, and beyond *ratio*, by *intellectus*, the principles of things.

Augustinian realism, in short, was being transmuted by the study of Aristotle. In the face of the new logic the defenders of the older view were often led to support positions that exposed them to criticism. John mentions some of these positions under his fourth division of contemporary philosophers. One was the doctrine known as *collectio*. A universal is an assemblage of particulars that are like one another in certain respects, unlike in other respects. But it was pointed out that this account entirely abandons realism of the older type. That realism maintained that every universal is prior in being to its particulars. A collection of particulars is a universal that is subsequent to the particular of which it is composed. It is a *universale post rem*, not a *universale ante rem*. Further, how can a collection of different men be an identity that is the same for every particular man, as realism requires? Nor could it be distinct from the particulars, for it would be exhausted by the range of particulars under observation.[1]

There were other attempts at compromise between the Christian-Platonic tradition and Aristotelian views. But the great school at Chartres and a few other centres continued to proclaim the Augustinian principles. John distinguishes two divisions of this conservative group, one emphasizing the theological view of Ideas as eternal supersensible exemplars in the divine mind, the other conceiving them in a more physical sense as the forms or principles of things.

But the intermediate view that closely followed Aristotle was beginning to prevail. John expresses it clearly. The mind thinks abstractly regarding things. Its concepts are not in reality separated from things, they are merely thought of as separated. For example, mathematical figures can be contemplated apart from bodies, though they do not exist apart from bodies. The mind is able to break up what is in fact continuous and to combine what is in fact separate. But thinking and being

---

[1] These criticisms are advanced by Abaelard.

are different. Universals, genera, and species, exist only as mental concepts, and concepts are derived from likenesses noticed between things; when compared with particular things they are no more than phantoms, and to attempt to grasp them apart from particulars is to pursue dreams. It is true that universality is implicated in particulars. Plato is a man, and no particular can be known unless it is known as such and such. But the universal element in particulars is not a thing nor a spirit nor a distinct essence. There is nothing in universals except what is found in particulars.[1]

Thought is moving towards a more moderate realism. John refuses to follow Plato in holding universals to be Ideas, in spite of Augustine and many other thinkers of his own time. In a later passage he accepts Augustinian principles in certain spheres. Ultimate mathematical and logical principles are the immortal *rationes* of which Augustine speaks. But here again our Aristotelian denies that they provide human thought with more than ideals. Men cannot see beyond appearances.[2] The activity of *ratio* is directed to the understanding of temporal things and is concerned with prudence; to the understanding of spiritual things belongs *intellectus*, or wisdom, and this depends on grace and revelation. Here it is better to believe without inquiry into matters that are beyond our capacities.[3]

Thus, the tendency of the new logic is to turn attention to the immanent principles of things and to withdraw thought from its exclusive preoccupation with the eternal order. This movement of thought was destined profoundly to affect the rational defence of the dogmas of the Faith. The entry of Greek and Arabic natural science, the renewed cultivation of the literature of antiquity, above all the recovery of the Aristotelian outlook on knowledge and reality contributed, in intimate association with the older tradition of thought, to the remarkable developments of the thirteenth century.

---

[1] *Metalogicon*, ii. 20 f.   [2] Ib. iv. 32, 33.   [3] Ib. 41.

THE ADVANCE OF ARISTOTELIANISM

I

In the thirteenth and fourteenth centuries the rich promise of the previous age was abundantly fulfilled. These centuries saw the appearance of comprehensive theoretical syntheses in which the older schemes of ideas were united with the new doctrines. Conceptions that had descended from Augustine and Dionysius the Areopagite were amalgamated with principles derived from Aristotle and from Arabic and Jewish philosophers. With this eclectic power there went searching criticism. Acute differences arose and the controversies they provoked led to fresh examination of accepted assumptions. It was the golden age of metaphysics. During this culminating period of Catholic reflection England nurtured a group of philosophers whose ideas roused interest and discussion throughout the West. The range and subtlety of their expositions render any general résumé unsatisfactory. The authors of the treatises and commentaries reveal perplexing differences of opinion in almost every branch of inquiry. It is difficult to assess the precise position of the prominent masters. Thomas of York, for example, offers so many solutions of philosophical problems, drawn from a mass of Christian and Arabian authorities, that it is not easy to discover which of them represents his own view.[1] Roger Bacon's vast investigations display several periods of development, and he denies in his later works the doctrines he asserts in his earlier treatises. The elusiveness of the teaching of Duns Scotus is notorious. Nor must we forget that our acquaintance with the works composed in this period is still sadly deficient. A large number of treatises have been lost, and many still remain in manuscript. It is unsafe to offer generalizations regarding schools and tendencies until these works have been printed and edited; and even on the interpretation of those philosophers whose writings are now available much remains to be done.

[1] The great scheme of theology and metaphysics composed by Thomas of York has not yet appeared in print. An account of its six books is given by E. Longpré in *Archivum Franciscanum Historicum,* t. xix, 1926.

Yet amid the inexhaustible variety of discussions that fill this remarkable phase of our thought it is possible to descry three systems of ideas. There was first the ancient body of conceptions that had descended from Augustine. A striking feature of the philosophy of the schools in England during the reign of Henry III is the vitality of the older principles of truth. Throughout the logical and scientific developments of the thirteenth and fourteenth centuries Augustinianism manifested a persistent vigour and an adaptability that enabled it to survive the mass of criticism pressed against it. The root of this tenacity was theological. The old intellectual vision was profoundly associated with the historic dogmas of religion, and the text-books and teaching of the faculty of theology, especially the *Sentences* of Lombard, controlled the lower studies in philosophy, and were imbued with the doctrines of reality that had descended from Augustine. The second group of theories that distinguish the reflection of this period is that which entered from the study of the great Arabian and Jewish philosophers of the eleventh and twelfth centuries. We have spoken in the preceding chapter of the discovery of Arabian physics by Latin Europe and of the part played by English scholars in this renaissance. The further phase of this influence was connected with the revival of Aristotelianism. As we have seen, Aristotelianism entered the thought of the West through the texts and commentaries of Mohammedan scholars. These interpretations of the teaching of Aristotle were strongly coloured with Neo-Platonic doctrines. In this form Arabian metaphysics penetrated the work of the schools and introduced a circle of beliefs, supported by the authority of Aristotle and of his greatest commentator, Averroes, that conflicted gravely with orthodox principles. The contradiction between some of the leading theses of Arabic-Aristotelianism and certain tenets of the Christian faith provoked the warmest controversies of the time. In other respects Arabian thought added weight to the Augustinian philosophy. The third and the most important development of thought was the construction of the edifice of Catholic Aristotelianism. As more accurate versions of the great texts became available through translations made directly from the Greek, a comprehensive reorganization of the theory of reality upon Aristotelian lines, freed from the distortions of Neo-

Platonic interpretation, was undertaken; and the new philosophy was adapted to the inviolable system of Christian doctrine. The chief labour in this immense reformation of ideas was carried through in Paris, but a line of eminent masters in the schools of England prepared the way for the fresh synthesis of thought; and at the end of the century the country gave birth to a thinker of the first rank, Duns Scotus, who united the strains of Augustinian and Aristotelian speculation in an original scheme of philosophy. But in England the new philosophy was already impregnated with Augustinian conceptions.

The intellectual activities of the age were marked by an extraordinary development of dialectical skill. Before we attempt to survey the movement of ideas it is well to touch on the method of scholastic discussion. The main condition of the remarkable growth of speculation in this country during the thirteenth century was the rise of the universities. The origin of the concentration of scholars at Oxford in the twelfth century is still obscure. The earlier teaching probably sprang up round some remarkable men who served the churches and monastic houses in the town. Even at the beginning of that century Theobald of Étampes describes himself as 'magister Oxenefordine', and he is recorded to have taught 'sixty or a hundred clerks more or less'.[1] A little later, a renowned theologian, Robert Pullen, was lecturing at Oxford, and a few other names relating to this primitive period of the university have survived. In the latter part of the twelfth century there was a striking increase in the body of scholars and masters; the increase has been attributed to the return of English students from Paris in 1167 when Henry II in the course of his quarrel with Becket recalled clerics from France and forbade scholars to cross the Channel without permission. It is probable that many came to Oxford. We hear of enlarged scholarly activities, of famous doctors, and of students so numerous that the town could barely feed them.[2] Halls were built, and a more definite organization appeared, modelled upon the great schools of Paris. In 1229 a dispersion of the scholars at Paris took place in consequence of the repressive measures imposed on the university by the secular authorities. Masters and clerks were welcomed at other

---

[1] C. E. Mallet, *A History of the University of Oxford*, 3 vols., London, 1924–7, i, p. 20.   [2] Ib., p. 23.

schools, such as those of Orleans, Angers, and Montpellier.
A number of celebrated Englishmen are reported by the
chronicler to have withdrawn from Paris, among them Allan
of Beccles, Nicholas of Farnham, and John Blund.[1] The last-
named was a notable Aristotelian. Many of these English
scholars made their way to Oxford. The masters of this period
include some distinguished figures, such as Alexander Neckham
and Alfred of Sareshal, both of whom signally promoted the
study of Aristotle. But a fresh intellectual ardour was kindled
when the mendicant Orders arrived in Oxford. The Dominicans
had appeared in 1221 and set up schools for their brethren; but
a stronger impulse to thought came from the Franciscans who
built their cloisters among the marshes near the town. The
friars minor aimed high. They chose as the first master of their
school a man who was already the foremost teacher in Oxford,
Robert Grosseteste. He directed the studies of the Order from
1229 until he was appointed Bishop of Lincoln in 1235. His
erudition, scientific interests, and humane spirit founded a
tradition that spread far beyond the Oxford schools. Men who
had attended his lectures and the lectures of his distinguished
disciples were sent to give instruction at many monastic centres
in England. We learn of more than thirty teachers distributed
throughout the English provinces of the Order.[2] The long list
of Franciscan masters at Oxford and at Cambridge in the
thirteenth century comprise many impressive names, Adam
Marsh, Thomas of York, John Peckham, Roger Bacon, and
Duns Scotus. The Dominican Order also gave rise to such
teachers as Robert Kilwardby, Robert Bacon, and Richard
Fishacre. The intellectual authority of Kilwardby may be
inferred from the fact that when the Master General of the
Order desired guidance on certain points of philosophy, he
wrote for advice to two scholars, Thomas Aquinas and Kilwardby.[3] But at the head of this rich movement in English
speculation stands Grosseteste. In the fourteenth century we
find his name united with the names of Democritus, Plato, and
Augustine, and preferred to the authority of Aristotle.[4]

---

[1] Matthew Paris, *Chronica Majora*, iii, p. 168.
[2] A. G. Little, *Franciscan Papers, Lists and Documents*, Manchester, 1943,
p. 62.   [3] *Mélanges Mandonnet*, i, Paris, 1930, p. 126.
[4] Wyclif, *Trialogus*, Lib. ii, Cap. 3.

A migration of scholars from Oxford in 1209 had founded the schools at Cambridge. At the close of the century an elaborate organization of university officers, rules of discipline, faculties, and schemes of study had arisen. But we are here only concerned with the organization of the universities in so far as it bears on the quality of the age. The usual periods of study demanded were seven years in the faculty of arts, eight years in the faculty of theology; and it was a common practice for scholars who had qualified in the faculty of arts to proceed to the full course in the higher faculty of theology. The length of the course of study was due in part to the fact that scholars entered the university at a tender age, in part to the slow and laborious process of acquiring knowledge from texts directly available only to a few. But it was also a consequence of the huge range of texts that was required thoroughly to be studied. Philosophical inquiries formed the main work of the faculty of Arts. On the one hand, they constituted an independent sphere of learning parallel to the doctrines acquired in the faculties of theology, of law, and of medicine. On the other hand, they provided the system of ideas that underlay much of the technical investigations of the other faculties. In particular theology leant strongly upon philosophy. But throughout the Middle Ages, and beyond them, philosophy, as we have seen, was in turn profoundly influenced by theology. The scope of what could be rationally demonstrated was controlled by the environment of the Faith.

The overspreading influence of biblical study upon intellectual habits remained. A thorough grounding in the text and in the interpretation of the Scriptures was required in order to prepare for an academic as well as for an ecclesiastical career. The theological training at Oxford began with four years' introductory study of the Scriptures, during which the student committed large portions of the text to memory. Theology was learnt principally through the *Sentences*, which also formed the basis for philosophical discussion. The two fields of thought were intimately associated. During the final stages of the long course the students worked at the *glossa ordinaria*, a vast compendium of patristic and later exegesis, and here he acquired skill in the multiple interpretation of the Bible that we observed in the Saxon theologians of the time of Bede. The literal, the allegorical, the anagogical, and the tropological senses were unfolded by the master with endless subtlety in lectures on both the Old and the New Testaments; and the clerk learnt that 'Holy Scripture is not merely to be understood according to its literal or grammatical sense, but with equal truth according to the mystical or moral sense'.[1] The minds of scholars were trained to search for spiritual meanings in all departments of inquiry, and though there was a movement towards a more objective and historical method, the traditional authorities continued to dominate the schools.

It is interesting to refer to a classification of the field of knowledge that appeared during the period. In Robert Kilwardby's *De Ortu et Divisione Philosophiae* knowledge is divided into two broad sections, the philosophy of the divine realm and the philosophy of the human realm. Under the first head are placed natural philosophy, mathematics, and metaphysics. Human philosophy comprises two fields, practical philosophy and logic; and practical philosophy is divided into ethics, private and public, and mechanical arts. Logic is described as *scientia rationalis*, and is distinguished from *scientia realis*. The scheme strikingly reveals the mental perspective; natural philosophy and metaphysics are theological investigations. Philosophical inquiries looked towards theology for their consummation; the faculty of theology crowned the scheme of studies, and the theologians lectured on philosophy. Yet philosophy tended increasingly to be pursued independently of theology, and this division was the source of the critical problems of the age.

Let us observe more closely the contents and methods of the intellectual training of the schools. Students in the faculties of arts and theology were occupied in collating a vast array of authoritative opinion and in construing the significance of highly abstract discussions by means of the *lectio*, *expositio*, *quaestio*, and *disputatio*. The master usually began by reading through the book under consideration to the audience of clerks. In the next stage he proceeded through the text section by section, offering a close commentary on its purport and citing many authorities on the topic under notice. In a further stage

---

[1] Robert Rypon, quoted in G. R. Owst, *Literature and Pulpit in Medieval England*, Cambridge, 1933, p. 58.

of exposition passages that called for further discussion were
picked out; these topics were termed *quaestiones*. A final stage
of study was the propounding of *quaestiones* for disputation.
Such was the method applied to the text of *De Anima* or the
Sentences of Peter Lombard. The prolonged investigation of
the texts rarely included criticism, and little historical sense
was brought to bear upon the intellectual circumstances of the
writers. The written word was reverently accepted, even when
it recorded wonders contrary to common experience. But the
method ensured an accurate understanding of the authorities,
and it promoted the immense learning that is displayed by the
masters of the Oxford schools. In the treatises and *quaestiones
quodlibetales* the problems are approached and explored by way
of a concourse of authorities. Four classes of authorities may
be observed.

In the first group are the logical, metaphysical, and scientific
works of Aristotle and the standard commentaries on them.
The range of these works will be referred to on a later page.
Other ancient philosophers were also read and discussed. Plato
was indirectly known through other writers; Porphyry, Cicero,
and Seneca were philosophical authorities. In the second class
are the Fathers, who were naturally cited far more frequently
than the pagan writers, except Aristotle. Those most often
quoted are Ambrose, Jerome, Augustine, Gregory, and Anselm.
In this class we may include also Boethius and the *Sentences* of
Lombard. We have quoted Bacon's complaint that the *Sentences* were more studied in the schools than the Bible. A
hundred and sixty-four *Commentaries on the Sentences* are known
to have been composed by English theologians, and many
more have disappeared. These commentaries are, in fact, the
principal sources that we possess for the philosophical inquiries
of the Middle Ages. The Sentence commentary was the chief
medium by which a schoolman offered criticism of contemporary
ideas and put forward his own opinions. The numerous commentaries and fragments of commentaries that have survived
present many textual difficulties to the modern scholar, for they
include several different types. There is the authentic edition
of the author; there is a Sentence commentary that is composed
of notes taken at the lectures of the master, the *reportatio*; and
there is the *abbreviatio*, a summary of the lectures for the use of

the students, made by a later hand. But in whatever form they were passed down to the following generations of copyists, these commentaries provided the leading channel of critical thought.

The third group of authorities comprised the Arabian and Jewish philosophers, Averroes, Avicenna, Alfarabi, Rabbi Moses (Maimonides), and others. The disturbing impact of Arabian thought upon Christian philosophy will be described below. The sanction of the metaphysical opinions of the great Arabian thinkers was appealed to by all the leading masters at the universities. Finally, there is a collection of titles whose authorship is anonymous or obscure, such as the writers of the books *De Causis* and *De Universo*.[1]

This accumulation of authoritative learning was the necessary condition of further advance. Beneath the heavy encumbrance of citations moved the living spirit of thought. The incessant effort to reconcile divergent texts is a mark of this life. For it was possible to quote authorities on either side of the same case. Aristotle himself was cited in support of contrary views, for example, on the problem of matter, for he had propounded different solutions in different works. Such divergences compelled independent discussion. The writings of masters like Peckham and Kilwardby are not merely collations of texts. On the contrary, they display the influence of another feature that dominated the mental training of the schools, a feature that encouraged unparalleled agility of thought.

The main work of the schools at Oxford and Cambridge was directed towards formal disputation. From the beginning of his career the student was practised in debating *quaestiones*. A large number of disputations, embracing examples at all the stages of the long preparation for the licence as master, have survived, many of which were taken down on the occasion of their deliverance.[2] They vividly reveal the energy of intellectual life at Oxford and Cambridge in the thirteenth century. They bring before us not only the strenuous formal methods of the schools, but also the principal topics of discussion during

[1] Ueberweg-Geyer, *Geschichte der Philosophie*, Berlin, 1928, p. 351. D. E. Sharp, *Franciscan Philosophy at Oxford in the 13th Century*, Oxford, 1930, pp. 3–4.
[2] A series of such disputations is printed in *Oxford Theology and Theologians*, c. *1282–1302*, by F. Pelster and A. G. Little, Oxford, 1934.

this period. In the early stages the scholar was expected to deliver little more than a brief summary of the case. One argument in favour of the problem, one against it, and a solution were sufficient. And we often find the argument *pro* and *contra* to consist of quotations from authorities, from one of the Fathers or from Aristotle. In later stages the argument in response to a *quaestio* becomes increasingly elaborate. In debating such matters as 'Whether the substance of the intellect is generated from matter?', 'Whether personality is composed of relations?', 'Whether everything that comes to be naturally tends towards nothing?', the respondent begins by giving a summary of the reasons for and against an affirmative answer to the question. The reasons are supported by authorities. There may be as many as ten reasons on one side, six on the other. The bare statement of the principal reasons *pro* and *contra* forms the introduction. The candidate now enters upon the discussion of the problem with the formal phrase *Dico ad quaestionem*. He puts forward the solution that he and orthodox opinion favours, explaining the grounds for asserting it and citing texts in support. The defence often rests on cardinal principles of philosophy or of theology, such as the principle of the simplicity of the Godhead or the distinction between essence and existence. The respondent concludes his exposition by meeting all the contrary arguments that he has quoted, concluding '*sic patet ad argumenta*'. The opponent now rises and offers a series of objections to the position that has been defended. The objections adduce a chain of damaging texts from Aristotle or from Boethius or from one of the Fathers. But they also include a reference to metaphysical and theological principles at variance with those maintained by the respondent, and often a reduction of the position that has been defended to awkward or absurd consequences. It is now that the mettle and the scholarship of the respondent is tested. He has to reply to each of the objections. His refutation usually shows that the opponent has misinterpreted the meaning of the texts that he has cited against the position asserted and that he has understood the principles brought against the position in a one-sided or superficial sense. At this point the candidate may be subjected to further criticism from the scholars present. In one disputation at Oxford, for instance, the luckless respondent is faced

with fourteen further objections against his position brought
forward by bachelors present at the disputation. To several of
these the respondent may reply comprehensively by showing
that they rest on an erroneous assumption, e.g., a false dichotomy. The respondent concludes the disputation with a firm
declaration of his position.[1]

When the respondent was a candidate for the mastership at
the end of his course, his duty was to preside over a disputation
and at its conclusion to 'determine' the argument by an authoritative survey of the topic under discussion and a judgement
pro or *contra*. Every scholar during his course in arts or
theology was required to debate in public several *quaestiones*
each year, concluding his studies with the prolonged disputations of the *vesperies* and the *inceptio*, after which he was
formally received into the rank of master. The solemn disputations named *quodlibet* were held twice yearly at Advent and
Easter. The leading masters and professors of the university
took part in them. No other source exhibits the immense range
and the intensity of thought at the universities more strikingly
than the record of these debates.[2]

The limitations of the method did not pass unnoticed; even
in the first period of its development Alexander Neckham
described it in satirical terms and Roger Bacon made some caustic
observations on it. The method could become stereotyped.
The thirteenth-century scholar was trained to know a host of
set problems and to have ready to hand chains of arguments
pro and *contra*. He had to be acquainted with scores of orthodox
solutions. The method laid stress on definitions and invited
verbal distinctions. It encouraged what F. Pelster terms 'the
reckless etymology of the Middle Ages'. He quotes some
examples from Oxford disputations. 'Sententia quasi sensum
tenentia.' 'Penuria est pena proveniens ab extra quasi pene

---

[1] In *Preaching in Medieval England*, Cambridge, 1926, p. 312, Mr. G. R.
Owst calls attention to the influence of the form of disputation in the schools
on the style of sermons. He quotes from a treatise of the time, 'Predicatio est
thematis assumpcio, ejusdem thematis divisio, thematis subdivisio, concor-
dantiarum congrua citacio, et auctoritatum adductarum clara et devota
explanatio.'

[2] See the fascinating description of the quodlibet by P. Glorieux, *La Littéra-
ture Quodlibétique*, Paris, 1925 and 1935. As counterbalance cf. M. D. Chenu,
Mélanges Mandonnet, i. Paris, 1930.

urens, quia carebat scientia adquisita.'[1] The verbal play, the formal antitheses, and the artificial divisions of the argument, retain the rhetorical apparatus of the Roman schools; we have seen how the design had descended to the curriculum of the ecclesiastical era. There was a superficial identity of aim, namely, skill in disputation. And looking more closely at the procedure we perceive that the discussions move on the support of established theses and texts. The method often appears mechanical owing to its *a priori* reliance upon traditional technical definitions and conceptions, as well as upon a mass of authorities. There is small admixture of concrete examples, of direct observation, and of practical experience. Later centuries contemptuously pointed out these limitations. But the scorn of men of the sixteenth and seventeenth centuries obscured the signal merits of scholastic instruction and prevented later thought from recognizing how much it owed to its methods.[2] The persistent effort to meet objections against a philosophical position was an education in agile and searching thought. It promoted the habit of drawing subtle distinctions and produced a mental environment favourable to great metaphysical achievements. An Oxford or a Cambridge scholar of the thirteenth century was obliged to penetrate deeply into the principles in which he believed. He learnt to distinguish between superficial and fundamental interpretations and to relate conceptions to broad underlying postulates. The philosophical discussions of the schools were concentrated upon the most general and fundamental classification of things, being and its modes, change, qualities, relations, universality, individuality, mind, matter, knowledge, God. It was the supreme period of metaphysics. The universities afforded a more thorough training in strenuous abstract thinking than was afforded in any later period in England; for in this sphere of reflection there soon followed a noticeable decline in standards. The methods that governed thought during the thirteenth and early fourteenth centuries produced in a brief stretch of time one of the finest efflorescences of philosophical intellect that our history has seen.

---

[1] Pelster and Little, op. cit., p. 27.

[2] But there was a strong revival of disputations in the sixteenth century. They were not finally abolished until 1852.

II

The salient feature of speculation during the thirteenth century was the advance of Aristotelianism. But the doctrines of Aristotle were assimilated in two distinct stages. In the earlier stage the peripatetic philosophy was interpreted through the glass of Neo-Platonic and oriental conceptions. John of Salisbury had expounded portions of the genuine teaching of Aristotle; the versions of the logic that now began to be current in the lecture-halls of Paris and Oxford were suffused with the notions of the school of Plotinus, and the doctrines of the metaphysics and cosmology were recovered in forms deeply coloured by the views of the great Arabian translators and commentators. And some works of Neo-Platonic origin were received as the authentic utterances of Aristotle. The treatise known as the *Liber de Causis* was the most influential of these spurious works; it was in fact part of a treatise by the Neo-Platonist, Proclus. In this first period, therefore, theses arising in late Greek thought were attributed to Aristotle. Prominent among these doctrines were the following positions; that the intellect apprehends universal essences that are separated from matter; that the intellect is an entity one and identical in all human minds; that the universe is an hierarchy of Intelligences proceeding from the Absolute One; that the lowest Intelligence is that which presides over the moon and the earth, and constitutes the intellect of man. These theories were absorbed with the expositions of Avicenna, Averroes, and Avicebron (the Jewish philosopher Ibn Gebirol). The second phase of the development of Aristotelianism fell in the third quarter of the thirteenth century. There now appeared a series of fresh translations of the principal works of Aristotle made directly from the Greek. The extensive labour of translation and revision was followed by massive reinterpretation of the entire range of philosophical inquiry in which the encyclopaedic investigations of the Stagirite were adapted to the interests and knowledge of the age. A main part of this great reconstruction was naturally directed to the task of adjusting the new philosophy of nature and of mind to the tenets of the faith. The systematic exposition of the doctrine of the *Physics*, of the *Metaphysics*, and of the scientific treatises in terms of Latin and Catholic thought, a blend that resulted in an original scheme of rational ideas, opened a new phase of thought in the West. This signal achievement in the history of speculation was principally the work of two Dominican scholars on the Continent, Albert the Great and Thomas Aquinas, but masters in England contributed to the revolution in ideas. Yet when we turn from the critical developments in Paris to the debates at Oxford we find ourselves in the midst of discussions that exhibit qualities strikingly distinct from those on the Continent. Philosophical exploration at Oxford was marked by a persistent concern with Augustinian principles and these principles dominated the interpretation of the new knowledge and the new metaphysics. The comprehensive reorganization of thought by St. Thomas did not gain the ascendency in England that it rapidly acquired in Paris and in the other great centres of thought. Inquiries in England, though they were profoundly affected by the recovery of Aristotelianism, pursued a course relatively independent of scholastic reflection in other parts of Europe. Let us glance at the course of philosophy at Oxford.

Aristotelianism was introduced into Oxford almost as soon as it appeared in Paris. There is evidence of its presence in the schools from the first decade of the thirteenth century.[1] Lectures and discussions on the whole range of works available grew steadily, and by the middle of the century it had attained the compass of the *corpus vetustius*, as it came later to be named, in distinction from the *corpus recentius*, which included the newer translations and commentaries. The older body of writings comprised the *Physica, De Generatione et Corruptione, De Anima*, the biological treatises embraced in the *Parva Naturalia, De Caelo et Mundo, Meteorologica*, the pseudo-Aristotelian *De Plantis, De Causis, De Differentia Spiritus et Animae* (attributed to Costa-ben-Luca), and parts of the *Metaphysica*. A number of commentaries were produced on various portions of this Aristotelian corpus by English masters.

But from the first introduction it was faced with serious difficulty. When the translations and commentaries of the Arabs began to be studied in the faculty of arts, the theologians and prelates expressed misgiving and there were moments of

---

[1] D. A. Callus, O.P., 'The Introduction of Aristotelian Learning to Oxford', *Proc. of the British Academy*, vol. xxix, 1943, p. 253.

severe tension between the philosophers and the theologians. In 1210 and again in 1215 the study of Aristotle was forbidden in the schools of Paris. The intercourse between Oxford and Paris was constant, and the injunctions caused considerable uneasiness among scholars in England. There were signs of serious strain between the guardians of the Faith and masters of the schools. The authority of the *philosophi* and *pagani* was resisted by the authority of the *sancti* and *theologi*. The hierarchy had many reasons for alarm. A powerful protest against the new learning came from churchmen who felt inveterate distrust of rational inquiry that unsettled men's minds and opened questions that had been decided by revelation and Catholic doctrine. *Non enim regnat spiritus Christi ubi dominatur spiritus Aristotelis*; such was the opinion of many leaders of ecclesiastical thought. But there were more particular reasons for disturbance. The new philosophy was putting into currency theories that were contrary to Catholic doctrine. Two theses were especially singled out for condemnation, the Aristotelian view of God and of His relation to the world, and the Aristotelian theory of the duration of the universe. The view of God as the unmoved mover of the universe, indifferent to the life of the world, and concerned with timeless contemplation of Himself, was a complete denial of the Christian belief in Providence. And from Aristotle's conception of matter there followed an equally serious admission. Since the material element in things must exist as a pre-condition of any production, the matter of the universe is eternal. It followed that the Christian doctrine of creation was denied. Looking back to the earlier part of the century Roger Bacon observes that the philosophy of Aristotle came late into use among the Latins, for the material philosophy and the metaphysics with the commentaries of Averroes and the treatises of other authors were translated only in his own day, and they were excommunicated at Paris on account of the doctrine of the eternity of the world taught in them. And he adds that many passages had been wrongly translated.[1] But it was in the shape of Arabian Peripateticism that Aristotle was condemned.

---

[1] *Compendium studii theologiae*, H. Rashdall, Aberdeen, 1911, p. 33. We shall find that the Aristotelian doctrine was still being energetically refuted by English divines at the beginning of the eighteenth century.

The influence of the great Arabian philosophers on the Aristotelian thought of the leading teachers in England in the earlier half of the century is pervasive. In certain writers we can detect the domination of one of these authorities. In John Blund's treatise on the soul the main source is Avicenna. The commentaries on Aristotle by Adam of Buckfield owe much to Averroes; many passages are little more than paraphrases of sections from the commentator. Thomas of York's *Sapientale* makes considerable use of the *Fons Vitae* of Avicebron; though this master draws liberally upon a wide range of Arabian and Jewish authorities, upon Averroes, Avicenna, Alfarabi, Albumasar, Algazel, and Rabbi Moyses (Maimonides).[1] The list indicates the extent of this influence. Nor is it remarkable that Aristotle was interpreted under Arabian guidance. There were few other translations available besides those that had been made from Arabic versions. And no other commentaries could stand comparison with those of Averroes in scholarship and in philosophical grasp. The deep reverence that Averroes felt for Aristotle shed its influence on scholars; for him the teaching of the Stagirite is the crown of truth and in his writings the human mind attained its consummation. Aristotle was created and given to men by Divine Providence in order that they might know what it is possible to know.

In these Arabian treatises there now entered the stream of thought in England an oriental current of speculation that, mingling with Neo-Platonic and Jewish ideas, carried forward a course of mystical and magical theory to later times. We shall observe some later developments of this oriental doctrine in the sixteenth and seventeenth centuries. In the condemnations of 1277 directed against erroneous principles circulating at Oxford, to which we must refer later, a number of Averroist theories were proscribed. Nevertheless, the interpretation of Aristotle continued to be coloured by the sources from which the texts had reached Europe. Some of these interpretations that profoundly disturbed the course of speculation in England will be described in a succeeding section.

A conspicuous mark of reflection in England, however, is the persistence of Augustinian views side by side with Aristotelian

[1] D. E. Sharp, *Franciscan Philosophy at Oxford in the 13th Century*, Oxford, 1930, p. 55.

formulae. In the thirteenth century the close study of the texts of the Philosopher did not cause any serious departure from the system of ideas that lay deep in the mental outlook. Augustine himself had used Aristotelian terms in describing the nature of things, for these terms formed an integral part of the Neo-Platonic scheme. We have noticed in the first chapter that portions of the *Metaphysics*, besides sections of the logical treatises, had survived in the versions of Boethius throughout the schools of the West from the sixth to the twelfth century. But the logic and the theory of being were suffused with Augustinianism. The Franciscan and Dominican masters who commanded thought in England continued to maintain Augustinian positions, serenely combining them with the new learning of the schools. The leader of thought in Oxford, Grosseteste, reasserts the main theses of Augustinianism, such as the argument from change to the changeless Being, the doctrine of exemplary forms and of the eternal reasons. The new Aristotelian principles of matter and form, potency and act, and the four causes, take subordinate positions in his philosophy. Roger Bacon even managed to turn Aristotle into an extreme realist, loudly proclaiming that Aristotle had been wrongly translated. And in Peckham and his pupil, Roger Marston, we find the main lines of the older philosophy once more asserted.

Yet the authentic teaching of Aristotle was gradually coming to the front encouraged by the incessant concentration of the schools on the texts. A second phase opened when there appeared new translations of the main works, made directly from the Greek text. The chief author of these translations was William of Moerbeke, the Flemish Dominican scholar. A general demand for more accurate translations had arisen, nowhere voiced with greater insistence than by Bacon. These versions were much more faithful to the original Greek than were the Arabic translations. The new texts reached Oxford about 1270. They were quickly followed by a tremendous event in the world of thought, nothing less than a comprehensive refashioning of the entire range of Christian philosophy on Aristotelian principles. The author of this achievement was Thomas Aquinas, the great Dominican master of the Paris schools. The new philosophy separated itself decidedly from Neo-Platonic and from Arabic attachments. The conflict of ideas in Paris had become acute about 1260, when Siger of Brabant led a group which advocated Averroist doctrines. The distrust of Aristotelianism was fanned into flame among the conservative theologians. Thomas threw himself against the Averroists by exposing at every point the dangerous consequences of their view of knowledge and experience. But his strength was devoted to the rigorous pursuit of Aristotelian thought to its logical end, and to the incorporation of this philosophy with Catholic doctrine. This development roused further conflict. The great master was vigorously attacked by the conservative theologians, headed by Bonaventura. The questions round which the vital controversy raged can be examined in the *Quaestiones Disputatae* that Thomas wrote at this time in reply to the charges brought against his position. These debates, fraught with such momentous consequences for the subsequent course of philosophy and theology, were deeply felt at Oxford; the letters of John Peckham manifest the intellectual disturbance. In 1277, three years after the death of Aquinas, the alarm of the theologians came to a climax. The Bishop of Paris, who was instigated to take action by the Roman Curia, promulgated an official condemnation of two hundred and nineteen theses that were being taught in the schools of the university. Most of these assertions were Averroist, but at least fifteen of them were teachings of the new Thomist-Aristotelian school of thought. A few days after the action of Bishop Tempier in Paris the storm descended upon the English scene. Kilwardby was now Archbishop of Canterbury. On 18 March 1277 he issued a solemn condemnation of thirty propositions circulating at Oxford, four concerning grammatical points, ten concerning logical questions, sixteen concerning principles of natural philosophy. The trend of these criticisms reveal the attachment of the archbishop to the older perspective in philosophy and his alarm at the new movement of opinion; he declared that all the Oxford masters were in agreement with him. It is interesting to observe that the condemnations are prominently directed against a principle of the new Aristotelianism that had not been mentioned by the injunctions in Paris, the principle of the unity of form in man. The condemnations provoked acute discussions at Oxford. The interference with the teaching of the university was resented, and there

were those who wondered that the archbishop had condemned
as intolerable errors views that were now held by many to be
well established. In fact, the movement in favour of Aristotelianism was gathering strength. The cloisters and halls of
higher learning in England became the scene of lively polemics.
The tension between the adherents of the old philosophy and the
new broke out in works that unsparingly condemned the leading theses of Thomas. Such a work was *The Correction of
Brother Thomas* of William de la Mare, a friend of Roger Bacon.
The treatise, composed about 1279, condemned no less than one
hundred and seventeen points of doctrine in the writings of
Aquinas. A reply to these strictures quickly appeared, written
probably by a Dominican scholar at Oxford, Richard Clapwell.
A few years later in 1284 the vehement champion of Augustinianism, John Peckham, who had succeeded Kilwardby as
Archbishop of Canterbury, reaffirmed the injunctions of his
predecessor. He reproved the strange novelties that had been
introduced during the last twenty years on the fundamental
points of theology. But already the new philosophy had gained
considerable support in Oxford, despite these official condemnations of it.

Yet the spread of Thomism in England was not so rapid as
its diffusion on the Continent. It was never accepted in this
country as it was accepted in other parts of the Catholic world.
Masters in England struggled to remain faithful to Augustinian
principles without abandoning the new Aristotelian views. The
climax to the grand age of metaphysical discussion is reached
in the treatises of a young Franciscan philosopher. Born
probably in Scotland, Duns Scotus taught for many years in
Paris, but his most important works were written at Oxford.
Many tendencies of thought converge in Scotus. He is the critic
of Thomism and of Augustinianism; indeed there are few of the
doctrines of contemporary philosophical reflection in which he
does not find difficulties. This comprehensive criticism contributed to the sceptical and disruptive forces of the fourteenth
century. But the embracing attacks of Scotus on contemporary
thought are animated by a constructive purpose. The great
and original scheme of thought upon which he was engaged was

---

[1] See his letter to the Bishop of Lincoln of 1 June 1285, in *Registrum Epistolarum*, ed. C. T. Martin, iii, London, 1885, p. 840.

cut short by his early death at Cologne in 1308; and the sketches of this sytem that have survived are far from easy to interpret. Fortunately we are more concerned with the impress of these ideas on thought in England than with the attempt to compose the subtle distinctions and novel turns of thought of the *Questions on Metaphysics* or of the *Oxford Work* into an harmonious system. The character of the Scotist schools in this country during the fourteenth century will be described in the next chapter.

In order, therefore, to disengage the main lines of thought in this age of searching controversy, it is necessary to take notice of several currents of speculation. With the Thomist-Aristotelian synthesis there mingled conceptions from older traditions that remained in the mental perspective. Now blending with, now opposing, the main stream of Aristotelian-Catholic assumptions, they gave breadth and variety to later speculation. In many of its features this philosophy of nature and of man brought to fulfilment the principles of Augustinianism, in others it diverged sharply from them. We have to describe, not a coherent body of beliefs, but a complex and loosely co-ordinated range of doctrines. Taking our stand at the centre of the new synthesis we must observe the variations and divergences that were preserved in English thought, and the problems raised by these divergences. And in tracing some of the cardinal features of this composite structure we are recalling moments of an enduring system of ideas. Until the middle of the seventeenth century it formed the unquestioned intellectual framework of experience. It is assumed by Chaucer, by Shakespeare, and by Milton. And even when it had been repudiated by the novel doctrine of truth that began to prevail among cultured men at the close of the seventeenth century, it lived on in disguised shapes and influenced the conceptions of the latest age.

III

All complexions of thought presumed the theology of Catholicism and justified their findings by the authority of the Scriptures and the saints. Lecturers and disputants are surer of the truths of faith than of the conclusions of reason. The ancient distinction of the Fathers of the Church between the certitude of revelation and the fallibility of human reason continued to dwell at the core of philosophical inquiry. The bearing of any discussion upon the beliefs of theology, whether it concerned the nature of universals or the distinction between essence and attributes, was constant. 'Hoc etiam auctoritatibus sanctorum confirmatur.' 'Hanc autem veritatem sacra scriptura confirmatur.' Such assertions were included in almost every division of the quodlibet and the Sentence commentaries. Most of the quodlibet were devoted to points of theological philosophy, to questions relating to the simplicity and absolute actuality of God or to His knowledge of contingent things; and many concerned the central dogmas of the creed, such as the dogmas of the Incarnation and of the Trinity. The doctrines were assumed as unimpeachable premisses; the traditional distinction between principles that are accessible to reason and principles that are revealed was maintained; but the rational meaning of the doctrines was indefatigably explored and the most abstruse metaphysics of the age is to be found in these discussions. It was the elaborate arguments concerning the twofold nature of Christ or the hypostatic union of persons in the divine being, rather than the more strictly philosophical portions of the labours of the schoolmen, that provoked the ridicule, of the practical humanists of the early sixteenth century.

The doctrines of theology govern the elaborations of philosophy. Yet in this period of acute polemics on fundamental problems a decided opposition between the sciences of logic and physics on the one part and theology on the other is apparent. Many instances could be cited of this conflict. There were sharp disputes over the pure actuality of the divine nature, over the distinction between the essence and attributes of God, over the question whether matter is present in the celestial bodies. Such differences were indications of a profound cleft between a philosophical theology constructed in accordance with the perspectives of St. Augustine and the novel philosophies of the schools. Certainly the opinions selected for condemnation at Paris in 1277 embraced some startling assertions. 'There is no higher life than the philosophical.' 'There is no wisdom but philosophy.' 'Nothing should be believed save only what is self-evident or can be deduced from self-evident propositions.' The quotations of Bishop Tempier from the Averroists included the extraordinary pronouncement that 'Theology rests upon fables'.[1] These defiant utterances are not found among the Oxford Averroists. But it is not uncommon to see disputants at that university, after quoting theological authority for a position, remarking that 'philosophia oppositum affirmat'. And when the philosophical case is argued at length the inclination of the master's thought is scarcely in doubt. Early in the century we can witness this double mode of arguing in Adam of Buckfield in the course of a discussion on the plurality of forms in man. And Richard of Cornwall mentions philosophers 'who take little notice of what the saints have to say since the saints speak in the name of the Holy Ghost in dealing with doctrines pertaining to the Faith, but in natural and philosophical matters they are just like ordinary men'.[2]

These signs of division between the philosophical cycle of studies and the theological must not be overlooked. Nor must they be exaggerated. The strongest impulse of thought was directed towards the task of bringing the Aristotelian theories of knowledge into conformity with the *intellectus fidei* of the theologians. Averroist rationalism was attacked as strongly by modern Aristotelians such as Thomas of Sutton as by the conservative theologians such as Peckham. At the same time the arguments of natural reason for theological truths were enlarged. Of the older arguments, the reasoning from the fact of change and contingency to a first cause, unchanging and self-sufficient, was frequently adduced. Thomas of York, in his comprehensive survey of the proofs for the existence of the Deity, lays much emphasis upon the argument of Anselm in the *Proslogion*. The most important innovation, though the argument can be discerned in earlier thought, is the doctrine of analogy of being. By this doctrine thinkers of the time learnt from Aristotle to evade the dilemma of applying terms to the Deity in either a univocal or an equivocal sense. In the former use, such terms as being, existence, goodness, have the same meaning when applied to divinity as they possess when applied to the realm of human experience. In the latter use the employment of the same terms in the two cases is accidental; the notion

---

[1] E. Gilson, *Reason and Revelation*, New York, 1939, p. 64.
[2] D. A. Collins, 'Two Early Oxford Masters', *Revue Néo-Scolastique*, xlii, p. 419.

of being when considered in relation to God and when referred to creatures is wholly disparate. The doctrine of *analogia entis* denies this disjunction. It maintains that there is a genuine *analogia*, proportionality, between the metaphysical principles apprehended in human experience and their transcendent dwelling in the Absolute.

But we cannot understand the rich speculative developments of the time without first considering the theories introduced by Aristotelianism into conceptions of mundane reality. The tendency of the new logic of experience has been descried in the work of John of Salisbury. The principal novelty was the belief that the only substantial being is the individual thing. The proper object of human inquiry is not the separate universal entity but the essence of particular things, the embodied universal. Singular individuals, trees, horses, and men are primary substances; classes and universals are secondary substances. The individual existents that constitute in their species and genera the created order are each metaphysically composite, for composition is the fate of all finite being. Composition denotes imperfection, mutability, dependence. Now the elementary factors into which all created things can be analysed are supplied by the Aristotelian principles, especially the principles of matter, form, privation, act, and potency. Matter and form, states Thomas of York, are the two roots of all things and into them all things can be resolved. The principles had been present in the philosophy of the earlier generations of thinkers, but they now assume the leading positions in the vision of reality. A long succession of masters in the English schools discussed them with inexhaustible subtlety. Our view of these ultimate categories must ignore all but the most striking refinements. But in order to understand the earlier phases of reflection and also the revolution in ideas that was accomplished in the seventeenth century a general picture of the principles is necessary.

In broad terms the principles seek to describe the confluence throughout the created universe of stability and instability, of repose and activity, of independence and dependence. In these reciprocal moments of the indivisible substances, stocks and stones, animals and men, elements and stars, one group signifies stages of accomplishment and definition, the other stages of

immaturity and limitation. The outlook is teleological. There
dwells in all things an amorphous element and this is *materia*.
The term, matter, is used in a sense quite different from the
'matter' of later natural philosophy. *Materia* is the nebulous,
undetermined principle that is the necessary correlative of definite
structure. The principle of definition that is associated throughout the universe with indefinition is *forma*, form. Form is used
by the schoolmen to mean both the activity that produces
determined structure and the determined structure itself.
Since in this latter sense it is the characteristic mode in which
a thing manifests itself, it often means the thing as an essence
or being. 'Forma est vere essentia ipsius rei et dat esse proprie.'
In its other sense form is the principle of movement and of
growth. It is in virtue of this principle that anything is shaped
to perform its proper function. It brings the passive matter of
things to completion, guiding them from an imperfect, ill-
adapted state, to a perfect, adapted state. Working with matter
it is the natural cause of change and development. The formal
cause is the principle of becoming. Its operation is most strikingly
seen in the phenomena of growth in living things. The vegetative, sensitive, and rational forms control respectively the
generation and growth of plants, animals, and men. But forms
also direct the changes of the physical world. At the lowest
stage, the amorphous *prima materia* is impressed with the form
of corporeity, *forma corporeitatis*, and this abstract pure ex-
tensity is further differentiated by incoming forms so as to
produce the structures of the elements, water, earth, air, fire;
and upon these there supervene a countless multitude of forms
that bring into being the character of things in their kinds.

Accordingly, the substance and behaviour of every class of
things are derived mainly from their forms. They account for
the fact that things are what they are and behave as they do
behave. In the terms of the schools, they aim at the perfection
of things in their species. It is by virtue of its appropriate form
that fire burns and man thinks. The mode of their impression
into matter provoked a wealth of discussion. The general view
was that they lie dormant in the natural world until they are
brought to bear on matter by the operation of some agent. For
it was generally held that forms cannot decay nor disappear.
When a being changes or grows, the forms that endow it with

its specific character were believed to be superseded by new
ones, while the old were understood to recede before the incoming ones and to remain in a potential manner in the composite
being. But there was a flood of discussion relating to the status
and appearance of forms, the consequence in part of the
obscurity of the Aristotelian texts on these questions. Elaborate
divisions and classifications of the hierarchy of supervenient
forms were propounded by the Oxford masters, notably by
Roger Bacon. The classification ranges from the most general
form that provides the bare quality of existence to the specific
form that defines the character of an individual object. But in
these explorations grave differences of opinion arose. The
question of the plurality of forms in things and especially in
man was a leading issue in the crisis that occurred in 1277,
as we have remarked. We must revert to it on a later
page.

The philosophical inquiries into the operation of forms led to
a development of physical theory. For the presence of some
agent was deemed to be required in order to call forth the
activity of forms. On a broad view the schoolmen recognized
three types of natural agency: physical contact, animal conju-
gation, and ideas in minds. The first produces physical changes;
it is exemplified in the action of the sun on ice, to cite a favourite
example of the masters. The second generates living beings;
the third makes artificial objects, implements, houses, books.
Naturally philosophers were not content with so general an
account of these operations. English masters, and especially
the Franciscan thinkers at Oxford, are distinguished by the
close attention that they gave to the details of these processes.
Roger Bacon discusses the factors of animate generation at
length in the *Communia Naturalium*, noticing those that are
contributed by the two parents and those that enter from other
sources, such as the sun. The analysis of the complex processes
that determine the activity of forms promoted the strain
between the philosophical and theological faculties, for the
theologians stressed the action of celestial and divine influence
in the work of forms, while the new school of philosophers
unfolded the interaction of natural operations. The metaphysical character of these accounts, however, allowed many
compromises between the two approaches; masters argued for

both the immanent activity of the natural world and the creative power of God in all the motions of the world.

The inseparable correlate of form is matter. Formal activity cannot function apart from matter. God alone is pure form, *forma formarum*, and some thinkers questioned the propriety of applying the term to Him, or of speaking of pure form at all. For our human experience form is the organizing principle of matter, and is always associated with matter, however refined and tenuous matter may be. Some mode of the common stuff that pervades the universe is necessary in each thing in order to suffer organization. With the first form the Creator made also the first matter. All being is composite, a unity of matter and form; forms are embodied. Primary matter is the elementary substratum that receives all forms; and everywhere matter is the subject of the formal activity that gives determination to things. In contrast to the formal element it is the seat of corruption and privation in things, and is often spoken of as gross and vile in comparison with the nobility of form. The primordial matter becomes qualified in countless kinds of things, each qualification being a preparation to receive the forms that come to life in it. Any matter for our experience is *materia signata*, matter determined by form. Following certain observations of Aristotle, it was generally held that the material element in the universe is the cause of particularity; it makes things in their kinds individual things. Many things and many persons possess the same form, but the material embodiments of the form, the wood and the stone, the flesh and bones, differ in each particular instance. This is the usual view; here again there are different positions. Some philosophers, e.g. Thomas of York, cited utterances of Aristotle in which form is referred to as the principle of individuation. Later in the century when the interpretations of Aquinas began to penetrate the schools in England the view was upheld that material quantity or the extension of substance through parts is the ground of the plurality of things. This is the position of Thomas of Sutton.[1]

The refinements and contradictions of the masters were endless, but in general philosophers held that all natural substances, from elements to men, compose unities of matter and form.

[1] D. E. Sharp, 'Thomas of Sutton', *Revue Néo-Scholastique*, vol. xxxvii, p. 93.

The form is a quickening spirit that imparts to a thing its specific nature, its qualities, powers, and motions. It is in virtue of the substantial form that heavy bodies descend and light bodies rise. The substantial form of gold endows the species with its weight, colour, fusibility, and all the other properties; in an animal, its powers of nutrition, movement, and growth spring from the vegetative and sensitive forms active in a body apt to receive them. And when an animal dies, the primary matter of its body, stamped and informed while living with the forms that gave it the qualities of its species, loses its specific forms and reverts to the basic forms of the elements.

Other Aristotelian principles were enlarged upon to the same metaphysical purpose. *Actus* and *potentia*, the ἐνέργεια and δύναμις of the *Physics*, supported the vision of universal growth and decay, of the waxing and waning of all things in their kinds. In fact act and potency are linked in the writings of the university teachers with form and matter, and are frequently spoken of as the material and formal causes of change. At any stage of its existence any natural thing, whether animate or inanimate, is in respect to one stage 'in act', in respect to another stage 'in potency'. In so far as it is changing it is incomplete. It is moving towards its specific condition, or it is receding from it. So far as it has attained stability it is in act, so far as it is still proceeding to a more determinate condition of existence it is in potency. Neither act nor potency, any more than form and matter, can occur in isolation. Act presupposes potency and potency presupposes act. Act is the culmination of process or potency, and process is defined in relation to its outcome. Potency is frequently named possibility. The end of activity that is present in every class of things in the created universe is implicit throughout their changes and governs all their stages. All change is a transition from potency to act; it is a movement towards fulfilment of being. Indeed the movement of potential matter towards its form and act is often compared with the process of attaining the ends of desire. In many contexts potency and matter, on the one hand, act and form on the other, are united. It is important to notice that what is potency and matter, what is act and form, are points of relative emphasis. In different references what is potency may be viewed as act, and what is act may be viewed as potency. The stones

of which a castle or cathedral are built are in potency in relation
to the finished structure, but in relation to the elements they
are in act. From one point of view a seed is in act, from another
it is in potency. Again it is in the organic realm that the operation of these categories is seen most clearly. The growth of a
flower or of a man is readily explained in terms of *potentia* and
actus, for here development in general and each detail of the
process is intelligible in relation to the maturity of the species
or of the organ. Growth in organisms points throughout to a
culminating stage in which the structural plan found in detail
throughout the organism attains completion. But the rhythm
of potency and act is universal, and is applied by the masters
of the schools to every kind of process. It is applied to moral
life; any activity judged good is in potency to its fulfilment in
act. It can equally well be described as a process controlled
by an immanent form. The category is also manifest in the
sphere of knowledge. Act and form are what are primarily
known.

Closely associated with potency is *privatio,* privation. This
term indicates negation, deficiency, and considers matter and
potency from the point of view of absence of form. But subtle
distinctions were drawn by the masters between matter and
privation, so that the latter becomes a further category.

IV

The formal principles of being that have been sketched were
present in the older logic of experience. The conceptions of act
and potency had been received from the standard text-books of
Boethius and from the works of Augustine himself. But these
principles now assumed a fresh significance and became issues
for prolonged discussion. The relation of one side of these
correlative principles to the other side in the structure and
process of things was debated by the Oxford masters with
infinite labour. Those who advocated Aristotelian theses were
obliged to defend their views and to point out the misinterpre-
tations of the accepted positions. For the conservative tradition
forms were the grounds of things. It fastened its gaze upon
the necessary and unchanging essences, not upon individual
existents, the unity of which depended upon the play of potentiality and actuality, of matter and form. The new philosophy

was divided from the old in substituting form-in-matter for transcendent form. The flexibility of the discussions on these doctrines that are found in the writings of the Oxford Franciscans forbids any sharp distinction of parties; the division of theory accentuates a general tendency, and, as we have seen, the older system of ideas continued to prevail at Oxford. But the effect of the new Aristotelianism in these respects was to point philosophy towards the analysis of mundane causes. The processes of the natural world are stated to require the influence of appropriate agents in order that the indwelling activity of the formal element of the material thing may be elicited. Philosophers paid increasing attention to the conditions of change and motion. The elaboration of the theory relating to the metaphysical principles of being directed thought towards an abstract physics. These recent developments of philosophy appeared to many theological masters, as we have seen, to diminish the direct operations of the Creator and the celestial powers in the processes of nature. In some of the protests levelled at the Aristotelians by the ecclesiastical authorities, such as Peckham, an Augustinian standpoint is presumed. But there was another vein of thought that opposed these developments. It was one that exercised a powerful influence over many religious thinkers. This scheme of ideas was Arabian.

The doctrines of the *Fons Vitae* of Avicebron had been absorbed and were expounded in the schools. We have observed that the work of Thomas of York owed much to this source. Now the teaching of this treatise gave strength to the simple theological outlook of tradition that regarded all natural processes and things as subject to the divine will. They are sustained in their existence and activity by the constant power of God. But the Arabian doctrine developed this view of the relation of God to the operations of nature in terms of a metaphysic that offered a rival scheme to that of the new Aristotelianism. It included a divergent theory of matter and form. It sharply divided the material mode of being from the formal creative element. The material substance of things is purely passive; activity and development is due to the pure forms that are imposed on matter from outside. And the operations of these forms ultimately descend from the divine will. The first will acts on matter through the forms as a writer acts on a clean page.[1] The Arabian doctrine, in fine, went far to deny the efficacy of secondary causes in natural events. But the Aristotelianism of the time was affected by the Arabian explanations. It was suffused with Neo-Platonic cosmological speculation. From the First Intelligence, the divine Absolute, there are engendered a chain of Intelligences whose bodies are the planets and fixed stars. The Intelligence that governs the earth is embodied in the moon, and the moon engenders the intelligent souls of men and also the active principles of the four elements that provide the basic properties of the natural world. Matter is made adaptable to receive the forms that animate it by the operation of the lunar and other celestial bodies. The intelligible forms of nature and of human minds are conferred by the celestial Intelligences and especially by the moon. Men's understanding is adapted by the heavenly forces to receive the rational ideas and universals that emanate from the lunar Intelligence. The entire tendency of this system of thought was to minimize, if not to abolish, the work of mundane natural causes and to transfer their explanation to a supra-mundane region. And its theory of knowledge taught that the intelligible forms enter wholly from above and that even the preparation of the mind owes little to human endeavour. It renounced all efficient development in nature and all intelligibility in minds to the impress of ideas or forms transported from without. The stability of things, the laws of growth, the achievements of knowledge, are explicable only in relation to spheres of Intelligibles external to mundane nature and to minds. The doctrine penetrated reflection largely through the writings of Avicenna. Roger Bacon's declarations in the *Opus Majus* concerning the divine content of philosophy are imbued with this doctrine.[2] It was the work of the new generation of thinkers to free Aristotelianism from these Arabian accretions. And despite their agreement with Augustinian positions, the Franciscan and still more the Dominican philosophers in England, opposed the theosophic theories of causation.

Another issue provoked acute controversy at Oxford. A number of philosophers advanced the doctrine of the active

---

[1] E. Gilson, 'Pourquoi St. Thomas a critiqué St. Augustin', *Archives d'Histoire Doctrinale et Littéraire du Moyen Age*, Paris, 1926, i, pp. 25–35.

[2] Op. cit., ed. J. H. Bridges, Oxford, 1897, i, pp. 33 ff.

potentiality of matter. They denied the Aristotelian view that matter is the passive correlate of active form. They held that matter possesses a lowly conative activity; it is not wholly the inert recipient of organization. The theory had descended from St. Augustine and is one facet of the Augustinian divergence from the Aristotelian school. In *De Genesi ad Litteram* he had attempted to reconcile the two accounts of the Creation given in Genesis. One account stated that the Deity created all things at one moment of time; the other described the successive production of creatures. Augustine supposes that creatures were created *potentially* in one moment of time, and *actually* in successive stages. In instantaneous potential creation creatures are said to exist in their *rationes seminales*. Augustine enters into the theory of these seminal natures in some detail. The gist of the theory is that they are spiritual propensities that govern the appearance and growth of things; and active causality is said to reside even in the earth and in the sea, waiting to produce new species of plants and animals in the course of time.[1] The Oxford philosophers applied these suggestions to the theory of matter. 'The seminal principle is nothing else but the essence of matter in its striving and desiring aspect.'[2] The material element is not inert, it contains an intrinsic power of development; it shapes itself in manifold ways to receive specific forms. The theory that matter is one in all its manifestations was strongly rejected. Matter is as specific as its forms. Its unity is only a logical unity; in nature every form requires a corresponding disposition in matter. This view of matter is the source of the doctrine of plastic nature that we shall find put forward in the seventeenth century in opposition to the mechanical teaching of Descartes and of Hobbes; and we shall notice other revivals of it in English thought. In the hands of the thirteenth-century masters the view that matter possesses an aptitude for the special form to be realized in it was worked out in connexion with the theory of the generation of living beings. According to a typical account generation requires four main factors, a pre-existing agent (the parent body), matter appropriate to the special form, the special form, and remote movers, such as the celestial bodies.

[1] Augustine, *De Genesi ad Litteram*, v. 23–vi. 18.
[2] Roger Bacon, *Communia Naturalium*, ed. Steele, 85. 1.

The insistence on the active potency of matter blurred the distinction between matter and form, and a vast amount of intricate discussion is to be found in the pages of the Oxford masters relating to the quality of being that should be accorded to matter. It was felt that matter must possess a being of its own distinct from the being of form. The passage in the *Timaeus*, where Plato speaks of matter as lying between being and non-being, was recalled. The Franciscan thinkers went farther and ascribed a positive character to matter, an innate activity. But neither they nor others maintained that matter existed apart from form; and some philosophers who explored the problem later in the century under the guidance of Thomism rejected the *rationes seminales* as superfluous.

The most interesting application of the metaphysical principles derived from the study of Aristotle lay in the theory of mind. The human *compositum* occupied the central place in the scale of beings. In the body-mind of man are united terrestrial and celestial forms. The human body is composed of the four elements and their mixtures, and over them there operate the vegetative and the sensitive forms with their appropriate matters. But at a point in the embryonic development of the body that is difficult to determine there supervenes the rational form that fulfils and unifies the tendencies of the lower forms. The intellectual apprehensions of the rational soul and its consequent relative independence of the body, links man with the pure intelligences who rule the celestial movements. Man is thus a microcosm, an epitome of the universe, a view that occasioned numerous analogies between parts of his nature and the order of the world. But the striking point in the new theories was a fresh conception of the relations between mind and body. The traditional view was a dualism. The mind is entirely distinct in substance from the body. It is active, totally present in every point of its operations, and not subject to corruption. This spiritual principle animates a body that is a complex part of the material order; though a lowly form of life was allowed to it. Under the teaching of the Arabians an intermediate position was maintained; a spiritual type of matter was allowed to combine with form in the substance of the mind. But a new theory was put forward by the Thomists. They asserted an essential relation between body and mind so intimate that the body taken apart from the mind is said to be a mere abstraction; it does not exist as a body. And it is equally true that the mind viewed in independence of the body ceases to be mind. Each part of the complex, body-mind, must be defined by reference to the other part. As Peckham says, 'Apart from the mind the body does not exist, save in an equivocal sense. Therefore the body and mind, since they are defined by reference to one another, are not two different things.'[1] The human individual is the whole composite, not the mind alone, as the Arabians maintained. The Oxford writers insist on this unity of man under the diverse aspects of body and mind. The mind is the substantial form of the body and this implies that it is not a kind of being that is exterior to the body, the directing agency of an alien type of existence; but an aspect of a single compound being. The union of form and matter is here so close that the one interpenetrates the other in all its organs, and the two compose a single unique substance.

Yet the nature of the mind is not fully described by defining it in relation to the body. It is the form of the body; but the rational form, as we have already observed, surpasses its bodily expressions. The schoolmen draw a distinction between primary and secondary acts of the mind. As primary act the rational mind co-ordinates the organic activities of the lower minds of the body, the vegetative and sensitive minds, and raises them to a new level. As secondary act the mind reaches beyond the bodily level and apprehends universals and spiritual realities. It engages in experiences which the body cannot share. The human mind cannot attain to the understanding that is possessed by the angelic intelligences, but in a limited fashion it can, by the operation of *intellectus* with which its reason is united, have some part in the knowledge of the universal intelligible forms of things.

The account of these higher functions of mind brings forward a distinction of vital importance between the human mind or soul and all lower terrestrial minds. The human mind does not come into being by the processes of generation. It is not an emanation from the potency of the vegetative and sensitive minds, those minds that Duns Scotus names 'partial actualities'.

---

[1] Quoted from *Quaestiones Disputatae*, 50. 26, Sharp, *Franciscan Philosophy*, p. 185. Thirteenth-century masters owed the doctrine to Thomas Aquinas.

The rational mind is created, not generated; and we have seen that in accordance with the postulate of theology, only Absolute Being can create being. The rational mind is infused into an organism prepared to receive it by God. The *forma intellectiva* does not emerge from the inferior forms that animate man's body. Its rational and intellectual powers and its spiritual desires preclude any such theory. It must have its origin in the source of spirit. The practical bearing of this theory on Christian beliefs is obvious. And of equal interest to Christian faith was the belief in the immortality of the soul that followed from the same principles. The argument that rationality implies freedom from the body, an argument that descends from the *Phaedo*, was adduced; and it was pointed out that an incorporeal and simple being cannot suffer dissolution, and that the soul possesses a desire for immortality and eternal blessedness that presumes a state in which the desire finds satisfaction.

We meet here the principal issue in the condemnations of Oxford thought by the heads of the Church in England. The most general form ascribed to the body was the *forma corporeitas*, that provides the body with the elementary quality of existence. Upon this bare quality of body were superimposed further forms, in order to account for the specific features of things, such as terrestrial and material form, *forma corporalis noncelestis*; the form of composite material things, *forma mixti*; the form of living things, *forma animati*, and numerous further divisions of forms.[1] Now the traditional view was that the lower forms remained in the body and mind of man after he had been endowed with the intellectual and highest form. The multitude of forms persist beneath the *forma intellectiva*. It is interesting to observe the theological arguments that were pressed in favour of this doctrine of plurality of forms. If the bodily forms do not remain in man, resurrection would be impossible, for the bodily characteristics would not be preserved. Again, there would be no identity between venerated relics and the original body of the saint. And, more generally, the doctrine of the Eucharist would be undermined, for the whole substance of the bread is believed to be changed into the whole body of Christ, not into its matter only.[2] But philo-

[1] Cf. Roger Bacon, *Communia Naturalium*, ed. R. Steele, pp. 87–9.
[2] Peckham, *Registrum Epistolarum*, ed. C. T. Martin, iii, London, 1885, p. 841.

sophical reasons for this position were also adduced. The theory of *rationes seminales* was relied upon; there must be a chain of potential forms in creatures. Moreover, when the soul leaves the body we see that the forms appropriate to body in general and to the individual body are still present in the corpse. It contains the forms and matters of the four elements and of their compounds, the *mixti*. And since he is an animal, the living man embraces the vegetative and sensitive forms. Many difficulties in the view that the intellectual principle supersedes all lower forms in man were pointed out. It would follow that the intellectual principle would be the cause of the bodily characteristics of man even after death, a conception repugnant to the belief in this principle as the form of spiritual life. And if the intellect were united only with primary matter, the resulting composite would not be man.

The difficulty was to combine the essential unity of the incarnate soul with its diverse operations; for every operation presumes a formal cause. The difficulty illustrates the problems that sprang from the basic principle of matter and form. Does the rational soul inform matter directly or is matter in the body already informed? Few thinkers went to the length of Roger Bacon, who related every perfection in a creature to a different form and supposed a multiplicity of individual forms as well as a multiplicity of universal forms. But many sided with Kilwardby in holding to the orthodox view that there are several forms in the human substance. Pluralism was now challenged by the Thomist theory. Man is a body-mind possessing one substantial form. Numerous adjustments were attempted. The unity was preserved by taking the lower forms to be incomplete; each grade points beyond itself to a higher grade and the human being constitutes an incomplete composite that is unified and fulfilled by the intellective form. There is a hierarchy of forms in man, but not a number of distinct souls. This is the compromise offered by Peckham, who was later to renew the injunctions against the Thomist teaching. 'The rational mind brings to fulfilment all natural forms and perfects them.' The Franciscan masters, in fine, tried to preserve the unique character of the rational soul while maintaining the relative independence and reality of physical and biological functions; the lower forms are subordinate to the ultimate form, which is the perfection of the human creature. But the orthodox position stood upon the conviction that the human organism embraced a series of substantial forms and that the intellectual faculty was distinct. Some of the arguments in favour of this position put forward in the English schools have been mentioned. 'The prevailing view at present in England', remarks Thomas of Sutton, 'is that the intellectual and sensitive forms are distinct.' He himself boldly argues for the Thomist theses.

V

The Aristotelian theory relating to the procedure and scope of human understanding steadily won its way in the schools. Here, as elsewhere, thinkers adapted the recent accounts to the old Platonic methods of truth, to the dialectical path that ascends to the Ideas. They sought to combine the belief that comprehension of reality is the task of *intellectus*, which must seek to detach itself from the realm of changing sensible things, with the new doctrine that human knowledge is throughout dependent upon perception. It was admitted that knowledge is concerned with the forms in things. We do not perceive nor think of the momentary items of sensation. Meaning requires universals, permanent characters amid the flux of impressions. But for the *moderni* understanding is attained by the process of abstracting the concepts from the matter given to it by the senses. Aristotle had given an elaborate analysis of the elementary processes of cognition and his account was followed by lecturers and disputants at Oxford, though with considerable differences of interpretation. A summary description of the theory may be presented.

Objects propagate 'species' that convey likenesses (*similitudines*) to the sense-organs. These likenesses are not material particles; the theory is not a form of the theory of physical transmission propounded in the seventeenth century. Yet the species cause activity in the sense-organs and this is transferred to points within the body. So far there are no more than unrelated sensations. Each of the five senses transmits a distinct type of likeness, but the different types are correlated by the general sense, the *sensus communis*, the source of which is placed by some writers in the brain, by others, following Aristotle, in the heart. The species thus correlated are preserved by the *imaginatio*, and thus can persist in the mind after the stimulus is removed. Further subconscious activities now occur; the activity of the *vis cogitativa* or *apprehensiva* that compounds and divides the complex impressions, and of the *vis aestimativa* that instinctively perceives whether the impressions are favourable or unfavourable for the animal life of man. All this complicated activity that goes to produce the experience of perceiving is the cognitive attainment of the sensitive order of mind, and is common to men and the animals. Some of the schoolmen went farther and accorded a primitive ability to think in universals to the animals.[1] But all thinkers agreed that the conscious recognition of the general features of the world is the unique prerogative of the rational form and of man.

The product of the subconscious responses of the sensitive level of the mind to the species emanating from the object is the *phantasma* or perceptual impression. It is the function of the rational activities of man to educe the concept from the phantasm. This is the work of the active intellect, the *intellectus agens*. As passive intellect, *intellectus possibilis* or *materialis*, the rational mind is in potency to understanding, receiving the material for knowledge from perception. In its active aspect it constructs the rational forms by freeing them from their potential and immanent status in the world that is perceived by the senses. The stages by which the universals are abstracted from the perceived complex are described with varying refinements by philosophers. But the upshot of the Aristotelian influence is the doctrine that the work of thought is to isolate the common features in the scattered items given in perception, and to reach after the abstract unities and connexions there descried. The signal difference from the conservative outlook is the insistence upon the dependence of thought at all levels upon any sensory experience. The position brings forward a vitally different conception of the being of universals.

But before we turn to this aspect of the new movement of ideas, let us notice the heretical notions carried into the discussions on the psychology of knowledge under the authority of the Arabian commentators. The doctrine that agitated orthodox thinkers related to the status of the rational faculty, the *intellectus agens*. The capacity to seize the universal forms

---

[1] Cf. Bacon, *Op. Maj.*, ed. Bridges, ii, pp. 127–9.

of things endows man with his unique character in the hierarchy
of the universe. By this power he is connected with the angelic
intelligences. As we have seen, it was a cardinal principle that
the rational part of man was not generated but created. The
intellectus is on a different plane of reality to other processes of
the mind, including *ratio*, the discussion of temporary and
mundane regulations of nature. In operating with purely
logical principles the intellect is conversing with entities that
are eternal, necessary, transcendent. Now the Arabian interpretation of the active intellect transformed it into the Augustinian process of illumination. In virtue of its capacity to
discern the intelligible essences of things the *intellectus agens* is
itself divine. For many masters it becomes God Himself active
in human beings. It is primarily God, secondarily the angel
intelligences. 'Intellectus agens est Deus principaliter et
secundario Angeli, qui illuminant nos.'[1] The active intellect
that distinguishes the universal characters of things is the
divine light. This faculty cannot be part of the natural human
soul, for in principle it knows things as they are, it is incorruptible, and it is always in act; that is to say, that in contem-
plating intelligible realities it is fulfilling its being. It seeks and
finds itself. And this means that it is divine.

This is the view of many of the leading thinkers of this time,
of Grosseteste, Bacon, Peckham, and of others. It is another
testimony to the tenacity of Augustinianism in English thought,
despite the advance of Aristotelian metaphysics. Indeed these
masters could refer to many passages in Aristotle that asserted
Platonic theories. But the belief that intellect is divine suggested alarming consequences. Among the injunctions by
Bishop Tempier against the erroneous theories that were being
uttered in the schools of Paris were condemnations of the
doctrines that the active intellect is a separate substance
superior to the possible intellect, and that the essential infallibility of the active intellect makes it divine. It was the
inference drawn from these doctrines that was especially condemned. 'This is error, because it holds that there is one
intellect in all men, and equality in all minds.' And the belief
that the intellect is one in all men denied immortality to the
individual souls of men. The intellect that deals with necessary

---

[1] Bacon, *Opus Tertium*, ed. J. S. Brewer, London, 1859, p. 14.

truths and universals as such is part of the eternal order of things; it is not part of the individual man who thinks. Socrates and Plato are not two distinct intellects. As reasoners on the intellectual plane they become merged in the one universal reason; they become God. This was the teaching of Averroes, and such was the weight of his authority that there were masters in the schools who taught that there was a single reason active in all human beings and that, in this region of mind, there were no personal minds. The recoil from this heresy was violent. Even those who leant towards Augustinianism in England condemned it in the strongest terms. The active intellect is superhuman, it is distinct from the rational or discursive powers, it is created, not derived from generation. All this is admitted. But the further conclusion was energetically rejected. An Oxford master wrote that the Averroistic theory undermines all moral belief, for it makes virtue and vice identical. The wicked and the blest are one. It also destroys the laws of nature, for each individual matter has its individual form. And another asserts that the view of Averroes could be held only by a madman. The rational mind of an individual person is his peculiar form, to which his body is adapted. The error of Averroes, according to Peckham, is founded on the assumption that the intellect must be universal because it operates without matter. In its purity, among the angelic intelligences, it must do so. But with men it is joined with the bodies that it perfects. It is circumscribed by its particular setting in a particular body, of which it is the form and perfection.

From the agitations stirred by the Averroist heresy let us return to the discussion concerning the nature of reality that thought reveals. Reasoning is concerned with both the particular and universal elements in things, with the sensory as well as with the intellectual factors of experience. Thought begins with particular presentations entering through the senses and advances by detaching the general elements from their sensible embodiment. So far the procedure appears to conform to the Augustinian ladder of the intellect. But the essential difference is that the general characters that thought descries amid the diversity of perceived things, separating and combining their qualities, are not now conceived of as realities transcending the things. The universals that constitute the essences of things are distributed through the particular things and possess no existence apart from them. The new logic asserted the association of sense and thought in all human knowledge. Knowledge arises from perception and must always return to perception. Reality, so far as human understanding can grasp it, is not a system of forms; it is a system of embodied forms. The recognition of the pervasive presence of matter directs attention to the multitude of particulars, to special and temporal factors, to movement and development. For this philosophy apprehension of the system of forms can never be more than approximate and provisional. At all levels our knowledge is governed by its relation to corporeal things, and we can understand incorporeal things, including God himself, only by analogy. What we apprehend is indeed always a system of universals. We cannot seize an individual thing in thought, for we should have to become it. But our concepts are not fictions. The nature of things that thought discovers are genuine aspects of reality, but they are necessarily simplifications and abstractions of reality. Reality is not composed of *genera* and *species*.

This union of sensory perception and intellectual knowledge, of particularity and universality, of matter and form, is the note of the new philosophy. The proper objects of our intellect are the qualities and relations of sensible things. '*Proprium objectum intellectui nostro proportionatum est rei sensibilis.*' Nevertheless, the older realism remained obstinately alive in the schools in England. At the opening of the century Grosseteste unequivocally asserts it. We have mentioned that he was among the first band of scholars in England to absorb the new Aristotle and the scientific learning of the Arabians. He wrote commentaries on the logical works, on the *Physics* and *Metaphysics*, and translated the *Ethics*. His writings on natural philosophy frequently cite Aristotle. But the trend of his philosophy is not Aristotelian. In order to reach demonstrative knowledge the mind must be brought into conformity with the eternal ideas existing in the divine mind. These prototypes provide the universal principles of knowledge and being. The ultimate reality of a tree exists in the divine idea or exemplar, and truth lies in the correspondence of our concepts with this substantial universal.[1] Indeed, Grosseteste reaches farther back than Augustine; he refers to Plato. The principles of knowing and of being are the eternal reasons 'that Plato named ideas and archetypes of the world'. These are the causes of genera and species. There is little recourse to Aristotelian views in this metaphysics. The function of sensation is conceived on lines that follow Augustine's account. Rational principles are in our minds in potential modes, and the stimuli of sense are the occasions for their actualization; Aristotelian abstraction is ignored.

If we turn to masters of the Dominican Order we find, in the earlier part of the thirteenth century, the same direction of thought. The work of Richard Fishacre on the *Sentences* affords us a clue to the philosophical teaching of the early Dominicans at Oxford. Where he touches on the theory of perception, on intellectual knowledge, and on the potency of matter, he writes in a pronounced Augustinian vein. And he has no doubt that these opinions are in harmony with those of Aristotle.[2] Robert Kilwardby, who as Archbishop of Canterbury was later to pronounce condemnation of Averroist and of Thomist theses, displays a similar conjunction of ideas. He is recorded to have composed a prodigious number of works on Aristotle, but in his best-known treatise, *De Ortu Scientiarum*, an Augustinian position is developed. He begins his account of knowledge by describing the process of abstraction in Aristotelian terms. Thought rests on the senses from which the *species sensibiles* are conveyed to the intellect; the intellect extracts from these species the universals that disclose the essences of things. But he passes from this position to a decided Platonic position. Human knowledge depends upon divine illumination by which it discerns the eternal reasons, the sources of being. In contrast to the principles that are received from intellectual apprehension, those that are derived from inferior things invite us to knowledge that stirs our concupiscent nature and encourages a craving for riches and power. Human science, divorced from illumination, opens the way to the dominion of evil spirits over us, and degenerates into the perils and the wickedness of

---

[1] Sharp, *Franciscan Philosophy*, p. 32.
[2] D. E. Sharp, 'The Philosophy of Richard Fishacre', *The New Scholasticism*, vii. 4.

magic.[1] This echoes tradition; and Augustinian also is the belief that the union of body and mind is 'accidental'. The view that the intellect is independent of the senses presumes this belief. Since the intellect is united with the animal body of man *per accidens*, its activity is not ultimately dependent on the senses. As in Grosseteste's psychology, the senses provide no more than the occasion for the independent activity of the intellect. The intellect is not a natural product, the outcome of generation. It is created by God.[2]

The Platonic trend of these Oxford thinkers, associated with their interest in Arabic science, produced a special quality of thought in England in this phase, the attempt to apply mathematical ideas to physics. Adam Marsh and Grosseteste sought 'to unfold the causes of all things by the power of mathematics'.[3] Grosseteste wrote that it is impossible to grasp natural philosophy apart from the consideration of angles and figures. He illustrated this principle mainly from optics upon which he made some penetrating suggestions. He unfolded an elaborate doctrine of light to which he assigns a central place in the universe. It is the source of space and of body, a fundamental energy, akin to spirit. Roger Bacon's observation that 'It is impossible to understand the world without knowing mathematics' has been much quoted in recent times, but his attempt in the *Opus Majus* to show that all departments of knowledge are based on mathematics is fanciful. In a number of fields he made astonishing scientific prophecies; he proclaimed with solitary force the necessity of experiment; but this insight had little effect upon his contemporaries, and it has been unnecessary to consider his discoveries here, or to describe his magnificent plans for the reform of knowledge.[4] In 1277 his

---

[1] E. M. F. Sommer-Seckendorff, *Studies in the Life of Robert Kilwardby*, O.P., Rome, 1937, p. 152.   [2] Ibid., p. 159.

[3] R. Bacon, *Opus Majus*, ed. Bridges, i, p. 108.

[4] For example, in *De Erroribus Medicorum* he writes: 'The third deficiency is that the ordinary doctor spends his time in discussing an infinite number of questions and in useless argumentation, and has no leisure for gaining the experience which he should have. By means of the *Topica* and *Elenchi* they multiply an infinite number of incidental questions and dialectic arguments and countless sophistries, in which they are always seeking but never learn the truth. For learning comes by way of the senses, of memory, and experience, and especially in the practical sciences of which medicine is one.' Translated by M. C. Welborn, *Isis*, vol. xviii, p. 30.

opinions were condemned by Bishop Tempier, and many of his works remained unpublished. His reputation for centuries was that of an alchemist and magician, and the large number of references to his magical experiments in the manuscripts of the fourteenth and fifteenth centuries testify to his influence in this province.

The most erudite philosopher of the century in England, Thomas of York, invokes the authority of Aristotle on almost every page of his vast work, the *Sapientale*. But he also leans heavily upon the great Arabians and the Jewish writers, and on many important questions he argues in favour of Neo-Platonic solutions. His pre-eminent authorities among the *sapientes Dei* are St. Augustine and Boethius, but amid the mosaic of citations that comprises much of the *Sapientale* passages from Avicebron occupy considerable space. In addition to an Aristotelian account of knowledge Thomas embraces the doctrine of divine illumination. Knowledge obtained from above is surer than that acquired from the senses. It passes from idea to idea and does not depend upon instruction coming from outside, but rests only upon inward illumination.[1]

Augustinian principles persisted in England, now in combination with, now in opposition to, Aristotelian theories. At Oxford they were in the ascendant in the latter part of the century. The reaction from Aristotelianism was due to its condemnation by the Church. By degrees the shock lessened and the theses of Thomism were revived.

VI

The external plan of the universe that attained definition in the thirteenth century stood with slight modifications the accepted frame of thought for over three hundred years. The vision of the cosmos pictured a complex hierarchy of spiritual orders. The account of the creation of the world in Genesis was amalgamated with the cosmologies of the *Timaeus*, of Neo-Platonism, and of Aristotle. The universe is composed of two regions, one celestial, the other terrestrial. The terrestrial region lies below the spheres of the sun and moon. It is arranged in degrees of nobility and perfection, but it is pervaded by the

---

[1] Sharp, *Franciscan Philosophy*, p. 100.

dividing and corrupting influence of matter and is infected with
confusion and opposition. At the basis of the terrestrial order
are the four elementary forces, earth, water, air, and fire. The
fiery element occupies the highest place in this fundamental
structure, the earthy element occupies the lowest. The earthy
element moves in a downward direction, the fiery element
moves upwards; water tends to follow the motions of earth, air
those of fire. The heaviest bodies are thus collected at the centre
of the world, the lightest and the noblest occupy the extreme
circumference of the terrestrial region. Out of these active
elements are formed the mixtures or compounds that fill the
world, all physical things including the bodies of animals and
men. In the inanimate region the forms that give the mixtures
their characteristic qualities are immersed in matter and are
named material forms. The elements can be transmuted into
one another, as, for example, air into water and earth into fire;
and their dominating properties, heat, cold, dryness, and
humidity, combine and conflict with one another in the composition of things. Numerous phenomena are explained by
reference to these properties. Thus man is erect because he is
warmer than other animals and heat tends to move upwards.

Above the region of the physical composites, the *mixta*, is
superimposed the region of the immaterial forms, of plants and
animals. Many distinctions are made by thirteenth-century
philosophers, following on those made by Aristotle, relating
to the peculiar properties of plants and animals. Vegetative
forms have life, the ability to nourish themselves and to grow.
Sensitive forms that rule the animals give them the capacity
to perceive and to respond to the world in movement, and the
capacity to reproduce their kind. There are grades within these
sensitive and vegetative forms, and we find encyclopaedists of
the period attempting to classify plants and animals on an
ascending scale of nobility.

Next in order comes the region of rational forms, which are
men. The peculiar mark of man is reason. He occupies the
central position in the scale of the universe, for while his body
and mind share in the inferior properties of the elemental,
vegetative, and animal forms, his intellectual soul links him with
the angels and the life of the heavens. The hierarchy of being
is repeated in small in him; he is a microcosm of the whole.

The difficulties that arose from the application of the hierarchy of being to man have been mentioned.

The world, created for the habitation and school of man, rests motionless at the centre of a chain of concentric spheres. Immediately beyond it circle the spheres of the four elements; for each element has its own region. The outermost sphere is naturally that of fire, and here we reach the line that divides the terrestrial from the celestial regions of the universe. The celestial regions comprise eight spheres formed of celestial matter upon which are borne in successively widening arcs the seven planets and the fixed stars, each sphere moving at a different speed according to the length of its passage. The largest and outer sphere of the fixed stars imparts the diurnal movement from east to west to the lower planetary spheres. We have spoken of celestial matter and it is an important principle in all medieval speculation that the matter of the celestial bodies differs profoundly from the matter of the terrestrial elements. It is often described as a fifth element. Its chief difference from the four terrestrial elements is that it is not liable to generation or corruption. Its mode of movement also differs, for while the sublunar elements and their compounds move in linear directions, celestial bodies move in circles. Circular movement is the perfect type of motion for it is eternal. The celestial bodies are guided in their contrasting and perfect motions by the angelic intelligences, for movement ultimately requires an immaterial and changeless mover. The question whether the stars were animated by the angelic minds was, however, much debated at Oxford. In their descriptions of the motions of the planets Oxford philosophers hesitated between the new Arabian system and the old Ptolemaic system. The Arabian theory was that the planets revolved in concentric circles round the earth, the circles being equally spaced from one another. The theory of Ptolemy was that they moved in epicycles, that is to say, that they described circles about points on the celestial spheres. The conflict between the two theories raised an interesting tension in the natural philosophy of the schools, for while it was known that the distances of the planets from the earth varied, the Ptolemaic system contradicted the axioms of Aristotelian physics.

The celestial bodies influence the form and matter of terrestrial substances and are factors in their generation, growth, and decay. It is frequently asserted that the potency of matter is set in motion by the celestial bodies to produce mixtures. But all the inner activities of the world involve the influences of the stars in addition to the operation of their specific forms. This principle is the foundation of the passionate concern with astrology and horoscopes that runs rife through these centuries.

There is a further moving sphere beyond the spheres of the planets and the stars. It is the sphere of the 'first moved', the *primum mobile*. This outermost sphere of the natural universe is directly moved by God, and its motion sets all the spheres below it revolving. Lastly, outside the natural order of the finite universe there lies the empyrean, beyond space and time, eternal, infinite, the dwelling-place of the blessed spirits.

The details of this scheme of the universe are not important for our purpose. Its conformity with the assumptions that we have distinguished is obvious. The perspective is profoundly final, purposive. In the operation of each process as well as in the large patterns of the natural order there is an immanent tendency to the fulfilment of ends. Each process expresses, more or less adequately, a form that is the perfection of the process. Things and their processes are at every point in potency to acts. Whether the change be substantial or accidental it is understood in relation to its end, and the ends appropriate to things, be they rocks or trees or men, determine their material qualities and their behaviour. In the great chain of being each grade includes and presupposes the grade below it, and points beyond itself to a further grade; and the whole looks beyond nature to the absolute being who is its origin, its sustainer, and its goal. A life courses through the universe and strains towards an ideal order beyond it. But on every side the attainment of ends, whether proximate or remote, is frustrated by the material element in things. Matter introduces division and irrationality into the heart of nature.

As we have already pointed out, a corollary of this final philosophy of experience is the principle of function. Since the explanation of anything or any activity lies in its end, its true being consists in its contribution to the particular system to which it is related, and to the wider systems, the *species* and *genera*, that lie beyond. The lower and more confused levels are

conditions of the work of the higher grades of being; but they
fulfil their own work in the order of things. A being is defined
by its purpose in nature, not by its external characteristics.
The innumerable classes of things are substantially different
from one another. Each class possesses an essential nature, an
essentia or *quidditas*, and its essence is not a static quality but
a source of activity. These principles govern the conceptions of
change and generation with which the created world is permeated. Movement of any kind, whether it be change of
position, or of colour, or of temperature, or whether it be
growth or decay in living organisms, is *potentia*, an inner metamorphosis of being from one qualitative state to another.

The detailed study of the writings of Aristotle poured into
the mental life of the age a vast new range of scientific information and theory. The scope of the faculty of philosophy now
embraced the Greek accounts of meteorology and anatomy.
The providential care of God is admitted in the substance and
operations of natural objects, but it was recognized that natural
beings possess also efficacy in their own right, and the interplay
of causes in the corporeal world, especially the conditions
governing change and generation, increasingly occupied the
attention of the Oxford and Cambridge scholars. But the
intellectual habits of the schools gave little impulse to empirical
exploration. Scientific development was restricted by the concentration on metaphysical and theological problems, and it
was hampered by the logical forms that ruled thought. At the
centre of the scheme of logical relations with which the thinking
of the schools operated was the category of substance. Reality
is composed of innumerable beings or essences, and the task of
philosophy is to apprehend these essences. The method proceeds more by formal definition than by observation and
generalization; it seeks to reach the essence by distinguishing
between the species and its inessential attributes and accidents.
The method presumes the existence of real things and divisions
of things in nature. But it is dominantly a method of classification. The typical logic is the logic of the syllogism. The process
may be succinctly described as follows. Here is a body, a mind,
a tree, a man. Each is an instance of something that possesses
a unique and essential nature. The something that possesses
this essential nature is a species, a kind; if the instance is an

instance of the species it will possess the essential nature of the species. A property is assumed to belong to all members of a species or class; a particular object is recognized as belonging to the class; and it is accordingly inferred that it possesses the property. The search for essences is bound up with the syllogistic method. The essence of anything is the ground of the thing's being. It is what the thing really is, what determines its nature. This must be a general character, for it is in virtue of its essence that any particular thing, say, this flower, is a flower, that is to say, a class of things. The real nature of a thing is a system of general relations and any individual thing or process is a specimen of the system. Essences, then, are universals, appearing in a multitude of different aspects to our senses. They are unities-in-difference; and unity-in-difference is the basis of the syllogistic mode of reasoning. Its characteristic movement is the process of bringing under, or subsumption. Reasoning consists of bringing attributes or particular manifestations under the general entity, into relation with the general permanent natures that compose reality. The guiding principle is the connexion between individual instances and universal essences; and the universal essences form the middle terms of syllogisms.

The noticeable character of this scheme of thought is its concern with qualities, with substantial forms. But the controlling mode of thought was that expressed in the subject–attribute proposition. The syllogism of the 'first figure' was esteemed the perfect type of inference, and induction from particular observations was not considered philosophical proof. The substantial forms are not static entities. They are incarnate ideas; we may even name them ideals. Reality is fundamentally active and purposive. A thing in act, or as it really is, is that which it has in it to become.

Substances are, we have seen, of two kinds: first substances or individual things, and second substances, species and genera, in a word, universals. But the substance of these is never more than potential. The categories that express the forms of predication, the various senses in which it is possible to assert that something is something, all qualify substance. Quality, quantity, relation, place, time, state, activity, passivity refer to the modes in which substances may appear. But the subject

of all assertions is a substance, and modes of predication are
conceived as accidents. They are external to the essences; they
may change and disappear. The infinite plurality of substances
abides. Here, as we shall perceive, lies the capital division
between the medieval and the modern outlook on nature.

VII

The rich diversity of rational discussion in the thirteenth
century cannot be comprehended in a brief survey. The sharpen-
ing of disputatious logic and the collision of authoritative
theories provoked ingenious refinements and compromises on
all the current problems of philosophy. The signal feature of
this phase of our thought is the apprehension of the genuine
doctrines of Aristotle and their incorporation into the catholic
universe. We have noticed the stages of this movement. But
a remarkable characteristic of the course of ideas in England is
the way in which the older Augustinian tenets persisted, at
times in association with, at times in opposition to the new
philosophy. Often the two traditions can be observed existing
side by side in the writings of the same master. The development of Thomism was shadowed by the censures of the archbishops and never dominated the intellectual scene at Oxford
and Cambridge.

Nevertheless, Aristotelian conceptions relating to the principles of being, to the nature of human thought, and to the physics of terrestrial and celestial motion, steadily advanced. In this
concluding section let us look back over the mental history of
the period and attempt to mark some of the contrasting views
of existence that had arisen.

The divine verities remain. The Catholic scheme of faith was
still the central preoccupation of inquiry; but the new tendencies in metaphysics were modifying the ancient relation
between divine revelation and natural reason. In the historic
philosophy some of the main assertions of faith were deemed
capable of demonstration by the path of Ideas. Such demonstration was denied by the new party in the schools. The
human mind cannot directly know spiritual substances in
separation; it can apprehend them only in an indirect way
through sensory experience. Spiritual realities can be rationally
inferred from man's moral being and from the evidences of

purpose in nature. But such reasoning cannot take us far in theology. Thomas of Sutton who, as we have observed, was a prominent supporter of the new philosophy, remarks that demonstration may give some aid to our religious beliefs, but it cannot communicate anything of value relating to the divine essence.[1] One result of this development was that the circle of theological belief was tending to be conceived as organized apart from the body of philosophical theory.

The general interpretation of experience recommended by the new schools of thought shows similar contrast with the old. The older thought fixed its gaze upon necessary and eternal essences freed from the contingency of sense. The foundation of the new metaphysic is the individual thing, essentially composite and limited. The theory of the composition of substances is explored in detail, according to the Aristotelian principles of form and matter, act and potency, and the ten predicables. Again, the view of knowledge now being proclaimed in the schools conflicts with the conservative doctrine. For the conservative view mind is not subject to the impressions received by the bodily organs. It is superior to the body and apprehends independently of the body elements of intellectual knowledge at the outset of experience from which it advances to the understanding of the timeless Ideas. It submits itself in its search for immutable principles to the light of divine illumination. The Aristotelian masters find the source of knowledge in sense-experience. Knowledge takes its rise from images that are likenesses of the impressions passively received by the organs of the body. In consequence the old Platonic realism that was associated with theology becomes modified. We have seen Aristotelian realism asserted in England in the twelfth century. The modern Aristotelians expounded the position of second substances or universals in greater detail. The mind forms abstract universals upon the data of the senses, and the business of human thinking is to apply the principles elicited from experience to the species that compose reality. For the older perspective the concepts of thought refer to essences that subsist independently of the material particulars. For the new the essences are embodied. Accordingly, there expands an interest in natural processes and a mass of physical information

[1] D. E. Sharp, *Revue Néo-Scolastique*, xxxvi, p. 351.

and theory streams into the thought of the time from the scientific writings of Aristotle. Yet causal explanation still looks to what is superior in knowledge and being. The assumption that whatever exists in the effect must have existed either formally or eminently in its cause, still governs intelligible understanding. There is little direct observation; philosophers repeat the lore of the authorities. But philosophy at the universities is becoming differentiated into branches. First philosophy or metaphysics is growing more distinctly defined in relation to physics and mathematics, which are recognized as possessing their own principles and methods.

The form of intelligibility that rules rational inquiry is founded in the union of Aristotelian logic and Christian theology. It rests upon the belief that essence or substance is the subject of all assertion. Other predications are accidental, adjectival. The determining logic of thought is syllogistic and exploration of reality proceeds by way of definition and classification. The universe is composed of a multitude of real kinds of things into which substances fall; and the central problem of metaphysics is the analysis of the nature of substances, while the task of natural philosophy is to distinguish the genera and species of things by formal definition. Objects are not different modes of one order or substance but different beings irreducible to one another. Reality is a chain of orders, sublunary and celestial, stretching from pure potentiality to pure actuality, from unconditioned matter to God, in Whom all the diverse abundance of nature is eternally contained.

But the great developments that we have been tracing had opened serious issues. We return to the dominating preoccupation with which our survey began, the problem of the relation of reason to the dogmatic contents of the faith. No one throughout the medieval phases of reflection questioned the belief that truth had been revealed by God to the Church. The problem concerned a special type of truth and a less special type. It asked, what are the intellectual processes involved in apprehending the truths of theology and how are they related to those employed in metaphysical and physical inquiry? On this central question many thinkers in England were in sympathy with the tradition that had passed down from St. Augustine and Anselm. They held to the conception of a unitary knowledge in which metaphysical reasoning can explicate the doctrines of theology. The advance of the Aristotelian view of knowledge had induced the leaders of thought to distinguish more clearly between the provinces of faith and of rational theology. The great dogmas of faith compose a scheme that is necessary for salvation; their divine authority is attested by unimpeachable signs; they perfect and crown the discoveries of reason. But our understanding cannot grasp the essence of purely intelligible and spiritual being since it is throughout its range dependent upon sensation; still less can it demonstrate the divine truths of faith, and the attempt to do so is absurd. Reason cannot contradict these truths, for the truths of reason and those of faith both proceed from God. But the doctrines of sacred theology are incomprehensible to natural reason, and though metaphysical inquiry can lead by strict reasoning to the existence of God and to many truths relating to His nature it cannot prove the truths of revelation. Now for many philosophical theologians, still nourished on the treatises of Anselm and his successors, this position was profoundly unsatisfactory. To them the view that for the wayfaring man sacred theology is not knowledge, *homini viatori non est scientia* as William of Ware bluntly put it, was fatal. They saw the drift from theology to philosophy, the growing insistence on the impotence of reason to resolve the problems of faith, the affirmation that the content of the creed of the Church is inaccessible to understanding. The crucial problem was the nature and the limits of human reason in relation to theology, and it is this vital issue that inspires the striking debates of the fourteenth century.

V

CRITICISM AND STERILITY

I

At the close of the thirteenth century Aristotelian conceptions were invading all the researches of philosophers and theologians. But in England the transformation of ideas advanced under the shadow of the condemnations of the archbishops. Thomism never became the official philosophy of the schools. The names of Robert Grosseteste and, among the newer thinkers, of Henry of Ghent, appear more frequently in the commentaries on the *Sentences* pronounced at the universities during the early years of the fourteenth century than the name of Thomas Aquinas. And there is a striking revival of interest in the philosophy of Anselm. A more remarkable note was the prevalence, in the face of sharp censure, of the doctrines of Averroism. Before we pass on to review the novel theories of truth that arose during the fourteenth century let us notice that extreme realism continued to be preached throughout this period of acute controversy.

The Augustinian view of the divine illumination of the intellect was maintained by a succession of masters and in terms that allow little to the human mind in the work of discovering essences. The passivity of the intellect is emphasized rather than its activity; the process of knowledge is described in many passages as a submission to irradiation by the divine Ideas. The apprehension of truth depends upon powers that lie beyond the native capacity of the human mind. Several thinkers came near to Averroism. Thomas Wilton, for example, declares 'on the authority of the Commentator (Averroes), of Avicenna, and of all the Peripatetics' that the active intellect is a self-subsisting substance, distinct from our minds and uniting with human cognitive faculties in the act of knowledge.[1] The active intellect, by which knowledge of material essences and spiritual substances is acquired, is interpreted in the Arabian manner. The genuine Aristotelian doctrine expounded for a quarter of

---

[1] K. Michalski, 'Le criticisme et le scepticisme dans la philosophie du XIVe siècle', *Bulletin International de l'Académie Polonaise, Cracovie*, 1926, p. 50.

a century by the new generation of scholars is ignored. Other famous lecturers propounded similar opinions. Osbert, a member of the Carmelite order and a master who acquired an extraordinary reputation in his day, cites the Arabians, Augustine, and Albert the Great in defending the thesis that the active intellect is God.[1] Such utterances called forth vigorous protests and John Baconthorpe (d. 1340) charged Wilton with yielding to the heresy of Averroes. He was accused of holding the belief that the active intellect is identical in all men and of denying the rational virtue of individual minds. But Baconthorpe himself allows in another passage that mono-psychism is a theory worthy of consideration and expresses the opinion that the arguments of Thomas Aquinas in refutation of it are not conclusive. Richard Fitz-Ralph (d. 1360) is another writer who protests against the doctrine of the unity of the active intellect, but who maintains also that the active intellect is the first form, that is to say, God, and that by sharing in it the human mind is prepared to receive the concepts of material things.[2] The strong realist current in the universities is reflected in the philosophical writings of the great reformer. In the earlier period of his career at Oxford Wyclif wrote treatises in which, despite all the criticisms of the Scotists and of the Nominalists, he asserted exemplarism and extreme realism. Universals exist *ex parte rei*; *animalitas* is an Idea of God. He went farther and propounded without reserve the Averroist position. The operation of intellectual knowledge in us is God. On being charged with heresy he was obliged to develop his view more carefully, and he went back to Grosseteste for a detailed exposition of realism. A created thing participates in the divine essence so far as concerns its rational ground, not in regard to the defective mode of its mundane existence. Yet in so far as it has a share of being it partakes of the divine being. There is a scale of being descending from absolute being to the lowest created form. Created things possess analogous being. But all of them are joined, by the fact of being, with divine being. Now being is possessed primarily by universals, secondarily by particulars, for universals are the exemplary essences of particular things. In *De Universalibus* different types of

---

[1] B. M. Xiberta, *De scriptoribus scholasticis saeculi XIV ex ordine Carmelitarum*, Louvain, 1931, p. 256.   [2] Michalski, op. cit., p. 52.

common natures are distinguished; besides the analogical identity of being there are generic, specific, and numerical types of identity. The classification owes much to Grosseteste. The doctrine of the identity of all being is enforced by the doctrine of potential being. All things in the universe exist potentially in the mind of God. In the theological treatises which incurred the severe criticism of the Church authorities, this realist metaphysic is applied to the dogmas of the Trinity and of the Incarnation. And, on the other hand, the realism is proved by the dogmas. For example, the relation between universals and singulars is explained by reference to the relation between the deity and the humanity of Christ.[1] The metaphysic of extreme realism is the philosophical basis of Wyclif's revolutionary ideas in theology, such as the denial of transubstantiation, and in the fifteenth century faculties of theology forbade the teaching of realism on account of its association with the errors of the reformers. Wyclif turned from philosophy and theology to ecclesiastical reconstruction, but his metaphysics were advocated by the Lollards at Oxford.[2]

The tenacity of Augustinian fashions of thought and of Arabian interpretations of Aristotle is an important element in the situation that gave rise to the heterodox ideas of the fourteenth century. The revolt from extravagant realism encouraged radical theories of experience, and the empirical fibres in the new Aristotelianism were emphasized. Meanwhile, the moderate realism of Aquinas obtained a hearing despite the ecclesiastical ban that lay upon certain parts of his teaching. The great synthesis of theology and philosophy was widely read and discussed. Résumés of the *Summa Theologica* were circulating among members of the Dominican order in the English province. The most notable defender of Thomism among the Preachers was Thomas of Sutton, who has been mentioned in the preceding chapter. He argued vigorously for Thomist principles in opposition to rival theories, including those of Duns Scotus. And others who promoted Thomist ideas in the schools were Richard Clapwell whose utterances were censured

[1] S. H. Thomson, 'The Philosophy of Wyclif', *Journal of Religion*, xi. 1, 1931.
[2] Realism at Oxford, as we have seen, was associated with the study of mathematics. Wyclif pursued optics in his youth. John of Holywood, William Rede, Simon Burdon, John Ashingdon, and others did notable work in this field.

by Archbishop Peckham, and that universal scholar Nicholas Trivet (d. 1328). In 1323 Aquinas was canonized by the Church and the official condemnations of his doctrines were withdrawn.

But fresh currents of thought were flowing. Remarkable thinkers and controversialists appeared in England whose reconstruction of contemporary principles further divided philosophical discussion, and shook the assumptions upon which the inquiries of the schools had stood. It was at Oxford that the novel theories of philosophical and religious truth were first developed, and from Oxford they were carried to Paris and to the other centres of reflection in Catholic Europe. This age of radical criticism, of acute division, and of disillusionment with the historic methods of reason was also a time of national catastrophe. The war with France drained the manhood of the country and dislocated its economy. Plague and famine at home followed upon the disasters abroad. The Black Death ravaged the land in several waves from 1348 to 1375, blighting scholarship together with all other pursuits. Monastic schools were closed, the universities waned, and numbers of promising masters succumbed to the pestilence. Hard upon these calamities ensued the great rising and the capture of London by the rebels. Spiritual unrest and discord were rife. There was wide loss of confidence in the ancient fountains of moral authority. Men complained bitterly against the oppression of the priests. The literature of the age levels charges of ignorance, corruption, and tyranny at the monks and clergy; Langland, Chaucer, and Wyclif voice the general resentment against the Church.

During the early decades of the fourteenth century the brilliant philosophical energy of the preceding age continued in the schools. The new generation of masters had learnt at the feet of the great scholars, and the detailed reconstruction of thought by Duns Scotus inspired clerks to fresh attacks upon first principles. In scores of lectures on the *Sentences,* in countless disputations and quodlibets problems were stated and argued according to the dialectical method that has been described in the foregoing chapter. The distinction between essence and existence, the relationship of potency to act, the burning question of the unity of forms in man, the basis of individuation, the status of universals; these and many other fundamental

issues were debated with unflagging zest. Much of this activity
was laboriously eclectic. The quodlibets of John Baconthorpe
are typical. This master was a Carmelite scholar from Norfolk,
who united vast erudition with a diminutive figure. When we
examine his discussions we find that the question in dispute
advances through such a maze of distinctions, citations, objections, and replies that the mind, the twentieth-century mind
at least, becomes confused and fatigued long before the 'determination' of the question is in sight.[1] But the mind of an
Oxford clerk of the early fourteenth century was not fatigued.
These methods were models for his own disputations. The
increasing number of communities in which philosophical
inquiries were pursued is noticeable. Beyond the universities
the great monastic houses contained schools of special studies
in which renowned scholars taught; and groups of theologians
dwelt at the cathedral churches and at the household of bishops. A
notable band attended upon the learned Richard of Bury, Bishop
of Durham; the circle included Walter Burleigh, Robert Holcot,
Thomas Bradwardine, and Richard Fitz-Ralph, men who made
important contributions to the philosophical debates of Europe.

As the century moves on more divisions of thought appear.
Wyclif, writing of the scene at Oxford in the latter period of the
century, protests that a new logical system springs up in the
schools every twenty years.[2] Established systems of ideas were
exposed to destructive criticism; a radical scepticism of knowledge was advocated; men lost confidence in reason and turned
to mysticism and unquestioning faith. And parallel with this
disruption of the ancient metaphysical assumptions there
appeared a passionate uprising against the spiritual authority.
Our principal task is to record the innovating notions that
impugned not only the Augustinian outlook of the theologians
but even the Aristotelian theories of knowledge and reality.

II

Four features marked the development of the new intellectual
situation, and it is not difficult to perceive that they all sprang
from the same rational impulse. They sprang from the Aristo-

---

[1] See an example in Xiberta, op. cit., pp. 208-9.
[2] Wyclif, *De veritate sacrae scripturae*, iii. Bradwardine also voices the
sense of interminable controversy in *De Causa Dei*.

telian reconstruction of ideas that had invaded the schools during the previous generation. They express, too, a vehement reaction from the excessive realism which, as we have seen, prevailed at Oxford. One tendency of the new school of thinkers was the inclination to seek for reality in the individual thing in preference to the universal entity. Associated with this trend there appeared increased emphasis upon intuition or sensory apprehension in knowledge. A further consequence of this outlook was the propensity to restrict the scope of demonstrative reasoning and to enlarge the province of dialectical or probable reasoning. Accordingly central questions of philosophy were now frequently said to be incapable of logical proof. When, finally, this tentative and empirical spirit was applied to the dominating problems of natural and supernatural theology the habitual outlook on experience was profoundly disturbed. A further step was taken in the severance of human reason from the truths of revelation.

All these tendencies are present in the discussions of the previous age, but it is in the writings of the Scotists at Oxford that they first come prominently into view. These features are far from forming the sole or main constituents of the intricate labyrinths of inquiry contained in the work of Duns Scotus. But it is principally through him and his disciples that they passed into the world of thought.

Scotus proposed a subtle reorganization of the conceptions that were current in the main schools of thought. He attempted to combine into one system the demands of faith, the Augustinian view of necessary truths, and the exigencies of Aristotelian logic. In relation to the direction of ideas that has been distinguished the analysis of the elements of knowing propounded in the *Opus Oxoniense* and *Reportata Parisensia* (both commentaries on the *Sentences*) is especially interesting. The account is on the one hand in sympathy with the new Aristotelianism, on the other it points towards the Franciscan and Augustinian philosophy. The view that knowledge arises through the operation of the active intellect upon the phantasms of sense is accepted, and here Scotus is on common ground with the Thomists; and in his elaborate criticisms of the theory of illumination he appears to range himself with the Aristotelians against the Augustinians. He argued that the extreme

Augustinianism that was being strongly revived by teachers in France and in England led to sheer scepticism. The ancient arguments, now once more brought forward by these philosophers, were directed to proving that immutable truth cannot be concerned with the changing objects perceived by the senses. The fact that the mortal and erroneous minds of men can distinguish between truth and falsity was taken to show that the human mind can apprehend exemplars, divine truths, by the path of illumination. Scotus's reply to this historic position is a most interesting contribution to the great debate on knowledge. He agrees that there must be a stable element in the flux of perception. If sense-perception were concerned wholly with passing items the mind could perceive nothing. If each item vanished as it came we could not be aware of objects; for objects suppose a certain enduring character. Nor can it be true to suppose that the human mind is wholly mutable. It must be in possession of fixed principles in the light of which things are understood. Consciousness and that to which consciousness refers, therefore, presume certain necessary and universal principles. Such necessary principles include the principle of similarity in virtue of which the mind is able to compare things with one another; the principle of contradiction that asserts that the same thing cannot both be and not be; and the principle of the relation of parts to whole. To these Scotus adds, in a prophetic passage, the principle that presumes the necessary causal connexion of things.

'I maintain that although experience does not embrace all particular instances, . . . yet when anyone knows, (that an effect is due to a cause) he knows with certainty that it is always so, and in all instances; he is aware of this by the following judgment residing in the mind, that whatever occurs in a great many cases as the result of some cause that is not free (that is to say, which is not a will) is the natural effect of that cause. This proposition is known to the understanding even though it had received the terms from the deceiving senses.'[1]

The discovery of causes must be made in experience, in the process of distinguishing accidental sequences from necessary

[1] Scotus, *Opus Oxoniense*, i, dist. iii, qu. 4; R. McKeon, *Selections from Medieval Philosophers*, London, 1930, ii. 327; C. R. S. Harris, *Duns Scotus*, Oxford, 1927, ii. 46.

and uniform sequences; and Duns admits that in many cases we do not reach farther than a low degree of understanding, apprehending superficial and empirical connexions, disconnected from other principles. He gives as an instance the judgement that 'a particular kind of herb is hot'. He describes the methods of induction that were named by an English philosopher 650 years later the methods of Agreement and Difference; and he points out, as Mill does, the difficulties that spring from the intermixture and plurality of causes. He agrees so far, then, with the Augustinians in recognizing that in all our attempts to distinguish reality from illusion we are guided by necessary principles. But he refuses to admit that we must have recourse to a theory of illumination by the divine ideas to account for these principles. They are as requisite a part of our natural understanding as the species of perception. The men who can distinguish the essential connexions from those that are accidental are not endowed with illumination but with better natural powers. And he sides with the Aristotelians in grounding knowledge upon sensory experience.

On the other hand, he asserted a novel type of realism, the difficult doctrine of formal distinction.[1] The shifting and relative information that is given by the senses is controlled by *formalitates*, but these are not logical concepts imposed on things by the mind. They are discovered in things. A formal distinction is not a *res*, it is *rei*. It is not a reality as the Platonists maintain, it is a section of reality. It cannot exist apart from the individual thing; Scotus writes that not even the divine power can separate the formal distinction from the essence. Numerous examples of formal distinctions are found in the works of Scotus. The most fundamental instance is that of the union of a common nature and an individual nature in an object. Other instances are provided by the universal attributes of being, unity, truth, and goodness, and by the metaphysical grades of being, such as substantiality, materiality, animality, and rationality. When it is applied to universals the formal dis-

[1] E. Longpré, *La Philosophie du B. Duns Scot*, Paris, 1924; D. E. Sharp, *Franciscan Philosophy at Oxford in the Thirteenth Century*, Oxford, 1930; M. J. Grajewski, *The Formal Distinction of Duns Scotus*, Washington, D.C., 1944. Traces of the doctrine are found in several English masters, in William of Ware (reputed to be the teacher of Duns Scotus at Oxford), in William of Macclesfield, Roger Marston, and William of Nottingham.

tinction becomes a mode of realism. Universals are products of the mind but they are not fictions, for there are genuine counterparts of them in things. But the universal in things exists as a potential universal. The objective natures from which the intellect extracts the intelligible species are not strictly universal nor strictly particular, or rather they are capable of being viewed as one or the other. And this conception of their universality refers to a real character, for otherwise as Scotus says 'we should know nothing about reality, but only about our concepts, and our opinion would not change from the true to the false with change in the existence of a thing'. The theory of *distinctio formalis* appears to show that the demarcations and connexions of our thinking approximate to real distinctions in things, though they do not completely describe them. It attempts to acknowledge both the abstract nature of thought and its validity in respect of reality. In seeking to define and to understand objects the mind discovers a hierarchy of partial realities, a system of general qualities that are distinct from individual things, and yet are not symbols imputed by the mind. But the most original doctrine of Scotus lay in the notion of individuality.

The potential common nature of any particular thing is one aspect that is always present, formally distinct from the particular aspect. But the nature of the thing lies truly in its individuality, not in its generic or specific natures. Its individuality is a unique determination that cannot be resolved into any general factor, such as form or matter. This principle is named *haecceitas*, thisness. It is the *haecceitas* that gives the individual its perfection and ultimate reality. And this unique character is not a contraction of universal principles; it is not due to the reception of form into matter as the usual belief held. It is an *ultima realitas entis*. The individual thing is not composed of matter and form but of *this* matter and *this* form. It is one, incommunicable, and *per se existens*. The stress of the Scotists on individuality sounds a new note in speculation. It promoted in metaphysics and natural philosophy interest in particular phenomena. This movement away from a preoccupation with universal entities towards a concern with individual items marks a turning-point in the history of western thought. But the emphasis on individuality did not take Scotus into sympathy with the novel teaching of the conceptualists and nominalists that was now heard at Oxford. He exposed at length the difficulties to which a nominalist view of reality leads. If there were nothing outside the mind save singulars, our understanding of reality would be false, since we think in universal terms. The divisions and the general characters that we attribute to things exist in nature. But they are less real than the unity of particular beings. Thus Scotus constructs a bridge between the extreme realists and the nominalists, and between the Thomists and the Augustinians. He agreed with the Aristotelian account of the process of knowledge in which the active intellect abstracts the intelligible species from the sensory species. He asserted as firmly as any of his contemporaries that the universal is *ab intellectu*. He declared with equal emphasis that it is a property of the thing itself. But his theory that a thing is essentially indeterminate, neither singular nor universal, yet potentially both (a conception that he accepted from Avicenna) separated him from the Platonic tradition.

The formal distinction is applied by Scotus to every type of problem. It is prominent in his elaborate discussion of the question of the relation between the soul and its faculties. The Thomists taught that the powers of thinking and of willing did not belong to the essence of the soul, since the soul is always in act; the faculties operate intermittently and are therefore accidental. Scotus denied that there is any real distinction between the soul and its faculties. The faculties are diverse *formalitates* of the same substance. They are logically distinct from the soul and from one another but they are essential properties of the soul; the distinctions are formal distinctions, intermediate between real and purely logical divisions. Scotus, therefore, is able to treat the disturbing problem relating to the forms in man according to the same principle of unity amid difference. He combines an assertion of the plurality of forms in man with an affirmation of the fundamental unity of the soul; the sensitive and vegetative souls make one soul with the intellectual soul. In theology, we find the same principle present in discussions on the Trinity. The complete unity of being in God is said to be compatible with the formal distinctions between the Persons. And there are other notable applications of the principle. But we must now turn to the capital problem of the age, for it was from Scotus's treatment of this problem that the new departures in philosophy took their rise.

We have seen that in the eleventh century the range of reason had been widened by the school of Anselm to embrace deduction of the truths of revelation. Under the strong tide of Aristotelian conceptions the scope allowed to demonstration in theology had become contracted. The old logic of the theologian-philosophers had been able to demonstrate the truths of theology by recourse to the Augustinian Ideas. The new logic showed that the Ideas were immanent in matter and shared in the contingency of sensible things. The Aristotelian strain in the schools rejected the *a priori* arguments for the existence and nature of God; it rejected also arguments resting upon immediate intuition. The existence of the Deity was proved by analogy from the nature of change and movement in the universe, from contemplation of the chain of causation, and from the postulate of the hierarchy of beings and perfections. The formulas of theology supplied the ideal limits of these rational inquiries. Revelation and faith presented to the consciousness of all men a system of sacred beliefs, some of which can be rationally proved. But there are other beliefs that reason is incapable of demonstrating; for reason takes its rise from the sensible species and cannot attain any direct knowledge of purely immaterial and intelligible substances. It cannot know God and the angels as it knows the essences of material things. This method of rational theology agreed with the historic tradition of Christian thought in confidently asserting that the truths of philosophy accord with the truths of revelation. But its method of argument was notably different from the old methods. Guided by Aristotelian principles it drew its conclusions from the evidence of sensible and contingent processes. It reached its theological goal by winding and indirect routes, by considering the nature of movement and change, by analysis of the notion of cause and of grades of being, and by the novel distinction between essence and existence. On such lines reasoned the new school of Dominican philosophers, among whom Thomas of Sutton was an important figure at Oxford. To the minds of conservative thinkers and especially to masters of the Franciscan Order the procedure of the Thomists was profoundly distasteful. The

Aristotelian path to the rational knowledge of God appeared to turn its back on the direct approach that had been opened by Augustine and Anselm. It rejected the immediate rational demonstrations of the latter, and, what was more serious, the doctrine of eternal reasons of the former. To theologians such as Peckham it appeared grievously to divide man's reason from divine truth. And, as we have seen, this modern philosophy carried with it theses that seemed to threaten capital points of faith, particularly the thesis of the unity of substantial form in man. The anxiety of the theologians had mounted to the formal condemnations of Thomist Aristotelianism in 1277 and 1285. The rational theology of Scotus is put forward under the consciousness of these authoritative injunctions.

The injunctions were equivalent to a censure of much of the contents and method of philosophy. Scotus was convinced of the truth of considerable portions of the Aristotelian way of conceiving our knowledge of reality. But his interpretations of Aristotle are suffused with Arabian readings of the doctrines of the philosopher, especially by those of Avicenna. Accordingly, the arguments of natural theology take a strikingly different turn in his hands to that which had been given to them by the Thomists. The central notion in his philosophy is the notion of being. Being is present in the same sense to everything that exists; it is univocal. It can be applied indifferently to all that is. Being as such is wholly indeterminate, transcending all specific determinations. In order, therefore, to understand reality we must look beyond the order of temporal causation and change and seek to descry the properties of being as such. In a long and closely reasoned passage Scotus unfolds the cardinal modes of being. They appear as infinity and finitude, necessity and possibility, end, intelligibility. These modes are contained in that which supremely is, the primal source of being. The philosophical arguments for the existence and nature of God rest on a vigorously deductive demonstration of the modes of being as such; they are not derived in the manner of the new Aristotelians from examination of the sensible and contingent world. But there was much in the conclusions that philosophy could infer relating to the primal being that was entirely discordant with the doctrines of the Church, and there were some cardinal points of faith that reason could not prove.

Above all, reason could not admit the notion of a free creative act by which all contingent things are made. It could conceive a cosmology in which the undifferentiated eternal being engenders by logical necessity an hierarchy of existences, but it could not accept the activity of an unconstrained and all-powerful Will in the operation of temporal processes. Metaphysics presents one picture of the ultimate order of things, scriptural theology another. In this situation Scotus does not hesitate to choose the scheme of revealed truth. The possible or dependent order is due to an act of will. The eminent position occupied by free will in his philosophy owes something to the circle of ideas that had descended from St. Augustine to the Oxford Franciscans of the thirteenth century. But Scotus gives the principle a capital place in his theology and his psychology. In the latter context he asserts that man's will can allow him to reject an end proposed to his consciousness by his intellect; he can act irrationally by refusing to accept a good understood to be good. The usual doctrine of the schools was that moral evil was contrary to the real intention of the will. The will is naturally conformed to the good and a man who chooses to do evil acts *praeter intentionem.* A wholly free choice in which a man deliberately prefers a course of action contrary to the *ratio boni*, the rule of good, to which his intellect determines him was regarded as impossible. The intellect adheres of necessity to the first principles of things; in like manner the will necessarily adheres to the final goal of activity, that is, blessedness. The end of voluntary endeavour was held to be parallel to the self-evident theorems of knowledge.[1] Scotus agrees that the intellect is moved of necessity by its natural object but the will moves itself freely.[2] Voluntary action is not pointed to a universal end. It is essentially self-determining and can turn its attention to any object, even to that which it knows to be evil. The will governs the intellect, and the nobility of the soul is derived more from willing than from knowing. The signal importance of this turn of thought for moral theory is obvious. It rejected the ancient doctrine, reaching back to Socrates, in which the will must conform to the knowledge of

---

[1] Thomas Aquinas, *Summa Contra Gentiles*, iii. 4; *Summa Theologica*, i, qu. 82. 1.

[2] Scotus, *Quodlibeta*, qu. xvi, n. 6; Harris, op. cit. i, p. 176; ii. 295.

the good, and brought to the discussion of the moral issues of the age a sense of indeterminism. But it is in theology that this voluntarist position was immediately seen. Duns applies his view concerning the self-originating direction of the will to the divine will. He emphasizes the absolute liberty of God. The only reason that can be assigned to the operation of the divine will is that will is will.[1] God cannot indeed will what is irrational or contradictory. But since He is absolutely free, the operation of His will cannot logically be deduced from conceptions; it is not amenable to philosophical treatment.[2] The works of creation are the acts of a spontaneous will, which cannot be traced to necessary grounds immanent in the divine nature. The universe is completely contingent and cannot be understood by apodeictic reasoning.

Such an outlook opened a wider breach between philosophy and theology. It declared that the rational theology that stood upon the distinguishing principle of Christian truth could not be a demonstrative science. It could not infer necessary conclusions from self-evident premises.[3] Theology becomes rather a practical science than a department of philosophy, and a number of theses that had been included in metaphysical inquiry are relegated to theology. An impassable gulf hangs between human thought and divine truth, and terms that are attached to the nature and action of the deity, terms such as wisdom and goodness, possess little of the significance that they bear in relation to human experience. It is impossible by reason to prove the omnipotence and providence of God or the creation of the world or the immortality of man's soul. The theologian can adduce many considerations to show that the great beliefs of the faith are very probably true, but he cannot offer demonstrative reasons in their favour. These questions and many others that men crave to know are inaccessible to our faculties. They are answered only in the sacred doctrines.

On the one hand, then, metaphysical reasoning can infer the nature of God from the properties of being by a necessary and orderly demonstration. It is these Augustinian arguments in the work of Scotus which Ockham submits to searching criticism. On the other hand, the actual content of the Faith cannot

---

[1] Scotus, *Op. Ox.* i, dist. viii, qu. 5, n. 24; Harris, op. cit. i. 181.
[2] Harris, op. cit. i. 94.　　　[3] Scotus, *Op. Ox. Prol.*, qu. 3, n. 26.

be reached by philosophy. These characteristic marks of the teaching of Duns Scotus that have been selected from the immense range of his writings appear in the debates of the schools early in the fourteenth century. Thomas of Sutton defended the doctrines of Thomas Aquinas against those of Scotus at Oxford about the year 1312, and a number of later masters, William of Alnwick (d. 1332), John Rodington, and the renowned Thomas Bradwardine (d. 1349), reproduce amid other theories various themes of the subtle doctor. And there is evidence of a lively party of Scotists at Oxford who disputed sharply with the disciples of St. Thomas and more bitterly with the followers of Ockham. One of the early critics of Scotus was Henry Harclay, Chancellor of Oxford and Bishop of Lincoln. The chief traits of Scotism were maintained by the Franciscan scholars, and the cardinal positions, the univocity of being, formal distinction, and the restricted competency of reason in theology were affirmed in many treatises and disputations. But, in the meantime, discussions concerning the relation of thought to reality and the competence of reason in sacred theology questions had been advanced by a fresh and radical departure in philosophy . Rational scepticism became visible in connexion with theological truth in the writings of Duns Scotus; in the teaching of William of Ockham it was extended to reason itself.

III

The fresh development in fundamental conceptions had its birth in the preoccupation of the younger generation of masters at Oxford with the science of theological truth propounded by Scotus. Well versed in the logic of Aristotle these critics pressed the empirical elements in the teaching of the Stagirite to extreme limits, and in their attacks on the rational assumptions of the Scotists they were carried towards a pronounced nominalism. But the new nominalism was not animated by any tincture of theological scepticism. On the contrary, it was inspired by an unquestionable belief in the divine will. The foundation of the new philosophy of knowledge and reality is the union of this religous outlook with a strictly empirical theory of truth.

The leader of this striking movement was a young Franciscan

logician, William of Ockham. About the year 1320 the doctrines
that he had put forward in his course on the Sentences were
provoking a storm of discussion at Oxford. There was a considerable weight of opinion favourable to the new analysis of
philosophical and theological problems, and in 1322 the Chancellor of the University, John Lutterell, was dismissed because
of his opposition to the modern schools of ideas. He appealed
to the tribunal of the Pope. Edward II and his government at
first resisted Lutterell's determination to proceed to Avignon in
order to lay his case before the curia, but after a discussion at
the council held at York in October 1322 when the two parties
to the dispute pleaded their cause, he was permitted to make his
departure. He had convinced the council that the new ideas
were dangerous to true philosophy and the faith. On his arrival
at Avignon towards the end of 1323 he lost no time in proffering
fifty-six theological errors in the lectures on the Sentences by
brother William of Ockham. The Pope, John XXII, appointed
a commission to examine the charges and Ockham was summoned to Avignon to answer them. But during his residence at
the papal court he became involved in the debate on evangelical
poverty which was agitating the Church. He naturally expressed
himself in accord with the views of the general of his Order,
Michael de Cesena, who was vehemently antagonistic to the
views of the Pope in this matter. He was arrested but escaped
with Cesena and placed himself under the protection of the
Emperor in Italy. It was his association with the spirituals that
provoked the severe condemnation of his doctrines by the commission of doctors in 1328. During the ensuing years Ockham
put his polemical powers at the service of the Emperor, Louis
of Bavaria. He died at Munich, probably in 1349, a victim of
the Black Death.

The issue that provided the spring of Ockham's philosophical inquiries was, as we have said, the dominating question of
the capabilities of reason in relation to the system of faith. The
Prologue of the *Commentary on the Sentences* opens with the
question, *utrum sit possibile intellectui viatoris habere notitiam
evidentem de veritatibus theologicis?* The discussion is closely
concerned with the thesis developed by Duns Scotus; there are
many other commentaries of the time devoted to the same
commanding problem. Now for Ockham the question is a

question of logic; it concerns the different ways of obtaining knowledge. In the *Commentary* he examines point by point a rational theology that proceeds by an hierarchical series of necessary deductions, moving from certain very general affirmations to a chain of precise conclusions relating to the divine nature. The inquiry is conducted with extreme care and every phrase and argument is critically assessed, every expression is cleared of ambiguity. But from the dense analysis of terms and demonstrations there appears a well-defined view of knowledge that is strongly opposed to the conceptions not only of Scotus, but also of leading traditions in the schools. And in setting forth his theory of knowledge Ockham believed that he was offering a faithful interpretation of the views of Aristotle. Later works, the *Expositio aurea* and the immense *Summa totius logicae*, are elaborate commentaries on Aristotle's logical works, full of penetrating discussions and subtle distinctions. Everywhere he is at pains to disembarrass the doctrine of the Stagirite from elements that had, in his view, corrupted it. The outcome is a conception of knowledge and reality that started many fresh currents of ideas which coursed far and deeply into the thought of later phases of English and European reflection. From the analysis of knowledge undertaken by the *venerabilis inceptor* there arose the depreciation of abstract thinking, the subjectivism of later philosophy; from the same source there sprang the subsequent distrust of metaphysical knowledge and especially of rational proofs of the grand dogmas of religion. The tendency towards empiricism in theory and in the study of nature that characterizes the mind of the Renaissance had its source in the work of Ockham. In truth, it is possible to trace many divergent streams of thought in the fourteenth and fifteenth centuries to his prolific and searching inquiries. The insistence on implicit faith in the traditional beliefs of revelation may be seen to have its origin in his writings equally with the theological doubts and indifferences of the succeeding period; and one may perceive in him the culmination of the movement in favour of Aristotelianism or a vindication of the religious principles of Augustine. It is clear that he cannot be held responsible for all the diverse consequences that flowed from his criticisms of current philosophy; we must understand his discussions in relation to the problems and opportunities of the early fourteenth century. It is also manifest that he was one of the most decisive thinkers in the history of Western ideas. Nominalism, as we have observed, was already attracting philosophers at Oxford when the *Commentary* was composed. From Oxford it rapidly spread to Paris and to other centres of learning and for two centuries it continued to divide the schools of Europe into hostile groups.

In seeking to discover the grounds of truth Ockham proceeds by decomposing into their elements the complicated material of judgements and demonstrations. Chains of reasoning presuppose the clear apprehension of their propositions, and the propositions presuppose the grasp of their subjects, predicates, and middle terms. Pursuing the inquiry beyond complex terms to the simple terms that are found at the base of complex terms we reach ultimately the apprehension of individual or undivided entities. These are singular things. *Intellectus nullam propositionem potest formare nec per consequens apprehendere, nisi primo intelligat singularia, id est incomplexa.* The perception of singular things provides the origin of all judgements concerning reality. But there are two modes of simple knowledge; one is intuitive, the other abstract. Incomplex abstract knowledge furnishes us with immediate and necessary judgements; there are propositions *per se notae* that are self-evident to every intelligence as soon as it is confronted with the terms. Such abstract simple judgements form the basic material of scientific and logical reasoning. The other mode of simple knowledge, intuitive knowledge, which comprises an intellectual as well as a sensitive factor, has this unique quality; it alone refers to what exists. It alone presumes the actual presence of an object, for some singular thing is its efficient cause. By sensory intuition I apprehend 'white' and 'Peter', by an abstract judgement I can assert that 'Peter is white'. The further elaboration of the distinction between intuitions of existence and abstract judgements reveals the fundamental distinction that governs Ockham's philosophy of knowledge. It is the division between a *scientia realis* and a *scientia rationalis.* The logical order is separated from the world of things; objects as they exist are divided from mental representations of them. Of a thing we must ask what it is; of a concept, what it means. All the spurious problems of philosophy and theology have arisen, in Ockham's view, because of the failure to preserve this distinction. The cardinal error is to transfer to reality what belongs only to discourse. The concepts or terms that enter into the structure of discursive reasoning are not copies or precise portrayals of things. They are signs of them. They stand for (*supponunt*) abstract aspects of things that can form the subjects and predicates of judgements. There are various types of 'supposition', *simplex, materialis,* and *personalis. Suppositiones materiales* are grammatical symbols, such as 'nouns'. There are several kinds of 'personal' terms, proper names, pronouns, and universal terms standing for individuals. Simple suppositions are substitutes for 'intentions' of the mind, or general concepts. The important consideration is that these connotative concepts assert not what things are in themselves but partial views of several things taken together. Logical and demonstrative reasoning is not therefore a *scientia realis.* It treats of truths that are proper to the association of signs, to ways of signification. The rules and postulates of this synthesis of terms and propositions are those of the Aristotelian logic. But the concepts and intentions of logic are fabricated by the mind, within itself. Demonstrative reasoning proceeds by syllogisms, but terms that refer to existence, to individual and unrelated things cannot be included in the premisses of demonstrative syllogisms, for the propositions in which such terms appear are not necessary, but contingent. A strict deductive proof can depend only on necessary premisses, and necessary premisses refer not to reality but to that which is *quid nominis.* They define entities that are abstract views of the single quiddities. A nominal definition does not bear in itself the guarantee of its truth; it requires the confirmation of direct experience. A strictly necessary proposition is equivalent to an hypothetical proposition. Its terms stand for what can or may be. In the *Summa totius logicae* Ockham maintains that the conclusions of demonstrations are doubtful in comparison with what can be known immediately without demonstration. We can infer that a certain kind of herb possesses healing properties, or that the moon can become eclipsed. These conclusions may also be known by experience and such knowledge is most certain. And there are many propositions that can be known in no other way save by experience; such assertions are indemonstrable.[1]

The radical division between reasoning as the logic of signs and intuition of singular realities gives rise to many remarkable consequences. It leads to an uncompromising rejection of the prevailing forms of realism, not only of those forms that were being advocated in England by adherents of the Augustinian tradition, but also of the modified realism of the Thomists and of Scotus. Many of Ockham's criticisms of realism are variations on the theme that it is unnecessary to suppose general types of being side by side with the particular objects known in perception. The realists describe universals as kinds of objects, distinct from particular things. But if they are objects, having the separate existence proper to objects, they cannot be present in a number of particular things at the same time. All the difficulties about the relation of universals to particulars spring from the attempt to make them contradictory types of objects, that is to say, singular beings and general conceptions at once. Species and genera are presumed to be both individual substances and abstractions. Ockham insists that all real objects are singular and there are no other kinds of real objects. Realism is due to verbalism, the confusion of words with things. When philosophers assert that the universal is real, they are saying that the word 'man' is part of the individual person. The upshot of these criticisms is the dismissal of the age-long belief in the objective reality of universals. '*Sufficiunt singularia et ita tales res universales omnino frustra ponuntur.*'

The great critic did not confine his objections to forms of Augustinian realism. The modified realism of the Thomist and Scotist syntheses was also impugned. Indeed, Ockham devotes more labour in his *Sum of All Logic* to refutations of the theories of Duns Scotus than to any other school of realism. The formal principles of Scotus are taken to mean that general entities are attached to the individual essences of things. The *formalitates*

---

[1] There are at present no modern editions of Ockham's logical works. The following books contain ample quotations from the philosophical treatises and valuable discussions of the intricate arguments developed in them. N. Abbagnano, *Guilielmo di Ockham*, Lanciano, 1931; R. McKeon, *Selections from Medieval Philosophers*, vol. ii, London, 1931; E. A. Moody, *The Logic of William of Ockham*, London, 1935; R. Guelluy, *Philosophie et théologie chez Guillaume d'Ockham*, Louvain–Paris, 1947.

inherent in matter are real beings, and the difficulties noticed in more extreme forms of realism recur. If there exists in an individual person a universal human nature that is contracted to the individuality of the person, we should have something that was both universal and particular at the same time. It is impossible to distinguish a formal difference from a real difference. And if species and genera are individual there are no universals. As for the Aristotelian psychology of knowledge expounded by Thomas Aquinas and others, it is pointed out that if universals are arrived at only by a process of abstraction from phantasms or sensory images, then they do not actually exist together with particular things; they are no more than mental inventions. It is true that we think in terms of universals; but it does not follow that universals exist apart from the mind, and the new school of thought denied that they did so exist. They are natural signs employed in reasoning. The grand problem of universals that had descended from Porphyry is due to a confusion of logical meaning with things. Since a universal is a sign of many it cannot be a real thing, for that is individual. If we oppose individual to universal, we can only oppose them as signs. We cannot oppose them as things, for everything is an individual.

The separation between *quid rei* and *quid nominis* is brought to bear on the whole range of elements that are present in rational thought, to all the relations between subject and predicate in propositions, to the primitive principles of systematic reasoning, and to the logic of inference. It is applied to the fundamental relation between a property and its subject. A property is not a reality inherent in a subject or, as Scotus taught, formally distinct from it. It is a concept fabricated by the mind associating realities really distinct. This position completely destroys the deductive arguments of classic scholasticism which proceeded by analysing substances in order to demonstrate qualities that they necessarily entail.

By dividing the science of valid inference from knowledge of the real world Ockham abolishes all the ontological assumptions of the traditional logic. He attacks the tendency to treat the Aristotelian predicables, genus, species, difference, property, and accident as metaphysical realities. The predicables are logical not metaphysical classes of predicates. They are not forms of existence, nor parts of things; they are mental 'intentions'. The ten categories receive similar treatment. They are ways of signifying things in abstraction from the contingent circumstances of the actual existence. They are modes of predication, not universal entities dwelling in things. Throughout his exhaustive analysis of logical forms Ockham is concerned with fashions of statement and inference, natural and conventional, in distinction from metaphysical assertions. A proposition does not affirm that one thing is actually another thing. It asserts a relation between signs.

Other principles of the schools are swept aside. The distinction between essence and existence upon which the Thomists laid stress is said to be superfluous. The terms are two ways of signifying the same thing. Everywhere Ockham insists on the rule of economy, the demand for simplicity in explanation. *Nunquam ponenda est pluralitas sine necessitate. Frustra fit per plura quod potest fieri per pauciora.* The principle is asserted by Duns Scotus and by other Franciscan thinkers of the thirteenth century, but it became particularly associated with the disciples of Ockham and passed from them into the scientific thought of the Renaissance. Under the guidance of the principle he refuses to admit the distinctions between essential nature and the principle of individuation, between form and matter and many other distinctions of the schools.

The view of reality implied in this nominalist conception of thought has already been indicated. All realities known directly by intuition are individual things. The relations which unite them for thought are not metaphysical elements but functions of human interpretation. Things are actually distinct and separate, unique, individual and singular. There are no general principles distinct from them or prior to them that contribute to their structure. The general features and relations by which we seek to understand things are not internal characters of them, but external and accidental. Things, for example, resemble one another in various ways, but such resemblances do not point to any kind of substantial unity. The primary data of knowledge include inward experiences, pleasures, and pains and efforts as well as particular items presented to our senses. Ockham recognizes the immediate intuition of several factors in a complex object, but even here the judgement that relates them is abstract, a form of signification. The intuition of one singular thing does not entail the intuition of another thing; if I perceive the objects on the earth and had never seen those above, I cannot know the sun and moon and stars. But we have not yet revealed the fundamental principle that inspires this metaphysic of disconnected singulars. The principle is religious. The sovereign notion of Ockham's outlook on experience is the supreme will of God. The independent realities that compose the order of things are related by causes extrinsic to their quiddities because God can dissociate all items that are not actually one. The entire order of things is contingent, suspended on His will. He can abrogate the secondary causes that govern the normal course of events and exercise His influence directly on the sequence and connexion of things. No created cause necessarily produces an effect, since it is ultimately dependent on the free consent of God; nothing is essential to a reality since the Almighty can alter the mediating factors according to His pleasure. The only causes essential to a being are those that belong to its individual nature. The only necessity to which God himself must submit is that of allowing a thing to be itself and not some other thing. Each reality is identical with itself and distinct from every other; its relations with others are extrinsic and accidental. The omnipotence of God entails the contingence of the rational order of existence.

At this point we may glance at some of the consequences of these principles in the realm of natural philosophy. Ockham rejected the idea of primary matter. As we have seen, the principle possessed a number of important functions in the cosmological scheme. It provided for the underlying physical connexion of things; it stood for the formal continuity of the material order. Matter also constituted the passive element that was universally moulded by the activity of form into the definite substances that filled the cosmos. It was the inert stuff in which generation was shaped. And finally, it was the principle of individuation, the source of limitation and particularity. Now, since this primary universal matter was amorphous, it had been held in the older philosophy to be pure potentiality. In the period immediately preceding the time of Ockham the notion of a pure potentiality had been sharply criticized by Duns Scotus and his followers and the Ockhamists carried forward their criticisms. 'Matter', says Ockham, 'is not to be pictured as an independent type of existence, a potential being, apt to be realized in this or that manner. It is in itself real and can by no means be reduced to mere potential being.' Primary matter is an abstraction; matter is always embodied in particular things. But the new critics went farther than this. They maintained that the particular embodiments of matter are all uniquely different. 'In all generated and existing things the various primary matters are each distinct and different, in the same way as various white objects are different.' And again, 'My primary matter is different from your primary matter'. As for the belief that things owe their particular nature to matter, we have seen that it is rejected. Things are singular in their own right and require no further metaphysical factor to make them so. There is no principle of individuation because there is no universal essence to be contracted into individual instances. An even more striking mark of this empiricism is the dismissal of the conception of essence, of substantial form. The phenomenalist bent of this school of thought is here evident. 'When we see a fire we know that it is a fire, yet in reality we do not know fire in itself, but only the accidents of fire, such as its heat.' Essence can only be described in abstract and negative terms, such as 'an entity that is not in another entity', or 'a being that under-lies all accidents'. This strict phenomenalism is boldly applied to the momentous doctrine of the rational soul. Our knowledge of the mind is confined to intuition of particular inward pro-cesses; knowledge of its essence is beyond our grasp. The question that had formed a vital point of discussion since the earliest days of western thought and that had been so com-prehensively explored in the thirteenth century is abandoned as irrational. The fundamental belief that the intellectual soul is an immaterial and incorruptible form is stated to be a doctrine that 'cannot be accepted as evident either from reason or from experience'. The doctrine can be held only by faith.

The method is applied to causal connexion. As we have seen, Ockham declares that the notion of one particular object is never the sufficient cause of the notion of another particular object. Items are presented to us distinct from one another and their connexion cannot be rationally deduced. The cause of heat can-not be proved by a syllogism; we have to observe the connexion between the sun and heat in order to attain the idea that they are causally connected; and the idea has no necessary force.

But it was in relation to theological truth that the most disturbing consequences of Ockham's criticisms were felt. For here, too, he declared that rational theologians had argued on false premisses and raised illicit problems. He maintained that it is impossible in the manner of Scotus and, one might add, of Anselm to offer strict proofs of any of the attributes of God. His views of knowledge precluded any attempt to proceed by *a priori* reasoning from general self-evident concepts, such as the concept of being, to necessary conclusions touching the chief doctrines of revealed religion. The point of departure cannot be a general concept but the intuition of a reality or several distinct realities, and in the realm of theology intuition is impossible. Our concepts of the deity are nominal and we have no means of comparing them with the real. In theology all judgements proceed from faith and the truths that we are incapable of knowing save by revelation cannot be known as we know other truths. No idea, not even an exemplary and Platonic idea, can be a reality, and the ideas of theology are connotative terms, possessing only logical character. So in creating things, God did not create ideas; He created things in the light of ideas. A divine idea is an *esse objectivum*, a mental concept. Existences are particulars. For every created thing in the universe there is a distinct idea in the mind of God. Augustine's doctrine that the ideas are eternal may be accepted, but only in the sense that God's thoughts are eternal, not in the sense that there are eternal substances. Some philosophers maintain that things exist as ideas in the divine mind potentially; but this view cannot be allowed. All we are entitled to say is that it was at any time possible for God to produce things. The exemplary idea, in short, is merely the knowledge that is required in order to produce anything and resembles on the human level of being the knowledge that is presupposed in the production of a house.

The arguments propounded at length by Aquinas in the *Summa contra Gentiles* are found to rest on false premisses. His arguments turned upon the theory of motion, and the basis of them was that motion requires an external agent to initiate it. When it is applied to the operations of the universe this principle leads to the necessity of postulating a first mover, the unmoved cause of all change. Ockham refuses to admit the basic principle. He declares that self-induced motion can exist; it appears, for example, in minds. And he denies that an infinite regress, which the Thomists made the main argument in favour of their conclusion, is an impossible conception. Other arguments daily discussed in the schools are treated in a similar manner. The concept of God is a composite concept formed by uniting many ethical and physical notions separately found in the natural order and among men. But we have no genuine knowledge of such a Being as is expressed in this composite notion. For such concepts suffer the defects of all concepts; they cannot establish existence. The only way by which certain knowledge of God could be attained would be the way of intuition, and this is impossible. And passing from the problem of the existence of the Deity to the problem of His attributes, Ockham criticizes the proofs of the unity, infinity, and eternity of God. We shall notice the repetition of these criticisms by later thinkers in England. The belief that there is one God cannot be demonstrated; there is nothing contrary to reason in supposing that there are many Gods, and many worlds. Aristotle's argument in *De Coelis* drawn from the universal operation of the movements of the elements lack cogency.

The criticisms of *a priori* reasoning amassed by Ockham involve the criticisms of theology. The definitions of theology are nominal; they do not refer to the divine essence but to representations constructed by our minds. Neither the dialectical path from temporal phenomena to the eternal mind, nor the deductive analysis of the necessary qualities of a subject can disclose the true order of things, for the reasoning by which these arguments proceed is not an instrument of metaphysical truth but a synthesis of symbols. Yet Ockham's philosophy is dominated by a central religious conviction, that of the absolute freedom of God's will in all the measures of the world. In consequence all the causes and relations of things are contingent and properties are extrinsic to their quiddities. The opposite view, the procedure of the Augustinians and the Scotists, is a denial of the transcendence of God. It is also a repudiation of the genuine logic of Aristotle. Ockham's nominalism is the fruit of a twofold preoccupation, a rigorous exposition of the

Aristotelian logic and a profound belief in the omnipotent will of God. The division between concepts and reality, the impossibility of expressing simple realities in propositions, the whole apparatus of *suppositiones* and of logical operations, derive from this double concern. Nominalism and empiricism spring, not from a reaction against faith, but from a sense of the total dependence of the created universe on the power of God.

IV

The nominalist logic was eagerly embraced at Oxford early in the fourteenth century, as we have seen; and it was soon pressed to further conclusions. Teachers such as Adam Wodham (d. 1358), and Robert Holcot (d. 1349) represented the new theory of truth. Wodham, lector of the Franciscans, defended the views of Ockham in his course on the Sentences in 1332. He argued that the belief in one first cause and in other fundamental positions in theology and metaphysics cannot be logically upheld. Holcot, who was an influential teacher at Oxford and Paris, expounded the nominalist theses without reserve. The items that compose the material of judgements are *suppositiones*, verbal symbols expressing intentions of the mind, possessing no counterparts in things as they are. The categories of Aristotle must be understood as a classification of terms, not of things. Some thinkers moved farther in the direction of logical scepticism and even the deliverances of intuition were impugned. Ockham had opened the door to this development when he had declared that God could produce an intuition without producing its corresponding object. An intuitive cognition could be supernaturally caused when an object did not exist. The suggestion that intuition does not necessarily require an existing object gave rise to radical theories which were hotly discussed. Richard Billingham was one of the most daring of the new critics. He maintained that all experience may be illusory, for the certainty contained in a cognition does not afford evidence of the existence of anything beyond the cognition. It does not even guarantee the existence of the self, as Augustine contended. And no one can be certain that any external substances exist.[1] The twofold basis of this epistemo-

---

[1] K. Michalski, 'Le criticisme et le scepticisme dans la philosophie du XIVe siècle', *Bulletin de l'Académie Polonaise des sciences et des lettres*, Cracow, 1925.

logical scepticism that we have recognized in Ockham must be recalled. The metaphysical foundation is that individuals are separate entities existing independently of one another, and intuitive awareness is an event distinct from its object. But the theological basis of the principle is faith in the omnipotence of God. The divine power is limited only by the rule of non-contradiction and the causal independence of things asserts no contradiction. The roots of this supernatural scepticism lie deep in scholastic thought. Masters of the thirteenth century had discussed the miraculous powers of God in suspending the regular connexions of causes, especially in the sacrament of the Eucharist where the accidents can be separated from their proper substances. The emphasis on omnipotent will was, in fact, a correlative feature of the Aristotelian development; it was increasingly felt that the naturalistic account of the uniform order of the world and of knowledge required to be supplemented by the article of faith which declared the absolute freedom of the Deity. But the new scepticism of the fourteenth century fastened also on the doctrine of subjective intuition. From the possibility that a cognition might, by supernatural means, refer to nothing beyond itself it was argued that the same may be true of natural cognition. The modern empiricism maintained that it is illegitimate to infer the existence of any-thing that is not given immediately by a particular intuition. The new Oxford logicians proceeded to question whether it is possible to infer the existence of the object of the intuition.

The course of this movement in England is still obscure. No teacher appears to have set forth a coherent scheme of empirical scepticism in the manner of Jean de Mirecourt or of Nicholas of Autrecourt, but it is evident that a number of lecturers at Oxford and Cambridge were expounding at this time highly empirical theories of knowledge in which experience is declared to be confined to accidents and even to images in the mind. But the interrelations of doctrines were so confused that some of these utterances must be attributed to the revival of Aver-roist conceptions rather than to applications of Ockhamism. John Rodington (d. 1348) and Richard Fitz-Ralph (d. 1360), for example, appear to have reached the principle that no certain knowledge of external things can be attained by insisting on the distinction between divine illumination and natural knowledge.

Yet the vigour with which the views of the nominalists were combated testified to their influence. A formidable champion of realism was Walter Burleigh, a great scholar who was tutor to the Black Prince. In his attacks on the '*incipientes de novo philosophari*' we catch echoes of the trenchant disputes that stirred the schools. Burleigh emphatically declared his belief, that universals are elements of the real order of things and protested against the thesis that in the work of thought the mind unites and distinguishes symbols. Genera and species are *in multis*; they are not merely conceived *de multis*, and this is the proper interpretation of Aristotle. Burleigh was too lively a mind to stand rigidly within the old circle of ideas and on several points he expressed agreement with the logic of the Ockhamists.[1] Others were less yielding. They were dismayed by the new ideas. They followed Lutterell in denouncing the entire scheme of knowledge proclaimed by the terminists and especially the doctrine that it is impossible to attain of God any knowledge but nominal concepts. They viewed the division between reason and the truths of faith with distress. The *Quodlibeta* of Holcot manifest the positions that faced conservative theologians. In his discussion of the question whether theology is a science he claims that the judgement affirming the existence of God cannot pretend to certainty. For only analytic judgements in which the predicate is already included in the subject are certain, and judgements that involve existence are not analytic. And if God's existence is not demonstrably certain, other attributes that are applied to Him cannot be proved, for they all depend upon His existence. Such truths must be reached through faith. Theology is not *scientia*. 'Hoc non potest ratione naturali demonstrari.' 'Haec veritas sola fide tenetur.' These are the conclusions of Holcot in numerous discussions on the dogmas of religion. Other masters expressed similar opinions. John Rodington contended that it is impossible to prove that God is infinite, or that He is omnipotent, or even that He is one. These principles must be accepted on the authority of scripture and faith. Richard Swineshead repeated the arguments of Ockham in rejecting the reasoning of the Thomists concerning the necessity for a first cause of

---

[1] L. Baudry, 'Guillaume d'Occam et Walter Burleigh', *Archives d'histoire doctrinale et littéraire du Moyen Age*, ix. 160.

motion: the demonstration from contigency to a first cause rests on the gratuitous assumption that the chain of causation cannot be infinite.[1]

There were many other critics, John Buckingham, William Heytesbury, and others who are at present little more than names. Neither from evident premisses by strict syllogistic reasoning nor from *a posteriori* proofs could the truths of theology be admitted to follow. They were matters of faith; *theologia nostra non est scientia sed est credita.*

Nevertheless this philosophical scepticism was by its decisive stress on faith controlled by religious interest. To the modern school of thinkers the theological lectures and debates that crowned the pursuits of the schools were far from vain. The destructive criticisms of the rational arguments in favour of the dogmas of belief did not lead to any criticism of the dogmas themselves. Some writers juxtaposed philosophical conclusions and theological beliefs in marked contrast, but naturally no philosopher uttered rationalist opinions in the sense of the rationalism of the eighteenth and nineteenth centuries. On the contrary the teaching of the new philosophy was emphatically directed towards vindication of faith. Convinced that the traditional reasoning that was associated with spiritual and theological beliefs was invalid, they were anxious to preserve the supreme truths upon which rested men's hope of salvation. They asserted that these truths pertained to a realm in which human reason is incompetent. The wisdom of God, enshrined in the scriptures and in the creeds, lay above the limits of natural reason. Revealed truths can neither be proved by reason, nor disproved. But from the principles of revelation that were taught in the theology of the Church deductions and applications could be made, and the elaboration of this system is sacred theology. And as the range of sacred truths capable of rational demonstration became restricted the circle of beliefs attained by faith was enlarged. Distrust of reason opened more widely the bounds of ecclesiastical authority. As a result of the critical logic of the Ockhamists an alliance between philosophical scepticism and implicit faith developed in England, as elsewhere, during the fourteenth and fifteenth centuries. The association between faith and scepticism was enforced by a

[1] Michalski, op. cit., pp. 77, 79.

singular circumstance to which we have already referred. The heretical movement in religious doctrine and practice led by Wyclif was the work of men who held conservative positions in metaphysics. The conjunction of reforming zeal with realist ideas threw the bishops into the arms of the nominalists.

But the relationship between philosophical scepticism and theology was an uneasy one. When Holcot argued that such articles of faith as the Virgin Birth and the Resurrection were contrary to natural reason, it appeared to many theologians a desperate procedure to resort to declarations concerning the feebleness of our understanding. Fideism, or loyalty to the teaching of theology even when philosophy contradicted it, was buttressed by the new stress upon the place of will in the scheme of things. The accent laid by Scotism on volition has been mentioned. The emphasis on the divine will was pushed to startling lengths by many theologians, of whom Thomas Bradwardine (d. 1349) was the most notorious. In his hands the doctrine became a theological determinism: every act of human will is determined from eternity by the omnipotent and omniscient will of God. This fatalism represents one side of the development of discussions at Oxford on the problem of free will and responsibility; it is a symptom rather of the perversion of Scotist ideas than of the development of them. Theologians were alarmed at the spread of that which they termed the Pelagianism of the Scotists, and Bradwardine complained that in his student days he rarely heard a word concerning grace. In his *De Causa Dei contra Pelagium* he argues that human actions in themselves are devoid of merit, and that no single temptation can be conquered apart from grace. This position called forth strong criticism and the question of man's freedom became an inexhaustible topic of debate; Chaucer refers to it in his *Troilus and Criseyde* and in the *Nun's Priest's Tale*, where he mentions Bradwardine. The followers of Ockham did not shrink from drawing from the Scotist premisses the conclusion that God must be responsible for evil as well as good, and Robert Holcot went so far as to maintain that God's absolute will could enjoin any one to hate Him, a doctrine that aroused a tempest of debate at Cambridge and at Oxford. By the middle of the century this aspect of Scotism has developed into a philosophy where the metaphysical difficulties of revealed doctrines could be settled by reference to the omnipotent will. Theologians increasingly referred to God's will rather than to His wisdom and maintained that no other reason can be given of the world-order nor of the mysteries of faith than that they express the arbitrary decree of God. 'With Him a thing becomes right solely for the reason that He wants it so to be.'

In many places where scholars lectured and debated, in the universities, in monasteries, and in the circles attendant upon bishops, the tendencies that have been mentioned advanced in spite of strong challenge from Augustinian realists, from the disciples of Scotus, and from the adherents of Aquinas. In the province of philosophy many thinkers embraced the radical empiricism of Ockham, dismissing the traditional apparatus of metaphysical principles, essences, species, substantial universals. In the realm of natural theology they accentuated the divorce between reason and faith that had appeared in the previous century and contracted further the scope of demonstration in theology. Scepticism and empiricism in philosophy united with implicit belief in religious truth. But we must now mention another tendency in philosophical inquiry that was strengthened by the work of the nominalists. From the days of Abaelard there had been philosophers who interested themselves in exploring the relations between grammatical forms and logic. In the thirteenth century an important figure in this line of inquiry in England was William Shyreswood who died as Chancellor of Lincoln in 1249. Others pursued these researches and a *logica moderna* developed, concerned with the examination of the various modes in which words and propositions are used to express meaning. One of William Shyreswood's pupils when that master was lecturing in Paris was Peter of Spain who afterwards became Pope John XXI, and who cultivated the science *de modis significandi* in a work that was widely studied. He explored the properties of terms, and developed the doctrine of *suppositio*, which was adopted by Ockham. In the hands of these writers logic became a *scientia sermocinalis*, a science of meaning, and interest became directed more upon ways of expression and usage than upon the relation of thought to reality. Ockham and the nominalists of the fourteenth century seized on the *logica moderna*. In Chapter XI of the *Sum of All Logic* William set forth an elaborate scheme of signs. Words are classified into words of first imposition and words of second imposition, words applied in a wide and in a strict sense, words used at first intentions and as second intentions, and so on. We need not follow these interesting classifications in detail. The development of this logic had important repercussions. The accumulation in the *Parva Logicalia* and other text-books of a mass of refinements and subtle distinctions contributed to the contempt for the philosophy of the schools that began to be expressed towards the close of the fourteenth century; and many teachers bewailed the corruption of the philosophy by this analytical logic. We have recorded the sarcasms of a great humanist writer of the twelfth century, John of Salisbury, concerning the logical niceties of his day. We shall find that the literary prophets of the fifteenth and sixteenth centuries echoed the scorn of John for the verbal elaborations of the schoolmen.

V

Destructive criticism and the sense of interminable divisions issued in a decline of confidence in metaphysical and rational inquiries that is widely apparent in England before the close of the century. The authorities of the Church and the masters of the theological faculties were encouraged by the modern logicians to invoke the supra-rational acceptance of the tenets of the faith. A popular line of attack upon the Lollards was to accuse them of bringing reason to bear upon the Holy Mysteries. A treatise of the time on the Sacrament of the Mass bewails the use of reason by the reformers.

'Both this luf and drede (of Christ in the Sacrament) wantes many gret clerkes, the which leven so mich upon ther owne kindely (natural) resoun and the princepales of philosophi th^t is mannes wisdom, groundede onely in kindely resoun of man, th^t thai will not leve (believe) the trew faith taght be holy chirch of this blessed sacrament.'

Men have been deceived by the 'kunnyng of philosophi' and have given more credence to the doctrine of Aristotle than to the doctrine that is above reason.[1] Yet the call of Wyclif and the Lollards was equally a call to simple faith. On all sides men were turning to revelation and grace in preference to rational

---

[1] G. R. Owst, *Preaching in Medieval England*, p. 137.

theology and the wave of piety and mysticism threatened to submerge intellectual discussion. Scholars as well as illiterate folk imbibed preaching that taught Christians to labour rather in charity and godly living than in disputations and nice theoretical inquiries. Mystical writings attained an extraordinary vogue. Already in the early decades of the century the books of Richard Rolle (d. 1349) were widely copied and studied; it is said that more manuscripts of his works survive than of any other medieval writer in England. *The Mirror of Simple Souls* and the *Scale of Perfection* by Walter Hilton (d. 1396) were eagerly read. A deepening sense of personal religion is evident in the rapid circulation of such works as the *Scale of Perfection*, but it is accompanied by a withdrawal of intellectual curiosity. In an earlier chapter we have referred to the profound influence exercised upon religious speculation by the transcendental theology of Dionysius the Areopagite. In the fourteenth century the *Mystical Theology* was freely translated into English. The effect of the work was to impress upon men, wearied by the disputes of the schools, the incomprehensibility of the divine nature and the futility of rational investigations. 'Also we ascending and beginning our denyings and our doings away at the highest of understandable things say that he is neither soul, nor angel, nor hath fantasy, nor opinion, nor reason, nor understanding; nor he is said, nor understood.' And the writer proceeds through a catena of negatives to the conclusion. 'For the perfect and the singular cause of all must needs be without comparison of the most high height above all, both setting and doing away. And his not understandable overpassing is understandably above all affirming and denying.'[1]

In the experience of the great contemplatives of this century, such as Richard Rolle, Walter Hilton, and Juliana of Norwich, this negative way led not to ignorance and scepticism but to unity with the divine. Through the darkness of unknowing seekers attained a profound illumination of the spirit. Yet the super-intellectual manner of reaching reality was naturally associated with distaste for the methods of discursive thought. The wide mystical interests of the fourteenth century encouraged a sense of the inadequacy of human knowledge. 'The most

---

[1] *The Cloud of Unknowing and other Treatises*, edited by Dom Justin McCann, New York, 1942, pp. 146-8.

godly knowing of God is that which is known by unknowing.'
The Cloud of Unknowing proclaims the method in its title, and
in several passages it condemns 'curiosity of much learning and
letterly knowledge as in clerks'. *The Mirror of Simple Souls*
speaks in slighting terms of reason and of the activities of the
schools. And in the lecture-halls themselves the disparagement
of the old mental disciplines met sympathetic ears. Clerks were
ready to echo the cry of Thomas à Kempis, 'What do we care
for genera and species?' And the interventions of authority
repressed the spirit of intellectual adventure.

In the year 1411 the archbishop and his council visited the
University of Oxford. An order was issued that no book should
be read in any College or Hall until it had been examined and
approved by twelve commissioners. The writings of Wyclif
were investigated and two hundred and sixty-seven dangerous
errors were found in them. All the members of the university
were commanded to renounce these opinions. The schools
became faithful mouthpieces of the Church and of the king.
The reformers had already been expelled from Oxford in 1382,
but the movement had persisted. Hundreds of scholars now
left the university and the intellectual life of the schools declined. For the action of the authorities checked not only new
developments of religious belief, it stifled freedom of discussion.
The courses in the faculty of arts languished. Theological
and philosophical learning had been depressed by the Statute
of Provisors of 1390 which restricted the right of the Pope
to appoint graduate clergy to benefices. The master's degree
no longer offered a path to preferment and men turned from
metaphysical studies to more lucrative pursuits, such as the profession of civil law. Latin scholarship degenerated. The suppression of the reforming doctrines at Oxford was not surprising.
The disciples of Wyclif threw doubts upon the sacramental
system and were sceptical of the Real Presence. But the repressive measures of the guardians of tradition checked philosophical
activity as well as heresy. The Lollards had been deceived by
the 'kunnyng of philosophi'. They had followed 'kindly resoun'
rather than the faith which is above reason. 'Naturale science'
denies the miracle by which the accidents of the bread and wine
are present apart from their natural substance. Such inquiries
were sternly condemned. The barrenness of thought at the

universities during the fifteenth century in England must be ascribed in part to the uncompromising policy of the ecclesiastical government.

Nevertheless, the debate between the *reales*, the partisans of Scotism and Thomism on one side and the *nominales* or *terministae* who followed Ockham on the other, continued. The intellectual rivalry often issued in unseemly brawls. The northern 'nation' stood for Scotus, the southern for Ockham and nominalism. But this strife brought forth no striking development of principles. Further refinements were added to the *Parva Logicalia* of the terminists, but the most obvious consequence was a dense growth of verbal distinctions. The wits of the time made play with the logicians. Ockhamism was not the source of new departures in physical theory in England as it was on the Continent. In other respects an air of sterility hung over the schools. The texts of the masters, especially those of Scotus, were expounded with infinite care and a literature of glosses and commentaries flourished. It is an industry that naturally succeeds a period of brilliant advances in speculation. Philosophy was passing into the hands of men who collected and repeated the positions of the past. The arguments of the *antiqui*, for example, in opposition to the *moderni* were endlessly retailed; but no new synthesis of ideas emerged. Men of ability were turning to other pursuits.

The scheme of studies in philosophy and theology was preserved, the Aristotelian system of knowledge, the theology of the Fathers and of the *Sentences*. It could produce critics if not philosophers. The affair of Bishop Reginald Pecock is doubly interesting in relation to the circumstances of the fifteenth century. It illustrates the direction in which vital thought was flowing and it throws a sharp light on the restraints exercised by the hierarchy.[1] Pecock did not offer any new proposals in general philosophy though he possessed an enthusiasm for scholastic logic. And he was the first writer to attempt rational discussion in the English tongue. The leading purpose of *The Repressor of Over-Much Blaming of the Clergy* is to refute the views of Wyclif and the Lollards upon ecclesiastical abuses, but in the course of his argument he unfolds opinions on natural

[1] For Pecock, see *Bishop Reginald Pecock*, by V. H. H. Green, Cambridge, 1945.

reason in relation to faith and authority that are far-reaching. The recurrent theme of his argument is a call to the 'doom', or judgement of reason. He accepts the orthodox position which held that the great dogmas of the Church, the dogmas of the Trinity, the Creation, the Fall, the Redemption, the Virgin Birth, are given to men by divine revelation. But he rejects the view that Scripture should be reverenced above all other sources of information, especially when question of 'natural law of kind and moral law of kind' are concerned. Even when the Bible treats of supernatural matters it must be interpreted in a reasonable way, and a rational faith must eschew the 'allegorik and tropologik' method of exposition. Pecock does not give a clear or systematic account of the processes of rational inquiry upon which he places so much emphasis, but what he does say is an interesting reflection of the mental tendencies of the period. In addition to the formal rules of the syllogism and certain axiomatic truths, he recommends attention to experience, for it gives 'the greatest certainty which may be had in our knowing'. In the critical observations upon the narratives of the Old Testament and upon some of the miracle stories it is moral judgement rather than assessment of evidence that provides his criterion. But though his definition of reason is obscure he insists that it is the sovereign guide to truth. It is independent of authority, common to all men, the inner eye of man, written 'in law of kind' in the soul. Scripture ought to be drawn to reason and not reason to it. Points of doctrinal practice can be decided without recourse to texts. Even when he is discussing the truths of revelation the bishop distinguishes between truths that are reasonably certain and those that are merely probable. And in one passage he disputes the authority of the Catholic Church, observing that a simple person may gain a truer understanding of Scripture by long study than a general council. The 'doom of reason' leads him into other audacities. The opinions of the Fathers are not to be deemed final either on points of doctrine or on the interpretation of the Scriptures, and St. Jerome's 'tongue was not the key of heaven and earth'. He went so far as to reject the article of the creed which asserts the descent of Christ into hell.

These rationalist utterances are embedded in professions of orthodox faith, but they were sufficient for his political and clerical enemies. His trial and condemnation in 1457 was provoked in part by the prejudice of the Yorkists against a prominent Lancastrian; but the hierarchy had little interest in Pecock's endeavour to meet the strong feeling that the Church in England was hostile to rational inquiry. The policy of the leaders of ecclesiastical rule was directed above all towards encouraging practical devotion in a period when laxity was widespread; and any movement that tended to depreciate faith received unqualified condemnation. Pecock was made publicly to confess that he had preferred the judgement of natural reason before the New and Old Testaments and the authority of the Church. His opponents, Gascoine, Lowe, Bouchier, and others representing the established order, could not allow any concession to a rational defence of theological truths according to the principles of the *Repressor* and of the *Book of Faith*. It was a challenge not only to the episcopate and the basic principles of society, but also to the historic view of salvation. Yet popular and intellectual changes were gathering force that were undermining the old philosophy of life and knowledge, and Pecock's ideas, though they were steeped in the logic of the past, indicate poignant dissatisfaction with the intellectual guidance of the Church and of the schools.

HUMANISM AND REFORMATION

I

THE social transformations of the fifteenth century affected men's views on ultimate questions. The growth of a commercial class, the tide of nationalism, the multiplication of books, the new grammar schools, the voyages of discovery, broadened interests and directed them into practical channels. Leaders of the modern culture expressed scorn of the exercises of the schools, but they offered no philosophy that could supplant the old perspective, and denunciations of Aristotle appeared side by side with restatements of the Aristotelian logic and metaphysics. Sceptical wit and puritanical earnestness were levelled at 'the barbarous and unprofitable disputations' of the terminist logicians and the wrangles of the Scotists and Thomists, and the tide of anti-clericalism weakened attachment to the time-honoured discussions. Towards the close of the century the claims of other philosophies began to be heard. The flow of learning from Italy opened the way to unorthodox schools of ancient thought. Besides the theories of Plato and Plotinus those of Epicurus and Democritus, of Heracleitus and Pythagoras, of Cicero and Seneca, were cultivated. Occult visions from the hermetic and cabbalist literature mingled with rumours of astronomical discoveries, and a vogue of astrology competed with a wave of scepticism. The mind of the sixteenth century was carried forward on a flood of unorganized knowledge and surmise, the product of new sources of literature, of new independence of thought, of wider sensibility and experience. It was a period of confused assimilation and of hasty eclecticism.

We must take flight at a considerable elevation above the variegated developments of this age, marking a few prominent features of the moving scene. The salient events are the revival of classical literature, the ecclesiastical revolt, and the advance of an esoteric philosophy of nature. These developments served to detach thought from its ancient modes, but they led to no rational reformation of the principles of knowledge, and after the ecclesiastical and political convulsions of Henry's reign,

after the poetic and biblical inspirations of the period of Elizabeth, the frame of ancient conceptions remained the settled
assumptions of most thoughtful men. A few were conscious of
revolutionary principles in cosmology that pointed to a fresh
vision of truth. But the new literary culture and the break
with Rome did not seriously affect the historic conceptions of
the universe and of man's place within it. They loosened confidence in those conceptions, they diverted attention from them,
and they provoked sentiments that encouraged a more practical,
a more concrete, a simpler philosophical creed. But the intellectual fruits of this spirit did not ripen until the following
century.

Let us observe some features of the literary revival in relation
to men's general conception of experience. In the year 1443
Pier Candido Decembrio sent from Italy his Latin translation
of Plato's *Republic* to Humphrey, Duke of Gloucester. The
incident marks the faint stirring of a new element that was
entering English intellectual life. A strange wind of ideas had
arisen in Italy a century earlier, the source of which was an
enthusiasm for the literature of classical antiquity. Scholars
searched for manuscripts, pursued the study of Greek as well
as of Latin letters, and under the patronage of powerful rulers
formed associations to promote the appreciation of the modern
learning. In these Italian circles the ancient literature was
welcomed and cultivated in a spirit strangely different from the
spirit of the schools. The imitation and discussion of the great
classics were pursued in a tone recalling the literary revival of
the twelfth century at Chartres which had captivated John of
Salisbury. The new revival was sensitive to the artistic form
and elegance, to the imaginative and personal qualities of the
ancient writings. But it moved far beyond the earlier renaissance. It moved towards conceptions of truth and of value that
opened a fresh view of life. The Italian scholars absorbed and
proclaimed not only the art of the classical authors but also their
cultural standards, their urbanity, their interest in men, their
humour, their passion, and their freedom. Such a spirit clashed
with the intellectual forms of the schools, and in Italy acute
conflict sprang up between the advocates of the new scholarship
and the majority who were educated in the metaphysical and
theological ideals of the Church.

The new classical learning passed beyond the Alps and secured a position in the mental life of the great centres of France, Germany, and Spain. It was long before its influence was deeply felt in England. The first touch of the classical revival may have been connected with the visit in 1418 of the renowned Italian scholar, Poggio. He was contemptuous of the literary taste that he found in the country. Other Italian men of letters who were attached to the Papal representative in England followed Poggio, and certain of these scholars kindled the ardour of the royal Duke of Gloucester. Humphrey invited Italians to his household, commanded Greek works to be translated, and formed a large library of ancient and of modern texts. He gave many hundreds of books to Oxford, and by this deed he encouraged the reading of the classics at that university. The copy of the *Republic* that has been mentioned and new translations of Aristotle were frequently transcribed and circulated among masters at Oxford. There soon appeared other patrons of the new knowledge, Thomas Bekynton, William Grey, the notorious John Tiptoft, and many others.[1] Men from Oxford and Cambridge went to read at the universities of Italy; there was an English 'nation' at Bologna. The interest in polite letters began to creep into the monastic schools; the great monastery of Christ Church at Canterbury, for instance, introduced the writings of the Italian humanists into its library about the middle of the fifteenth century.

There is a signal difference between the manner in which this new culture was first accepted in England and its reception in Italy and in France. Abroad, and especially in the country of its birth, the new culture was greeted as a revelation. It beckoned the minds of its votaries in the Florentine Academy to strange vistas, and the ideas that were proclaimed there and in other circles were sharply divided from the current debates of the schools. Some of them were openly pagan. The result was that humanism became tainted with heresy, and in many places fierce conflicts broke out between the new type of scholars and the old. In England, the reading and imitation of the classics and of the modern *belles lettres* were absorbed into the traditional scheme of medieval thought. The craving for improvement in

---

[1] R. Weiss, *Humanism in England during the Fifteenth Century*, Oxford, 1941, Chapters V–VII.

Latin style was a strong inducement to study with fresh ardour the texts of Cicero and Seneca; English diplomatists were concerned at the barbarism of their Latinity when they perused the letters of Italian correspondents. But even when they savoured the civilization of the ancient writers in the new translations of Plato or of Xenophon they were not conscious of any vital conflict between the conceptions of the world that they found in them and the metaphysics of the schools. There was assuredly no tendency among the humanists in England during the fifteenth century to embrace pagan ideas. The men who cultivated the new learning were, with few exceptions, ecclesiastics and schoolmen, and their reading effected little change in their philosophical perspective. It was placed at the service of the customary intellectual habits and beliefs. Accordingly, in England, a large proportion of the texts translated for patrons from the Greek were theological and philosophical works. Translations of the Greek dramatists and historians proved less attractive. And commentaries on the philosophical texts now made accessible conformed to the historic modes of interpretation. John Doget's discussion, for instance, on the recent translation of the *Phaedo* explains the dialogue in terms of Christian doctrine. The text becomes the occasion for short sermons wholly unconnected with Plato's views, and so far as the theory of the work is considered it is seen in the light of the Christian Neo-Platonism that descends from St. Augustine and the Pseudo-Dionysius. Doget shows acquaintance with modern translations; for example, he quotes Ficino's version of the *Poimander*, one of the hermetic writings of which we shall have to take notice later. But his approach to the *Phaedo* is scholastic, not humanist.[1]

At the turn of the century the new cult became less dilettante and began seriously to affect the general outlook. Few of the earlier patrons and readers of the classics knew any Greek. There now appeared a number of scholars who were proficient in Greek, and among them some entered on a study of philosophy in its original tongue, free from the misleading associations of contemporary scholasticism. Greek, in fact, was the

[1] Ib., p. 166. Doget, a Dorset man, went to study at Padua and Bologna, and was appointed shortly before his death in 1501 Provost of King's College, Cambridge.

key that opened the door to the new landscape of mind. The study of Greek writers and of the Greek tongue led to fresh conceptions in theology, in physics, in medicine, in philosophy. Hythlodaye in More's *Utopia* takes a set of Greek works on literature and science to that country. The greatest figure in this advance was William Grocyn (d. 1519) who on the one hand was a student of the works of Aquinas, Scotus, and Ockham, and on the other was widely read in the Latin and Greek classics. He spans the old and the new tendencies, but he remained untouched by the zeal for Platonic ideas that he had encountered in Italy. 'I think the difference between these great philosophers, Aristotle and Plato, is simply the difference between a man of science and a man of myth', he remarked. But he was the herald of the new outlook as teacher of the marvellous knot of men whose conversation enchanted the young Erasmus. The picture of the English scene in 1497 is well known.

'The air is soft and delicious. The men are sensible and intelligent. Many of them are even learned and not superficially either. They know their classics and so accurately that I have lost little by not going to Italy. When Colet speaks I might be listening to Plato. Linacre is as deep and acute a thinker as I have ever met with. Grocyn is a mine of knowledge and Nature never formed a sweeter or happier disposition than that of Thomas More. The number of young men who are studying ancient literature is astonishing.'[1]

In a later portrait of Colet the broadening culture of the age is shown. In youth he studied scholastic theology. He then read Cicero and Plato and Plotinus and made himself a first-rate mathematician. He pursued his education in France and Italy, keeping up his Scotus and Aquinas, but worked also at the early Christian Fathers, while Dante and Petrarch polished his language. The members of this wonderful circle of scholars, statesmen, and churchmen, Colet, Linacre, Lily, More, Fisher, and others, differed from one another in belief and policy, but they manifested common interests and ideas that reflect the new tendencies of thought. The wider appreciations of existence that were brought to life by the pursuit of the literature of Greece and Rome have been touched upon; our concern is with the rational qualities of the new culture.

[1] Erasmus to Robert Fisher, *Erasmi Epistolae*, ed. P. S. Allen, Oxford, 1906, i. 273. The version is Froude's.

The salient character of the movement is the moral change of attitude in relation to the old intellectual material, the Scriptures, the dogmas of faith, the corpus of metaphysical doctrine and method. The sentiments that moved these men to study and reflection were eminently practical. They sought knowledge not for its own sake but for the sake of its ethical quality, for its bearing on the conduct of life. The movement towards religious sincerity that we have witnessed in the previous epoch attains in this group and in numbers of young students of the time a fresh power. The impelling motive of mental activity is devotional and the devotional purpose is associated with moral discipline in private and in public life. 'This kind of philosophy is situated more truly in emotions than in syllogisms; it is a life rather than a disputation' wrote Erasmus in his *Paraclesis*. It is the motto of the Catholic reformers and humanists.

The search for the rational forms of this spirit led men to the original sources of goodness and right living. They turned to the Gospels, the letters of St. Paul, and the early Fathers, reading them freshly for their human lessons rather than for their theology. In the celebrated lectures on St. Paul Colet expounded a more realistic and historical conception of the Epistles than had been heard before. William Tyndale in his *Obedience of a Christian Man* described the theologians of the schools as still engaged in interpreting the Scriptures according to the theory of the four senses that prevailed, as we have seen, in the earliest period of our civilization. And he finds that for the masters of theology the tropological, the allegorical, and the analogical senses remain more significant than the literal. The new outlook stresses the literal sense. 'Nor is one thing said and another meant, but the very thing is meant which is said, and the sense is wholly literal.'[1] It was to be taken literally because it was to be understood in relation to common practice, not in relation to esoteric truth. The concern of the new generation of scholars with the correction and translation of the texts of the New Testament is directed by urgent ethical purposes. It is governed by the desire to recover the unsophisticated message of the Gospel and to encourage its practice among men. The work of the Catholic reformers, and above all of Erasmus in his edition

[1] Colet, *Treatise on the Hierarchies*, tr. J. H. Lupton, London, 1909, p. 107.

of the New Testament, marks a profound change in the intellectual problems pressing upon men. The words in the introduction to the edition of the New Testament are famous. 'I long for the husbandman to sing parts of them to himself as he follows the plough, for the weaver to hum them to the accompaniment of his shuttle, for the traveller to beguile the tedium of journeying with them.' The direct critical examination of texts is inspired by an evangelical aim, but it imposed a method in one department of inquiry which was soon to spread to other fields. The search for original simplicity, for literal meaning, for historical understanding, in the region of biblical and patristic study is the prelude to a fresh logic of experience. Sir Thomas More recommended the University of Oxford to seek for knowledge of God from the Scriptures and the early catholic Fathers, not from the scholastic conundrums. For the return to simplicity, obviousness, and the original purity of the Faith is accompanied by a revolt from the methods of the contemporary schools. The new scholars are never tired of denouncing the theology of the universities, and their assaults on theological logomachies naturally embraced the topics of traditional philosophy. Preoccupied with the scandalous abuses incessantly proclaimed against the Church by the Lollards and the disciples of Wyclif, with the faithlessness of the new generation in England, and with the rising heresy of Luther, they were out of patience with the problems and methods of the schoolmen. They abhorred their logical subtleties and abstract dialectics. 'To cavil about different sentences and words, now to gnaw at this and now at that and to dissect everything bit by bit seemed to him to be the mark of a poor and barren mind.' So wrote Colet to Erasmus who warmly agreed. That mercurial genius hated the philosophers almost as violently as he hated the monks, and found their 'notions and instants, formalities and quiddities' incomprehensible. These were 'things no eyes ever saw, unless they were eyes which could see in the dark what had no existence'.[1] The new propensity towards the practical and the concrete is evident. In *Utopia* More expresses contempt for the activities of the schools, and Colet refused to allow logic and disputation to be included in the curriculum of his new foundation of St. Paul's school. He begged men not to become

[1] Erasmus, *Encomium Moriae*.

readers of philosophers, 'companions of devils'.[1] It was not merely the scholastic method in theology and philosophy that was dismissed by the new prophets, it was the pursuit of the questions that occupied the philosophers and theologians. The problems were deemed futile. Erasmus again is the spokesman of the revolution in ideas.

'We dispute how the Father differs from the Son, and both from the Holy Ghost, whether it be a difference of fact or a difference of relation, and how three can be one when neither of the three is the other. . . . Then there are endless questions about baptism, about synaxis, about penance, when no answer is possible, and the answer, if we could find one, would be useless to us. . . . Hundreds of such questions are debated by distinguished theologians, and the objects of them are better unknown than known. It is all vanity.'[2]

This utilitarian scepticism is extended to metaphysics. The great reformers are no longer interested in the clarification of fundamental conceptions. Fisher, in his controversial work on the burning theological questions of the time, falls back on Scripture and on the unanimous voice of the Church. He rarely considers the philosophical principles involved in the points under dispute.

In fine, the living interests of thought had suffered an extraordinary change. The sceptical treatment of knowledge, the religious revolt, the call to discipline, the mechanical conservatism of the schools, had united to produce a revulsion from the historic problems and modes of inquiry. The impelling call was the call for ecclesiastical reform. The diatribes of *The Praise of Folly* vented a general sentiment, and in the bookshops of Oxford Erasmus's satirical pictures of priests and monks were in larger demand than the treatises of the masters and the works of Aristotle. The rising repugnance against superstition and magical practices, and the universal alarm at the threatened divisions of the Catholic Church, precluded logical speculation. The disputes over the primacy of the Roman pontiff and the nature of the Mass held men's minds. What filled More and his friends with anxiety were proposals that threatened to divide the historic unity of Christendom. The Lutheran doctrines that were being openly discussed at Cambridge raised issues beside which the rational debates of the Scotists appeared idle chatter.

---

[1] J. H. Lupton, *Life of Colet*, p. 76. In his letter to Radulphus on Genesis he relies on scholastic categories.   [2] Erasmus on 1 Timothy i. 6.

'I wish there could be an end of scholastic subtleties, or if not an end, that they could be thrust into a second place, and Christ taught plainly and simply.' The cry for plainness and simplicity, for moral discipline and Catholic unity, silenced the ancient explorations into the nature of knowledge.

These propensities mingled with the visions that had been breaking in from the revival of Greek literature. There was a tendency to replace the philosophy of Aquinas and Scotus by a Christian Platonism. Several scholars, who journeyed from England to learn Greek in Italy, came under the spell of the Platonic Academy in Florence. Linacre is reported to have shared the studies of Giovanni di Medici. The translations of Plato and Plotinus by Marsilio Ficino were carried home and eagerly read. The attempt of Pico della Mirandola to reconcile Plato with Christian dogma attracted the new generation. More composed a life of Pico, and Colet in the lectures on St. Paul quoted Ficino, Pico, and Plotinus. The *Utopia* is the fruit of More's study of the *Republic* and the *Laws*. A manifestation of the distaste for logical analysis in association with the revival of personal religion, was the continued interest in the transcendental mysticism of the Pseudo-Dionysius. Colet, in particular, made a close study of the work *On the Divine Names*. The way of negation which we have seen to have offered an alternative to the minute rationalism of the schools during the fourteenth century accorded also with the intellectual sentiments of the later leaders of religious thought. Nor did Grocyn's embarrassing discovery that the works attributed to Dionysius the Areopagite were not written by that author shake their influence over devotional minds in England.

A visitor to Oxford in 1535 found the quadrangle of New College filled with swirling pages from the works of Duns Scotus. A certain gentleman of Buckinghamshire was 'gathering them up to make sewells or blaunshers to keep the deer within the wood'. Forty years earlier a course of lectures on the quodlibeta of Scotus had drawn large audiences. Now undergraduates were burning copies of his treatises in the market-place.[1] This violent revulsion from the old ideas was the consequence of a revolutionary change in the ancient religious jurisdiction of the land.

[1] Anthony à Wood, *Historia et Antiquitates Universitatis Oxoniensis*, Oxford, 1674, i. 62; ii. 108.

II

It is not necessary to recall here the tangled motives and circumstances that culminated in the sweeping reconstruction of the Church between 1529 and 1536 by which the king became the supreme authority of the ecclesiastical as well as of the civil order of the country. It may safely be asserted that the act by which the dominion of the 'bishop of Rome' over English life and thought was cast off was principally a political act. It was an act of State policy, but it was supported by a widespread indignation against alien interference that attained bitter intensity beneath the autocratic rule of Wolsey; and into it was poured the passionate resentment against the powers and privileges of the monks that had been rife since the days of Chaucer. The anti-papal wave of feeling was not at first associated with doctrinal nor with philosophical innovations. Henry VIII and his ministers had no intention when they broke with Rome of departing from the articles of the Catholic faith. The critical Acts of 1534 firmly repudiated any interpretation of their provisions in a sense contrary to the accepted dogmas, and the dogmas were rationally substantiated by the philosophy of the schools. The independence of the Church in England was declared by men who were vehemently opposed to the novel principles that were entering the country from Germany and from Switzerland. At this stage of events those who preached Lutheran and Zwinglian ideas were liable to be burnt as heretics. The reformed doctrines of faith and salvation did not become prominent until the time of the Protectorate of Edward VI, and even then they were not voiced in any strength outside groups at the universities and in London, and with more emotional fervour among extreme communities in Kent and Essex. Towards these extreme sects, such as the Anabaptists, the leaders of the Church were as ruthlessly intolerant as towards those who followed the 'idolatrous practices' of the Papists. But the pronouncements of the government upon religious questions were frequent and confusing and even the leaders of opinion vacillated from one position to another. The general uncertainty, the incessant conferences, the stream of publications, distracted men's minds; sensitive and learned men, such as Cranmer and Gardiner, found themselves confronted with the gravest and most delicate problems arising from the conflicting claims of the civil and spiritual orders. Hundreds of saintly persons, Romanists and Reformers, faced agonizing death rather than betray their convictions.

The controversies and declarations that filled the air during the reign of Edward VI often touched questions of first principles, but no systematic development in the view of knowledge and reality emerged. Yet change in the categorical modes of interpreting experience was occurring. Sacred sentiments and the immemorial schemes of ideas that were attached to them were becoming loosened. Cardinal principles that had been assumed without question were now openly criticized. The mental soil was broken up and prepared for fresh planting; men were becoming familiar with new ways of thought; but the harvest did not mature for a generation. The impact of religious reform upon the old philosophical principles can be illustrated from the discussions over the central issue of doctrine, the nature of the Sacrament of the Eucharist. If we take the positions upheld by the advanced group of reformers on the one hand, and the views maintained by the supporters of theological tradition on the other, we can discern, amid the strictly religious and scriptural arguments, signs of revulsion from the old metaphysics. The conservative theologians stood intellectually upon the Aristotelian scheme elaborated in the thirteenth century. The rational foundation of the doctrine of transubstantiation was the distinction drawn by the schools between substance and accidents. The transformation of the Elements that followed upon the act of consecration was explained by reference to the substantial essence of the Elements. The transformation was said to take place in the essences of the material objects, not in their accidents. The accidents are the sensible qualities of the bread and wine, and these suffered no alteration at consecration, but the normal essences of the bread and wine became transmuted into a new and transcendent spiritual essence, the body and blood of Christ. The extreme wing of the reformers were forced to criticize the theory of the relation between substance and accidents in objects, since they rejected the belief in the Real Presence in the Sacrament. They pointed out that the arguments of the theologians presumed a complete separation between accidents and their appropriate substances, with the result that, as Cranmer put it, 'the accidents hang upon the air'. The sensible qualities of whiteness, sweetness, and roundness are present to the senses of the worshipper, but the things themselves are neither round nor white nor sweet.[1] The radical spirits went farther. They would have nothing to do with these subtleties. They took their stand upon the plain deliverances of common sense. John Hooper, Bishop of Worcester, the stubborn leader of Zwinglian teaching in England, bluntly asserted that a piece of bread can never be other than a piece of bread. Its substance can never be transformed into anything else. Christ's body is in heaven and to suppose that it can exist upon a thousand altars is to suppose what is incredible. And faith in that which is incredible is irrational faith. Hooper presses sensory and empirical arguments against the metaphysics of the theologians with rough vigour. 'Is God so much the enemy of man to give him his senses to destruction? No. He hath of his abundant mercy given them to discern white from black, sour from sweet, chalk from cheese, the glorious body of Christ from the sign of a sacrament, which is bread.'[2] In naming the sacrament a sign Hooper and his party asserted its subjective virtue. It is a symbol possessing intrinsic spiritual value; it is a token by which the faithful may call to remembrance the religious associations of the Last Supper.

The reliance on simple empirical criteria runs through all the doctrinal controversies of the sixteenth and seventeenth centuries. It will be sufficient to refer to a passage from Archbishop Tillotson's *Discourse against Transubstantiation* (2nd ed., 1684) in which the same criteria of proof as those used by Hooper are applied to the same sacred context.

'It might well seem strange if any man should write a book, to prove that an egg is not an elephant, and that a musket-bullet is not a pike: it is every whit as hard a case, to be put to maintain by a long discourse, that what we see and handle and taste to be bread is bread and not the body of a man; and that what we see and taste to be wine is wine and not blood. And if this evidence may not pass for sufficient, without further proof, I do not see why any man, that hath confidence enough to do so, may not deny anything to be what all the world sees it is, or affirm what all the world sees it is not; and this without

[1] Cranmer, *Answer to a Crafty and Sophisticated Cavillation*, quoted by C. S. Smyth, *Crisis and Reformation*, Cambridge, 1926, p. 18. The work was a reply to Gardiner.   [2] Quoted by C. S. Smyth, op. cit., p. 102.

all possibility of being further confuted. So that the business of transubstantiation is not a controversy of Scripture against Scripture, or of reason against reason, but of downright impudence against the plain meaning of Scripture, and all the sense and reason of mankind.'

Much had occurred in the realm of thought since the time of Hooper, and Tillotson's conception of reason was wider than the quotation suggests. But in spite of his denial there is here a controversy of reason against reason. The historic metaphysics of the schools in alliance with theology are dismissed in favour of plain tangible evidence in association with practical goodness. It was in Puritan teaching that a philosophy of unsophisticated common sense, a distaste for subtle analysis and for 'occult principles' passed from the age of the Reformation to the scientific empiricism of the eighteenth century. Tillotson echoes Hooper, and Hume opens his essay on Miracles with a quotation from Tillotson.

But many of the reformist leaders in England were not prepared to adopt such easy and popular methods. The views of Cranmer, Ridley, and of other leaders who had absorbed the teaching of Bucer were more subtle. They were equally as anxious as the Zwinglian group to avoid the implications of a substantial transformation of the Elements in the sacrament. They, also, rejected the division between accidents and substance that was derived from the Aristotelian doctrine by their orthodox opponents. They regarded the theory of transubstantiation as an invitation to return to the old superstitions that they were in earnest to destroy. But they were deeply concerned to save the belief in the Real Presence. Accordingly they resorted to the theory that the sacrament is a genuine but a spiritual communication of Christ's presence. His presence is a reality but a reality that is not perceived 'by the senses nor by any natural understanding, nor in any way an understanding of this generation, but by faith and by the inward working of the Holy Spirit'.[1] The doctrine is justified neither by the metaphysics of *essentia*, nor by transferring it entirely to the mental attitude of the participants of the rite, but by postulating a spiritual realm apprehended only by mystical faith, to which the conditions of natural existence and the methods of mundane reason do not

[1] The words are Bucer's. Smyth, op. cit., p. 171.

apply. The solution tended in one direction to encourage the drift of the reforming movement in England towards a pious irrationalism. In this direction it fulfils the work of the terminists, supplanting reason by faith. But it also promoted the Puritan insistence upon the authenticity of spiritual knowledge.

But ancient habits of thought die hard. Amid the clash and flow of religious controversy there was no marked advance towards new philosophical positions. Venerable assumptions were being freely questioned within the practical contexts of ecclesiastical reform, but when the Elizabethan compromise had united the Church the old frame of ideas, qualified it is true by renaissance and by Protestant sentiments, was seen to retain its position in men's minds. The cosmology and metaphysics of the schools provided the essential philosophy of Churchmen and Puritans, scholars, poets, and dramatists. The rupture of the historic body of religious practice generated a variety of sects in England, each of which asserted a special doctrine of organization and worship. The fierce laws against heresy, cruelly enforced by Henry VIII, were relaxed at his death and extreme theological opinions were openly professed. Under Elizabeth the sects grew. Many of them were moved by crude theories of moral action, notably the Anabaptists. Some were more critical, the Presbyterians, Socinians, and Congregationalists. But none of the sects gave birth to theories relating to the order of things that departed in any important point from the accepted forms of thought. The appeal to artless common sense in the controversies over the Eucharist and over other practices of worship promoted no philosophical exploration in England. Two attempts to formulate a comprehensive theology were made by sectarian teachers later in the century; *Sacra Theologia* by Dudley Fenner (1585) and *Armilla Aurea* by W. Perkins (1590). These works cursorily repeat the theological tenets of the historic faith before passing on to reformist declarations concerning the organization of the Church. The intellectual development of Puritanism was restricted by several factors. It was controlled by the practical impulses of the movement. The spirit of the advanced reformers was fixed upon moral fruits, not upon doctrine. In it there lived again the religion of the disciples of Wyclif, the recoil from ceremonial and external performance, the call to inward conviction, the demand for private access to God without the intervention of priests. The bitter struggle between the nonconformists and the bishops, above all between John Whitgift and Thomas Cartwright, rarely touches upon broad philosophical issues. It is taken up with principles of ecclesiastical authority, with details of public worship, and with the interpretation of the liturgy presented by the Anglican church. The leader of the Puritans did not differ from the State church on theological questions. Even the opponents of Cartwright recognized agreement between themselves and him on the fundamental points of doctrine.[1] And as in public policy so in personal matters practical ideals extruded rational activities. Spokesmen of the nonconformists declared that the heart takes precedence over the head. Edward Dering bade Christians shun vain and curious searching of God's mysteries and the attempt to measure things revealed according to our understanding; and Richard Greenham, another Presbyterian teacher, advised the Christian to be prepared to renounce his reason.[2] Further, the Puritans concentrated their studies and reflections upon the Bible and renewed the old claim to find in it an infallible source of truth and a sure guide to conduct. The Bible contained all the truth that it was necessary to know, for this truth had been divinely revealed to men. The Puritan concentration on the Bible to the exclusion of other means of thought was undertaken in a Protestant spirit. The leading reformers from the days of Latimer and Hooper preached the right of individual access to the Word and vehemently repudiated the doctrine that the elucidation of the Scriptures should be left to the masters of theology and the Church. The Bible could be understood by any faithful Christian without aid, and this principle meant that the literal and plain sense of the sacred text was to be followed in preference to the allegorical and tropological senses. We have already quoted Tindale's pronouncement; it is echoed by many writers among the Presbyterians. The principle was soon involved in difficulties, for the simple moral lesson was often not easy to discern, and in practice nonconformist preachers reverted to allegorical modes of exegesis.

[1] A. F. Scott-Pearson, *Thomas Cartwright and Elizabethan Puritanism*, Cambridge, 1925, p. 407.
[2] M. M. Knappen, *Tudor Puritanism*, Chicago, 1939, p. 342.

The radical religious movements of the period were debarred by their intense preoccupation with moral and practical interests from developing the philosophical suggestions that appeared in the early controversies over the Eucharist. In the later part of the century the theoretical differences between the old and new systems of thought had almost disappeared under the virulent conflicts over the problems of authority in the Church. But there is a further influence in English Puritanism that served to imprison the speculative spirit. The first principles of the leading nonconformist groups were supplied by the writings of the continental reformers. In all the more abstract problems of religious philosophy the English Puritans repeated the views of Bucer, Calvin, and Beza, especially the *Institutes of Christian Religion*. The main doctrines were accepted, the doctrines of human depravity, of predestined election, of particular redemption, of effectual calling, of the perseverance of the Saints; and with them there was implicitly accepted the theology upon which they were based. That theology descended from the school of William of Ockham and was indeed the most remarkable issue of the Ockhamist outlook. The Ockhamists, it will be remembered, had taught that the truths of faith pertained to a sphere where human reason is incompetent. The system of beliefs revealed in the Scriptures must be accepted on divine authority. The philosophical basis of this position was the view that the will has primacy over the intellect, and when applied to theology it maintained that God's will is above reason. His will for men is absolute and we cannot by searching understand it. The Calvinist theology is the heir to Thomas Bradwardine. The predestination of the elect depends upon God's grace, upon decisions for which no human reasons could be preferred. It does not rest upon faith or good works, but upon the secret 'counsel of His own will, whereby he extendeth or withholdeth mercy as He pleaseth'.[1]

Hooker in *The Laws of Ecclesiastical Polity* struck hard against the new irrationalism. He attacked the Puritan claim to possess infallible truth in the Bible, and vindicated at length the right of reason in the face of the Puritan distrust of all that is human. He, and to a lesser degree Whitgift and Bancroft,

---

[1] Calvin, *Institutes of Theology*, tr. Beveridge, London, 1845, iii. 21. 5. Cf. *Westminster Confession*, iii. v, and H. Y. Reyburn, *John Calvin*, London, 1914, p. 361.

appealed to reason and history in response to the insistence on the 'warrante of God's worde' for all doctrines. Nevertheless, the stream of Puritan religion and morality mingled with the tide that was flowing from the new learning and endowed the forces of thought with their peculiar inspiration. They added energy to the tendency to turn to simple origins for the truth and to seek reality among primitive elements. 'The water at the fountain head', wrote Hooper, 'is more pure than when it is carried abroad in rotten pipes or stinking ditches', and the sectarians shared the ideals of the conservative reformers in calling upon them to return to 'the chaste and simple purity' of the Apostolic age. It is the standard of Bishop Jewel in the celebrated *Apology* (1562) no less than Cartwright in the *Admonition to Parliament* (1572). There was considerable difference of opinion relating to the practice of the primitive Church, but the impulse of thought was similar throughout the parties. And in its gospel of sober morality and of independent common sense Puritanism helped to advance the march towards an unsophisticated empiricism, and to encourage the widespread revolt against the abstract logic of the schools. The principle of the priesthood of all believers promoted independence of judgement, but it also promoted naïvety. The new generation of Biblical Christians helped to establish the habit of freedom of thought and the habit could not stop at questions of religious practice. Puritanism was an undercurrent in the intellectual forces of the time and penetrated philosophy at the universities, especially at Cambridge where Emmanuel College was founded in 1584 to promote the reformed creed. But in general the sectarians were not active in intellectual fields. In a play of the period the Puritan is held up as a dullard who can make little of philosophy.[1]

The intellectual life of the universities was closely knit with the theology of the Church, and the assaults of the Government upon ecclesiastical jurisdiction and privileges had shaken the schools to their foundations. The official representatives of Oxford and Cambridge yielded easily to the demands of the Crown in the question of the Pope's sovereignty over the Church in England, but there was bitter dissatisfaction in the colleges and sharp divisions broke out. The suppression of the religious

[1] *The Pilgrimage to Parnassus*, ed. W. Macray, Oxford, 1886, p. 10.

houses removed much of the opposition to reform. It also encouraged the progress of the new learning with which the reform was now associated. And the abolition of the monastic schools altered the character of the undergraduate population. The monastic schools had been free. Laymen who could afford the rising cost of university life began to enter the universities, and new secular studies, especially the study of the civil law, came into demand. A number of colleges that depended on the monasteries disappeared. The popular emotion directed against the old system of thought is symbolized by the burning of the books at the universities and monasteries. Scores of great libraries were ransacked and piles of manuscripts were thrown into the flames. They included the works of the philosophers and theologians, as well as illuminated missals and books of devotion. At Oxford Duke Humphrey's collection was pillaged and cart-loads of manuscripts were burnt in the market-place. The sudden swing towards historic Catholicism and conservative philosophy under Mary did not check the new ecclesiastical movement. For a few years the old statutes were restored at the universities, and with the Mass there reappeared the old metaphysical principles. Reformist scholars fled to Zurich and other Protestant centres. Persecution and burnings followed; Latimer, Ridley, and Cranmer perished at Oxford where Spanish friars taught and disputed. But in 1558 Mary died. After a period of hesitation the Government of Elizabeth declared itself in favour of the principles of reform. But there was no imposition of doctrine until 1570 and this declaration was followed by harsh proceedings against the Roman Catholics on the one side and the nonconformist sects, which had multiplied in variety and numbers, on the other. But the controversies rarely rose to philosophical levels. They were concerned with vestments, the use of organs in churches, the number of holy days and, what was of far greater practical importance, the validity of the episcopate; and the basis of the conflict was the relation of the political authority to the Church.

Yet the ecclesiastical convulsion profoundly affected the old rational outlook on experience. Amid the groups of extreme reformers it promoted two tendencies that appear in many quarters of reflection. It promoted the tendency to rely upon simple and unsophisticated criteria of truth in contrast to the metaphysics of the schools; and it encouraged a vein of implicit faith that possessed an historical affinity with the Scotists and Ockhamists of the fourteenth century.

III

So far we have glanced at sentiments spreading from scholarship and from religious reform that obliquely influenced the life of thought. Let us now turn from these undercurrents to the broad surface of ideas. The voices that arrest attention are not those of divines in this secular age. They are the voices of a literature of unparalleled exuberance. The Elizabethans explore with overflowing passion the universe of human sensibility. Yet the general beliefs that the poets and dramatists assume are the beliefs of the medieval schools. For Shakespeare and Sir Walter Raleigh, for Marlowe, Spenser, and Sir Philip Sidney, the frame of ancient conceptions still stood. The natural scene is the language of the Deity. The physical universe and all life and mind and society reveal the same fundamental order, a system of hierarchies, a chain of being. The old cosmology is repeated. The earth abides at the centre of the spheres and from the lunar region to the *primum mobile* the spheres preserve the Ptolemaic order. All the features of the physics of the thirteenth century are accepted, the four elements, the compounds, the sensitive, vegetable, and rational grades of being. The rhetoricians and poets take for granted the Aristotelian principles of existence, form and act, potency and matter. Every created thing looks towards the perfection of its nature, the fulfilment of its specific form. The species are qualitatively different from one another. They are defined by the essences that uniquely characterize their class. The belief that all things possess essential natures that manifest special purposes in the system of the universe formed the metaphysical basis of the view, frequently expressed in Elizabethan thought, that every class of things and persons has its own function to perform. To preserve the hierarchy of duties and services in society is an aspect of the law that rules all nature.[1] And other aspects of the Aristotelian

---

[1] The classic pronouncement of the theory is the speech of Ulysses in *Troilus and Cressida* beginning:

> 'The heavens themselves, the planets, and this centre,
> Observe degree, priority, and place.'

The rational order is traced through the heavens, society, the elements,

philosophy that we have noticed in considering the thought of the thirteenth century are present. The view that all things are composed in their species and genera of permanent and distinct ideal characters is associated with the logic of syllogistic demonstration. The category of substance still governs the typical form of inquiry. The method seeks the essences of things by definition, and the search for essences is expressed in the syllogistic process. The art of reasoning for the products of the Elizabethan grammar schools and universities is what it was for the university teachers four hundred years earlier, a matter of bringing cases under a definition that expresses the real quality of a thing; it is a process of qualitative subsumption and views the business of knowledge as the relating of attributes to subjects. The universe is an infinite plurality of substances and the work of thought consists in distinguishing the various modes by which substances are qualified. These principles were perpetuated not only by commentaries and treatises but by epitomes of the doctrines of the schools and by popular handbooks of Aristotelian logic. In them the young student, who might now be the son of a merchant seeking culture for himself outside the universities, was instructed that 'when we go about to expound any matter, first we must begin with the definition to know the very nature of the thing'.[1] The very nature of anything is reached by formal classification of the thing in its kind. There are two modes of substances, singular things and general entities, but first substances are the fundamental type. They are the self-sufficient basis of the accidents and properties that are, with more or less relevance, attached to them and by which their presence is indicated to our senses. For in themselves substances cannot be perceived.

But for the great moralists and playwrights the position of man in the order of things is the central interest. Their treatment of man rests upon the psychology of the thirteenth century. Man resides in the centre of things, including the lower forms of inanimate, vegetative, and sensitive or animal being on the one side, and touching the higher forms, intellectual and angelic, on the other. Analogies between microcosm and macrocosm

morality, and psychology. See T. Spencer, *Shakespeare and the Nature of Man*, Cambridge, 1943, p. 21.

[1] T. Wilson, *The Rule of Reason*, 1551.

throng the literature of the period. And the prevailing view of knowledge is Aristotelian. By his reason man extracts the essences from the deliverances of the senses and seeks to contemplate the forms.

All these elements of the medieval phase of thought control the perspective of the Elizabethan poets.[1] There were differences of emphasis and some of those that had arisen during the renaissance of classical literature were substantial. And, as we shall see, there were profound doubts and forebodings regarding the historic panorama of reality and it is the presence of these skeleton misgivings that cast a poignant and a tragic pall over this final phase of the old philosophy. But no comprehensive alternative way of belief was offered. Let us turn from the surpassing splendour and bombast of the poets to some more sober and academic utterances of the conservative metaphysics.

A generously eclectic expression of traditional theories of knowledge was put forward in Everard Digby's *Theoria Analytica* (1579). Digby was senior fellow of St. John's College, Cambridge, and the leading authority on logic in the University. It is probable that the youthful Francis Bacon attended his lectures. He was deprived of his fellowship by Lord Burghley under suspicion of papist leanings. The *Theoria Analytica* finds place for the Thomist–Aristotelian view of sensory knowledge, the Augustinian way of ideas, and the path of divine illumination. There are three worlds, the world of sense, the world of intellect, the world of faith. The key that opens the first world to our understanding is the method of assembling universals from particulars. The intermediate world is approached by starting from universals and seeking the forms that are unmixed with things by the instrument of the most perfect intellectual reflection. The world of divinity is attained by submission of the human mind to the light of holiness, and the key of this illumination is faith.[2] In developing this threefold philosophy Digby draws upon a mass of ancient doctrine; Aristotle, St. Thomas, Duns Scotus, are confusedly amalgamated with Neo-Platonism, the Pseudo-Dionysius, and the Cabbala. Some of

---

[1] The reliance of the dramatists and especially of Shakespeare upon the scholastic philosophy of nature and man has been amply illustrated in recent works, such as E. W. Tillyard, *The Elizabethan World Picture*; T. Spencer, *Shakespeare and the Nature of Man*; H. Craig, *The Enchanted Glass*.

[2] Digby, *Theoria Analytica*, London, 1579, p. 130.

this learning is borrowed from *De arte cabbalistica* of J. Reuchlin, some from *De occulta philosophia* of Cornelius Agrippa.

The greatest systematic thinker of his age in England, Richard Hooker, shaped his massive inquiries much more in conformity with the old intellectual forms than did the Cambridge philosopher. Indeed, he was obliged to defend himself for his use of 'the distinctions and helps of the schools'.[1] He opens his consideration of the laws that should govern the Church of England with a review of the fundamental laws of things. In these introductory sections of the *Laws of Ecclesiastical Polity* (1594) the foundations of the moral, political, and ecclesiastical doctrine of the remaining seven books are set down. The familiar design of ideas at once appears; in fact the argument is clearly indebted to the *Summa Theologica* of Aquinas. The operations of all things are directed to ends. 'That which doth assign unto each thing the kind, that which doth moderate the force and power, that which doth appoint the form and measure of working, the same we term a Law.' Law is defined in terms of genus, of inward controlling influence, of end. Further, all things depend upon a First Cause in whose working 'Counsel is used, Reason followed, a way observed'. The order in the universe is rational because regularity and constancy are expressions of purpose. Hooker will not allow that the laws of things are the arbitrary manifestations of God's will. The issue raised by Duns Scotus and pointedly developed by Ockham and the nominalists was still alive among scholars. It was maintained by some clerical philosophers that the divine will is independent of and prior to reason, not merely to any reason that human thought can assign to its workings in the created universe, but to reason altogether. The divine ordering of the world is to be accepted without attempting to pry too closely into the secrets of nature. The attitude was strongly advocated, as we have seen. Hooker stands firmly on the belief that reason is always present with God's will, for all things are ordered to good purpose, though we cannot always trace the reason of events. Next, God's counsel is eternal. But there are several orders of His eternal law. Lowest in place is the law of inanimate nature under which the heavens and the elements keep the law of their kind; the obedience of created things to their natures is the stay

---

[1] Hooker, *Works*, Oxford, 1880, iii. 586; *Answer to Travers*.

of the whole world. Yet things natural often show defects, and the true original cause of these swervings is the divine malediction laid upon man for his sin, according to the revelation of God to the Church. The inward forms of things preserve them in their kinds and operations, and the forms are the work of divine providence. Natural things tend not only to their own perfections, they serve also one another's good and the good of the whole.

Far above the region of natural law is the realm of heavenly and divine creatures, the angels. They are intellectual, immaterial, dwelling for ever in celestial joy and adoration. Passing by Hooker's account of the 'inhabitants of those sacred palaces' and of their fallen brethren, the wicked spirits, let us turn to his view of man. Here the embracing principles that have been propounded are applied to human nature. God alone is; all other beings 'are somewhat in possibility which as yet they are not in act'. Possibility is an appetite or desire for greater perfection, and this desire appears most fully in man. All things seek the continuance of their being and the excellency of those operations that belong to their kind; in man these natural desires are manifested in the endeavour after truth and virtue to the end that he may become united with God. In the pursuit of his perfection man's freewill is directed by reason, and in following the law of reason he resembles in his voluntary actions the involuntary workings of nature. Reason discovers the main duties of man, those owed to God and those owed to men, and it discovers them without the help of revelation. The law of reason is the law of nature and for man to transgress the law of his nature provokes harm comparable to the ruin brought about by the failure of the heavenly bodies to perform their allotted work. Accordingly religion and virtue are not matters of opinion but 'nature itself teacheth laws and statutes to live by'.[1] Hooker then proceeds to expound the laws of societies and states that spring from the general laws of nature. The tones of the classical period of scholastic thought are evident in the noble passage of which we have given a summary. The finalism, the hierarchy of being, the orders of genera and species, the implicit forms, the association of natural aberration with the primal sin, all are there. And other notes are there to which we must revert.

[1] *Eccles. Pol.* i, ii–x.

The extent to which philosophical minds were still engrossed by the old inquiries is illustrated in the writings of John Case, who taught philosophy at Oxford at the end of the century. For him Aristotle stands 'omnium philosophorum facile princeps'. His *Lapis Philosophicum*, published in 1599, is a detailed commentary on the *Physics*. There is no hint of serious criticism of any item of the Aristotelian principles, except in relation to the old difference over the question of the creation of the world; and even here Case maintains the ultimate orthodoxy of Aristotle's opinions. For the rest, all the characteristics of the philosophy of the schoolmen are unfolded. The theological motives govern the investigation; the value of natural philosophy is affirmed to lie in the mind's ascent from second causes to the first cause. The principles of nature are interpreted teleologically; the leading cause is the final cause; and the grades of being crowned by man are faithfully reported. The old categories of being, matter and form, potency and act, are expounded at length; and there is a detailed discussion of the ancient conception of movement. Many of the questions raised for debate swing us back to the disputations of Peckham's day. 'Was primary matter created?' 'Is there matter in all natural things?' 'Is matter devoid of all forms?' 'Is form derived from the potency of matter?' A passage on the nature of universals illustrates the old context of ideas at Oxford in the last few years of the sixteenth century. There are four types of universals. There are first dialectic or logical universals; and of these there are two kinds, concepts of genera and concepts of individuals. The second type of universals is mathematical. These are mental forms or pure concepts, drawn from pre-existing realities and applied to existences. Metaphysical universals, the third type, are either things in their pure and divine state or the ideas of them in the mind, such as the idea of God and of all simple and absolute essences that are called the ultimate abstractions. Last, there are physical universals, namely, natural things and their principles, causes and elements, such as matter, form and the complex object, and all kinds of being universally found that result from act and potency by motion.[1]

The investigation of the theories of Aristotle is laboriously

[1] John Case, *Lapis philosophicum*, Oxford, 1599, i. 1, pp. 31–2.

thorough in the tradition of scholastic philosophy and it searches deeply metaphysical ideas. But Case and the Oxford scholars had little new to say. There is no hint of the recent developments in astronomy in the *Lapis philosophicum*, and little reference to any contemporary discussion. Machiavelli appears among the ancient atheists, and the foolish innovations of Ramus relating to the Aristotelian principles of being are contemptuously dismissed.[1] The only interests of the day that figure prominently are those concerned with the activities of the alchemists and there is a lively section on the virtues of the philosophers' stone. By means of it Sir Richard Kelly has succeeded in making pure gold, not to mention Haly, Guido, Agrippa, and Roger Bacon in former days.[2]

In short, scholarly men continued to look upon reality through the casements of the schools. A more independent mind was manifest at Cambridge, which was a stronghold, as we shall notice, of Ramist teaching. But the scholastic ring of conceptions was deeply rooted in the curricula of the Grammar Schools, in which pupils worked through the trivium, grammar, rhetoric, and logic, and competed with other schools in disputations. Such, no doubt, was the diet at the King's Free Grammar School at Stratford-on-Avon, and recollections of school-boy drill in the tropes and figures of rhetoric and in the formal distinctions and ripostes of logic appear in the Plays.[3] And the well-worn courses of the trivium and the quadrivium continued to provide mental training at the universities. The statutes of 1565 imposed the old subjects on Oxford. For the bachelor's degree two terms were to be devoted to grammar, four to rhetoric, five to logic or dialectic, three to arithmetic, and two to music. For the master's degree three years were to be given to geometry, astronomy, natural philosophy, moral philosophy, and metaphysics.[4] The text-books in these subjects were the writings of the ancients, Ptolemy on astronomy, Strabo and Pliny on geography; there is no contact with Copernicus, Columbus, and Vasco da Gama. And in philosophy the statutes of 1586 banned from the schools questions 'disagreeing from the

---

[1] Op. cit., *Prolegomena*, p. 16; i. 2, p. 47.   [2] Ib. ii. 1, p. 181.

[3] T. W. Baldwin, *Small Latine and Lesser Greeke*, 2 vols., Urbana, U.S.A., 1945.

[4] C. E. Mallet, *History of the University of Oxford*, 1924, ii. 120.

ancient and true philosophy'. The injunction was levelled against the new logicians who disparaged the authority of Aristotle.

For the most obvious commotion in the mental history of these years was the bitter dispute between the Ramists and the more orthodox logicians. The debate is a sign of the preoccupation of thoughtful men with problems of method; it reveals the sense of dissatisfaction with the scholastic approach, and the yearning for a new philosophy. But the innovations of the followers of Ramus exhibit the quality of thought that now offered to reform philosophy. Its quality is distinguished by sweeping intemperance of judgement, superficial criticism of the logic of Aristotle, and a narrowly oratorical view of the art of reflection. The ruling motive of logical study had once more become conspicuously rhetorical. In the middle of the century the most notable of a series of text-books on logic in English was published. This was Sir Thomas Wilson's *Rule of Reason* (1551). It was followed by Ralph Lever's *Arte of Reason* (1573), Blunderville's *Art of Logic* (1599), and other handbooks. These popular guides were closely associated with rhetorical skill. Logic is viewed as the art of effective discussion, and its rules are applied to the traditional divisions, the theses and antitheses, the tropes and figures of rhetoric. This training is visible everywhere in the Elizabethan literature, in the conversation of Shakespeare's clowns, for example.[1] The motive of this rhetorical logic is practical. Wilson dwells on the profitable virtue of a training in formal logic. It is true that he recommends the study on the ground that it advances the knowledge of God and all his heavenly works, but its chief value is in worldly affairs. Its purpose was forensic rather than philosophical.

In the earlier period of the century the sentiments that inspired scholarly inquiry were predominantly moral. Philosophical conceptions were explored in relation to the conduct of life. The penetrating effort to clarify ideas that distinguishes the thought of men in the thirteenth and fourteenth centuries is replaced by more immediate aims, and, as we have observed, the great humanists express impatience with logical subtlety and even hatred of such pursuits. A pupil of William Temple at

[1] H. Craig, *The Enchanted Glass*, Oxford, 1936, Chapter vii.

Cambridge testifies in the later period at which we have now arrived that he laboured to fit his pupils for the true use of that art (that is to say, logic), rather than for vain and idle speculations. The true use of the art was now persuasion and eloquence.

Any voice that offered to reform logic, especially when the reform moved towards practical simplicity, was sure of a hearing. An exciting figure had appeared at the University of Paris who drew the eyes of scholars in every quarter of the continent. Ramus had experienced a revulsion against the barren formalities of scholastic disputations. He startled the learned world by unmeasured abuse of Aristotle and thrilled the younger generation of students by proposals for a new method of logic. The new method of the *Dialecticae Institutiones* and other works attempted to adapt the traditional logic to the exigencies of practical life. In effect it sought to fit formal logic to the art of rhetoric. But Ramus argued that in order to observe the precepts of good reasoning it is necessary to examine the practice of the intellectual élite among men, and he proceeded to seek his models, not among the philosophers, but among the poets and orators of antiquity. The results of his inquiries into the methods of these masters of thought are not strikingly different from the forms of the accepted logic. That which emerges is the old logic with a renewed emphasis upon the deductive and syllogistic method, with a readjustment of the divisions of the subject in accordance with the parts of rhetoric, and with a show of rules designed to simplify the Aristotelian scheme.[1] It is in the last aspect that the chief merit of the Ramist reform dwells. We have seen that the invasion of the schools by nominalism and terminism had imposed upon philosophical study a mass of linguistic distinctions and subtleties that composed the body of the *Parva Logicalia*. These were the inquiries against which the literary conscience of the time revolted and the labours of Ramus signally promoted the general movement towards a plainer and more effective view of rational method. 'Ça a été toute mon estude,' he exclaimed, 'd'oster du chemin des arts libéraux les épines, les caillous, et tous empeschements et retardements des esprits, de faire la voye plaine et droite,

[1] Ch. Waddington, *Pierre de la Ramée, sa vie, ses écrits et ses opinions*, Paris, 1855.

pour pouvenir plus aisément non seulement à l'intelligence, mais à la practique et à l'usage des arts libéraux.'[1]

Such a programme was well calculated to attract progressive minds in England, who were fatigued by the artificial exercises of the schools. On all sides protests were audible against the lifeless expositions of the Aristotelian texts. Ramist logic was seized upon at Cambridge. Gabriel Harvey was among its early adherents, but its leading champion was William Temple, Fellow of King's College. In subsequent years he was secretary to Sir Philip Sidney, who favoured the teaching of Ramus; later he became attached to the Earl of Essex. This connexion damaged his fortunes, but in 1609 he was appointed Provost of Trinity College, Dublin, a position that he held until his death in 1627. His main opponent in the battle of logical method was Everard Digby, author of the *Theoria Analytica*.

The champion of the new way hurls abuse against Aristotle and the medieval masters, Aquinas, Scotus, Aegidius, and the rest, in the manner of his master, Ramus. The only rational criterion is nature. 'The Aristotelians have failed to grasp the fact that dialectic like other arts is derived from the observation of nature and therefore it must not be constructed on a plan that moves away from nature.'[2] But the appeal to nature leads merely to the discarding of much of the matter of the traditional logic, the predicables and predicaments, the opposition and contradiction of propositions, the conversion and reduction of syllogisms, and all the subtleties of the figures. The chief point of attack is Digby's double method of logical inquiry. He had expounded a twofold way of seeking truth, one proceeding from the sensory particulars to universal statements, the other descending from universal propositions to special cases. The former way is described as the way of synthesis, the latter as the way of analysis. In the former he rested upon the Aristotelian account of induction, in the latter he depended upon the process of syllogistic reasoning. Temple and the Ramists will have nothing to do with the first way. They are interested rather in the art of persuasion and exposition than in the art of discover-

---

[1] *Remonstrance faite au Conseil privé*, 1567. Cf. G. Sortais, *La Philosophie moderne*, Paris, 1920, p. 30.

[2] W. Temple, *Francisci Mildapetti Navarreni ad Everardum Digbeium Anglum admonitio de unica Rami methodo rejectis caeteris retinenda*, London, 1580, p. 4.

ing truth. Temple is fond of saying that logic can better be learnt from the speeches of Cicero than from the *Organon*. The insistence of the new logicians upon the one method of thinking, that from the general to the particular, is not an insistence upon the deductive or syllogistic mode of argument in preference to the inductive mode. The single way advocated by the Ramists is rather the movement of thought from what is vague to what is more precise, a movement that is manifest in many passages in literature where the author is attempting to develop and illustrate the principle he upholds. The interesting feature of Temple's eloquent diatribes against Digby is his refusal to perceive any form of reasoning in the inductive process. A collection of instances merely illustrates a rule already known, it cannot prove it.

The immense popularity of Ramist logic shows once more the withdrawal of interest from fundamental questions. Dialectic is a literary art; it is the 'art of discussing well'. But this drift of interest riveted a fresh array of formal rules upon thought, drawn from the regulations of rhetoric.

IV

The old philosophy of nature and of man was now accompanied by many revivals of unorthodox speculation. The renewed study of the ancient classics of literature and the opposition to Roman Catholicism awoke to life a number of theories that blended or competed with the Aristotelian corpus of beliefs. The Elizabethan mind made little attempt to fashion a patient synthesis of its intellectual gains. Fragments of pre-Socratic philosophy, of Plato and Plotinus, of Cicero and Seneca, are mixed incongruously with the orthodox outlook, and the men who reject or improve upon the logic of Aristotle fail to propose any important substitute for his view of knowledge. Thoughtful persons were poignantly conscious of the diversity of creeds, but no one in England undertook a resolute investigation of principles, and the mass of new revolutionary material drove many towards scepticism or towards a blind faith in revealed truth.

Platonic doctrines were received from the Italian scholars, and Spenser, Drayton, and other poets and dramatists express the contemporary study of the *Timaeus* and the *Phaedrus*. The vision of a world of intelligible forms, a realm of absolute truth and beauty of which the mundane world is an inferior copy, mixes in their verse with the Aristotelian cosmology. And the imagery of the *Timaeus* is once more blended with the doctrines of Neo-Platonism. The passing domain of sense is a shadow of the realm of Intelligence. What exists in this world exists in archetypal form in the sublime sphere; the earth, the animals and birds, the sea, and all inanimate things live yonder as well as here, and the soul of the world strives to return to the One from which it draws its life.

But this Platonic and Neo-Platonic strain mingled with another and more emotional tradition. It mingled with the visions of the hermetic philosophy. The mysterious doctrines comprised in this loose system had passed into England from Italy early in the century, the main influence proceeding from the writings of Ficino and Pico di Mirandola. Ficino had translated into Latin the corpus of hermetic writings in 1471 and twenty-two editions of the book appeared before the middle of the seventeenth century. Pico had enthusiastically proclaimed the mysteries of the Jewish Cabbala and they were eagerly studied in England in association with the hermetic books. We have seen that Doget had quoted Ficino's translation of one of the hermetic books, the *Poimander*; the title is derived from an Egyptian word. Other powerful influences that excited deep interest in the occult philosophy were the *De arte cabbalistica* of Johann Reuchlin and the *De occulta philosophia* of Cornelius Agrippa. We have remarked that portions of this body of notions had been transmitted to the scholarly consciousness by the Arabian Neo-Platonism of the twelfth century. There were two impulses that had readily responded throughout the later ages of scholasticism to the fascination of these strange doctrines. On the one part the mystical movement that became prominent in the fourteenth and fifteenth centuries, revolting from the minute logic of the schools, often found intellectual solace in the hermetic lore. On the other, the principles and the art of the natural philosophers, the astrologers, alchemists, and physicians, were suffused with the magical conceptions of the ancient wisdom. During the renaissance of learning the occult philosophy was everywhere revived.

We have indicated that there were two sources of this esoteric

tradition, the Hermetica and the Cabbala. The hermetic
doctrines had passed down the ages from the third century
when a collection of writings had issued from Egypt and spread
over the Roman world. In these writings there was gathered
a fanciful synthesis of Platonism, Neo-Platonism, Stoic theory,
Judaic allegory, and oriental mythology. They were attributed
to Hermes Trismegistus, thrice-greatest Hermes, who was
believed to have been a sage living in the time of Moses to whom
profound revelations had been vouchsafed. It was supposed that
Plato had derived his cosmological and theological views from
Hermes. The Greek writings treat in rhapsodical terms of the
nature of God, the origins of the world, the creation of man, and
the mystical knowledge of divine reality. Widely different
systems of ideas are confused in the several books, Platonic,
Stoic, and Mosaic, and it is a gauge of the critical sense of the
sixteenth century that this medley of doctrines was assumed
to comprise a coherent scheme of teaching issuing from the
mind of a single great philosopher. The other channel of occult
theory was even more extravagant. The Cabbala was a body
of beliefs that purported to have descended from the Jewish
prophets. It had been transmitted through the Hellenistic
Jews to later periods and appeared in the Jewish philosophy of
the thirteenth century. In these doctrines primitive Judaic
speculations are prominent, but they are mixed with Stoic and
Neo-Platonic principles. A closer description of the theories
that preside over the imaginative literature of the sixteenth and
seventeenth centuries in England would demand a full account
of the Cabbalistic theosophy. It is present in Spenser and
Raleigh, in Donne and Vaughan, and scholars like Browne and
Burton are acquainted with it. It is not necessary here to penetrate into the labyrinth of its mysteries. It will be sufficient to
mention the scheme of emanations that occupy a conspicuous
feature of the cosmology. From the supreme God there descend
ten sephiroth or intelligences, like rays from the sun. Each of
these possesses a mystic name and symbol, and they are elabo-
rately divided and subdivided in a complex design of triads,
each section performing its function in the order of the universe.
The sephiroth are moments in the being of God. There are four
grades of world, the material world being the lowest. In it there
dwell innumerable spirits, elemental and aerial forms, bene-

ficent, mischievous, and devilish. Above the earthly order reigns the archetypal and universal man, the cosmic Adam, who is composed of a union of the sephiroth. Into the intricate symbolism of male and female principles, the marriage of the sephiroth, it is not necessary to enter.

From the more esoteric convolutions of this hermetic and cabbalist lore let us turn to consider the ideas that especially bear upon the speculations of the time. First there coursed into discussion from the occult philosophy the belief in the fundamental unity of all being. All the multifarious substances and shapes of things on the earth and in the heavens are in principle one. The hidden God is present everywhere; He is in all things, from stars to stones. The cosmos is an organic being. It is a living creature. There are subordinate souls within the cosmic soul; there is an earth soul, and the world is often spoken of as an animal. Further, all that is in the world is living, and even minerals possess a form of life. No part of the whole dies; upon material disintegration the soul of any substance passes into another substance. All natural things and events are related by subtle ties to their similars; an active web of unseen forces unites all points of the universe. Finally, man holds a cardinal place in the scheme of things. He is a microcosm of the cosmos, combining many spheres of being within himself. The cabbalists worked out in minute detail a plan of correspondences between the parts of the human body and the spheres of nature.

These pantheistic and panpsychic doctrines coalesce in the literature of the sixteenth century with Italian Neo-Platonism. They appear in the poems of Spenser, together with more Platonic conceptions. There is evidence for the existence of a School of Night, a coterie of young noblemen and writers headed by Sir Walter Raleigh, which devoted attention, among other matters, to the hermetic theories.[1] The group included Marlowe, Chapman, and Matthew Royden. Marlowe and Chapman employ occult symbolism and ideas in their verse and Raleigh cites Hermes Trismegistus. But the chief application of this body of beliefs was astrology.

In fact the occult assemblage of ideas appeared most prominently in the activities of the natural investigators. Physical

---

[1] M. C. Bradbrook, *The School of Night*, Cambridge, 1936, p. 70.

researches and medical practice rested upon the theories of universal life, of secret sympathies and antipathies, of correspondence between the celestial bodies and the creatures of the earth. The science of nature according to this vitalist tradition received powerful impulse from the writings of Paracelsus, which were avidly studied in England by scholars interested in the secrets of nature. His writings are pervaded with the belief in the fundamental relation of man to the whole of nature, and he unfolds a complicated scheme of signatures in which every part of man is shown to have affinity with the outer world. The doctrine of the active principles in all material things, especially in metals and fluids, is enlarged upon, and the hermetic belief in secret attractions and repulsions is supported by a few original observations. Paracelsus excited interest by proposing a new scheme of elements; the basic elements in things are sulphur, salt, and mercury, and health and disease depend upon the proper combination of these mystic ingredients.[1] But he also insisted that a physician cannot understand or cure any disease without knowledge of the stars.

There were three great secrets that the disciples of Paracelsus in England were fervently pursuing, the transmutation of metals, especially the transmutation of the baser metals into gold, the elixir of life, and the philosophers' stone, the key to all power over nature. The theory of alchemy descended partly from the scholastic view of matter, partly from the Arabian and occult cosmology which, as we have seen, was vigorously revived in the sixteenth century. The teaching of the schools showed that all substances were modifications of primary matter. By removing by means of fire or chemical agents the superimposed substances the alchemists sought to obtain the primary matter of which all things are made, and from it to compose gold or any other substance. On the other hand, the cabbalistic and hermetic doctrines led to the search for the conjunctions of things that would awake the sleeping life in the depths of nature. The alchemists, believing in the unifying soul of things, experimented with chemical contraries and likenesses with the aim of setting free the harmonious and creative powers latent in the matter of the earth.

The principle of astrology had been established in the minds

[1] The same doctrine of elements had been put forward by Roger Bacon.

of natural philosophers since the dawn of thought in England. They had been fortified by the Arabian science of the thirteenth century and persisted throughout the ages of Chaucer and of Malory. But the sixteenth century was the golden period of the science. A diligent industry of horoscopes and prognostications sprang up, literature was studded with references to the stars and the zodiac, and enlightened men at the court and in the universities consulted the astrologers and discussed the influence of Leo or Sagittarius upon public events. Elizabeth appointed an astrologer to her court and frequently took counsel with him. Astrology formed part of the training of a physician and was included in the course for a bachelor of arts. But there was a dangerous side to the art and a number of books were published in condemnation of it. The gravest arguments against it were theological. Philip Stubbes in his *Anatomy of Abuses* (1583), William Fulke in a book *Against the useless predictions of Nostradamus, Cunningham, Lowe, Hill, Vaughan and all the others* (1560), and John Chamber in his *Treatise against Judicial Astrologie* (1601), brought two main arguments against the astrologers. The art encouraged intercourse with devils and it denied man's free will. Several practitioners were summoned for sorcery and black magic. Yet able scholars believed in astrology, for they accepted the theory of nature upon which it was based. The theory included, as we have seen, the view that every feature in the universe is mirrored in its counterpart, and that as Tycho Brahe put it 'the universe is woven together by mysterious connecting threads which the contemplation of the stars or of the elements of nature might unravel, and thereby lift the veil of the future'.[1] The theory also embraced the old belief in the divinity of the planets. The charges of the critics were answered in detail and the academical astrologers indignantly distinguished themselves from the quacks of the street who mixed 'magic' potions and told horoscopes for an angel. The writings of the celebrated Dr. John Dee portray the exalted enthusiasm of the astrologers, and also a sense of the alarming dangers of these investigations.

'And fore as much as for many yeres, in many places, far and nere, in

---

[1] Quoted by C. Camden, 'Astrology in Shakespeare's Day', *Isis*, vol. xix (1933), p. 53. This article gives much information relating to the debate over astrology and cites numerous astrological references in the plays of the period.

many bokes and sundry languages, I have wrought and studyed, and
with sundry men conferred, and with my own reasonable discourse
laboured, whereby to find or get some ynkling, glimpse or beame, of
such the aforesaid radicall truthes: ... And having allways a great
regards and care to beware of the filthy abuse of such as willingly
and wittingly did invocate and consult (in divers sorte) spirituall
creatures of the damned sort: Angels of darknes, forgers and patrons
of lies and untruths; I did fly to thee by harty prayer, full oft and
in sundry manners: sometimes crying unto thee, *Mittas lucem tuam
et veritatem.*'[1]

In his early *Propaedeumata Aphoristica* Dee unfolds the philosophy of astrology. He maintains that everything in nature
radiates virtue to every other thing. The invisible rays of the
planets influence human character and the course of events.
The sign that stands for the planet Mercury is a mystical
representation of all truth, pregnant with occult significance.
Innumerable phenomena, figures, lights, sounds, birds, beasts,
and precious stones are attributed to the powers of the celestial
bodies. And the old authorities that had governed natural
knowledge at the opening of our history, Galen, Dioscorides,
Pliny, are once again searched for information on the magical
virtues of metals and plants. The emerald disposes the bearer
to chastity, the jazule wards off melancholy.

Dee wrote not only on astrology and alchemy but also on
logic, mathematics, optics, navigation, and history. The
pursuit of natural philosophy was associated with occult investigations and with literary scholarship. Observation and experiment of natural processes were largely undertaken in connexion
with the search for transmutation of substances or for reading
horoscopes. But the main sources for facts and theory were
the written or printed works of the ancient authorities, Aristotle,
Theophrastus, Dioscorides, Pliny. An overwhelming example
of this literary mode of thinking is displayed in the last hours
of the phase in Burton's *Anatomy of Melancholy* (1621). In
order to decide a problem of disease or of metaphysics he
assembles an encyclopaedia of quotations on all sides, expressing
no opinion himself. On natural questions the Greek and Roman
texts were still indiscriminately revered. In 1559 a young
Oxford physician narrowly escaped punishment for venturing

---

[1] C. F. Smith, *John Dee*, London, 1909, p. 84.

to ascribe errors to Galen. An eminent historian of our own day considers that in some respects inquirers of the sixteenth century were less disposed to scientific scepticism than the schoolmen of the thirteenth, and that none of them surpassed Albert the Great in observation and descriptive power.[1] Yet a thin stream of original inquiry runs through the time. Persons interested in scholarly and philosophical questions had the habit of meeting together for discussion; a notable example is the circle that used to gather at the house of Dr. William Gilbert on St. Peter's Hill, London. Schemes for searching out the riddles of nature were promulgated. The field in which empirical methods were most usefully applied was that of the physician. In Italy had appeared Vesalius whose lectures and writings on the human body announced anatomical details discovered by careful dissections and observations. John Caius of Cambridge studied under Vesalius and in 1552 produced a book on the sweating sickness in England that departs strikingly from the old animistic notions. Other university doctors of medicine, especially at Cambridge, advanced the knowledge of anatomy.[2] Meanwhile naturalists were visiting Gesner at Zurich and bringing back new stores of zoological information and a zest for facts. Thomas Penny (d. 1588) is the most remarkable of these collectors. If to these activities are added the work of the compilers of herbals, men such as William Turner (d. 1568) and John Gerard (d. 1612), the stirring of a fresh approach to the world of nature is evident. A widening curiosity over the marvels of nature is evinced by the popularity of outlines of knowledge such as John Maplet's *A Greene Forest, wherein may be seene the soveraigne virtues of all kinde of stones and metals; next of plants as of herbes, trees and shrubs; lastly of brute beests, fowls, creeping wormes and serpents, and that alphabetically.* It was published in 1567.

But no important step in natural philosophy was taken until the publication of Gilbert's work *On the Magnet* in 1600. Few thinkers conceived that anything new might be discovered. The revolutionary ideas in astronomy that had been put forward abroad were little regarded in England. In *De revolu-*

---

[1] L. Thorndike, *History of Magic and Experimental Science*, v. 278.
[2] See the list in R. Gunther, *Early Science in Cambridge*, and *Early Science in Oxford*.

tionibus (1543) Copernicus, a Pole who taught in Italy, had proposed a new system of the heavens wherein the earth and planets turned round the sun and the earth rotated on its own axis. This proposal would have profoundly shocked men if it had been regarded as anything more than a speculative hypothesis, for, as we have seen, the established doctrine in which the earth stood at the centre of the created universe was connected by many strands with the entire rational and spiritual outlook on experience. But Copernicus himself thought there was nothing unorthodox in his conception, and the few English astronomers who mention it in the sixteenth century do so without expressions of alarm. Robert Recorde passes it by with a brief note of disapproval. Thomas Digges, writing in 1573, is the first mathematician to advocate the theory, and it was accepted by Gilbert. By the time of the publication of *De Magnete* it had begun to be discussed in learned circles. It was not, however, until the theory had been confirmed by the discoveries of Galileo that it was viewed as more than an hypothesis.

In the meantime the tide of Neo-Platonism and of Arabian philosophy had borne strange fruits. The belief in the infinite proportion of things relative to one another had revived in speculative minds vague theories of a universal mathematics. A strain of Pythagoreanism enters thought. Writers such as Digby play with the notion that the ultimate constituents of the universe are measurements. The visit of Giordano Bruno to England intensified this drift of thought. That apocalyptic figure had arrived at Oxford in 1582, but he found himself isolated from the scholastic preoccupations of the university. He named Oxford 'the widow of true knowledge so far as philosophy and mathematics were concerned'.[1] He quickly departed for London where at the court he became friendly with a number of eminent persons, among them Sir Philip Sidney and Fulke Greville who affected an Italian culture. Bruno's speculations were discussed in court circles, and a small coterie read the books that he published during his stay in London. The most important of these were *La Cena delle Ceneri*, *Della Causa*, *Principio ed Uno*, and *Dell'Infinito Universo e Mundi*. His ideas added strength to the growing distrust of the old principles, and

---

[1] W. Boulting, *Giordano Bruno*, 1914, p. 84.

turned men's attention to fresh and startling vistas. His ornate and fervent discourses loosened further the attachment of men's minds to the Aristotelian scheme of beliefs. He attacked the cosmology, avowing, for example, that there was no evidence for the traditional spheres of water, air, and fire, and declared that the stars are not kept in motion by the *Primum mobile* but by their own immanent forms. He rejected many points in the traditional physics, especially the Aristotelian doctrine of absolute motion. But it is by the magnificence of his cosmological visions that he impressed speculative minds in England. These visions were the products of immense reading in unorthodox authorities such as Heracleitus and Empedocles, among ancient inquirers, Cusanus and Copernicus, among recent writers.

Two innovating conceptions ran through his speculations, the doctrine of the infinity of the universe and the belief in the universal soul of things. From the first Bruno's friends in London learnt that 'the divine one extols his own glory and sets forth the greatness of his sway, not in one sun, but in uncountable suns; not in one earth, but in worlds without end'. 'There are countless suns and an infinity of planets that circle round their suns, as our seven planets circle round our sun.'[1] This vast extension of the cosmological picture shattered the anthropomorphic system established in men's thought. And with this revolutionary idea went the hermetic conception of the universal soul. Bruno taught that the fundamental distinctions offered by the metaphysics of the schools were aspects of a still more fundamental unity. Behind potentiality, matter, form, act, special essences, nature, and God, there is unity of being. Aristotle has divided that which is in nature and truth indivisible. The One is both matter and form, potentiality and act; it is present in all particular substances. There is a cosmic soul that informs every portion of matter in the universe. Its activity is analogous to the activity of the human mind in forming general ideas; it directs the production of things in their classes and fashions the trees and the bodies of animals. One in all things it takes on diverse configurations, guided on the one hand by the end appropriate to each species, on the other by the perfection of the entire universe. The world and all its parts,

---

[1] Quoted from *Dell'Infinito* by Boulting, op. cit., pp. 138, 144.

down to the atomic elements of things, is animate.[1] In Dialogue V of *Della Causa* Bruno exalts the One in the style and spirit of Plotinus. 'One is absolute possibility, act, thing, being, the greatest and the best, which cannot be comprehended, to which limits and completion cannot be set, which, for that reason, is infinite and unending and consequently established.'[2]

Such incandescent notions lit new vistas. For some who conversed with the eloquent Italian they fortified the philosophy of occult interpenetration, of sympathetic virtues, of magical influences, in a word the theories of Paracelsus. Others were awakened to the significance of the new astronomical hypothesis and to the suggestion of new methods of investigation. For 'Why', asked Bruno, 'turn to vain fancies when there is experience itself to teach us?'

V

Mixed with these veins of credulity and speculation there ran a stream of sceptical philosophy. Lord Burghley remarked that the court was the abode of sceptics. The writings of Sir Walter Raleigh present an example of ways of thinking that were followed by many cultured persons; it will be recalled that Raleigh was the leader of a group of inquisitive courtiers and poets whose discussions ranged over the occult beliefs, mathematics, and theology. Raleigh expressed his views in the *Sceptic* and in the preface to the *History of the World*. In *The Sceptic* he presents the old epistemological arguments in his own terms. The perceptions of animals probably differ widely from those of human beings. Fishes, men, lions, and dogs must see the same object in different manners, and the disparity between the organs of touch, hearing, and smelling throughout living creatures suggest that each species apprehends what is present to its senses in ways perculiar to itself. What, then, is the thing in its own nature? Why should human beings prefer their own idea to that of other creatures? Moreover men's senses frequently deceive them, 'so that what the quality of an apple is, of whether it hath one quality or many, I know not'.[3] In

---

[1] *Della Causa*, tr. in B. Rand, *Modern Classical Philosophers*, 1908.
[2] Boulting, op. cit., p. 131.
[3] *The Works of Sir Walter Raleigh*, ed. Oldys and Birch, Oxford, 1829, viii. 556.

the *History of the World* he points at the limitations of human knowledge. Every one knows that certain causes produce certain effects. 'The cheese-wife knoweth it as well as the philosopher, that sour runnet doth coagulate her milk into a curd.' But philosophy cannot explain the connexion; and yet man who is ignorant of all natural causes proposes to examine the art of God in creating the world. The doctrine of the eternity of matter is absurd, and the arguments of Aristotle relating to the everlasting nature of the world are unacceptable. All the processes of nature depend upon God, but to inquire into the secret of these processes and into the essence of God is madness. 'The heavens are high, far off and unsearchable.'

Raleigh and his friends incurred charges of atheism, and Marlowe was saved from trial only by his death in a tavern brawl. But scepticism of human knowledge tended to enforce a current of unquestioning belief that ran strongly at the turn of the century. The opinion that divine matters are unsearchable by human reason so far from detaching the minds of the critics from religion, threw them into the embraces of faith. The association of rational scepticism with implicit acceptance of the doctrines of revelation had been asserted by the nominalists of the fourteenth century. It was asserted, as we have observed, in more than one quarter in the sixteenth century.

The assembled influences of the movements of thought that have been surveyed produced a general sense of insecurity and uneasiness among thoughtful men. Public events during the latter years of Elizabeth's reign filled men with anxiety. The high spirit of the Armada period faded and the melancholy of the ageing queen was reflected in the forebodings of her counsellors. The profound disturbances in the traditional conceptions of the universe and of man's situation within it contributed to the mood of discordance. Men saw the very foundations of order and intelligibility dissolving before their eyes and they found nothing to fill the fearful void. Those who were steeped in the classic philosophy of the schools, such as Hooker, could still trust in 'the admirable order wherein God hath disposed all laws, each as in nature, so in degree, distinct from other'. These thinkers could still acknowledge the harmony of the world and perceive in the heavens and on the earth, in man's mind and in society, the evidences of universal law. But others were bleakly aware of innovations that had shaken the established forms in all these regions of experience. The system of beliefs was so organically composed that confusion in one section spread disruption throughout the whole. Doubts concerning the scheme of the celestial spheres affected beliefs relating to the hierarchy of natural forms on the earth; cynicism concerning man's position in the cosmos corrupted the philosophy of political society. As the unheard-of notions of Copernicus and Bruno, of Machiavelli and Montaigne, became adopted and discussed in England, many sensitive men felt as though reality itself were in process of dissolution. The feeling of horror and despair is expressed above all in the later tragedies of Shakespeare. A great critic has pointed out that in the earlier plays the traditional beliefs about man and the physical universe appear as part of the emotional and intellectual background. In *Hamlet, Troilus and Cressida, Othello, Lear,* and *Macbeth,* 'they are part of the consciousness of the protagonists and the splitting of a soul is the splitting of a world'.[1] In *Lear* the chaotic strife in the mind and in the political body is one with the disorderly tumult of the sky.

The old rational confidence sustained further assaults. After the year 1610 the strange cosmological theories that had been discussed in philosophical circles of the court and the universities took a more disturbing place in speculative minds. In that year the English ambassador in Venice, Sir Henry Wotton, sent a copy of Galileo's *Siderius Nuncius* to James I. 'It was', he wrote, 'the strangest news he had ever yet received from any part of the world.' Galileo announced the discovery of four new planets and many new stars. He confirmed the heliocentric hypothesis of Copernicus and refuted experimentally the Aristotelian theories of motion. Few accepted these discoveries in England, many were deeply disturbed by them. John Donne was imbued with the philosophy of the schools. His poems assume the doctrine of universal correspondence, the chain of spheres, the grades of elements and forms. Now in the year after the publication of Galileo's book he cries that 'the new philosophy has put all in doubt'.

[1] T. Spencer, *Shakespeare and the Nature of Man,* p. 166.

> And freely men confess that this world's spent
> When in the planets and firmament
> They see so many new; they see that this
> Is crumbled out again to his atomies.
> 'Tis all in pieces, all coherence gone,
> All just supply and all relation.[1]

The realization that the earth was not fixed at the centre of things shattered the orthodox view of man. The amazing idea that he was not the chief figure in the cosmic drama dawned in the consciousness of thinkers. And the writings of Montaigne undermined the old religion of human dignity. Readers learnt that man has no privileged position among the animals, that his knowledge of nature and of the soul is contemptible, and worst of all, that his notions of divinity are subjective. The wave of pessimism that followed on the destruction of the historic ways of reason is indicated by utterances such as *The Fall of Man* (1616) by George Goodman. He turns away from the universal corruption of the age to the old sources of security, to Aristotle and the scholastics.

Two remarkable expressions of the intellectual disillusionment may be cited. 'Man, dreame no more of curious mysteries', adjured Fulke Greville in his *Caelica*, written during the last decade of the sixteenth century. Greville was not a philosopher, but no one reveals with more bitter force the moral revolt from thought. In the *Treatie on Humane Learning*, composed in the first years of the seventeenth century, he disdains the pursuit of natural knowledge.

> Nature we draw to Art, which then forsakes
> To be herselfe, when she with Art combines,
> Who in the secrets of her own wombe makes
> The Loadstone, Sea, the Soules of men, and Windes;
> Strong instances to put all Arts to schoole,
> And prove the Science-monger but a foole.
>
> Nay, we doe bring the influence of Starres,
> Yea God himselfe even under moulds of Arts;
> Yet all our Arts cannot prevaile so farre,
> As to confirme our eyes, resolve our hearts,
> Whether the heavens doe stand still or move,
> Were framed by Chance, Antipathie, or Love.[2]

---

[1] *An anatomie of the world.*

[2] *Poems and dramas of Fulke Greville*, ed. by G. Bullough, Edinburgh, 1939, vol. i, p. 160.

The science-monger is not a fool because Nature infinitely surpasses his arts; he is a fool because he attempts to understand what is beyond his powers. There are no means of deciding between the cosmogonies of Ptolemy, of Copernicus and Bruno, of hermetic allegory. In many passages of his sombre poem Greville sounds the current notes of radical scepticism. All human knowledge lies under the curse of the Fall. The senses upon which man relies for information, memory, and judgement are vitiated at the source. No philosopher has ever succeeded in offering a perfect demonstration or discovered a true form. Our philosophy is no more than poetry, 'for where the judge is false what truth can show?' Let men turn from the vain idols of the schools and concentrate upon the moral discipline of himself; and for knowledge, let him attend to 'that sure rocke of truth, God's word or Penne'. Many influences contributed to the distrust of knowledge exhibited in the verses of the *Treatie on Humane Learning*. But the driving impulse in the minds of men such as Greville flowed from Puritanism. It is the passionate concern with individual salvation in the midst of a world that appeared politically and intellectually on the brink of collapse that commands the dark and despairing mood of the *Treatie*. The teaching of Calvin and of Seneca combine to urge even graceful courtiers like its author to abandon all hope in philosophy and to clutch the austere comfort of religious stoicism.

A parallel manifestation of the sense of intellectual bewilderment is a revulsion from learning and inquiry. A book that was widely read and quoted in England was *The Variety of Arts and Sciences*, a translation of *De Incertitudine et Vanitate Scientiarum* of Cornelius Agrippa. 'Nothing', proclaims that author, 'can happen more pestilential to men than knowledge: this is the true plague that invades all mankind with so much confusion, that subverts all innocence; subjecting us to so many clouds of sin and error and at length to death'. And again, 'To a commonwealth nothing can be more pernitious than learning and science.'[1] Agrippa proceeds to inspect the entire range of the culture of his day with the purpose of exposing the contradictions and variety of theories in every section of knowledge, devoting particular scorn to the scholastic theologians. The upshot is that since all learning is uncertain men must turn to the

[1] Edition of 1676, pp. 7, 8.

Word of God. There were many in England who were ready to respond to the old recourse to Biblical revelation. The work of Francois Sanchez, *Quod nihil scitur* (1581), added force to this movement; the book enjoyed considerable vogue in England. Sanchez describes vigorously the interminable multiplication of authorities, exposes the infirmity of human intelligence, and repeats on almost every page the refrain *ergo nihil scitur*.[1]

No passage expresses better the feeling of disintegration and confusion that weighed upon the minds of men at this turning-point in the history of our thought than the opening pages of Lord Herbert of Cherbury's *De Veritate* (1624). All the voices of philosophical thought are mentioned. Reflection has been enslaved by authority and distracted by criticism. The very goodness of the universe is now openly discussed, a proceeding that would have astonished earlier ages. What is there that is sound to which an uneasy and divided mind can turn? The wits of the learned and the consciences of unlettered men are distracted by the multitude of sects. It seems at present not the world but the philosophy of the world that is composed of antagonistic and fortuitous elements. One school of teachers declares that we can know nothing; another frames with remarkable temerity the structure of things from the laws of thought (which are subjective), maintaining that there is nothing that is not ultimately clear. Amid these dissensions a strange doctrine appeared that proposed to supersede reason altogether and attempted to impose doctrines discovered by means of implicit faith. This position approached the philosophy of those who teach that it is impossible to know anything.[2]

Herbert's book manifests the general feeling of bewilderment and the sense that the old system is no longer equal to men's intellectual demands. With his usual impetuosity he addressed himself to an independent examination of the basis of knowledge and certainly no other thinker pursued the inquiry with such systematic attention. But the outcome proved how difficult it was to detach the mind from its heritage: and Herbert's book is an eclectic string of incompatible doctrines drawn from a multi-

---

[1] But Sanchez is not wholly a sceptic. *Scientia* he defines as perfect knowledge modelled on the syllogism, and he promised a further work in which the true method of science would be described. This promise was never fulfilled.

[2] *De Veritate* (1633 ed.), pp. 1–2.

tude of sources. In it the minced Aristotelianism of the university courses is thrown together with fragments of the anti-Aristotelianism of the previous age. The main doctrine of the work is derived from the Neo-Platonic current of sixteenth-century speculation. All the processes of the mind, named by Herbert faculties, correspond to characteristics in things, for the microcosm reflects at every point the features of the macrocosm. The entire order of nature is represented in the elements and humours of man's body and the sympathies and antipathies of the material and animal world enter into his experience.[1] The passions of wrath correspond in the human frame to the hurricanes, whirlwinds, and meteors of the sky; and the 'secret analogy' between the form and essence of a snake and the mind is the cause of the alarm that the appearance of the creature excites.[2] Herbert applied this theory of universal correspondence to knowledge. To every difference in the physical and psychical nature of things there responds a different mental process. These innumerable processes, adapted to the infinite diversity of things, may be classified in broad divisions—the external senses, the internal senses, discursive thought or logic, and natural instinct. It is upon the last type of knowledge that Herbert insists in preference to all other modes of apprehension, and his theory of truth recalls the sixteenth-century resuscitation of Cicero, and, through him, of the Stoic school. For by natural instinct man is endowed with common notions, the κοιναὶ ἔννοιαι of the Stoics, self-evident truths of knowledge, morality, and religion, common to all mankind. The development of common notions in the pages of De Veritate, though extremely confused, brings its doctrine into touch with the older traditions of Augustinianism and Neo-Platonism; the common notions provided theologians with arguments against mechanism later in the seventeenth century. In Herbert's hands the doctrine becomes an inductive rationalism that belittles both perception and logic. The denunciation of logic is, as usual, aimed at 'the academies'. It is the greatest source of error, deceit, and blasphemy, and possesses no value unless it is based upon the common notions. The end of logic is to disengage the common notions, which it is not lawful to dispute, from the wrapping of words that enclose them.[3]

---

[1] De Veritate (1633 ed.), p. 91.   [2] Ib., p. 33.   [3] Ib., p. 157.

Herbert's book attracted the interest of Descartes, and a theological section that was added to the main body of the argument is a leading source of the stream of natural theology that agitated religious thought in England during the seventeenth and eighteenth centuries. But in its belief in universal analogies, its scornful rejection of the logic of the schools in combination with an uncritical reliance upon the old method of formal definitions and distinctions, in its Protestant assertion of independence and democratic rationality, and in its Stoic theories of truth, *De Veritate* is symptomatic of much of the confusion and desperation at the beginning of the seventeenth century. Omnivorous readers, such as Herbert, struggled in a sea of contending authorities; the metaphysics of St. Thomas, perceived through the commentaries of Suarez, mingled with the radical attacks on the methods of the schools by Telesio and Patrizi, Stoic views combined with Neo-Platonism and the occult science of Paracelsus and the alchemists. No critic of the stature of Ockham appeared to sift the heterogeneous elements of this intellectual culture. And few of the erudite scholars of the time were prepared to seek in the 'catechisms and alphabets of unconcerning things' answers to the fundamental problems of philosophy.

THE NEW PHILOSOPHY

I

A CRUCIAL moment in the life of English thought had now arrived. The vision of reality that had supported the rational consciousness of men for a thousand years was fading. Cardinal beliefs relating to God, to man, and to the physical universe were being openly questioned. Habitual modes of inquiry and traditional standards of reasoning were condemned and the venerable authorities of the schools held up to scorn. Forms of investigating experience were proposed that appeared scandalous to conservative minds. A revolutionary outlook on the panorama of the world was constructed and within a hundred years the ancient methods and interests had been eclipsed.

Let us pause at this turning-point in the history of our thought and throw a backward and a forward glance over the stream. The long epochs of reflection in the past, from the distant cloister schools at Jarrow and York to the Cambridge of Dr. Caius, had been commanded by theological and metaphysical conceptions. The search for truth in every sphere had been infused with a religious faith. The numerous philosophies of these centuries had been engaged above all in the task of understanding and of justifying the universal religion. They were adapted in various forms to a system of divine truths and the system provided a chain of presuppositions that directed the forms by which experience was interpreted. The chief postulate was that the universe had been fashioned by a personal God who had revealed Himself to men in specific ways; and the metaphysical doctrines of being, creation, becoming, and end, were consequences of this postulate. These and other governing principles penetrated the successive rational resources that inquiry found at its disposal. Speculation continued through all its forms to be pointed to that which is eternal, absolute, supernatural, and holy. In the earlier phase natural reason explored a metaphysic, derived from St. Augustine, that concentrated upon the primary truths from which all other truths descend. During the twelfth and thirteenth centuries the range of lesser and mundane truths was immensely enlarged. The Aristotelian corpus supplied a logic of demonstration, a psychology of cognition, and an elaborate physics of terrestrial and celestial bodies. Principles proper to the several fields of knowledge were defined and the wider principles discussed by logic and metaphysics underwent important modifications. Serious conflicts occurred between the older and the later conceptions of knowledge and reality, but the new developments were subtly adjusted to the older philosophy, and the comprehensive scheme was adapted to the overarching beliefs of the Christian faith. Above the tensions and interplay between Aristotelianism and patristic Platonism the eternal verities of theology remained at the heart of thought, and certain conclusions of Greek speculation that called in question the convictions of belief were unhesitatingly rejected.

A long period ensued in which confidence in the traditional forms of reason declined. The science of logic and the philosophy of reality became divorced. An intricate system of conventional terms was substituted for rational knowledge and the great questions of human thought were declared to be incapable of solution. The provinces of reason and theology, necessary and natural truth, were sharply divided. Scepticism in theology threw men on to the rock of sacred authority, and the rise of Protestant movements in the fourteenth and fifteenth centuries enhanced the dogmatic position of the Church. Philosophical scepticism and the formal ingenuities of the terminists also turned men's minds to empirical matters. The disciples of Ockham offered revolutionary opinions in astronomy, dynamics, and mathematics, and suggested the illimitable possibilities of the experimental method in natural philosophy. But the problem of ecclesiastical reform engrossed attention and the agitating conflicts of moral authority that filled the air diverted interest from fundamental issues of knowledge.

The broadening culture of the new learning tended to break the customary moulds of thought and the rupture with Rome loosened respect for the ancient authorities. The exercises of the schools became blunted and dulled by repetition and an incoherent aggregation of competing theories, taken from Neo-Platonism and the hermetic books, sprang up. Nevertheless, the grammar schools and universities preserved the old logic and the old structure of belief amid the flood of humanism, and scholastic Aristotelianism continued to provide the main order of experience. But by the year 1600 there were many indications that a fresh phase of thought was at hand. Aristotelian mechanics had been undermined, a wealth of information was being accumulated, the value of precise observation of natural phenomena was increasingly asserted, and fresh moral impulses, secular, practical, and progressive, were transforming the mental habits of men.

In the present chapter we shall observe the construction of the modern perspective in England. A general glance at its character and course may be attempted here. The earlier approach to knowledge held, as we have seen, two dominant features; it was theological and it was metaphysical. The new is governed by physical science and is concerned, not with real natures and causes, but with sensible appearances and the laws of their connexion. We shall have to record an astonishing expansion of human knowledge, immensely surpassing the scientific renaissance of the days of Adelard. Freed from the inveterate assumptions of Aristotelian astronomy and physics natural philosophy advanced with unparalleled celerity, and before the close of the seventeenth century the frame of the modern theory and of the material world had been fashioned. Speculation followed its triumphant march. The qualities of rational inquiry and the conceptions of reality that now appeared reflected the axioms and procedure of Newtonian physics. Investigations into first principles assumed the mathematical and experimental view of things as implicitly as the older investigations had assumed the Aristotelian and theological views. Philosophical thought became imbued with the logic of scientific activity, with the search for elementary data and mechanical laws. Holding the findings of science to be the truth, it retracted its interest to problems of perception and thought. It became, largely owing to the influence of Descartes, increasingly subjective, concerned with modes of consciousness. Nature, the primal reality, becomes a self-sufficient mechanism; mind is divorced from matter; and the mathematical structure of blind force and material threatens to absorb the kingdom of ideals. When closely pressed, the scientific foundations of the philosophical inquiry led to startling results. They led to the conclusion that the realm of scientific reality is a realm of mental sensations, and they were pushed to the discovery that the beliefs upon which scientific knowledge is built cannot be logically explained. Science is based, according to this account, upon irrational instinct. But the scientific philosophy of experience survived these awkward inferences, and the principles set forth in the seventeenth century under the victorious shield of Newtonian mechanics continued unshaken in English thought for two hundred years. The nineteenth century saw striking advances in physical theory, and confidence in the capacity of scientific method to unify and explain the whole arc of experience became unbounded. The idea of a universal system of determined mechanism was revived with sweeping force.

The fundamental dualism of the Newtonian phase of English thought may be observed in relation to another principle. The conception of cause is a governing assumption of rational explanation. The unquestionable postulate of the earlier phases had been the postulate of eminent causation, that the cause must contain more than the effect, that something cannot be produced by nothing. The axiom had been associated at every point with the Augustinian constituents of the traditional perspective, with the belief in the dependence of the temporal on the eternal, of changeable things on the unchangeable. All the attributes of creatures must be possessed in some fashion by the primal cause; and the same principle was carried into the understanding of all mundane changes. The nobility, or superior being, of a cause over its effects is applied in detail to physical phenomena, such as the generation of composite things and the movement of the celestial bodies. This cardinal axiom had been challenged by the fourteenth-century logicians, but it remained at the heart of thought until the seventeenth century. There now appeared a radically different notion which, as it became more generally applied, produced a revolution in men's fundamental ideas. The new notion conceived natural events as associations or rearrangements of simple and pre-existing elements, the total number of which remains unchanged. Further, the modes of relation between these elements continue unaltered through all the combinations into which they enter. For this outlook there is nothing ultimately in complex effects that is not already in the simple elements; the complex effects are the result of elaboration of the self-same elements that enter into all events, from stones to human bodies. Explanation becomes analysis, and since the relations between the components at any level are determined, uniform, and precise, it becomes mathematical analysis. But this ideal was very imperfectly worked out. The mechanistic conception was brought to bear too comprehensively on the entire range of experience soon after its invention, and Hobbes's contention that all knowledge is nothing but addition and subtraction could be met by pointing to many things that could not be adequately described as rearrangements of simple bodies in motion. Yet in the eighteenth and nineteenth centuries the principle gained ground. Its greatest moments were the revival on a new and substantial basis of the atomic theory of matter and the formulation of the law of the conservation of energy. But the vindication of Newtonianism as an account of reality depended for its plausibility on the dualism which has been mentioned. By assuming a basic division between the objective world and mind it was able to assign to subjective processes many factors in experience that were hard to reconcile with the principle of quantitative constancy.

We have to observe then, in this phase of philosophical belief in England, the birth and growth of the scientific theory of truth, and the view of mind and knowledge that accompanied it. And we must review briefly the ways in which the ancient metaphysics of Christian theology were adapted to the new naturalist prospect. Let us now turn to regard the rise of the new philosophy in England. The rapidity of its development, the revolutionary character of its principles, the brilliant sagacity of its leaders, its practical successes, and its splendid visions, distinguish this period of thought among all the phases of English speculation. The swift flowering of fresh technique and theory was nurtured by parallel departures of thought in the West, by the labours of Kepler, Galileo, Descartes, and Huyghens; it shared in the general impulse of mind that was stirring in Europe. But this country produced some of the directing geniuses of the movement and contributed its own quality of doctrine to the new system of beliefs. And the men who wrought the intellectual revolution pursued their researches during the darkest moments of our political history. The first society of new philosophers were conducting their experiments in London during the year of the battle of Naseby.

But we shall gain a false picture of the seventeenth century if we concentrate our attention upon the new philosophy and ignore the more traditional interests and conceptions that were active among the majority of scholars. At the universities the core of beliefs in first principles remained scholastic. Even in natural philosophy discussions continued to be untouched by recent advances; the primary source of information for studies pursued in connexion with the new chair of natural philosophy at Oxford was the *Metaphysics* and the statutes of the Savilian professorship of Geometry and Astronomy, founded in 1619, enjoined a deep knowledge of the theories of Plato and Aristotle; the only modern author mentioned in the scheme of studies is Copernicus. The conservative methods and subjects were but slightly affected by Laud's statutes for the university, promulgated in 1636. The first year was to be spent on rhetoric, the second and third on logic and metaphysics; and the works authorized for study were Porphyry's *Isagoge* and the logical works of Aristotle. At Cambridge the reformed logic of Ramus had taken hold. George Downham, in his eloquent inaugural oration to the undergraduates in 1590, had praised Ramus for his herculean labours in purging the barbarous augean stable of logic and daring to disinter the true doctrine from the shades of the past. 'So I venture to ascribe all the praises that I have pronounced on logic to logic as set forth by Ramus.'[1] In the *Commentaries on the dialectic of Ramus*, 1616, he pleads for an extension of the art of logic, unfolds the provinces of *inventio* and *judicium*, the collection of types of argument and the application of them, and touches on the classical theories of form and matter, end and substance. For physics the end is man; for man, God. Downham agrees with those who maintain, with Ramus, that there is one method of knowledge, from universals to particulars, and he follows his master in illustrating the method from Virgil, Ovid, Cicero, and Livy. Other popular text-books were more traditional in matter. Samuel Smith's *Aditus ad logicam*, 1633, repeats all the divisions of the earlier epitomes; Edward Brerewood's *Elementa Logicae*, 1638, invites the youth of Oxford in a flowery introduction to shine

---

[1] *Commentarii in P. Rami regii professoris dialecticam*, Frankfort, 1616.

in the strife of letters by means of logic, and follows this
oratorical prelude with a dry and stereotyped summary of the
old formal distinctions, most of which relates to the classification
of propositions. The chief exercises of higher education were
still the Latin disputations, and the ancient topics were mechani-
cally debated by the young bachelors of arts. For the master's
degree candidates were expected to defend a thesis for four days
and their arguments were obliged to adhere strictly to the
Aristotelian rules. Text-books newly composed for undergraduates reflect the metaphysical preoccupations of the schools.
Even optimists such as George Hakewill, who were anxious to
rebut the widespread belief in the age's decay, base their argument upon the divine activity present in the essences of things;
'and as for the formes of naturall bodies, no sooner doth any
one abandon the matter it informed but another instantly
steps into the place thereof'.[1]

Further declarations of scholastic principles occur throughout
the century; John Sergeant's *The Method to Science*, 1696, is the
last of many reaffirmations of Aristotle.[2] The mental environment of the new experimental inquirers was composed of school
metaphysics and syllogistic logic. To men engaged in the teaching of philosophy at the universities the activities of the recent
school of anatomists and physicists were distasteful. John Cotta,
at the beginning of the century, expressed what many earnest
scholars felt about the new empiricism throughout the period:

'The Empiricke is he who rejecteth the disquisition of diseases
and remedies, their causes, natures and qualities according to judgment and understanding and carefull perpension and balancing of
his action and practise unto a just proportion with reason; but onely
informeth himselfe by such things as oft appeare evident and manifest unto sense and experimentall proffe, carrying his heart and
understanding (for the most part) in his hands and eyes, taking
nothing but what he sees and handles.'[3]

The charge of irrationality is frequently brought by the

---

[1] *An Apologie or Declaration of the Power and Providence of God*, Oxford,
1627, iv. 1.

[2] But Sergeant gives a strange turn to the historic conceptions. Knowledge
is derived from identical or tautological propositions.

[3] Quoted in R. F. Jones, *Ancients and Moderns*, St. Louis, 1936, from John
Cotta, *A Short Discovery of the Unobserved Dangers of several sorts of ignorant
and unconsiderate Practises in England*, 1612.

Aristotelians against the men who carried their understanding in their hands and eyes. They lamented the tendency to trust, as the Duchess of Newcastle put it, rather in deluding experiments than in rational arguments. The antagonism between the customary and the novel methods of seeking truth cut deep. It was far more than a conflict between the views of revered authorities and the upstart theories of an unorthodox coterie. The new theories were suggesting conceptions of logic and of rational order that to the minds of men steeped in the old learning were immoral as well as fallacious. Reason looked to a hierarchy of qualitative orders, to transcendent ends that precede and determine change. And from these conceptions the new way, as we shall perceive, was turning aside. The protests of the conservatives on behalf of reason were associated also with feelings of disgust at the vulgarity of the new approach to truth. The men of experiment were termed common mechanics. Boyle was obliged to defend his willingness to handle coarse and repulsive materials in pursuing his researches. Hobbes described the votaries of the Royal Society as apothecaries and gardeners, and scholars who hated Hobbes were ready to agree with him in this matter. There was, in fact, an active intercourse between the manipulative skill, the trial and error methods of craftsmen, and the new experimental technique of Boyle's invisible college. Bacon was always pointing to the examples of the 'mechanical arts'; and his greatest disciple asserted that ground for expecting considerable advantages from the experimental philosophy is provided by the discoveries of illiterate tradesmen. The academic doctrines had vigorous defenders. But for the disciples of Bacon they had become topics for bitter jokes and there were many utterances of scorn against the 'tyranny of subtile rules, distinctions, terms and notions'. The abuse of the old logic and metaphysics resounds through the century, but not all who were dissatisfied with the philosophy of the arts courses were prepared to embrace the new gospel.

As for the philosophy that 'pretendeth to discover that correspondence or concatenation which is between the superior globe and the inferior', it continued to absorb many thoughtful persons during and after Bacon's day. In the writings of these illuminati an elaborate tissue of allegory was woven round the worlds of nature and of spirit. A plethora of mystical explanations were drawn from the biblical narratives, especially from the story of the creation of Adam in Genesis; and a mass of occult cosmology was culled from the hermetic books and from the Cabbala. Here, once more, were unfolded at length the doctrine of the ten sephiroth, the lore of the tetragrammaton, and the theory of emanations. The writings of Robert Fludd form the crest of this wave of magical conceptions. In them all the hermetic doctrines are revived, and a wealth of ancient Persian lore was poured into the stream of English reflection. The opposing principles of light and darkness, for example, play an important role in the scheme of things. The mind is light, the body darkness. Every feature of the heavens and the earth has its counterpart in the body and mind of man, for God has made two images of Himself, the world and man. The analogies between the macrocosm and the microcosm are endlessly drawn out. The claims of astrology, alchemy, and sympathetic magic are pressed at every point; for all things are permeated with secret affinities and antipathies.[1] As regards method, the old symbolism of numbers, of geometrical forms, and of letters, is lavishly employed. Aristotelian and scholastic science is controverted in detail; but Fludd also rejects Gilbert's views on the loadstone and denies the Copernican theory. His views aroused considerable discussion among leaders of thought. Abroad Mersenne attacked them on the score of magic. Gassendi defended them on this charge, but accused Fludd of turning the Bible into a handbook of alchemy. Kepler was also interested in Fludd's theories. In England his ideas received the approval of King James and of several bishops, and his defence of sympathetic cures against sceptical critics excited great interest. Indeed, a considerable part of this Cabbalistic philosophy persisted in conjunction with the philosophy of naturalism and was frequently drawn upon to overcome the deficiencies of scientific knowledge. The stream of occult belief courses through the century. Henry More, who responded to

[1] The application of these principles to physiognomy and disease provided the seventeenth-century student with many instructive pieces of information. If the nose of a person is naturally red, he will have many friends; if his feet are oblong he will have many thoughts. Creeping under a bramble that grows in the earth at both ends will cure boils. On Fludd see J. B. Craven, *Doctor Robert Fludd*, London, 1895.

so many of the intellectual currents of this time, laboured to reveal the mysterious meaning of the text of Genesis through the symbolic significance of numbers, and collected examples of apparitions and witchcraft in order to open the door to religious belief. Joseph Glanvil, who was a member of the Royal Society, found that there was one argument that shook the infidels, namely, the evidence for witches; and the prebendary of Worcester and his friends eagerly gathered stories of evil spirits and magic influences for the purpose of confuting the Hobbists and Spinozians. A number of writers transmitted the hermetic teaching of Fludd, and many earnest persons preferred to read of the intercourse between visibles and invisibles and of the magic analogies of sulphur and mercury rather than of the new researches into physics and anatomy. They preferred Thomas Vaughan's *Magia Adamica* to the transactions of the invisible College. The visionary science of the Paracelsians and the Cabbalists persisted far into the eighteenth century. It appeared, mingled with the mystical conceptions of Boehme, in the works of William Law and Christopher Smart.

But we must now turn from these conservative habits of thought to the new philosophy of the seventeenth century. Revolutionary modes of natural inquiry had been put forward during the preceding fifty years. About the year 1577 a very young student at the University of Cambridge conceived an immense ambition. He discerned in the work of contemporary writers the shape of a new way of truth and determined to make the chief vocation of his life the task of promoting it. The first notable issue of Francis Bacon's discovery was the *Advancement of Learning*. But the new gospel must be seen in relation to currents of thought that were flowing at the end of the sixteenth century; and it must be related to the influences that were stirring in Paris where Bacon spent three formative years at the English embassy. Like other inquisitive young scholars he was moved by strong distaste for the methods and topics of the schools and readily responded to the scornful utterances against the philosophy of Aristotle that, as we have noticed, were especially fashionable at Cambridge. The first book of the *Advancement of Learning* reviews the main intellectual pursuits that were engaging the minds of Bacon's contemporaries in the lecture-rooms and at the court. It is an invaluable survey of the philosophical temper of the age. Here are arraigned the powerful tendency to belittle human knowledge in the interests of religion, the fantastic learning of the astrologers and alchemists, the rhetorical exercises and verbal subtleties of the schools, the excessive preoccupation with literary style. The *Advancement of Learning* appeared in 1605, *Novum Organum* in 1620, *De Augmentis Scientiarum* in 1623. These works declared in majestic tones the bankruptcy of the ancient ways of thought and traced the lines of a new philosophy of nature. Soon after Bacon's death in 1626 his aphorisms began to appear in books on a wide variety of themes, and later, when the civil war was over and the restrictions on academic pursuits were lifted, many of his proposals were recalled and became possessions of the reconstructed system of ideas. The writings of Robert Boyle, which did more than any other to establish the new philosophy as an integral portion of the intellectual life of cultured persons, contain numerous expressions of veneration for Bacon. In the treatise on the *Mechanical Origin of Heat and Cold*, he observes that 'Bacon was the first among the moderns who handled the doctrine of heat like an experimental philosopher'; and elsewhere he extols the author of *Novum Organum* as 'the great ornament and guide of the philosophical historians of nature'. The vision of co-operative research in the sciences that is set forth in the *New Atlantis* gave birth to plans for the foundation of philosophical colleges, and the first historian of the Royal Society, Thomas Sprat, finds the works of Bacon the best preface to the history of the Society. By the middle of the century he had become 'our new Aristotle' and observations and experiments as well as general precepts are frequently cited from his pages. And he inspired the educational reforms of John Durie and of Samuel Hartlib, no less than the activities of the natural physiologists.

But in the meantime the new examination of natural facts that was rhetorically advocated by Bacon had been undertaken by a number of inquisitive persons. We have noticed that coteries interested in the theories of Copernicus and of Bruno had appeared in Elizabeth's reign. Thomas Harriot had collaborated with Kepler, and Thomas Digges corresponded with Tycho Brahe. The new logic and the new physics of the heavens were eagerly canvassed in the circles of inquirers that gathered in London. A leading figure in these pursuits was William Gilbert, the Queen's physician. He was an ardent experimenter, and in his book, *De Magnete*, published in 1600, he described a long series of experiments on the behaviour of the loadstone and drew fresh conclusions from his observations. Rumours of the remarkable activities of natural philosophers abroad were carried to the court by intelligent travellers such as Sir Henry Wotton, and the news of Galileo's astronomical discoveries occasioned a ferment of discussion. Young men had gone to pursue their studies in the universities of Italy. William Harvey, for example, made the journey to Padua in 1598 in order to work at anatomy under the celebrated Fabricius. He found a considerable English 'nation' established at that university. This movement of ideas produced a number of publications in which a fresh outlook on phenomena mingled with the older ways of thought. Harvey's *De motu cordis* is the most notable of these works. Seth Ward, William Petty, and others were in touch with Mersenne who was bringing together the mathematical and physical thinkers of France.

After 1640 the movement gathered volume. There had been many proposals to establish societies for the pursuit of natural philosophy, but 'Minerva's Museum' and similar projects failed to reach fulfilment. The examples of the Italian societies attracted the ambitions of learned men who were in the habit of assembling together in order to discuss questions of natural philosophy. The most important of these groups was one that met weekly in London to discuss what was already termed the new philosophy. The members included John Wallis, John Wilkins, Jonathan Goddard, George Ent, Francis Glisson, Samuel Foster, and Theodore Haak, mathematicians, physicians, and physicists. A noticeable feature of the discussions is that they deliberately precluded theology and politics. They ranged over anatomy, geometry, astronomy, statics, magnetism, chemistry, and mechanics; and members reported on work that was being accomplished in these fields in England and abroad. When opportunity occurred experiments were performed. These gatherings took place about 1645. In 1648 the society divided, some repairing to Oxford where they met at Wadham College and at the lodgings of Robert Boyle in High Street. Boyle's house was soon fitted with a laboratory and it became the centre of the experimental philosophy at Oxford. The Oxford society continued to meet and read papers until 1690, but meanwhile other groups had been formed. It was from the London body of philosophers that had been assembling at Gresham College in Bishopsgate Street that the Royal Society was born. After the lecture by Christopher Wren on 28 November 1660, a number of eminent members, including Lord Brouncker, Boyle, Wilkins, Goddard, Petty, and Rooke, decided to found an academy for the promotion of 'Physico-Mathematicall Experimentall Learning' and in 1662 the society received its charter of incorporation at the hands of Charles II. In the brief interval between the first meetings in London and the establishment of the Royal Society an astonishing range of knowledge had been surveyed, extending from the properties of the air to the effects of powder from the horn of a unicorn. And looking beyond the investigations of the society we must recall the incessant advances in mathematics, in pathology, in knowledge of animals and plants that were accomplished in these wonderful years. In mathematics these few years beheld the discoveries of William Oughtred, Lord Brouncker, Thomas Baker, and above all the profound researches of Isaac Barrow and of John Wallis. The former explored the fields of optics and geometry; Wallis's *Arithmetica Infinitorum*, 1656, is a landmark in the history of mathematics for it generalized under a comprehensive rule the work of numerous predecessors and opened the way to nearly every mathematical discovery in the next two centuries.[1] Similar series of capital names could be taken from the history of the physiological investigations that were built upon the achievement of Harvey, or from the account of botanical and zoological progress that was compassed at this time. But it is important to observe the constant intercourse of scientific and humane interests in the minds of these thinkers. They were concerned with many sides of nature, not with one compartment of it. And they were eager to relate their natural science to theology.

II

Let us now observe the qualities of the experimental philosophy in relation to the broad problems of experience that we have discerned in the earlier phases of speculation in England.

[1] J. F. Scott, *The Mathematical Work of John Wallis*, London, 1938, p. 30.

Four notes of the revolution in ideas may be distinguished. First, the movement of thought is marked by the diversion of rational interest to the structure and processes of the external universe. A second quality is the rapid development of a new logic, a new method of truth. But more fundamental than these characteristics is the theory of reality that now becomes expressed in the minds of the great investigators. The leaders of natural philosophy in England adopted, we shall find, a cautious attitude to the metaphysical implications of the system of principles that they were vindicating in the course of their exploration of the physical world. This cautious position of mind in relation to primary questions of experience is a notable trait of the new philosophy in England and it entered deeply into the outlook of the succeeding period. The comprehensive designs that were offered by Descartes, Hobbes, and Spinoza served only to confirm the characteristic empiricism of English reflection. But the experimental philosophy, for all its caution in relation to metaphysics, inevitably assumed theories of reality and of knowledge. Conceptions that were found to be cogent within the regions of 'physiology' tended from the birth of the movement to be applied to wider provinces of experience ; the story of modern beliefs concerning first principles is the story of this extension of the methods and categories of natural science. Finally, the development of the new logic and the new vision was associated with a profound change in the moral conditions of thought. The means of knowledge and its goal accorded with the sentiments that had been growing among the religious sects and among Protestant scholars since the Reformation.

The men who met at Dr. Goddard's lodgings in Wood Street or at Gresham College in London explored a boundless range of subjects.

'We then discoursed of the circulation of the blood, the valves in the veins, the venae lacteae, the lymphatic vessels, the Copernican hypothesis, the nature of comets and new stars, the satellites of Jupiter, the oval shape of Saturn, the spots in the sun, and its turning on its axis, . . . the weight of the air, the possibility or impossibility of vacuities, the Torricellian experiment in quicksilver, the descent of heavy bodies, and divers other things of like nature.'[1]

[1] J. Wallis, quoted by C. R. Weld, *History of the Royal Society*, London, 1848, i. 30. A few items have been omitted.

The scope and complexity of the new material was sufficient to absorb the intellectual energies of the most capacious minds. The groups of inquirers who led the activities of the invisible college naturally turned away from those searching questions that had engaged the philosophers of the past. But this detachment was deliberate; it was the expression of an explicit policy. The prophet of the new way of truth had proclaimed it. *The Advancement of Learning* and *Novum Organum* had exhibited not merely a revulsion from the doctrines of the schools but a repugnance to the investigations of metaphysics in general. Bacon gives a cursory recognition to the office of *philosophia prima*, the critical examination of the principles assumed in various departments of human belief. But he displays little interest in such inquiries. He concentrates his attention upon the prospects of natural philosophy. He goes further. Metaphysics receives a novel designation; it becomes an extension of physics. 'Physic' is concerned with the local, variable, and relative causes of phenomena; metaphysic seeks the wider, fixed and constant causes.[1] And the phenomena to which these sciences apply are material processes. The investigation of these processes, that subordinate investigation which the philosophy of the thirteenth century had named, after Augustine, the rational knowledge of temporal things, defines the scope and limit of human thought. Regions of experience that lie beyond this boundary are the concern, not of knowledge, but of faith. A vast range of topics that had engaged the main attention of earlier thought is dismissed. Questions, for instance, relating to the nature of the rational soul 'must be handed over to religion to be determined and defined'.[2] The fundamental processes of experience and the problems of theology are put aside in favour of a comprehensive investigation into sensible and material things. It is in relation to theology that the narrowing of the perspective is most explicitly stated. The old division between sacred revealed truth and reason, which thinkers in England had been driven to maintain in the fourteenth century, is now asserted in uncompromising language. 'The articles and principles of religion are placed and exempted from examination of reason.' Theology requires us to 'step out of the bark of human

[1] *Advancement of Learning*, II. vii. 3.
[2] *De Augmentis Scientiarum*, IV. iii.

reason and enter into the ship of the Church'. For Bacon the
separation of divine and natural knowledge is complete, and in
the manner of the fourteenth century he asserts that faith must
believe what it finds incredible.[1] In conformity with this position he urges a return to the simple and literal text of the inspired scriptures. He dwells on the weakness of the analogical
method of interpretation; 'to press too far into it cannot but
cause a dissolution and overthrow of the spirit of man'. And
to seek philosophy in divinity is to seek the dead among the
living. God does not provide natural information in the scriptures except passingly and for edification.[2]

The acceptance of this dualism of faith and reason was largely
an affair of policy. It allowed natural philosophy to be free to
pursue its work independently of the suspicions of ecclesiastical
authority. It also reflected the agnosticism of Bacon's mind in
relation to theological questions. We have seen that the new
philosophers who met in Oxford and London twenty years after
Bacon's death deliberately excluded theology and metaphysics
from their discussions. And later Robert Hooke declared that
the business and design of the Royal Society was to improve the
knowledge of natural things and not to meddle with 'Divinity,
Metaphysics, Moralls, Politicks, Grammar, Rhetoric, or Logick'.[3]
The exclusion of the academic topics saved the inquirers from
becoming entangled in the controversies of the schools and
allowed natural knowledge to progress in security from the war-
fare of philosophy and theology. The new investigators avoided
such questions because the very formulation of them presented
them with conceptions of nature and with methods of exploration that were completely at variance with the methods and
conceptions they were discussing. They were asking questions
of phenomena that were fundamentally different from the old
questions. Many of these pioneers were observers and laboratory
workers first and metaphysicians in a secondary manner; the
task before them was enough, and since general theory meant
the metaphysics of the schools it was evaded as far as possible.
Few leaders of the Baconian movement, however, possessed
Bacon's cool detachment from religion. They excluded theology

---

[1] Ib. IX. I.
[2] *Advancement of Learning*, II. xxv.
[3] C. R. Weld, *History of the Royal Society*, i. 146.

from their discussions but the chief minds of the movement were constantly occupied with the reconciliation between natural philosophy and religion. The ways in which this reconciliation was effected will be noticed on a later page.

The concentration of reason upon the exploration of the external realm was one mark of the new philosophy. We must now consider some features of the new logic of method. Bacon provided the movement with an elaborate introduction, the greater part of which is occupied with condemnations of conservative thought and with eloquent denunciations of scholastic logic. These towering invectives set the fashion for a fresh effusion of protest against the philosophy of the schools and, indeed, for renewed misrepresentations of Aristotelianism. The opulent scorn of the *Advancement of Learning* is echoed in many passages in the writings of Seth Ward, Noah Biggs, John Webster, and other reformers in the period. Bacon's arraignment of Astrology, Natural Magic, and Alchemy helped also to clear the ground for the reconstruction of knowledge. But he undertook a deeper scouring of the mind. He compelled men to make a strenuous attempt to loosen their thinking from habitual prejudices and age-long postulates. He collected from the works of Telesio, Patrizzi, Campanella, Cardano, and others a long list of preconceptions that beset the mind of the investigator of nature. He sharpened the suggestions that he found in the writings of the innovators of the sixteenth century. The Proemium to the *De rerum natura* of Telesio was especially influential in this part of Bacon's work. These predispositions include the tendency to find greater order and regularity in things than the facts warrant, and the inclination to select evidence in accordance with desire and interest. The most troublesome confusions are due to language, 'whence it comes to pass that the high and formal discussions of learned men end often in disputes about words and names'. He cites as instances Fortune, the Prime Mover, Planetary Orbits, Element of Fire. These are fictions, and other words denote existences in several different senses at once.[1] The empirical trend of thought is conspicuous in this passage, and he returns to it in describing a last class of 'idols' due to false philosophical systems. On all sides 'philosophy is based upon too narrow a foundation of experiment and natural

[1] *Novum Organum*, i. lx.

history, and decided on the authority of too few cases'.[1] The philosophy of Aristotle is the manifest example of this error and the schoolmen who followed him have abandoned experience altogether. In this process of cleansing the mind at its entry into the kingdom of man, all the criticisms of the old approach to truth that had been gathering force for generations are assembled and defined. Bacon's powerful purge of the understanding helped many thoughtful men to open their minds to the novel theories of Galileo and Descartes. The list of idols in the *Novum Organum* was followed by similar surveys of intellectual prejudices, such as those of Sir Thomas Browne in *Pseudodoxia Epidemica*, of Joseph Glanvil in *the Vanity of Dogmatising*, and of Thomas Sprat in the *History of the Royal Society*.

In other sections of his works Bacon described the method of attaining truth in natural knowledge. His proposals bore the influences of his violent recoil from the rationalism of the academic teaching. He advocated a laborious collection of evidence; 'first of all we must prepare a Natural and Experimental History, sufficient and good'. Upon this follows induction which 'must analyze nature by proper rejections and exclusions; and then after a sufficient number of negatives come to a conclusion on the affirmative instances'. The investigator is required to muster all the instances of the phenomenon under examination that agree in the same nature though in sensible apprehension most unlike. No speculation is permitted at this stage. The next step is to observe cases in which the nature is wanting though it might be expected to be present. Then the inquirer must collect all the instances he can find where the nature is present in varying degrees. Induction sets to work by considering the presence, the absence, and the correlated variations of the factors in the conditions that accompany the nature in question and when the invariable conditions have been detected 'there will remain at the bottom a Form affirmative, solid, and true and well-defined'.

Bacon illustrated the method by investigating the nature of heat and arrived at the conclusion that it was a manifestation of motion. His account directed the thought of the time to leading principles of the new method, its recourse to perceptual evidence and its search for necessary conditions. The enthusiasm for

[1] Ib. 1. lxii.

facts, for 'histories' that distinguished the labours of the first scientific societies in England, is a legacy of Bacon. But in important respects his recommendations were deficient. We must inspect the transactions of the societies and the writings of the leading inquirers in order to perceive the practical logic upon which the changed conceptions of reality were being erected. We are not concerned with detailed processes of the experimental method as it is exhibited in such works as Glisson's *De Rachitide* (1651) or Boyle's work on the properties of the air. Our task is to descry those qualities that affected the general view of truth.

In England the new philosophy was controlled by Baconian empiricism. The earlier generation of investigators, among whom Gilbert and Harvey were notable figures, was moved by a passion for precise observation and for information acquired from first-hand scrutiny of the facts. The members of the London society collected evidence concerning the physical conditions of foreign lands, the anatomy of trees, the clothing trade, and the belts of the planet Jupiter. The minutes of the meetings at Gresham College record many 'exact narratives of everything observable'. The pursuit of information in many different fields was joined with a rapid refinement of the means of observation. The requirements of exact scrutiny and the need to increase the range of observation led to the invention of instruments, Wren's pendulum, Boyle's air-pump, and the numerous ingenious mechanisms of the indefatigable Hooke. Parallel with the supply of these aids to precise measurement and observation there developed skill in laboratory technique and in the handling of apparatus. These instruments and skills were means towards the new inductive logic which moved far beyond the programme of the *Novum Organum*. If we consider any of the innovating achievements of the period, Harvey's labours on the circulation of the blood, Boyle's work on chemical elements, Newton's discoveries relating to light, we can notice the characteristics of the modern method. The criteria of proof at which Bacon hinted are more delicately applied. The method of comparison and exclusions, by which the presence, absence, and parallel variations of the conditions of the phenomenon under investigation are tested in order to distinguish essential from accidental conditions, is brought to bear under stricter experimental conditions. But the critical feature of the method when it is viewed in relation to the historic modes of interpretation lay in the kind of mental expectations with which the new philosophers of nature approached the multifarious phenomena of the world. Bacon gave little recognition to the questions that the scientific inquirers of the time were directing to nature, but the salient characteristic of the work of these inquirers is the way in which observation and experiment are controlled by theory. The new mode of explanation consists of arranging phenomena under certain types of order and connexion. These schemes are put forward as suggestions and the objects under investigation are manœuvred and scrutinized in order to test the suggestions. The process consists of asking, 'what will result if the suggestion is true?' In the work of the men who met at Boyle's lodgings at Oxford or at Gresham College in London the investigations are guided by hypotheses, and the task of natural philosophy is to search by careful experiment for the facts that will confirm the hypotheses. The logic includes the activity of deduction as well as of induction, but the deductive logic is not that of the schools. The principles that form its premisses are not the principles of Aristotelianism nor of any of the modifications of scholastic naturalism that had been proclaimed in the fifteenth and sixteenth centuries. In order to perceive the nature of the revolution in reason that was now in progress, it will be necessary to consider the new ideal of knowledge that determined the methods of the new philosophers. We have glanced at the interests and at the empirical logic of the movement; we must now turn to consider the most revolutionary change of principle. We have referred above to certain types of order that were presumed to explain the material phenomena. What, in general, were these types of order?

III

Once more the herald of the new standard of intelligibility is Francis Bacon. The instinctive consciousness of scholars, rooted in a thousand years of Christian and Aristotelian reflection, conceived phenomena in terms of process and development. From the four elements to man all things were imbued with latent potentialities for development in ways appropriate to

their position in the chain of being. Natural objects were
realizations, in varied degrees, of the forms and acts that enter
into matter. The fundamental demand of rational interpretation is teleological. In Bacon's day even the pioneers of the new
knowledge were relating their discoveries to the historic modes
of interpretation, mingled with the Neo-Platonic doctrines that
had been revived in the sixteenth century. Gilbert viewed the
phenomena of electricity and magnetism in the light of the
metaphysics of the schools, though these principles are combined
with the theories of Bruno. The notions of matter and form,
potentiality and act, are associated with belief in the earth-soul
and in the living being of the stars. Harvey supposed the blood
to enjoy affinity with the celestial bodies and believed that all
the motions and changes in the inferior world were under the
control of the superior and incorruptible spheres. In academic
circles confidence in the ancient standard of interpretation persisted, as we have seen, far into the age. The novelty of the
proposals relating to the understanding of the natural world
that were offered by Bacon can nowhere be more strikingly
observed than in his discussions concerning form. He gives
the familiar principle a strange appearance. The forms of
natural things are not qualitatively different entities successively imposed upon matter adapted to receive them. They are
general configurations of the elements of bodies. This 'latent
configuration' is a determined arrangement of material properties underlying diverse sensible objects, and the 'compound
natures' are limitations of general natures. 'For when I speak
of Forms, I mean nothing more than those laws and determinations of absolute actuality that govern and constitute any
simple nature, as heat, light, weight, in every kind of matter and
subject that is susceptible of them.' The Forms are determinations, that is to say, they are fixed orders of matter, indifferent
to purpose and values; and in seeking them the human mind
moves 'from the complicated to the simple, from the incom-
mensurable to the commensurable, from surds to rational
quantities, from the infinite and vague to the finite and certain,
as in the case of the letters of the alphabet and the notes of
music. And inquirers into nature have the best result when they
begin with physics and end in mathematics.' Bacon catches
view of the ideal of the new philosophy in such utterances, and

the sharp break with the habits of the schools is apparent in his repudiation of finality in nature. He finds the natural philosophy of Democritus, 'who did not suppose a mind or reason in the frame of things, but attributed the form thereof able to maintain itself to infinite essays and proofs of nature', preferable to the theories of Aristotle and Plato, for they introduced final causes into nature. The new forms are mechanical frames, embracing substances that are most unlike one another. 'But whosoever is acquainted with Forms embraces the unity of nature in substances the most unlike, and is able therefore to detect and bring to light things never yet done. . . . From the discovery of Forms therefore results truth in speculation and freedom in operation.'[1]

Bacon's ignorance of mathematics and his failure to appreciate the activities of contemporary natural philosophers held him back from a fuller vision of the new world of thought. He was aware of the work of Galileo but displayed no interest in it. And he constantly reverts to scholastic modes of interpretation, clinging to qualitative theories of being. Much of the animism of his age is retained in his account of physical and chemical processes. He speaks of inanimate bodies possessing perceptions though not sense, and asserts that these perceptions precede 'operations'. Air, for example, has a 'subtile perception' of wind. He explains a number of phenomena in terms of spirits; the properties of quicksilver, to take one instance, are due to the presence of 'spirit' in it. Even the old doctrine of elements appears, and animal spirits are said to be compounded of flame and air. References to the irritation, the appetites, and the aversions of the spirits enclosed in substances show that Bacon, despite his revolutionary outlook, had not freed himself from fashions of thought prevailing in his generation.

But before his death the novel theory of natural order had begun to assume a more definite and a more comprehensive shape. Two great currents of ideas blended in its construction. One was the theory of atomism, the other was the mathematical method. The seventeenth century witnessed a powerful revival of Epicureanism. The leader of this restoration was Pietro

---

[1] The translations from the *Novum Organum* are taken from Bacon's works edited by Spedding, Ellis, and Heath, London, 1858.

Gassendi whose *De vita, moribus et doctrina Epicuri* appeared at Leyden in 1647. In other works, notably in the physical sections of the *Syntagma philosophica*, he set forth at length the corpuscular theory of matter assumed by Epicurus and Lucretius. After reviewing other theories of the ultimate constitution of things, especially the classic principles of Aristotle, he decides that the atomistic theory is the most successful, and he applies himself to working out the principles of a physics grounded upon indivisible corpuscles. The atoms, endowed with weight, figure, order, and position are the primary elements of things. All the qualities of nature are complexities of the primary atoms. Employing a simile which Bacon had also used and which became widely current in seventeenth-century thought, Gassendi likened the infinite combinations formed in nature from the atoms to the endless possible combinations of the letters of the alphabet to form words and sentences. The atoms are the alphabet of the universe. Nature presents ascending degrees of complexes of atoms. The primary complexes form various kinds of earth, secondary complexes form metals; and at far more elaborate levels there are ranged primary and secondary organic compounds. The theory readily associated with the empirical trend of natural inquiry, for it emphatically stressed the importance of sense-perception and scientific observation, and impugned the *a priori* methods of the schools. Moreover, it sought to unite corpuscular physics with orthodox Christian theology. The original motion of the atoms was directed by God and the development of things expressed His laws. It should be added that Gassendi ascribed a kind of sensation to the atoms, similar to that ascribed by Bacon to inanimate bodies.

The rehabilitation of the atomic theory of matter by Gassendi was welcomed in England. The groups of natural inquirers in Oxford and London frequently discussed it at their meetings and compared it with the Aristotelian principles of matter and form. And it took hold in circles that moved in orbits outside the invisible college. The *Physiologia* of Walter Charleton, published in 1654, reflects this interest. It is true that he avows that he is more indebted to the ancient philosophers of nature than to the modern, but he examines the views of some contemporary thinkers, particularly those of Descartes. The universe is composed of body and inanity, or emptiness; expressions that recall Lucretius'

Omnis ut est igitur per se natura duabus
Consistit rebus nam corpora sunt et inane.

The atomists rejected the notion of the continuity of elementary matter, which was fundamental to the conceptions of Descartes and also to those of Hobbes. The dualism of atoms and the void was defended by arguments from analogy; the atoms in a body were likened to a heap of grains of corn, in which there are minute intervals where the grains do not touch one another. Moreover, phenomena of compression and expansion point to the presence of a vacuum. And, in general, the motion of the atoms demands it. In describing the nature of the ultimate atoms Charleton shows how various were the interpretations given to these basic entities in contemporary speculation. For him the particles of matter were physical bodies, not mathematical points, and he refused to allow that geometrical demonstrations could be transferred to physics. For mathematics assumes infinity in space and time, and also precision of measurement; the composite parts of a material thing can never be exactly assessed, and its constituent elements are not infinite. Charleton and other Epicureans rejected mathematical accounts of the arrangement of the atoms. It was generally agreed, however, that all atoms are composed of the same substance, but that they differ incalculably in size, shape, and weight. They are incredibly minute. Consider 'the pulverized fragments of bodies which the beams of the sun, transmitted through lattice windows, makes visible in the air. One of these dusty granules doth consist of myriads of thousand of true atoms.'[1] To the properties that have been mentioned must be added the property of motion. Atoms are in perpetual motion, 'never desisting from internal evolutions, circumgyrations, and other changes of position'. The movements of atoms are governed by the laws of efficient causation, that is to say, by the varying force and direction of contact. There is no action at a distance; when no visible force is apparent between bodies, as in cases of magnetic attraction, we must suppose that the movement is due to 'swarms of subtle emanations'. The corpuscular theory renders

[1] W. Charleton, *Physiologia*, London, 1654, II. iii. 11.

nugatory not only the sympathies and antipathies, the appetites and repulsions, of the occult chemists, but also the substantial forms, the powers and acts, of the Aristotelians. In the hands of 'physiologists' such as Charleton, the Epicurean philosophy refuses to allow any genuine development in nature. The principle of the indestructibility of atoms is firmly asserted; and it is affirmed that no new atoms can be created. Things that appear to be new are fresh or more complex configurations of pre-existent atoms, and even the specific form of the schools, as, for example, the specific form of a horse, is 'not a new or freshly created substance but only a certain contexture of the most subtle and moveable atoms in the composition'.[1]

The universal genius of the new philosophy, Robert Boyle, was deeply influenced by his early reading of Gassendi and in many passages he defended 'the corpuscularian and mechanical' philosophy as being the most tenable hypothesis to account for the phenomena of nature. He declared that the aim of his experiments was to establish 'a good intelligence betwixt the corpuscularian philosophers and the chemists'. The vast array of qualities in things are all derived from 'the magnitude, figure and motion of the atoms'. In *The History of Particular Qualities* he describes eleven fundamental properties of matter, and these properties relate to the size, shape, motion, position, order, and association of the atoms. The endless variety of substances and qualities are the results of the permutations and combinations of these atomic properties. And, reverting to the favourite simile of the atomists, he represents the bulk, figure, and motion of the atoms as the alphabet of nature.[2] In other treatises he shows at length by reference to numerous practical experiments that the four peripatetic elements and the three chemical principles of the spagyrites or Paracelsians are insufficient to account for the facts, and that the atoms of the corpuscularian school were better fitted to explain the intimate nature of things.

Boyle's is the most celebrated statement of the new Epicureanism. But it was widely embraced by 'physiologists' and the title of a book published in 1664 refers to 'the now famous atomical hypothesis'. Philosophers concerned with the bearings of the new knowledge upon religious beliefs approved of the

---

[1] W. Charleton, *Physiologia*, London, 1654, IV. ii. 1.

[2] Boyle, *Works*, ed. T. Birch, London, 1772, iii. 197 f.

Democritean atomism that had been 'so successfully revived of late by Cartesius',[1] though they labour to show that it must be supplemented by spiritual elements. Atomism, in truth, became tainted with Hobbism and its supporters were obliged to risk the charges of atheism and irreligion. They took pains to declare their belief that the motion and disposition of the atoms were ordained by God and to disavow in the strongest terms the view that 'all the regular motions in nature should be from blind tumultuous jumblings'.[2] Conservatives in philosophy also attacked the theory. The author of *Arcana Microcosmi* criticizes at length 'the absurdities of this whimsical opinion concerning atoms' but his censures display considerable misunderstandings of the doctrine.[3]

But the corpuscular theory of nature developed in close alliance with a more important tendency the mathematical theory of nature.

IV

This influence began to penetrate English ideas during the lifetime of Galileo. His *Mechanics* was read in the French translation by Mersenne, and within twenty-five years of his death the *Dialogues on Astronomy* and on *Two New Sciences* were being circulated in the English version by Thomas Salisbury. A large number of copies of this translation were destroyed in the years after publication in the great fire of London. Meanwhile the universal possibility of these theories of physical reality had been perceived by Descartes, and upon many inquiring minds, already predisposed towards a mathematical vision of things, the *Discours de la Méthode*, published in 1637, burst as a revelation of truth. It was not the preliminary metaphysics of the *Discours* that thrilled English philosophers; it was the 'essays in this method', the *Dioptric*, the *Meteors*, and the *Geometry* that excited their enthusiasm. Other works of Descartes were widely read and discussed soon after they were published, and books and pamphlets quickly appeared presenting sketches of his doctrines. The new philosophy and its author called forth a wealth of encomia. Glanvil epitomized the admiration of a generation of writers when he wrote in 1661 of 'the grand Secretary of

[1] R. Cudworth, *The True Intellectual System of the Universe*, iii.
[2] J. Glanvil, *Essays*, London, 1676, iv. 32.
[3] A. Ross, *Arcana Microcosmi*, London, 1652, II. xvii.

Nature, the miraculous Descartes' as having 'infinitely outdone all the Philosophers who went before him, in giving a particular and Analytical account of the Universal Fabrick'.[1] The new doctrines had been defended at Cambridge in 1649 in opposition to the 'jejune peripatetick philosophy'; and in the course of the ensuing decade the reading and teaching of Cartesianism increased at the university. Among its fervent exponents was Henry More, who lectured on the *Dioptrics*, the *Meteors*, and part of the *Principles of Philosophy*. His admiration for Descartes at this period approached idolatry. In a letter to the great Frenchman, written in 1648, he says, 'All the masters of Nature's secrets, who have ever existed, or who exist even now, manifestly appear dwarfs and pigmies in comparison with your splendid genius.'[2] At Oxford the new theory was received less cordially than at Cambridge. Cartesianism was even acclaimed by the clergy, and leading prelates, such as Simon Patrick, vindicated the theological merits of the system. They deposed that the new science was in full accord with the Mosaic account of creation. Descartes was also found to be a powerful force in the fight against Hobbes. But this strong tide of approval was tinged with certain misgivings, and the criticisms grew by the end of the century into vehement opposition. More is a striking instance of this change of front. His earlier adulation of Descartes has just been illustrated. In the *Enchiridion Metaphysicum* (1671) he refers to Cartesianism as the enemy of religion, and in *The True Notion of a Spirit* warns his readers against Descartes who 'by his jocular metaphysical Meditations has so luxated and distorted the rational Faculties of some otherwise sober and quick-witted Persons'. Yet Cartesianism advanced with steady pace among thinking men, and the sharpest intellectual conflicts of the time arose in relation to its comprehensive claim.

The mathematicians and natural philosophers who debated the works of Kepler and of Galileo at the meetings in Oxford and London had become aware of an extraordinary departure from the traditional notions of matter. From Kepler they had received the suggestion that the real order of the sun and planets consisted in a system of quantitative relations, and from Galileo they received a far more precise account of the mathematical

[1] *The Vanity of Dogmatising*, 1661, p. 211.   [2] *Epistolae ad Descartes*, i.

relations of moving terrestrial bodies, verified by numerous experiments. In this philosophy units of space and time, of distance and intervals, serve to discover the exact laws of the behaviour of matter. 'True philosophy expounds nature to us; but she can only be understood by him who has learned the language in which she speaks to us. This language is mathematics, and its symbols are mathematical figures.' The world that interests the new knowledge is a world of measurable forces, accelerations, momenta, velocities. Number, weight, shape, magnitude, position, motion, are the primal realities; other features of things, colours, tastes, sounds, smoothness, softness, are irrelevant. But Galileo went farther. He maintained that these qualities are dependent upon the measurable qualities of things, and have no being in the things themselves. They are the products of human senses. 'Tastes, odours, colours, on the side of the object in which they seem to exist are nothing but mere names, and reside solely in the sensitive body.' The sensory qualities of things do not afford material for scientific knowledge. The mathematical relations with which mechanics is concerned alone give us knowledge, that is to say, information which is certain, objective, and immutable. The affinity of the new outlook with the original impulse of Platonism is evident. The qualitative inward powers that determine the essences and the changes of things were abandoned in favour of quantitative spatial and temporal relations.

The wider implications of this view of nature were revealed to English philosophers, as we have seen, by Descartes. The cardinal feature of the *Dioptric, the Meteors*, and *the Geometry* lies in the ideal of reducing the entire physical fabric of things to a universal mathematics. The invention of analytical geometry in 1619 had encouraged the vision that the physics that had till then been connected with medicine and philosophy might now be shown to be reducible to number. The essential step was the discovery of a method of expressing the correspondence between algebraic formulae and spatial properties, and this remarkable advance in mathematical generality led in Descartes's mind to the perspective of an all-embracing method applicable to every region of knowledge. From a few 'simple natures', understood with indefeasible clarity, the characteristics of countless natural objects and events might be strictly deduced. The 'simple natures' that lie at the basis of the method are extension, figure, and motion. Every natural law is deducible from certain primary propositions of geometry and mechanics, and these in turn rest on the fundamental assertions of metaphysics. A place for observation and induction is allowed in order to decide between alternative deductions.[1] But the salient logic of this philosophy of nature is mathematical demonstration from first principles. The explanation of all material phenomena follows from the principles of calculable pressure and impulsion. The demonstration was applied to the motions of the planets, the earth, and the sun, to the nature of light, to the phenomena of the tides, to the formation of metals and of glass, and to the anatomy of animals. The cardinal principle is that all the properties of things are reducible to the divisions and interactions of the universal matter. And it is to be observed that Descartes himself associates this embracing principle with the corpuscular theory. He distinguishes his theory of atoms from the revived theories of the Greeks, but maintains that all sensible bodies are ultimately composed of insensible particles, the relations between which are determined according to the rules of mechanics.

The proposal to deduce the fabric of the whole world from a very small number of principles and to subject all departments of natural knowledge to a universal determined order, excluding all considerations of ends, internal powers and natures, was received with deep interest and admiration in England, as we have noticed. By the leading thinkers of the new philosophy the Cartesian mathematical physics was quickly adapted to the empirical method of inquiry and to the cautious speculation of the Baconian gospel. The form in which the experimental and the mathematical, the Baconian and the Cartesian, methods of explanation combined together and qualified one another in English thought signally appears in the general theories of Robert Boyle. We have cited him as an ardent disciple of the Baconian method, the method of patient observation and experiment; and the author of *The Usefulnesse of the Experimental Naturall Philosophy* is never tired of insisting upon the creed of the *Novum Organum*. It is the road to truth as well as to the improvement of human conditions of life. But Boyle also

---

[1] Descartes, *Discours*, vi, *Œuvres*, ed. Adam et Tannery, Paris, 1908, vi. 64–5.

wrote treatises in support of the Cartesian theory and united it with the corpuscularian philosophy of matter. 'The Magnitude, Figure and motion of Atoms', and the permutations and combinations of these fundamental principles, afforded the most satisfactory explanation of heat and cold and all other qualities of things. Bulk, figure, and motion constituted the alphabet of nature; the universe is a gigantic machine the interrelations of which are determined by mathematical rules. Everywhere in his general philosophy of nature Boyle has recourse to Cartesian theories, but the pragmatic, Baconian influence, which is equally powerful in him, leads him to insist upon the tentative character of such theories. He finds them intellectually valuable but declares that other explanations may be possible. He thinks it highly useful that some speculative wits well versed in mathematical principles and mechanical contrivances should employ themselves in deducing the modes or qualities of matter from the motion and figure of primitive corpuscles. But speculation on the ultimate causes of phenomena must be distinguished from knowledge of special principles derived from experiment. The test of hypothesis—and Boyle associates this testing with usefulness—is variety of experiment and observation; and the mechanical philosophers have brought few experiments to verify their assertions. It is his hope to do no unreasonable service to the corpuscular philosophers by illustrating some of their notions with sensible experiments.[1] *The Specimens of an Attempt to make Chymical Experiments Useful to Illustrate the Notions of the Corpuscular Philosophy*, 1661, contributed to this purpose.

Boyle, accordingly, recommends a discipline of reason by the constant evidence of the senses, and this outlook is characteristic of the main body of thought. The union of experimental and mathematical methods steadily developed, but criticisms of the Cartesian system soon became fashionable. Many of these objections referred to various details of the natural theory, particularly to the theory of vortices. But the metaphysics also occasioned much criticism. Some academic thinkers recoiled from Descartes's sceptical method and defended the truth of common notions or innate rational principles against the radical doubt of reason in the *Meditations*. The scholastic proofs of the

[1] *Certain Physiological Essays, Works,* i. 308.

existence of God, which form the keystone of Descartes's philosophy of reality, were criticized. Glanvil, as we have seen, expressed the admiration of his generation for Descartes, but he concentrated also into the pages of his first book a number of the current criticisms of 'the grand secretary of nature'. The doctrine of the union of body and mind is obscure, and the manner by which one can affect the other is a mystery. The account of memory is inconceivable, and the theory of the coherence of matter, though the most ingenious and rational that has been offered, is full of difficulty. But the aspect of Cartesianism that provoked increasing alarm was the vision of universal mechanism that hovered over it. Descartes taught that, side by side with the determined universe of extension and motion, there existed a realm of incorporeal substance un-amenable to scientific treatment, and he argued that this spiritual reality was known with more convincing certainty than the world of matter. His recognition of spirit was gratefully acclaimed by theologians who were interested in the develop-ments of natural knowledge. They could pit the authority of the great mathematical philosopher against Hobbesian 'soma-tists', men who denied belief in immaterial beings. Neverthe-less, the vast mechanistic theory of Descartes was felt to be menacing, and a philosophy which taught, as Cudworth put it, that 'from the fortuitous whirling of matter there proceeds of necessity the whole frame of things without the guidance of any minds', played into the hands of Hobbes. We have observed the violent reversal of views that More suffered in relation to the doctrine of Descartes. The publication of *Leviathan* (1651) and *De Corpore* (1655) intensified the alarm of the new school of thought over the prospect of universal mechanism.

V

Hobbes proposed the first comprehensive application of the new assumptions to all divisions of experience. Early in his career he planned a system of philosophy under three capital heads, Body, Man, Politics. In the Preface to *De Corpore* (1655) he puts the scheme as follows. 'Therefore the order of con-templation will be reason, definition, space, the stars, sensible quality, man; and after man is grown up, subjection to com-mand.' The programme is audacious; the new physical principles are extended to the life of men and societies. The grand scheme is more explicitly described in the sixth chapter of Part I of *De Corpore*. Philosophical inquiry concerns the general causes of things that are the bases of particular causes. These primary and universal causes are known by reason, not by induction from particular phenomena. The method proceeds by abstracting the principles inherent in things until the most general elements are reached. But the one universal cause of things is manifest immediately; it is motion. The various forms and complications of matter in motion produce a necessary system of effects, figures, and properties, which system is named geometry. Further elaboration occurs when we pass to the effects caused by bodies in motion acting upon one another. After the working out of the principles of this science we arrive at the region of the senses and their causes; for the study of sensible qualities, light, colour, sound, heat, cold, and others depends upon knowledge of the senses. Hobbes names these studies 'physics'.

'After physics we must come to moral philosophy; in which we are to consider the motions of the mind, namely, appetite, aversion, love, benevolence, hope, fear, anger, emulation, envy etc.; what causes they have, and of what they be causes. And the reason why these are to be considered after physics is, that they have their causes in sense and imagination, which are the subject of physical contemplation. Also the reason, why all these things are to be searched after in order above-said, is, that physics cannot be understood, except we know first what motions are in the smallest parts of bodies; nor such motion of parts, till we know what it is that makes another body move; nor this, till we know what simple motion will effect. And because all appearance of things to sense is determined, and made to be of such and such quality and quantity by compounded motions, every one of which has a certain degree of velocity and a certain and determined way; therefore, in the first place, we are to search out the ways of motion simply (in which geometry consists); next the ways of such generated motions as are manifest; and, lastly, the ways of internal and invisible motions (which is the inquiry of natural philosophers). And, therefore, they that study natural philosophy, study in vain, except they begin at geometry; and such writers or disputers thereof, as are ignorant of geometry, do make their readers and hearers lose their time.'[1]

[1] *Elements of Philosophy* (the translation of *De Corpore*); *The English Works of Thomas Hobbes*, edited by W. Molesworth, i. 72–3, London, 1839–45.

The new categories of natural investigation are here exalted to a world-view that sweeps from simple motion to human cogitation and impulse. But Hobbes goes further. He pushes the new principles into remoter regions. He extends them, at least by suggestion, to civil philosophy and to 'the causes and necessity of constituting commonwealths'. He admits that the principles of government may be discerned from experience and by the analytical method, that is to say, by reasoning from the characteristics of human nature. And it is clear that he himself formed his views on politics in this manner. They were the outcome of his earlier studies in history and of the intense feelings provoked by the Civil War.[1] Nevertheless, when he came to formulate his general philosophy the political doctrines were assimilated in theory to the 'geometry' and 'physics'; 'for the principles of the politics consist in the knowledge of the motions of the mind, and the knowledge of these motions from sense and imagination'.[2]

The vast scheme here outlined was naturally carried out with unequal success. Many expanses of knowledge received scant attention, and there are obvious breaks in the commanding deductive argument. Not only is there much ethical and social discussion that is not brought into touch with the metaphysics, but there is much that appears to be inconsistent with that philosophy. And there were more patent limitations that brought him into violent opposition with competent authorities. His controversies with Boyle on the question of a vacuum in nature exposed his prejudices, and his bitter attacks on Wallis displayed his ignorance of the new geometrical algebra. In many points of his physics he showed himself to be out of touch with the knowledge of his time. Such technical shortcomings were serious in a philosophy that stood upon the principles of Galileo, and his opponents made the most of them. But though he was not abreast of some recent developments in mathematics, physics, and chemistry, and was perversely wrong in others, his outlook is charged with the new spirit. In the most notorious part of his work, his approach to the problems of man and society, he exercised a profound influence on the assumptions of his own and of the succeeding age. More than any other

[1] L. Strauss, *The Political Philosophy of Hobbes*, London, 1936, p. 25.
[2] *Elements*, i. 74.

thinker he recommended to English inquirers the new way of seeking the truth in these questions. It is to be discovered by an appeal to nature. Human actions are grounded upon the known natural inclinations of mankind and upon the articles of the law of nature.[1] The method of discovery is 'experience', that is to say, the cool description of human behaviour as it is and not as it professes itself to be nor as supernatural beliefs declare it to be. In his treatment of the motives that, in fact, govern the relation of men to one another Hobbes promoted a new realism in the understanding of the affections and impulses, and his spirit entered Dryden, the Restoration dramatists, and Swift.

But in his philosophical method he encouraged the Cartesian trend of speculation. In decisively rejecting empiricism he placed himself across the current of English reflection. We are not to account experience as part of philosophy. Observation results in 'prudence', practical sagacity, not in reason. Prudence is common to man and the beasts, and consists only in remembering and comparing past successive events. Reason and philosophy stand in contrast to such practical and doubtful knowledge, for reason proceeds from clear definitions and reaches certain conclusions.[2] And reason means the geometrical method. The ideal that he suggested was the ideal of understanding the physical universe and the world of mind in the manner by which a mathematician understands a complex problem. And as a mathematician reaches his conclusion by means of a strict chain of consequences from self-evident or clearly apprehended initial conceptions, so this method of philosophy sought to deduce the concrete features of the world from primary definitions, the universal postulates of thought, and the fundamental causes of things. Hobbes deemed Plato the best philosopher of the Greeks because he encouraged the study of geometry. He offers a new *Timaeus*. In the second part of the *De Corpore* he attempts to demonstrate the main shapes and figures necessarily described by bodies in simple or uniform motion. He attempts, in a word, to lay the foundations of a kinematic geometry as the ground-plan of all phenomena. He seeks to deduce the basic figures of things according to such factors as direction, speed, and confluence of lines transcribed

[1] *Leviathan, Review and Conclusion.*   [2] *Leviathan*, 46.

by elementary units of motion. He begins by defining the primary categories assumed in these operations; space, time, body, cause, identity, difference, and others. A central place in his argument is occupied by the principle of proportion, for the mathematical quantities of figures are discovered from a consideration of the proportions of lines and angles. In pursuing the geometry of motion and magnitude according to the method of proportions, Hobbes believed himself to be extending the work of the ancient Greek geometers. It is unnecessary to follow him into the details of this part of the philosophic enterprise, since his geometric method strayed from the fruitful algebraic geometry of Descartes that was being developed by leading mathematicians in England. But the general procedure of this philosophy was in line with the modern movement. The procedure is twofold. It consists on the one hand of analysis, reasoning from something given to principles, and finally to prime propositions which are definitions; on the other hand, it is synthesis, reasoning from first causes 'through all the middle causes till we come to the thing itself which is constructed or generated'.[1] And it is this deductive process that is able to reveal the structure of reality.

The one universal cause being motion, and motion always arising from the contact of a moving body, the system is materialist. The whole universe is corporeal. Substance is body. The immaterial substance and essence of the scholastics and of the Cartesians is a contradiction in terms. Even spirits are subtle kinds of bodies; and God Himself is 'a most pure, simple, invisible spirit corporeal'.[2] Final causes are rejected. 'A final cause has no place but in such things as have sense and will; and this also I shall prove hereafter to be an efficient cause.'[3] The entire cause of effects is a union of the material and efficient causes of tradition, but there are here no qualitative elements present as in scholastic thought. For all 'generation' consists of complications of motions. The arresting character of this comprehensive mechanics lies in its extension to psychology. Sensations are motions in human bodies. External bodies in motion press on the internal motions and produce phantasms or immediate appearances, and these are prolonged by memory and imagination which is decaying sense. The connexion of

---

[1] *De Corpore*, i. 312.   [2] Ib. 313.   [3] Ib. 132.

phantasms is thought; 'conceptions and apparitions are nothing really but motion in some internal substance of the head'; appetites and aversions are complications of the vital motions of the blood; and the control of the casual associations of the phantasms by desire is practical thinking or prudence, of which mention has been made.

Upon cultured opinion the impact of Hobbes' moral views was startling. The *Leviathan* provoked a storm in England comparable only to the ferment excited by the theories of Darwin in the nineteenth century. For generations the name of Hobbes spelt irreligion and licentiousness. Even in his own day he represented doctrines that 'have so great a share in the debauchery of this generation that a good Christian can hardly hear Hobbes' name without saying of his prayers'. He represented 'loose and licentious reflections upon piety and religion, the undervaluing and perverting of Scripture, and utter contempt of the Church', so that 'the very repeating all the particulars must be more grievous and offensive to most devout Persons than the most unclean discourse can appear to the chastest ears'.[1] And the flow of scandalized comment continued unabated far into the next century. There was in truth a storehouse of inflammable material in his writings. Moralists were horrified at the account of the nature of man and the practical teaching that was derived from it. Statesmen warmly challenged the authoritarian doctrine of political society. Theologians denounced the sections on religion as blasphemy. The surpassing force, lucidity, and wit by which these corrosive theses were conveyed to the public were themselves occasions for dismay. A steady stream of books, pamphlets, and sermons appeared in condemnation of the opinions of Hobbes. Most of them were pointed at the moral and political heresies. But the scientific principles and the metaphysics were also challenged. For they had revealed the atheistic implications of mechanism, and the scope of the new hypothesis now became the urgent issue of thought. We have mentioned the alarm with which some philosophical theologians contemplated the embracing mathematical rationalism of the Cartesians. The extension by

[1] Lord Clarendon, *A Brief View and Survey of the Dangerous and Pernicious Errors to Church and State in Mr. Hobbes's Book entitled Leviathan*, Oxford, 1676, p. 274.

Hobbes and his admirers of the geometrical method to politics and morals discredited the new philosophy still further in the eyes of many earnest persons and cast suspicions upon the labours of the Royal Society. Sermons were preached against the experimental and mathematical system of ideas. Dr. Stubbe, a physician residing in Warwick, violently attacked it in several books as destructive to the religion and Church of England, and the great scholar, Meric Casaubon, expressed the protest of humane learning against 'this way of Philosophy, of late years much cried up in London and elsewhere'. These philosophers, he says, advocate practical and useful learning and decry the notional and profitable way of study. If by useful they mean what affords some use for the necessities and conveniences of this present life, a brewer or a baker, a skilful horse-leech or a smith deserve to be named the lights and ornaments of their age. Man's soul is nobler than his body and those who promote godliness are worthier than inventors and mechanics. When the reading of the ancient authors is out of fashion, barbarism and gross ignorance will quickly follow. The new men affect scorn of Aristotle though he grounded knowledge upon sense and experience as much as they do. But the glory of God is not to be sought only among the wonders of nature. And the nobility of the land will be better employed in reading histories and in military exercises than attending on furnaces, or raking into the entrails of men or beasts. Casaubon does not omit to introduce the popular charge against the natural and experimental philosophy, that it is apt to degenerate into atheism. 'Men that are much fixed upon matter and secondary causes and sensual objects, if great care be not taken, may in time, (there be many examples) and by degrees forget that there be such things in the world as spirits . . . and at last that there is a God and that their souls are immortal.'[1]

The immediate effect of Hobbes's materialistic theories was to compel thinkers who were active in promoting scientific research, or who were sympathetic to the aims of the experimenters, to defend the new 'real philosophy', and especially to rebut the charges of atheism and religious scepticism that were widely levelled against it. The defence took several lines. One course of argument we have already noticed. It met the accu-

---

[1] *A letter of Meric Casaubon, D.D. to Peter du Moulin*, Cambridge, 1669.

sation that its philosophy was dangerous by denying that it had a philosophy. It claimed to be no more than a method, a fruitful and progressive method of investigating nature. This apology for the new approach to truth insisted upon the restricted character of its theories. There was no desire to set up some new system in philosophy. 'Their first and chief Imployment is carefully to seek and faithfully to report how things are de facto.'[1] Their business was to observe and to describe what they observed, to bring speculation to the test of the senses 'and by erecting a well-grounded Natural History to tie down the imagination to sober realities'. This line of argument manifested an important characteristic of English reflection, but the refusal to speculate was no reply to the criticism of the patent Cartesian tendencies of the 'real philosophy' and it was still less an answer to the charges of Hobbism and irreligion. More effective reasons were ready to hand.

The principal figures of the scientific movement were men of deep religious conviction. Boyle wrote *The Christian Virtuoso* as well as *The Sceptical Chymist* and showed in the former work 'that by being addicted to experimental philosophy a man is rather assisted than indisposed to be a good Christian'. The special argument for theological belief that was proclaimed by the new philosophy was the argument from design. Scientific inquiry reveals in all branches the marvellous mechanism of the Creator. The more precisely men pry into the arrangements and operations of the physical world the more profoundly are they impressed with the evidence of divine contrivance. The deity was now conceived not only as the first cause which set the atoms in motion but as the supreme designer of the laws of nature. The regularity and harmonious working of natural events declare the presence of a superhuman intelligent Being ever watchful over the good of particulars and of the whole. Admiration for the elegance and detailed contrivance of nature united mechanism with theology. Boyle in a celebrated passage compared the universe to the clock at Strasbourg.

'The several Pieces making up that curious Engine are so fram'd and adapted, and are put into such a motion, as though the numerous wheels and other parts of it knew and were concerned to do its Duty,

---

[1] Glanvil, *Essays on Several Important Subjects in Philosophy and Religion*, London, 1676, p. 37.

and the various Motions of the Wheels, and other parts concur to exhibit the Phaenomena designed by the Artificer of the Engine, as exactly as if they were animated by a common Principle, which makes them knowingly conspire to do so, and might, to a rude Indian, seem to be more intelligent than Cunradus Dayspodius himself that published a description of it.'[1]

Glanvil, in an elaborate essay, refers to divers instructors of the people who teach that the study of Nature is prejudicial to the interests of religion, and proceeds to show at length that the further philosophy scrutinizes the recesses of things the more it finds the marks of ingenious contrivance. Turning upon Hobbes and his followers he describes the view that all the regular motions in Nature proceed from 'blind tumultuous jumblings' as 'the most unphilosophical Fansie and ridiculous Dotage in the World'. The late restorers of the corpuscularian hypothesis teach that God created matter and is the supreme orderer of its motions; 'and hereby Piety and the Faith of Providence is secured'.[2]

The remarkable development of this theology during the ensuing age in England will be seen in the next chapter. But an alternative philosophy was at hand. In opposition to the materialism and nominalism of Hobbes there appeared a weighty revival of the ancient Neo-Platonic metaphysic, a re-animation, in conjunction with the new natural theories, of Augustinianism.

VI

The leading names in this notable movement were Benjamin Whichcote, Ralph Cudworth, Henry More, Nathaniel Culverwell, John Smith, and Peter Sterry. Several of them were fellows of Emmanuel College, Cambridge; others were attached to Oxford colleges. In religion these men and their pupils are witnesses to the striking development of toleration after the period of the Restoration. Before the Civil War Lord Falkland had assembled at Great Tew a band of scholars who debated in a spirit of freedom the problems of philosophy and theology.

---

[1] Boyle, *Some Considerations teaching the Usefulness of Experimental Natural Philosophy*, 1663, Pt. I, pp. 70–2. There are many similar descriptions of the natural order in the period. Nehemiah Grew, for example, declared Nature to be a great engine made by God and compared it to a watch.

[2] Glanvil, *Essays*, 1675, 4.

Chillingworth, Hales, Wotton, and others were detached from the ritual strife of the ecclesiastical parties and expressed in their writings the claims of freedom of inquiry and a charitable recognition of opposing beliefs. But among the divisions of Puritanism there arose intense struggles for domination. The furious denunciations of the Arminians or High Church party at the opening of the Long Parliament in 1640 were followed by sharp controversies between the sects. At first the Presbyterians triumphed and attempted to impose a rigid Calvinism upon the country. But the power of the Independent parties steadily grew, and innumerable religious groups sprang into existence. By 1648 the Presbyterians had been swept from power and the cause of toleration advanced, but during the Protectorate the conflict between orthodox Puritanism and the sects continued to be acute, and upon the death of Cromwell the extremists among the Presbyterians again bid for control. These leaders presented Presbyterianism as a system of infallible and exclusive truths. They suffered no dissent from the doctrines of the true Church and they advocated relentless suppression of the independent bodies. Their inflexible principles moved them to regard toleration as prodigious impiety and their invectives against all those religious organizations which did not accept the ideal of a Calvinistic Church reached a level of frantic denunciation.[1] The reaction from the intolerance of the fanatical Presbyterians was profound. On many sides there was a swift movement in opposition to clericalism and institutional religion that affected English culture for generations, and the rationalism of the eighteenth century is the fruit of the recoil from the harsh Puritanism of the seventeenth. But there were many authorities among the independent bodies who were champions of a wider and more charitable theory of religion, and especially the Cambridge group of thinkers eloquently promoted the cause of religious toleration. They expressed deep distaste for the bigotry of the more rigid factions and endeavoured to further a spirit of meekness and reason in theological matters. This attitude of moderation and open-mindedness earned for them the name of latitude men, and naturally called forth charges of laxity in dogmatic faith.

[1] Cf. W. K. Jordon, *The Development of Religious Toleration in England, 1640–60*, London, pp. 267–316.

They declared, however, their allegiance to the articles and discipline of the Anglican Church, while deprecating exclusive claims. 'Religion', wrote Whichcote in a noble passage, 'is not a hearsay, a presumption, a supposition; is not a customary pretension and profession; it not an affectation of any mode; is not a piety of particular fancy, consisting of some pathetic devotions, vehement expressions, bodily severities, affected anomalies, and aversions from the innocent usages of others; but consisteth in a profound humility, and a universal charity.'[1]

In this spirit they sought the rational justification of moral and religious insight. 'This I account, that in morality we are as sure as in mathematics.' Reason is an affair of moral and aesthetic vision as well as of scientific knowledge. Before the mental perspective set in the mould of Newtonian physics these scholars recalled to life a philosophy of Platonic idealism. And, as we shall see, this philosophy contributed elements to the doctrines of Newton himself.

The most considerable thinkers of the group were More and Cudworth, who drew upon immense stores of learning. Their dominant philosophical concern is the desire to prove the reality of incorporeal spirit in opposition to the new materialism and scepticism. They bring forward a large range of arguments to support belief in the substantiality and immortality of the soul, and they adduce the Augustinian theory of ideas to bear out the claims of theology. But Cudworth, and at first More, do not repudiate the mechanical principles of the material world proclaimed by Descartes and by Hobbes. On the contrary, they fully accept them. Divisible extension and motion are the true basis of all lifeless phenomena; there is nothing in the physical world besides these 'simple elements' and their combinations. There are no substantial forms, nor intentional species, nor any self-originating motion; for bodies are moved only by impulse from without. It follows from this view of the physical world that there are no colours in it, nor heat and cold, sweetness and bitterness. These are 'fancies contributed by our minds'. Cudworth is at one with the new philosophy in declaring that this view of the physical world has the merit of being intelligible when compared with scholastic doctrines that conceal their

[1] B. Whichcote, *Sermons*, quoted in E. T. Campagnac, *The Cambridge Platonists*, London, 1901.

ignorance under such terms as forms and qualities. The exclusion from bodies of qualities such as heat and cold frees the
system of mechanism from confusion. If they were qualities in
bodies, when a man is pricked with a pin or sword the pain that
he feels would be a quality in the pin or sword.[1] But these
theologians devoted untiring labour to the refutation of
materialism. They attempted, in the words of More, 'an inter-
weaving of Platonism and Cartesianism'; but they drew away
from Descartes's mathematical view of nature, and by 1671
More had reached a position that denied any pure mechanism
to the operations of nature. Three lines of criticism may be
detected in the diffuse examination undertaken by this school
of the mechanist philosophy. It is urged that mechanism
cannot account for consciousness; that the doctrine of motion
is inadequate; that knowledge is not confined to sensation. It
is plain that these objections are directed chiefly against
Hobbes and his followers.

Cudworth roundly asserts again and again that the primary
qualities of the new physicists cannot account for life and mind.
'The Atomical Hypothesis, allowing nothing to Body, but what
is either included in the Idea of a thing impenetrably extended,
or can clearly be conceived to be a Mode of it, as more or less
Magnitude with Divisibility, Figure, Site, Motion and Rest,
together with the Results of their several Combinations; cannot
possibly make Life and Cogitation to be Qualities of Body,
since they are neither contained in those things before mentioned, nor can result from any συζυγίαι or conjugations of
them.'[2] The new philosophers are right to reject the scholastic
type of explanation which is a mere tautology, proclaiming that
laughing and crying are due to laughing and crying principles.
But a mechanical explanation is not the only alternative.
Sensation and understanding are not the products of local
motion. The root error is 'ignorance of causes'. Cudworth and
his friends here stand upon the ancient principle that no effect
can possibly transcend the perfection of its cause. 'It is utterly
Impossible that Greater Perfections and Higher Degrees of
Being, should Rise and Ascend out of Lesser and Lower, so as
that which is the most Absolutely Imperfect of all things,

[1] Cudworth, *The True Intellectual System of the Universe*, i. 1; xxix.
[2] Ib. i. 1, 38.

should be the First Fountain of All.'[1] This is the cardinal
reason for the rejection of mechanism. The new theory supposes that a 'real Entity', that is to say, a new form of being,
can emerge from a different form of being that contains none
of the characteristics of the new being; and this is to say that
something can be brought out of nothing, or made without a
cause.[2] The traditional conception of cause was still sufficiently
potent to allow Cudworth to appeal to it with confidence. The
historic metaphysics continued to govern the view of the
universe, and in recalling the principle that an effect cannot be
greater than its cause the modern Augustinian expressed the
belief of many of the experimental school. But the Cambridge
group gave a special turn to the theory of order. They revived
the Neo-Platonic conception of plastic nature. It will be
recalled that the conception had descended to the schools
through Augustine's doctrine of *rationes seminales* and had been
asserted during the thirteenth century in terms closely similar
to those now employed by Cudworth and his fellows. Philosophers such as Thomas of York had denied the passivity and
negative character of matter and had described it as plastic,
possessing an attenuated kind of conation. They protested
against the belief that looked to the divine activity for an
explanation of terrestrial phenomena. In the same way Cudworth seeks to bridge the gulf between the mechanical and the
spiritual order, between the two realms of the Cartesian
dualism. The organic world is a subordinate instrument of
divine providence, possessing a certain independence of its own.
This mundane soul pursues its ends without clear understanding, impelled by its biological needs. The instincts of creatures
provide the best example of its character, 'as for Example, the
Bees in Mellification, and in framing their Combs and Hexagonal
Cells, the Spiders in spinning their Webs'.[3] The plastic life of
Nature constitutes a second head of being beside extension.
It cannot be resolved into local motion, for organisms determine
their own motions by a vital energy of their own. It is a form
of life and therefore incorporeal. Cudworth supposes that this
instinctive vegetative life is not only apparent in animals and
plants, but animates the whole corporeal universe, 'which

---

[1] Cudworth, *The True Intellectual System of the Universe*, i. 5.   [2] Ib. 4.
[3] Ib. 3, 37, 14.

makes all things, thus to conspire everywhere, and agree together into one Harmony'.[1] By this doctrine of a plastic nature the Cambridge group sought to overcome the sharp distinctions of the new thought; the worlds of matter and of mind are linked by the half-conscious instinctive world of organic life. And in opposition to Hobbes they reiterated the view that the world includes more than a lifeless concourse of atoms. More's absorbing interest in vitalist and abnormal phenomena led him to extend the notion of instinctive life to the world. Drawing upon Cornelius Agrippa and the alchemists he revived the ancient conception of the world-soul, *anima mundi*, that had been fashionable in the sixteenth century. The doctrine attracted attention and Boyle discussed it. He pointed out that it was an unnecessary hypothesis to account for the phenomena referred to by More, and observed that in any case it had not been proved.[2]

The argument against Hobbes' theory of motion can be shortly described. Since, according to that theory, body cannot move itself, motion must either have no cause or there must be something incorporeal to move it. Here again Cudworth charges the mechanists with 'ignorance of causes'; they cannot assign a true cause to motion. They are committed either to an infinite regress, or to the admission that there is some self-originating cause of motion. To say that motion has no beginning is to avow that it has no cause; and the self-originating cause can be perceived in ourselves and in animals.[3] The argument quickly leads in Cudworth's hands to a proof of the first mover. As for the psychology of knowledge, sensation cannot possibly be what Hobbes supposes. According to him sensation is the result of the pressure of particles of matter in motion pressing upon the body and producing corresponding internal vibrations in the nerves and organs. It is a subtle form of material reaction to external stimulus. More subjects this theory to a searching criticism.[4] The theory requires that each particle impinging on the internal system causes a particular corresponding reaction. But perceiving involves an apprehen-

---

[1] Ib. 23.
[2] Boyle, 'Free Inquiry into the Vulgar Notion of Nature', *Works* (1772), v. 183. [3] *True Intellectual System*, i. 4.
[4] *Immortality of the Soul*, bk. ii, chs. 1 and 2.

sion of numerous impressions at once. It requires a 'common
sensorium', whereby we perceive objects, not streams of
heterogeneous impressions. The external particles must produce
different reactions in the matter of the body that is affected
appropriate to seeing on the one hand and to hearing on the
other; yet we perceive the same object through seeing and
hearing. 'For we find ourselves to perceive the whole Object,
when in this case nothing could perceive the whole, every part
perceiving its part; and therefore there would be nothing that
can judge the whole. No more than three men, if they were
imagined to sing a song of three parts, and none of them should
hear any part but his own, could judge of the Harmony of the
whole.' Moreover, if our knowledge is composed of particular
physical impressions how do we apprehend width and distance?
Objects of greater breadth and at a farther distance must
impinge upon our bodies in the same way as those that are
nearer and narrower. And the difficulty is even greater in the
case of mathematical and logical notions. What corporeal
impressions can correspond to them? Hobbes had sought to
escape the difficulty by an extreme nominalism; these notions
are no more than names or words, by which particular impressions are spoken and thought of as though they were
universal. But this is absurd, for it would follow that logical
and mathematical truths would not be the same in all nations,
because they have not the same names.

More then proceeds to examine all the theories known to him
that hold the 'common sensorium' to be 'mere modified and
organized matter'. The discussion leads him to the conclusion
that the 'animal spirits' in the brain are the instruments of a
purely psychical entity, the soul, an immaterial substance
distinct from the body.

One line of argument entered deeply into the thought of the
time. It appears in several of the leading physicists and mathematicians as well as in the theologians. They descried in the
nature of space a proof of the pervading presence of spirit.
The view of Descartes that matter and extension are identical
was widely debated. More dwelt at length on the question. He
showed that space penetrates the universe and all material
bodies. It is indivisible while bodies are divisible. In a word,
it exhibits the features of spirit, and More introduced extension

into the nature of spiritual substance. Spiritual beings can penetrate one another. The point was vehemently pressed against Hobbes who had declared that since spirit was not extended it is nowhere and consequently nothing. But More proclaimed Descartes also to be the prince of the 'nullibists' and roundly denied his contention that spirits were unextended thinking substances. That mind or spirit possesses immaterial extension appeared manifest from the fact that it must be somewhere, and though spiritual extension differs from material extension in being indivisible and capable of penetration, yet it embraces some of the essential properties of space. This endeavour to make spirit correlative with matter is a fundamental feature of the philosophy of the great mathematical physicists of the time, of Barrow, for example, and as we shall see, of Newton. It is a revulsion from the Cartesian principle that matter occupies all space. Since space is not material it becomes spiritual, and since it is the framework of order and coherence it becomes an attribute of God.

In the mind of More, however, the incessant pursuit of spirit led to the discovery of indisputable evidence in sinister and even diabolical manifestations. The menace of mechanism impelled him to look for plain proofs of the operation of spiritual forces not only in sympathetic cures, but also in stories of apparitions and witchcraft. He was deeply interested in the collection of reports of ghostly appearances made by his friend Joseph Glanvil, and other eminent men as widely different as Richard Baxter, Robert Boyle, and Meric Casaubon lent their approval to the investigations concerning the demon of Tedworth and the witchcrafts of Elizabeth Style. The appearance of the devil in the form of a mickle black man was a piece of providence calculated to awaken a suspicion in the minds of the Hobbists and Spinozians that there are other intelligent beings beside those clad in heavy earth or clay; and the belief in wicked spirits invites belief in good ones and lastly in a God.[1] In the same way Baxter pointed out that the evidence relating to evil spirits had put any doubt of the existence of spirits out of the question.[2]

Cudworth and More brought forward other less eccentric arguments on behalf of theology. They repeated the usual

[1] H. More, *Letter to Glanvil* in the latter's *Sadducismus Triumphatus*, London, 1681.   [2] R. Baxter, *Saint or a Brute*, 1662, p. 135.

arguments from design. It is inconceivable that the organs of
the body should have happened by chance, from a fortuitous
concourse of atoms. 'As for example, the Eye, whose Structure
and Fabrick, Consisting of many Parts (Humours and Mem-
branes) is so Artificially composed; no reasonable person who
considers the Anatomy thereof, and the Curiosity of its Structure, can think otherwise of it, but that it was made out of
Design for the Use of seeing.'[1] The argument is applied frequently to the 'System of this Great World'. To suppose that
the 'Orderly and Regular System of this Whole World' is the
result of 'the fortuitous Motion of Dead and Senseless Matter'
is like saying that an illiterate man making scrawls upon paper
could produce a philosophic treatise. More applies the argument
from design so widely as to include the steadiness of the axis of
the earth and the action of gravity. He even declares that the
sea is made to bear ships, and offers an interesting explanation
of the presence of stinking weeds and poisonous plants; they
were created for the sake of the exercise that they afford men.[2]
The recurrent emphasis upon the evidence of purpose in nature
throughout the writings of More and Cudworth testifies to the
disturbance provoked by the Cartesian denial of teleology and
by the materialist speculations of Hobbes.

But we must now turn to notice the alternative philosophy
that was stamped upon the discussions of the time by the
Cambridge divines. The philosophy was in essentials a reaffirmation of Augustinianism. The ancient lineaments became
once more visible in England through the works of John Smith,
Nathaniel Culverwell, Cudworth, More, and Peter Sterry. The
ideas of the intelligible principles of things are not composed
of passive impressions received by the soul from without.
They are native and domestic to it, or actively asserted by the
soul itself.[3] Singular objects are not the only objects of our
mind and cogitation; we apprehend also universal entities. In
mathematics and in the logical principles that govern knowledge we apprehend an order of existence that is timeless,
immutable, and absolute. 'There are Eternal Verities, such as
were never Made, and had no beginning, nor can ever be
destroyed or cease to be; as, for example, such Common

---

[1] *True Intellectual System*, i. 4.   [2] More, *Antidote against Atheism*, ii. 6. 2.
[3] Cudworth, *True Intellectual System*, i, 4.

Notions as these, That Equals added to Equals, make Equals; That the Cause is in order of Nature before the Effect, etc. together with all Geometrical Theorems.' In his Essay on *Eternal and Immutable Morality* Cudworth extends the domain of these intelligible ideas to include moral conceptions and ideas of beauty. This Platonic realm of ideal truth and values leads him, as it had led Christian thinkers from the time of St. Augustine, to the conclusion that there is one perfect mind who is the source of all truth and value. And in his pages there is revived the vision of the ladder of perfections in nature; living creatures are ranged above senseless and inanimate things, and rational beings above the sensitive order, and all is crowned by infinite wisdom. We have turned back through the centuries to the ruling conceptions of Anselm and of Boethius. Cudworth, in fact, opposes the text of *De Consolatione Philosophiae* to the new 'democritic atheists'; 'neque enim a diminutis inconsummatisque natura rerum cepit exordium sed ab integris absolutisque procedens in haec extrema atque effaeta dilabitur.' Things in the universe do not ascend from lower perfections to higher but descend from higher to lower, 'so that the first original of all things was not the most imperfect, but the most perfect Being'. Cudworth's view of the temporal order is indeed widely different from the view of the earlier disciples of Augustine. The principles of the new physics of Descartes are accepted, as we have seen. But above the world of extended matter and motion he superimposes a world penetrated by the *rationes seminales* of Augustine, and beyond are the 'verities necessarily existing' in which all created intellects participate.

This resurgence of Augustinianism amid the context of the new philosophy was given further life by the appearance of a great work of idealist thought in France. The *Recherche de la Vérité* by Nicholas Malebranche had been published in Paris in 1675 and several translations of it appeared in England at the end of the century. It produced a deep impression upon philosophic theologians in England, and Malebranche was acclaimed as the Galileo of the intellectual world. The most striking token of this influence is the work of John Norris, rector of George Herbert's parish of Bemerton. He was a man of immense learning, well acquainted with the scholastic philosophers, and a voluminous writer. His most ambitious work is *An Essay towards the Theory of the Ideal and Intelligible Word*, the first volume of which was published in 1701, the second in 1704. He had before him, therefore, the cardinal expressions of the new philosophy, the writings of Newton and of Locke. In an earlier piece, *A Metaphysical Essay towards the Demonstration of God from the Steddy and Immutable Nature of Truth*, the Augustinian theses are developed. Since there are eternal truths in logic, physics, metaphysics, and mathematics, there are eternal essences. Such essences as centre and circle are eternal, not in their natural subsistencies but in their ideal subsistencies or realities. And these ideal realities entail the existence of an eternal mind. In the later book he explores further the ideal realm which is declared to be the model and exemplar of all created being. Several new points are adduced, drawn from scholastic authorities, such as the argument that the world before its creation must have existed in the mind of God. In the second part he discusses problems of knowledge and considers Locke's account at length, but the result is a loose confusion of Platonic idealism and recent empiricism. He returns at the end to the doctrine of intelligible principles that constitute the plastic natures and true substantial forms of things, and by which the harmonious order of nature is controlled. Norris's work is a testimony not only to the powerful resurgence at the end of the century of the ancient Christian Platonism but also to the continued absorption of theologians in scholastic philosophy. He studies the great medieval thinkers with the aid of Suarez to whom he refers as 'my metaphysical master'; but he is also deeply versed in the teaching of Aquinas. Here, as in all seventeenth speculation, we perceive the intermingling of the old and the new. The Christian heritage in philosophy is preserved side by side with elements of the new natural theory; Aristotle and Aquinas mingle with Gassendi and Descartes.

But from the Neo-Platonism and scholasticism of the theologians we must revert to further qualities of the new philosophy.

VII

A signal characteristic of the revolution in thought was its practical intention. At the outset of his career the *buccinator novi temporis* had recoiled from the unfruitfulness of the schools, and later in his chief work he proclaimed that 'the true and lawful goal of the sciences is none other than this, that human life be endowed with new discoveries and powers'.[1] Thought must be directed to the material benefit and use of men, not to abstract wisdom or logical subtlety. It must seek to advance the empire of man over things by inventions. 'Human knowledge and human power meet in one, for where the cause is not known, the effect cannot be produced.' The utilitarian motive is essentially united with the search for determined order. Natural processes can be predicted and controlled only when the fixed connexions that they embody are discovered by patient observation. The nature of things must be constituted on a plan that is indifferent to ends in order that man may use them for the production of arts and inventions. The guiding purpose of knowledge is the endowment of man's estate. The animating motive of this philosophy of science marks the changed quality of the moral impulses of the age. The old theological preoccupations have receded. Intellectual activity is no longer to be controlled by a philosophy the principles of which are conformed to a divine purpose beyond the world of existence. The basic assumptions of the ancient theological metaphysic had been weakening for centuries, as we have seen ; and the break with Rome, the conflict of the clerical parties, and the abundant secularism of the Elizabethan period drew men from the rational system that subserved religious faith towards theories of the temporal order. The association of natural truth with utility exhibits a change of theological and moral beliefs. The reform of knowledge conceived natural law as the expression of God's skill. Bacon relates utility and 'magnitude of works' to the divine government of the world. The order of nature presumed by the inductive naturalist expresses the true Ideas. God has made the world as a workman makes a tool; it displays rather His power than His will. It is power that interests Bacon. And he concludes, 'Truth therefore and utility are here the very same things, and works themselves are of greater value as pledges of truth than as contributing to the comforts of life.'[2]

The moral propensities of Puritanism lent countenance to the practical aims of the new philosophy. At the heart of the Puritan scheme lay the ideal of sacred calling, an ideal that united godliness with industry. To consciences that sought

[1] *Novum Organum*, i. lxxxi. [2] Ib. cxxxiv.

salvation in works the applications of the new knowledge were congenial. The greatest leader of Puritanism in the seventeenth century associates knowledge with use. Richard Baxter was no vulgar pragmatist. He thought little of the world; 'though earth were something, if there were no better to be had, it is nothing when heaven standeth by'.[1] He is never tired of striking at the pride of man's intellect, and he could look his own stupendous learning in the face and avow that he preferred George Herbert's *Temple* and St. Augustine's *Confessions* to all the works of the philosophers.[2] Yet he writes: 'We may therefore make use of all true humane learning, real and organical, and he is the happy scholar who fasteneth upon the *certain* and the *useful* parts, well distinguished from the rest, and truly useth them to their great and proper ends.'[3] The profound belief in the virtue of industry lent sanctity to the new methods of pursuing truth. The ideal of tireless sober activity in the service of God embraced with approval the ceaseless empirical and experimental activities of the natural philosophers. The evangelical conscience interpreted reason in terms of authentic experience made explicit in conduct, and by contrast purely intellectual processes, 'the way of mystical ideal reasons', in Seth Ward's phrase, were felt to be akin to idleness. Even after the Restoration most of the men of science were attached to one or other of the sects, though the Royal Society set out under the patronage of the king and of noblemen, such as Albemarle and York. And Puritan impulses lived on at the root of scientific pursuits during the eighteenth and nineteenth centuries.

The usefulness of natural knowledge is a frequent theme of the pioneers of science. Boyle wrote in 1646 that 'our new philosophical college values no knowledge but as it has a tendency to use', and later he published a book on the 'Usefulness of experimental philosophy' in which the Baconian aphorisms are confirmed and illustrated with many recent discoveries. Experiments, according to one writer, are not only full of pleasant surprise and information but are of valuable use in the service of men. The intellectual and the utilitarian interests coalesce during the early years of the Royal Society. A striking propor-

---

[1] *Right Method for Settled Peace of Conscience and Spiritual Comfort*, 1653.
[2] *A Treatise on Knowledge and Love Compared*, 1687.
[3] *Christian Directory*, 1673, p. 908.

tion of its investigations were devoted to improvements in the processes of manufacture, especially in the textile trade, in transport, in navigation, and in coal-mining. Technology rather than theory was the main concern of the society in these first years of its career. Ardent expectations were kindled by the practical achievements of physicists, anatomists, chemists, and botanists, and a number of books described the marvellous inventions that might soon minister to the relief of man's estate. John Wilkins's *Mathematical Magic*, 1648, is one of the earliest of these, Glanvil's picture in *The Vanity of Dogmatising* is the most eloquent. Looking back upon the age he sees 'those illustrious Heroes, Cartes, Gassendas, Galileo, Tycho, Harvey, More, Digby' as instances 'that will strike dead the opinion of the world's decay, and conclude it in its Prime'. And surveying the glorious prospect he conjures visions from the future.

'Should those Heroes go on as they have happily begun; they'll fill the world with wonders. And I doubt not but posterity will find many things that are now but Rumors, verified into practical Realities. It may be some Ages hence, a voyage to the Southern unknown tracts, yea possibly the Moon, will not be more strange than one to America. To them that come after us it may be as ordinary to buy a pair of wings to fly into remotest Regions; as now a pair of Boots to ride a Journey. And to conferr at the distance of the Indies by Sympathetic conveyances, may be as usual to future times, as to us in a litterary correspondence. The restauration of gray hairs to Juvenility, and renewing the exhausted marrow, may at length be affected without a miracle: And the turning of the now comparatively desert world into a Paradise, may not improbably be expected from late Agriculture.'[1]

These enthusiastic prophecies were made before the incorporation of the Royal Society. If the sanguine rector of Wimbush could have foreseen Dr. Denis Papin's communication to the Society on the steam-engine in 1687 and the subsequent demonstrations of models by Savery and by Newcomen he would have had further material for his speculations.

The concentration on technology reflects the close interaction between the new knowledge and the new economic needs of seventeenth-century capitalism. But the economic activities of the society were interrupted by the Dutch war and the great

---

[1] *The Vanity of Dogmatising*, p. 181.

fire of London.[1] The society was at a low ebb of its fortunes when Newton's *Principia* was presented to it in 1686.

We are brought to the picture of reality which, already before the work of Newton, was now informing many active minds in England. Such minds had learnt to think according to a logic that was incomprehensible to conservative scholars, to men such as Alexander Ross who bitterly attacked the 'new conceits and whimsies' and implored men to 'return to our Master's house; there we shall find pure fountains of ancient learning'. The Master was Aristotle. But Aristotelianism was now a losing cause. A writer of 1654 had described it as 'meerly verbal, speculative, abstractive, formal and notional, fit to fill the brains with monstrous and airy Chymaeras, speculative and fruitless conceits'.[2] A succession of broadsides from friends of the experimental way of reasoning were poured upon the sinking ship, though many critics took pains to distinguish Aristotle from his latter-day interpreters.[3] In place of the ancient metaphysical conceptions of natural beings, in place of the animistic principles of the sixteenth century, the new philosophy was substituting methods and hypotheses that approached the facts with wholly different interests and postulates. The method had already been wonderfully vindicated and its promises were illimitable. Its leaders in England expressed distrust of speculation and, with the dangerous consequences of Cartesianism and of Hobbism before them proposed to confine their theories to the range of empirical verification. The proposal inevitably failed. Metaphysical and even occult views were applied by the disciples of Bacon to phenomena in order to satisfy spiritual demands; theological beliefs were invoked; and a new philosophy of experience was sketched out in place of the old. The distrust of general hypotheses was itself a philosophical position that became, before the close of the century, a rational system of thought. And the fundamental simplification and generalization of the evidence presented to human perception by the new method was already being extended to all regions of experience.

---

[1] G. N. Clark, *Science and Social Welfare in the Age of Newton*, Oxford, 1937, p. 17.

[2] John Webster, *Academiarum Examen*, 1653, quoted by R. F. Jones, op. cit., p. 143.

[3] Glanvil, as usual, epitomizes the sentiments of progressive circles. See Essay 3 in *Essays*, 1676, for a sweeping condemnation of the old principles.

It was assimilating cultured belief concerning the fundamental reality of material objects. The rational impetus that propelled the new inquiries was an interest in how things worked and the desire to perceive with accuracy the structure and processes of natural phenomena called for measurement. 'How does this hypothesis show us', cries Boyle to the Paracelsian 'spagyrites', 'how *much* salt, how *much* sulphur, how *much* mercury must be taken to make a chicken or a pompion?' The question before the minds of the new philosophers was not 'What are the qualitative principles that compose the beings of things?' but 'What are the precise proportions of the perceived ingredients in natures'? But the qualitative ingredients were themselves specific determinations of more general entities that were being reduced, under the demand for precise description, to geometrical and calculable forms. The preface to an early volume of the *Transactions* of the Royal Society laid down the view that the mind cannot be allowed to apprehend physical matters except under a mechanical conception, and this means that we come short of a satisfactory information unless we suppose that knowledge is concerned with the magnitude, figure, situation, and motion of bodies; 'it follows that Number, Weight, and Measure must be applied to analize the problems of Nature'.[1] The new physics had begun by treating of the quantitative relations of things, the relation of the weight of falling bodies to the speed of their fall, the relation of the time taken by a pendulum to complete its swing to the length of the pendulum, and many other simple relations investigated by the groups in London and Oxford. It had accordingly tended to regard the scheme of precise measurements as the important consideration. Before the end of the century substances themselves had become resolved into quantitative spatial and temporal relations. Thought about the reality of bodies has become addressed to frames of reference by which material changes can be strictly determined. The theoretical construction in any special province was held to be established when the results that had been mathematically calculated were in fact found to follow. The mathematical theory of things unified the empirical observations and the observations verified the mathematical theory. The real nature of things was now being increasingly conceived metaphysically

[1] Weld, op. cit., i. 327.

as well as experimentally as a mechanical system regulated by
mathematically determined laws. And the mathematical treatment of experience required that phenomena be reduced to
homogeneous material; the quantitative differences must be
differences in the quantity of the same pervasive material. Here
the corpuscular theory supplied the system required. The ultimate homogeneous material consists of primitive units of matter
in dynamic relations to one another. Reality is seen as a system
of the measurable properties and connexions of particles.

The theoretical and practical success of this natural philosophy throughout wide reaches of knowledge infected general
beliefs. The conviction that the mechanical relations of things
constituted the primary order of reality induced the belief that
all those qualities of common experience that are irrelevant to
spatial and temporal determinations of bodies must be assigned
to the mind. 'There is in the body to which these sensible qualities are attributed nothing of real or physical, but the size, shape,
and motion or rest of its component particles.'[1] The sensible
qualities are light, colour, texture, sound, smell, taste. These
are phantasms of the sentient in Boyle's phrase; they are produced within our bodies by the agitation of external and internal motions. The hues we see, the notes we hear are not in
nature, they are imputed to the sky and to the birds by disturbances in our brains. The consequences of this philosophy upon
the literature of the time have been frequently traced.[2] Artistic
standards became assimilated to the norms of the new philosophers, and prose and poetry aimed at clearness, accuracy of
observation, neatness, and balance. They shunned imaginative
flights and romantic fancy, and Locke advised parents to stifle
the poetic vein in a child. There were several attempts to invent
a language of precise symbols; Seth Ward, Samuel Parker, and
John Wilkins published proposals for a philosophical language.
The ground of these developments was the belief that the
qualities perceived by human senses are appearances, 'they do
no more exist without our faculties in things themselves than
the images that are seen in water or behind a glass do really
exist in those places where they seem to be.'[3]

[1] Boyle, 'The Origin of Forms and Qualities', *Works*, 1666, vol. iii.
[2] See especially B. Willey, *The Seventeenth Century Background*, London, 1934.
[3] Richard Burthogge, *Essay upon Reason*, 1694, iii. 1. But Burthogge puts
forward a radically subjective theory; notions are also in the mind.

The outlook on experience that was gaining upon thought carried with it the view that the perception of things is an indirect and mediate process. It is the result of a causal sequence flowing from the real, that is to say, the mechanical nature of things. The visible image strikes upon the primary organ of vision in a certain order and position of particles and causes a sensation of colour. Motions travel from the mathematical entity to the sense-organs and thence along the nerve fibres to the brain where they become perceptions. This is the view of Boyle, of Barrow, of Glanvil. But there were more profound implications that were spreading over thought from the experimental-mathematical philosophy. A single type of explanation was beginning to be applied to all experience. The demand for simplicity and unity combined with the corpuscular and mathematical method to form a new habit of reasoning, a habit that looked to elementary and original traits in place of fulfilments and ends, to spatio-temporal co-ordinations in place of eminent causation. A comprehensive exposition of this modern metaphysic was set forth before the close of the century.

VIII

THE EMPIRICAL PHILOSOPHY

I

'THE celebrated Lord Bacon struck out new light in an age of general ignorance and corruption, and prepared the way for those subsequent discoveries and advances in every branch of science which have rendered the last century so distinguished in the annals of time. Newton and Boyle pursued the track which he had marked out for unfolding the system of nature, whilst Locke applied the hints he had given, to the investigation and analysis of the human mind.' In such terms and in association with four great English names, a writer in the *Monthly Review* for April 1771 epitomized the achievements of thought during the age of enlightenment. The first motions of the modern phase, the period commanded by Bacon and Boyle, have been sketched; it remains to observe the later career of the new philosophy in England, and here the tutelary geniuses are indeed Locke and Newton; though we cannot accept the belief in the dependence of these philosophers upon Bacon. We have seen that before the close of the seventeenth century the main current of speculation was running in channels shaped by the new sciences of nature. And it was already animated by the impulse to introduce the experimental method of reasoning into moral subjects, into the comprehension of man's mind as well as of the world. In the year 1685 Newton achieved the masterly synthesis by which the immense and complex motions of the solar system were deduced from a cardinal principle, the principle that every particle of matter attracts every other particle with a force proportional to the product of its mass and inversely proportional to the square of the distance between them. The movement of bodies from the fall of a block of stone to the orbits of the moon and the planets were brought together in one mathematical design and accurate observations and measurements, terrestrial and celestial, were found to corroborate the theoretical deductions. The printing of the *Philosophiae Naturalis Principia Mathematica* by the Royal Society in 1687 was the culminating point of the labours of the society, and the triumphant vindication of the methods of the new philosophy.

In his preface to the *Essay concerning Human Understanding*, published in 1690, John Locke described his inquiries as being those of 'an under-labourer in clearing the ground a little' leaving the task of extending knowledge to 'a Boyle or a Sydenham', 'the great Huyghensius' and 'the incomparable Mr. Newton'. The *Essay* was the most searching attempt of the age to render explicit the main assumptions of the new outlook on experience. Locke's investigations into human knowledge were qualified by the close association that he had enjoyed at Oxford with the band of experimental observers who worked there, and he himself became a member of the Royal Society in 1668; the dominant influence on his thought was that of Boyle. The *Essay* controlled the direction and procedure of subsequent speculation. It rapidly became the standard text-book of general philosophy and many abridgements of it were published in the eighteenth century. It determined men's thinking for generations and all the leading developments in the theory of experience flowed from it.

The *Essay* formulated systematically much of the underlying conceptions of the natural philosophy of the seventeenth century, but it gave a change of direction to ultimate inquiries by stating the main problem in terms of knowing rather than in terms of what is known. The main issue is confined to the question of the extent and validity of human knowledge. This diversion from metaphysical investigations to epistemological problems is a tribute to the success of natural science and to its independence of metaphysics. Holding before them the new physics as standards of what can be known and as guides to the way of attaining knowledge of anything, Locke and his numerous disciples conceived their task to be that of examining knowledge in the light of physical science. Philosophy in the strict sense became a criticism of human abilities in order to 'see what objects our understandings were, or were not, fitted to deal with'. But the inquiry was guided by the metaphysical assumptions that had grown up with the new natural philosophy, and these were confidently accepted owing to the explicit repudiation of metaphysical notions by the leaders of the new science of matter. The new science had carried with it from its birth, as we have seen, certain beliefs about knowledge and reality; in England these beliefs sprang in part from the basic dualism of mind and matter which had been the main working hypothesis of the new philosophy of nature, and in part from the decidedly empirical qualities of English physics in the seventeenth century. The general outline of the psycho-physical dualism has been noticed in the previous chapter. With differences in detail the Cartesian dichotomy had become the settled background of the scientific view of things; it assumed a material universe of spatio-temporal relations facing a world of thinking substances. The fabric of knowledge is woven on the one hand of scientific realities described in mathematical terms, on the other hand of qualities in which the sentient organs of human beings are entangled, the qualities of colour, sound, taste, and smell. These qualities are excluded from the domain of physical reality. The mind perceives itself and its ideas immediately, it knows material things through the mediation of ideas. The ideas with which it is occupied represent the true character of things so far as they are concerned with the mechanical conceptions of Newtonian physics; they distort it so far as they are concerned with the sensory qualities of the world. From the experimental and analytic character of natural philosophy there grew the tendency to seek the ultimate constituents of knowledge in simple ideas, and these were conceived as mental effects of impressions accepted from the spatio-temporal order. The governing norms of explanation are analysis, composition, and mechanical connexion. The primary units of knowledge are impressions or sensations. The philosophers of nature constructed the physical realm from the determined relations of moving corpuscles; the investigators of mind devoted themselves to fabricating knowledge and thought from sensory atoms united by natural laws. The system of knowledge depends upon a few laws of attraction between ideas, comparable to the laws that rule the behaviour of physical particles.

The explicit parallel assumed between the mental laws of association and the grand generalization of natural philosophy can be illustrated by utterances made at an early and at a later stage of this phase of speculation. Edmund Law, in a passage published in 1747, pronounced his conviction that the principle of association 'will not appear of less extent or influence in the Intellectual World than that of Gravity is found to be in the Natural'. And John Stuart Mill wrote in 1865 that the laws of association are to psychology what the law of gravitation is to astronomy.[1] The consequence of this theory of mental processes was that all the factors that are implied in the connexion and stability of the world of experience, all relations and metaphysical notions such as substance, causation, similarity, difference, time, space, were traced to the action of association. Since all knowledge has its source in the sequence and coexistence of ideas the mind possesses no knowledge of formal principles. It cannot treat conceptions that have arisen in the course of the integration of separate perceptions and ideas as though they had an independent origin and nature. The categories of substance and of causation, for example, are merely the recognition of the way in which sensations and the ideas that survive sensations occur in sequence or union with one another. And the sensationalist foundation of this method naturally supported nominalist theories of universals. Abstract terms are amalgamations of concrete particular references; they are rendered universal by convention. Concepts are words which by being substituted for selected elements of concrete ideas arrest our attention on those elements. They refer to nothing apart from the concrete ideas.

Such are some of the capital positions of the philosophy that dominated speculation in England from the end of the seventeenth century to the latter portion of the nineteenth, from the writings of Boyle and of Locke to those of Bain and Spencer. Its logic reflects the methods of experimental science and it is interesting to observe how the successive theories of mental analysis echo developments in physical theory; Locke is influenced by the corpuscular doctrine, Hartley is affected by the discussions of his time on the nature of sound, Priestley carries over recent chemical principles to his psychology, Bain's view of mind is imbued with the physiological discoveries of his day. Our preliminary view of the classic position ignores many important differences among the procession of philosophies during this phase of our thought. All the components of the

---

[1] *Metaphysical Tracts of the 18th Century*, edited by Dr. S. Parr, London, 1837, p. lvii; J. S. Mill, *Auguste Comte and Positivism*, London, 1865, p. 53.

empirical outlook underwent development, the doctrine of the elements of experience, the theory of the association of ideas, the belief in the representative quality of ideas, the view of abstract ideas and the conclusions relating to the scope of metaphysical knowledge. During the earlier sections of the movement there were borne forward from the past many conceptions that consorted ill with the empirical standards that it asserted. Locke employed scholastic principles at important points of his argument, the notions of essence and of eminent causation, for example. And despite his destruction of beliefs in all classes of 'innate ideas' he upheld in several passages Cartesian and even Platonic views of knowledge. This rational intuition is especially prominent in the theological controversies which agitated the times of Pope and Swift. Orthodox defenders of the Church as well as the critics of revealed religion professed belief in certain infallible and universal dictates intuitively apprehended by all normal men. Reason could perceive by its own light the essential truths touching the being and character of God and the duties of men. Rational religion had always existed and the religion of the Gospel is the true original religion of reason and nature. By reason the theologians meant the original light of truth that had been corrupted by the Fall; by nature they meant the eternal laws of things and fundamental constitution of man's mental fabric. This rationalism was accordingly composed of several strains. Much of it was derived from the persistence of ancient propensities, Augustinian and Neo-Platonic idealism, and the Stoic conceptions of common notions that had been recalled to life in the seventeenth century. But these dispositions mingle with recent Cartesian and mathematical principles and with the dazzling prospect of all-embracing natural law. Yet by the middle of the eighteenth century the profession of natural religion founded upon abstract reason was yielding to the current of empiricism and scepticism. It became common to reject completely the claims of self-evident reason in religion, and, like the fourteenth-century thinkers, theologians turned to arguments from probability and from the external evidences of Christianity.

Let us now observe some of the principal moments in the career of this system. We have to recall its first authoritative formulation at the end of the seventeenth century and the bearing of the grand advances in physical theory upon its construction. We must touch on the strange conclusion to which its doctrine was soon pressed, the conclusion that nothing exists but ideas and spirits. The sceptical tendencies that accompanied the empirical outlook from the beginning of its course moved next to the front of the intellectual scene and they were closely followed by applications of the empirical premises that reduced mental activity to material operations controlled by chemical laws. Of these disturbing applications it was the doctrine that the human mind is material and determined that raised the most serious concern in the eighteenth century. Berkeley's thesis that the world is composed of sensations in the mind was received with polite incredulity and had small influence on the trend of reflection. And Hume's brilliant exposure of the difficulties to which the initial assumptions of the scientific doctrine of knowledge led was not fully appreciated. His few important critics, such as Thomas Reid and, later, Thomas Brown, themselves accepted some of the chief principles of the theory which they attacked; a manifestation of the hold that the classic theses had obtained over the minds of thoughtful men. Throughout the eighteenth century it was the *Essay* of Locke that dominated philosophical opinion. It was the bible of cultured discussion in metaphysical matters, and writers such as Reid and Josiah Tucker were severely admonished for venturing to question its teaching. Fresh conceptions derived from German thought began to penetrate philosophical debate early in the nineteenth century, but the main tide of English speculation returned with confidence to the principles of the eighteenth century.

The analysis of knowledge brought forward by Locke and his successors illustrates one of the recurrent tendencies of which the history of our thought gives abundant evidence. Their account of knowledge vividly recalls in many passages the descriptions of the nominalists of the fourteenth century. Their doctrine of signs, their view of judgement, their criticism of the postulates of causation and substance, often reproduce verbally the discussions of the Ockhamists; and the theological basis of Berkeley's philosophy resembles the emphasis placed by Ockham on the omnipotence of God. What they were attacking resembles also the Augustinian realism criticized by the terminists. But now the time was more favourable to the development, in association with these conceptions of knowledge, of a positivist outlook on experience. One strange voice was uplifted on behalf of 'the ancient philosophy that continued to the days of Mr. Cudworth'. But Lord Monboddo's *Ancient Metaphysics or the Science of Universals* in six quarto volumes was received with indifference by readers for whom the doctrine of intelligible forms had long been exploded.

II

In tracing the familiar outlines of the tradition we must begin with the two men who stand at its head, Isaac Newton and John Locke. Newton's work united on a fresh plane the experimental and mathematical logic of the proceeding period. He built upon the researches of Boyle and Barrow, of Flamsteed and Wallis, and upon the labours of the great natural philosophers of the Continent, such as Galileo and Huyghens. The purpose of the experimental observations is to discover those characters in things that can be mathematically handled. Mathematical formulae are generalizations of the perceived facts. The ideal to be aimed at is to express experimental physics in mathematical form, 'but geometry is founded in mechanical practice'.[1] The conspicuous note of the method is its emphasis on perception. Newton insists constantly on the necessity for the experimental verification of hypotheses and mathematical calculations. In many passages he spurns the employment of hypotheses in physical inquiries, but by hypotheses he means speculations that cannot be brought to the test of perception and experiment. He refuses, for example, to indulge in theories concerning the real nature of gravitational attraction. He allows that the atoms that constitute the basis of matter are moved by 'certain active principles', but he immediately adds that these principles must not be understood as occult qualities, nor as specific forms, but as general laws of nature, that is to say, as descriptions of ways in which material bodies are found to behave. It is not the business of natural philosophy to discuss the metaphysical causes of these manifest operations. 'To derive two or three general Principles of Motion from Phaenomena, and afterwards to tell us how the

[1] *Principia*, Preface.

Properties and Actions of all corporeal things follow from these manifest Principles, would be a very great step in Philosophy, though the Causes of those Principles were not yet discovered.'[1] Newton accomplished the great step. He succeeded in deriving the two or three general principles of motion from phenomena and in applying them to the elucidation of many aspects of the physical universe, from the rise and fall of the tides to the behaviour of light. His cardinal scientific discoveries and generalizations are not at present our concern. In relation to the new phase of speculation in England the interesting feature of his thought is its empirical quality. He was anxious to keep apart the sphere of metaphysics or general philosophy and that of science or natural philosophy. Natural philosophy treats only of secondary causes, not of the real or primary causes of phenomena.

This cautious attitude towards theories of reality encouraged the tendencies that had been characteristic of the new philosophy in England since the days of the Oxford meetings, and had determined the attitude of its leaders to the rational deductions of Descartes and of Hobbes. Under the authority of Newton the term hypothesis became applied, at the turn of the century, not only to the speculation of the Cartesians, but also to the principles of the schools; and forms and essences, genera and species are now frequently dismissed under the opprobrious name of hypothesis. Nevertheless, the sweeping span of the new mechanics of nature inevitably overshadowed general beliefs relating to the truth of things. And despite the avowed disconcern with metaphysics the Newtonian prospect of the universe carried forward to modern times a number of philosophical principles that had been accepted by the natural thinkers of the previous age. It assumed the dualism of mind and matter. The world of mathematically determined matter is divided abruptly from the realm of mental life. It assumed that knowledge of the world is indirect. Immediate apprehension takes place at a point in the brain, to which point motions are conveyed by external and mathematical objects to sense-organs and nerves. We perceive only the distorted representations of things. This view of knowing presumes that sense qualities, such as colours and sounds, do not exist in the real

[1] *Opticks*, iii. 1.

objects that constitute the frame of nature. The awareness of colour, the green of grass, for example, is the result of vibrations propagated through the fibres of the optic nerve to the brain, and the shade that is perceived depends upon the size of the vibrations. In a word, sensory qualities are subjective. Those entities that are discussed by mathematical physics are the solely objective entities, extension, inertia, mass.

The revulsion from debates concerning ultimate causes and real natures that characterized the philosophers of the Royal Society is no less apparent in Locke's *Essay on Human Understanding*. The spirit of the *Essay* is wholly in accord with the current distaste for vain speculation, and its purpose is to warn men from seeking to extend their inquiries beyond their faculties and allowing their thoughts to wander into those depths where they can find no sure footing.[1] The philosophy of knowledge that springs from naturalism is anxious to impress a practical lesson upon men, that they should subordinate speculation to conduct. 'Our business here is not to know all things, but those which concern our conduct.' 'Morality is the proper science and business of mankind in general.' It was a lesson that the modern type of earnest Englishman was ready to embrace. The advice that it is futile to pursue questions which human understanding is unfitted to answer discouraged metaphysical inquiries in England and promoted the growing preference for moralization over speculation. It was the age of *Robinson Crusoe*, of the middle-class virtues of industry, thrift, sobriety, and caution.

But the attempt to proscribe the limits of knowledge involved many declarations of positive belief. The current definitions of matter are accepted, and approval is given to the corpuscularian theory. The Platonic or Cartesian features that had entered naturalism are carried into the new empirical structure. Locke related that he had been attracted to philosophy by the works of Descartes, and though he declared his disagreement with the Cartesian outlook, the presence of that outlook in the doctrines of the *Essay* is manifest.[2] The dichotomy that rules the Cartesian perspective is assumed throughout; the world of material extended things faces the world of immaterial mental

---

[1] *Essay*, i. 1, 17.
[2] J. Gibson, *Locke's Theory of Knowledge*, Cambridge, 1931, chapter ix.

substances. The mind is aware primarily of ideas, secondarily of material things and accordingly the representative view of consciousness, frequently expressed by the earlier English physicists, is adopted. Material substances affect the mind by indirect impact, and the ideas so generated represent or correspond to the real qualities of objects. The qualities are faithfully represented in the case of the mechanical ideas, 'solidity, extension, figure, motion or rest, and number', while colour, sound, and other sensible ideas do not represent qualities in the material things as they are in themselves but are produced by the mechanical qualities in the mind. Locke followed his friend Boyle in naming these two classes of ideas primary and secondary. In neither class are we in direct contact with things; ''tis evident that the mind knows not things immediately but only by the intervention of the ideas it has of them.'[1]

In this distinction the quantitative or mathematical view of things is taken for granted; in the object there is nothing in reality but the determined interaction of its minute parts. The new physics are assumed. But the Cartesian influence on the empirical view of knowledge appears most vitally in the ideal of knowledge that informs the *Essay*. Locke seeks, as Descartes sought, the ground of certainty; and the type of genuine knowledge he found where Descartes found it, in mathematics. The science of mathematics and especially the science of geometry, furnished the ideal form of knowledge in the light of which all other claims to knowledge were to be tested. Genuine knowledge consists in the intuition of irresistible truths,'and this kind of knowledge is the clearest and most certain that human frailty is capable of'.[2] Demonstrative knowledge consists of a chain of necessary connexions between intuitive truths. The mathematical criterion of thought that had developed in association with the exploration of phenomena in the seventeenth century dominates the new theory of knowledge. The abstract modes and relations in which things appear are *aeternae veritates*, and the illustrations of necessary ideas in the *Essay* are drawn from arithmetic and geometry.

[1] *Essay*, iv. iv. 3.
[2] Ibid. ii. 1. Prof. R. I. Aaron (*John Locke*, Oxford, 1937, p. 218) suggests that Locke found the doctrine in the *Regulae ad Directionem Ingenii* of Descartes, which was being circulated among Cartesians during his sojourn in France.

But this mathematical view of knowledge is set in an empirical frame. In accordance with the experimental and observational methods of Locke's friends the foreground of knowledge is occupied with data given by experience. Guided by the 'physiological' methods of analysis the new theory of thought seeks by 'a plain historical inquiry' the original, primary, and simple elements that provide the basis of experience. The original components of ideas are natural occurrences that underlie the processes of knowing as the material atoms underlie the processes of the physical world. These elementary constituents are 'simple ideas' of sensation and reflection, presenting the external and internal primary data of experience. From these elements complex ideas arise by combination, the combination being the work of mind which unites and separates simple ideas at will. This analysis of experience into elements and compounds influenced the psychology and theory of knowledge in England for two hundred years; but acute critics in Locke's own day pointed out that he himself failed to preserve the distinction between simple and complex ideas, and that he allowed ideas to be given originally in complex as well as in simple modes. Nevertheless, the repudiation of all notions that are not derived from external and internal sensations is the cardinal doctrine of the *Essay*. The mind is a *tabula rasa* upon which the characters are first written by outer and inner sensations. 'In all that great extent wherein the mind wanders in those remote speculations it may seem to be elevated with, it stirs not one jot beyond those ideas which sense or reflection have offered for its contemplation.'[1] This inductive position leads to a conceptualist view of universals. Mental operations begin with particulars and particular ideas are taken as representative of all ideas of the same kind. Our knowledge is not knowledge of real universal species, for it is dependent upon sensory experience. The universals of natural philosophy do not exist apart from the mind; they are formed by the mind from observation of those phenomena that are found to 'go together'. We attain only the nominal essences of things, not their real essences. Subjective activity is especially present in mathematical reasoning. Mathematical ideas do not refer to existence, nor are they fundamental forms of reality appre-

[1] *Essay*, II. i. 24.

hended by the pure intellect. They are creations of the mind,
though they exhibit necessary relations between ideas. Thus,
the empirical outlook of this theory of knowledge prevails over
the Cartesian elements that are associated with it. Mathematical reasoning remains the criterion of knowledge, but
owing to the sensory constitution of our minds it consists of
abstractions. Certain knowledge lies in the perception of the
relation between ideas, in 'the perception of the connexion and
agreement, or disagreement and repugnancy, of any of our
ideas'.[1] But these ideas are not the objects of the pure intellect
according to the Augustinian and Cartesian outlook. They do
not represent real objects; they comprise a necessary system of
ideas.

The sensory origin of human thought severely restricts the
extent of our knowledge of the external world. 'I am apt to
doubt that how far soever human industry may advance useful
and experimental philosophy in physical things, scientifical
will still be out of our reach; because we want perfect and
adequate ideas of those very bodies which are nearest to us
and most under our command.'[2] The coarseness of our senses
prevents us from perceiving the underlying corpuscular nature
of things. We cannot penetrate to the essential connexions of
qualities; we can only record coexistences, such as that yellow
and dissolubility in Aqua Regia are found with the object we
name gold. The sceptical trend of English philosophical thinking at the end of the seventeenth century is strikingly manifest
in the famous discussion concerning substance. The idea of
substance as that which supports the several qualities of things
apprehended by the senses is a necessary idea. But our ideas
are ideas of particular qualities and since substance is not
a particular quality we can have no idea of it. Material substance is the unknown substratum of simple ideas. When
we perceive a horse or a stone, we perceive a collection of several
simple ideas, of simple qualities that we find are united in the
thing called horse or stone. But we can have no clear idea of
this unity.[3] And similar considerations apply to mental and
spiritual substance; it is the unknown substratum of the
'operations which we experiment ourselves within'. It may for
aught we know be material. Two certain items of knowledge

---

[1] Ib. IV. i. 2.   [2] Ib. IV. iii. 26.   [3] Ib. II. xxiii. 4.

are admitted. We possess indubitable knowledge of the existence of the self and from this knowledge we can demonstrate the existence of God. These two objects exhaust our
knowledge of existence; the rest is belief or opinion. In all this
the parallel with the fourteenth-century critics is striking.

During Locke's own lifetime the doctrines of the *Essay* were
attacked and defended in a score of books. The attacks reveal
the continued virility of older principles and also the lively fear
of materialism. Locke's unlucky remark that for aught we
know thought may be a property of material substance was
singled out for warm condemnation and the debate on this issue
raged long after his death. It opened the way to the physical
psychology of Hartley and Priestley. The most celebrated
instance of conflict between traditional metaphysics and the
new mode of thought occurred in the course of the long controversy between Bishop Stillingfleet and Locke. The Bishop
maintains the realist, the Anselmian, position. There must be
common natures or universals in things. The common nature
man must reside in individual men and must be one and the
same thing despite their individual differences. Otherwise
there would be nothing but particulars and thought and language would be impossible. The universal essences of things
must be the fundamental realities. Locke's account of abstract
ideas is irreconcilable with the articles of the Trinity and
Incarnation.[1] Thus the new nominalism was confronted with
the same combination of realism and orthodoxy that had condemned the nominalism of Berengar in the eleventh century
and of Ockham in the fourteenth. Locke was charged by many
prelates with Hobbism, scepticism, and infidelity. But in his
discussion of religious faith he led the tendency to rely upon the
external signs and testimonies recorded in the Bible for evidence
of Christian truth. This line of defence ran parallel to the appeal
to natural reason in the eighteenth century, and a stream of
books pursued the evidence for miracles and prophecies.[2]

The most striking outcome of the way of ideas was a stricter

---

[1] Edward Stillingfleet, *Works*, London, vol. iii, p. 511 f. The Augustinian
position is affirmed in *Origines Sacrae*, vol. ii, p. 232, where an idea is said to be
the objective being of a thing.

[2] Charles Leslie, *A Short and Easy Way with the Deists* (1698), and Thomas
Sherlock, *Tryal of the Witnesses of the Resurrection of Jesus* (1729), are prominent examples.

interpretation of its empiricism. A more consistent adherence
to the sensory origins of experience quickly resulted in a radically mental philosophy of knowledge. This type of idealism
merged with a current of thought based on principles utterly
opposed to the new way of ideas. The Platonic school of thinkers
had sharply distinguished sense-perception from reason. What
we apprehend immediately are not physical objects but the
sensations produced by them. When I touch a coal of fire it is
not the fire I feel but the pain. I infer the fire by reason.[1] For
the disciples of Malebranche the function of sensation was what
it was for St. Augustine, to excite our minds to discern the
intelligible ideas that are the grounds of things. Norris deemed
Locke's way of ideas as 'lame and defective as any that can
well be'. Yet certain thinkers derived from the study of Malebranche and of Norris the conclusion which others were inferring from the study of Locke, that the external world possesses
no existence apart from the mind. Arthur Collier is representative of this development. Relying on arguments drawn from
Descartes and the Platonists he shows that the exterior world
of objects assumed by the philosophers is otiose, for it is invisible and unknowable. It is 'the same thing to us as if there
were no such thing at all'. The belief in the external world is
full of contradictions. For example, philosophers tell us it is
both finite and infinite, divisible and indivisible, motionless and
moving. The antinomies cannot refer to anything actual. The
external world has no independent existence. The argument of
Clavis Universalis (1713) attracted little attention; it was not
aided by the scholastic definitions and divisions by which it was
advanced; such methods were now out of fashion. But similar
conclusions were being offered from an empirical point of departure. In 1710 George Berkeley of Trinity College, Dublin,
published his *Principles of Human Knowledge*. His inquiries
were animated by the old desire to vanquish the materialism
that lurked in the new philosophy of nature, for he felt, with
the Platonic school, that the belief in the mathematical substance of things was a danger to morality and revealed religion.
He hoped that his account of experience would be welcomed by
moralists, divines, politicians, and experimental philosophers,

[1] John Norris, *Essay on the Ideal and Intelligible World*, London, 1701-4,
p. 199.

and he saw his opponents in 'mathematicians and natural philosophers (I mean only the experimental gentlemen)'.[1] He offered
a view of knowledge in which a strict empiricism, nominalism,
and a contingent account of natural science are united with
Locke's way of ideas so as to recommend an immaterial system
of reality. All knowledge is knowledge of particulars. The
general relations and ideas assumed in natural philosophy,
matter, substance, cause, power, are usages of words by which
names are made to stand for similar groups of particular
phenomena. Terms such as force, gravity, and attraction refer
to nothing real, for they cannot be perceived. The notions
of absolute space and absolute motion are unintelligible and
the mathematical hypotheses employed in mechanics do not
designate genuine causes in the world. The only real causation
known to us is that which is experienced in conscious volition.
Here Berkeley's speculations join the current of reflection that
flowed from the philosophy of Malebranche and that had in
turn descended from the teaching of Duns Scotus and William
of Ockham. The sole motive power in nature is the will of God.

But the arresting doctrine that Berkeley proposes is that
the objects of knowledge have no existence apart from the mind
that knows them. Not only are the qualities that are apprehended by the senses, colours, sounds, textures, and tastes,
nothing but sensations in the minds of the perceivers, but the
qualities asserted by the Newtonians to form the real nature of
the physical world are also mental sensations or ideas. Extensions, motion, substance, and figure are ideas, and no idea can exist
outside the mind. For the same arguments which prove that
the secondary qualities cannot exist apart from the mind prove
that the primary qualities are in the same position. Extension,
motion, and solidity are apprehended in the same manner as
the sensory qualities; they vary according to the state of the
perceiver, they are dependent upon the sense-organs, in short
they cannot be conceived apart from the secondary and sensory
qualities. The belief that knowledge is indirect since it is the
result of sensations generated by effects proceeding from
scientific realities is contemptuously dismissed. The world of
real things is composed of items that are immediately perceived,
and these are sensations in the mind. The order and objectivity

[1] Berkeley, *Life and Letters*, ed. A. Campbell Fraser, Oxford, 1871, p. 420.

of the world is contained in an infinite and omnipresent spirit. 'Men commonly believe that all things are known or perceived by God, because they believe the being of a God; whereas I, on the other side, immediately and necessarily conclude the being of a God, because all sensible things must be perceived by Him.'[1]

The immaterialism of Berkeley was widely discussed but few were prepared to defend it. Samuel Clarke, who was regarded as an oracle, refused to discuss a theory so inept, and most of the writers on first principles in the period sharply reject Berkeley's conclusions. Two later expressions of opinion concerning the Bishop of Cloyne's 'ingenious sophistry' may be taken as representative of the prevailing attitude. Abraham Tucker refers to Berkeley's scheme 'that bodies subsist only in our idea, and are, or cease to be, according as our ideas fluctuate. So that when everybody goes out of the room, the tables, the chairs, the pictures they left behind, become instantly annihilated; and upon the company's return, become as instantly re-existent.'[2] James Beattie refutes the doctrine by a declamatory appeal to common sense. 'Where is the harm of my believing', he asks, 'that if I were to fall down yonder precipice, and break my neck, I should be no more a man of this world? My neck, Sir, may be an idea to you, but to me it is a reality, and an important one too'; and much more to the same effect. He admits that he has known many who could not answer Berkeley's arguments, but he has never known one who believed his doctrine. It is contrary to common belief and leads to universal scepticism.[3]

These consequences of Locke's premises were received with incredulity. More popular was a philosophy that, discarding all the intellectual notions that had been surreptitiously incorporated into the *Essay*, reached a position of sensory phenomenalism. The mind at birth is a *tabula rasa* and all knowledge enters through the five senses. Knowledge has no further origin than simple ideas of sensation which in respect to all conceptions of the mind may be compared to the first particles of

[1] Berkeley, *Three Dialogues between Hylas and Philonous* (1713), ii.
[2] *Man In Quest of Himself* (1763), by Cuthbert Comment (Abraham Tucker), Metaphysical Tracts, ed. S. Parr, London, 1837, p. 190.
[3] James Beattie, *An Essay on Truth*, Edinburgh, 1776 ed., pp. 179 f.

matter of the natural philosophers in respect to compound substances. These simple sensations are immediate, direct, and clear. They are passively received by the mind and lodged in the imagination. There are no purely intellectual ideas as the Platonists assert. All of our notions of spiritual beings are drawn by analogy from the observation of material and sensory things. The teaching of Descartes and of Locke that we have direct knowledge of ourselves cannot be admitted; it is as true to say that the body is in the spirit as to say that the spirit is in the body. Such are the opinions of Peter Browne, Provost of Trinity College, Dublin, at the beginning of the century. Nominalism is necessarily a feature of such a philosophy. But the salient consequence that is derived from the principles of Locke and Newton is the extreme deprecation of the search for real causes. 'All the real true knowledge we have of Nature is entirely experimental, insomuch, that how strange soever the assertion seems we may lay this down as the first fundamental inerring rule in Physics, that it is not within the compass of human understanding to assign a purely speculative reason for any one phaenomenon in Nature; as why grass is green or snow white? Why fire burns or cold congeals?' He defines a speculative reason as the true and immaterial efficient cause *a priori*. Observation and experiment show us that certain effects are produced, but any attempt to go beyond the facts is precarious.[1]

Other teachers reverted more nearly to the framework of Locke. But we have now to notice the most remarkable consequence of this philosophy. Before the middle of the eighteenth century the principles of Boyle, Locke, and Newton had been pressed to completely sceptical conclusions. No rational basis for human knowledge can be discovered, and we are obliged to believe by natural propensities of the mind the notions upon which common sense and science rely. The way to this sceptical conclusion was opened by Francis Hutcheson (d. 1746) whose theory of knowledge closely adhered to the scheme of Locke. He reproduces the familiar circle of doctrines. All the materials

---

[1] Browne, *The Procedure, Extent and Limits of Human Understanding* (1728), bk. ii, iv. Browne's argument that the notion of spirit is reached by analogy from sensible experience was used by the critics of the deistical view that the notion of God is an innate common notion. Cf. Philip Skelton, *Ophiomachus or Deism Revealed*, London, 2nd ed., 1751, vol. ii, p. 65.

of thought are traced to external and internal sense; the mind compares the elements thus received, discerns their relations, and inquires into their causes.[1] *A priori* notions are explicitly rejected, though a number of non-sensory ideas are allowed to accompany simple sensations. Hutcheson upholds the distinction between primary scientific qualities and secondary sensible qualities; our ideas of sensible qualities resemble nothing in objects themselves, but our ideas of primary qualities, duration, number, extension, motion, and other mechanical factors, correspond to the real natures of things.[2] But he accepts the orthodox conception of the limits of our knowledge. We cannot grasp the essences of things. We are assured of the reality of the external world only by natural instinct; the substance of both body and mind is unknown. For the rest, Hutcheson's metaphysics reproduce the Cartesian division between mind and body and other features of the philosophy of naturalism. His strength lay in ethical and aesthetic investigations. But the significant note in his application of the naturalist philosophy is the recourse to instinctive belief. He develops Locke's opinion relating to the ordinary confidence in the reality of the world of objects; it is a confidence founded upon the practical requirements of our nature, not upon theoretical conviction. Hutcheson refers this problem and other problems raised by philosophical inquiry to the natural propensities of man. We are led to embrace a number of important principles in dogmatic philosophy not through arguments and reasons drawn from the intelligible nature of things but rather by a kind of internal sense, habit, and impulse or instinct of nature.[3]

These suggestions had already been expressed by Hutcheson in earlier works on moral theory published in 1725 and 1728 and they had deeply influenced the strenuous reflections of a brilliant young man whose mind was possessed with ethical problems. David Hume's *Treatise of Human Nature, being an Attempt to introduce the Experimental Method of Reasoning into Moral Subjects*, appeared in three volumes in the years 1739 and 1740 when the author was twenty-eight. The doctrine of moral sense propounded by Shaftesbury and Hutcheson had led him

---

[1] Hutcheson, *System of Moral Philosophy*, published posthumously, 1755, bk. i. 1.

[2] *Synopsis Metaphysica* (1742), ii. 1.   [3] Ib. 3.

to distrust accounts that attributed the source of moral activity
and understanding to reason. He had rejected the rationalist
theory of the Platonists, embraced also by Locke, 'which
establishes eternal rational measures of right and wrong' and
had become convinced that moral perception is a mode of
feeling, 'so that when you pronounce any action or character
to be vicious, you mean nothing, but that from the constitution
of your nature you have a feeling or sentiment of blame from
the contemplation of it'.[1] But could not the principle of
natural propensity be ascribed equally to knowledge? Hume's
attempt to apply it to the fundamental assumptions of knowledge constitutes part of his great contribution to English
speculation. But the principle of natural instinct is associated
with the standard positions of the experimental philosophy
instituted by Locke, Newton, and Berkeley. The other side of
Hume's signal achievement is the rigorous and comprehensive
way in which he applies their conceptions. All perceptions of
the human mind resolve themselves into impressions and ideas,
the latter being faint images of the former; all our ideas are
particular and separate from one another; the bond of union
between them is supplied by modes of mechanical association
that display a kind of attraction comparable to the law of
gravitational attraction in the physical world. From these
bases he conducts a penetrating analysis of the beliefs that are
presupposed in knowledge, the result of which is to show that
the orderly connexion assumed to exist between particular
items in the world of objects cannot be rationally proved. The
belief in the continued existence of objects apart from our ideas
'is soon destroyed by the slightest philosophy, which teaches us,
that nothing can ever be present to the mind but an image or
perception' and these cannot give us any intimation of any
thing beyond nor, since the impressions are separate, can they
rationally provide us with the notion of continued existence.
The idea of substance is nothing but a collection of simple ideas,
the notion of the self no more than a bundle of different perceptions. Of all the relations upon which science is founded the
central relation is that of causation or necessary connexion of
phenomena. Hume submits the idea to a searching investigation. The rational principles upon which the scientific analysis

[1] *Treatise*, bk. iii, pt. i, sect. i.

of phenomena was presumed to rest, power, force, energy, efficacy, productive quality, and others are shown to represent nothing in reality. 'All our ideas are derived from, and represent impressions. We never have any impression that contains any power or efficacy. We never therefore have any idea of power.'[1] Our notions of spirits and of the Deity are derived from impressions and cannot give us ideas of force or efficacy; the arguments of Malebranche and of the Cartesians must be dismissed. In the manner of Newton the ultimate force and efficacy of nature is declared to be unknown to us. After examining the natural belief he concludes that our universal confidence in the principle of necessary connexion arises from an internal propensity of the mind constituted by custom. A number of conjunctions between impressions produces through the natural forces of association a prevailing belief that the conjunctions are necessary. When we are accustomed to see two impressions associated, the appearance or idea of the one immediately carries us to the idea of the other. Our experiences present us with constant conjunctions of phenomena and we suppose a general rule as a result of these experiences, but the assurance of necessity arises from our imaginations. We cannot penetrate into the reason for the conjunctions. Our minds are determined by custom which induces a lively expectation that the same causes will be followed by the same effects. The belief in the uniformity of nature is not founded on arguments of any kind but springs from a habit of mind. No reason can take us beyond the particular impressions or connexions that we have experienced, for all experiences are distinct and have no union but in the mind. Necessity 'is nothing but an internal impression of the mind, or a determination to carry our thoughts from one object to another.' Reverting to the cardinal notion offered by Hutcheson, Hume asserts that our ineradicable beliefs relating to the objectivity and rational order of the world are more properly acts of the sensitive than of the cogitative part of our natures. He refers them to 'a kind of instinct or natural impulse' that no philosophy can destroy. Philosophical inquiry shows 'the whimsical condition of mankind, who must act and reason and believe; though they are not able, by their most diligent inquiry to satisfy themselves concerning

[1] Ib. i. 3. 14.

the foundation of those operations, or to remove the objections which may be raised against them'.[1] Our intellectual postulates are dependent upon propensities of which we are not masters.

This annihilating criticism of the fundamental assumptions of natural philosophy excited a few incredulous comments from Hume's contemporaries. To some of the misrepresentations of his position Hume was able to reply. He protested, for example, against the charge that he had asserted that a thing could be produced without a cause.[2] But the *Treatise*, as its author confessed, fell dead-born from the press, and twenty-five years passed before serious examination of its arguments was undertaken. The *Enquiry concerning Human Understanding* (1748), in which the scepticism of the earlier work is modified, received scarcely more attention from philosophers. It was among the theologians that the conclusions of Hume were discussed and the polite public became vaguely aware of the doctrine of the *Treatise* through its association with the author of the notorious essay 'Of Miracles'.

The deductions of Berkeley and of Hume from the empirical philosophy of ideas did little to deflect the course of that philosophy. The outlook of Locke and Newton continued to rule the educated opinion. Yet there are signs of the effects of Hume's destructive inquiry upon thoughtful men. The effects appear in a shrinking from the investigation of first principles common among leaders of opinion in the latter part of the century. Dr. Johnson was averse to philosophical discussions and Burke expressed a dislike of metaphysics. Beattie, in a letter to a friend written in 1767, declares his 'conviction of the insignificance of metaphysics and scepticism'—the two are for him one—and in a later epistle he describes the philosophy of Hume as 'a frivolous, though dangerous, system of verbal subtility, which it required neither genius, nor learning, nor taste, nor knowledge of mankind, to be able to put together; but only a captious temper, an irreligious spirit, a moderate command of words, and an extraordinary degree of vanity and presumption'.[3]

---

[1] *Enquiry concerning Human Understanding*, XII, Part ii.

[2] The charge, typical of the general failure to understand the argument of the *Treatise*, was made by Prof. John Stewart of Edinburgh. The correspondence on the subject is given in N. K. Smith, *The Philosophy of David Hume*, London, 1941, pp. 411 f.

[3] *Life of Beattie*, by Sir William Forbes, Edinburgh, 1807, vol. i, p. 168.

The Rev. Mr. Knox of Tunbridge School was kindled to similar heat at 'the new infidelity'. And there was acclamation when the doctrine of the *Treatise* was refuted by Thomas Reid and by Beattie upon the commodious principles of common sense.

Meanwhile there had appeared a further development of the scientific conception of knowledge that had a powerful influence on subsequent thought in England. David Hartley, a physician who practised in London and Bath, published in 1749 his *Observations on Man* in which he put forward a theory of experience derived from certain suggestions of Newton in the *Optics* relating to the connexion between vibrations and sensations of colour. Hartley combined this theory with the account of the association of ideas that was added by Locke to the fourth edition of the *Essay*. He acknowledged also the work of John Gay, a fellow of Sidney Sussex College, Cambridge, who had discussed the psychological doctrine in a *Dissertation* introducing Edmund Law's translation of the 'Origin of Evil' by Archbishop King (1731). According to Hartley's view of the physical aspect of the process, material changes in the nerves and brain are produced by physical impulses entering the body from external objects. The material changes consist of vibrations set up in the infinitesimal particles of the medullary substance of the brain. When the exciting causes, the external objects, have been removed, the vibrations persist in the brain, and this persistence is the cause of sensations. The order and arrangement of the sensations reflect the order and arrangement of the original impulses that excited the vibrations. A mechanical and atomic theory of the association of ideas is elaborated upon this basis. The succession of physical vibrations and the psychological association of sensations are two aspects of the same phenomenon. The complex associations of affections in the nerves and brain excite corresponding complex perceptions and ideas. The difference in the degree, kind, place, and direction of the vibrations correspond to the differences in the sensations and in the simple ideas that are the traces or vestiges left by the sensations. Now when several vibrations occur simultaneously in the brain or when they follow one another, a single vibration may in time excite the other vibrations that accompanied it. The chief condition that causes this reproduction of the original vibrations is repetition; a further condition is the strength of the excitement. The physical phenomena correspond to the mental. When sensations are frequently or vividly associated, one element in the group will call up other members of the group; 'thus the names, smells, tastes and tangible qualities of natural bodies suggest their visible appearances to the fancy, i.e. excite their visible ideas'.[1] These simple ideas become united and merge into unique complex ideas the original factors of which cannot be easily distinguished, just as the various ingredients in Venice treacle cannot be separately tasted. This psychology is applied in detail to each of the sensations, to the formation of complex ideas and trains of ideas, to muscular habits, to memory, and to imagination. Hartley brings out the cardinal part played by words and phrases in exciting ideas.[2] The empirical basis of his view of mathematical ideas is manifest in the following passage. 'Now the cause that a person affirms the truth of the proposition, twice two is four, is the entire coincidence of the visible and tangible idea of twice two with that of four, as impressed upon the mind by various objects. We see everywhere that twice two and four are only different names for the same impression. And it is mere association which appropriates the word truth, its definition, or its internal feeling to this coincidence.'[3] He approves of 'the ingenious bishop Berkeley's' denial of abstract ideas and maintains that the propositions of science are derived from experiments performed a sufficient number of times, and from the observations of scientifical persons of 'the constancy and tenor of nature'. Here, and in many other passages, he takes much for granted. In his concluding remarks on the mechanism of the human mind he defends his doctrine against the philosophical theory of free will. He holds the view that actions result 'from the previous circumstances of body and mind in the same manner and with the same certainty, as other effects or from their mechanical causes'.[4] But he declares that this position has the merit of making us dependent upon the grace of God.

These practical consequences of the theory attracted immediate attention and Hartley was charged with denying personal responsibility for action. But the hypothesis of Hartley was

[1] *Observations on Man*, part 1, chap. i, sect. 2.
[2] Ib., chap. iii, sect. 1.   [3] Ib., sect. 2.
[4] Ib., Conclusion.

soon pressed to materialist conclusions. The belief in the two independent orders of mind and matter that had descended in its modern form from Descartes was abandoned. The whole man is composed of a uniform substance and his mental powers are the result of the organic structure of the brain. Mind is a kind of matter; but this conclusion is reached through re-defining matter in terms of attraction and repulsion. Matter is not solid, it has penetrative properties. This materialism draws upon recent experimental work in physics and chemistry, and asserts that the new conceptions of matter as a system of activities is not incompatible with the phenomena of sensation and thought. These processes are never found apart from brains and sense-organs and the distinction between ideas and their objects cannot be maintained. Reversing the idealist argument this philosophy declared that ideas must possess extension and parts if they represent objects.[1] No arguments from the ex-quisite subtlety and complexity of mental powers can prove their immateriality, for the affections of matter are as subtle and as complex as those that are called mental affections. Hartley's theory of mind is a practical answer to all objections of this kind.[2] Theological difficulties were boldly met by Priestley and those who agreed with him. For instance, the materialist hypothesis entailed the belief that the mind perished with the body. But Priestley held that God would reassemble the material and therefore the mental elements of the dead at the last day. A fierce controversy arose over the necessitarian consequences of the doctrine. Priestley stoutly defended a rigorous determination, a 'mechanism of the mind, depending upon the certain influences of motives to determine the will; by means of which the whole series of events, from the beginning of the world to the consummation of all things, makes one con-nected chain of causes and effects, originally established by the Deity'. Hobbes was the first to discover this great truth; it was promoted by Collins and Hartley. Abraham Tucker and Lord Kames are also cited in support of it. The will is determined by certain invariable laws depending upon the previous state of mind, but this view does not imply fatalism nor Calvinist

---

[1] Joseph Priestley, *Disquisitions relating to Matter and Spirit*, 2nd ed., Birmingham, 1782, vol. i, p. 58. The first edition appeared in 1777.
[2] Ib., p. 113.

predestination, for our own determinations and actions are necessary links in the chain of causation.[1] A rain of pamphlets descended on Priestley's head. Joseph Berington, a Roman Catholic, attacked him in a series of 'Letters on Materialism' (1776), in which it was pointed out at length that the powers of consciousness are incompatible with a matter composed of exclusive parts, a point which the author acutely pressed also against Hume's doctrine of association. A full and frank correspondence between Priestley and Richard Price on philosophical necessity appeared in 1778; and exchanges on the same question occurred between the great controversialist and the Rev. John Palmer. A swarm of other combatants rushed into print against the man who appeared to subvert the doctrine of a future state and to deny all moral responsibility. A few defended his theory of volition; no one was prepared to support in public the view that the animation of the body depended, not upon an immaterial principle, but upon a certain arrangement of matter.

III

The way of ideas had led to mentalism, to scepticism, and to determinism. It was the materialism of Priestley that aroused the most lively concern, but towards the end of the eighteenth century an effort was made to meet Hume's position on logical grounds. 'Philosophy is indebted to Mr. Hume in this respect among others, that, by calling in question many of the first principles of human knowledge, he hath put speculative men upon enquiring more carefully than was done before, into the nature of the evidence upon which they rest.'[2] The inquiry was undertaken by a long series of Scottish thinkers who addressed themselves to the task of maintaining a theory of experience that should preserve the inductive outlook of Locke and Newton while evading the consequences pointed out by Hume.[3] The notable figures in this succession were Thomas Reid (d. 1796),

[1] Priestley, *The Doctrine of Philosophical Necessity Illustrated* (vol. ii of *Disquisitions*).
[2] T. Reid, *Essays on the Intellectual Powers of Man*, 1785, Essay VI. vi.
[3] T. E. Jessop in a *Bibliography of David Hume and of the Scottish Philosophy*, London, 1938, gives a list of seventy-nine names under the head of the Scottish Philosophy, extending from Gershom Carmichael (d. 1729) to Lord Gifford (d. 1887).

Dugald Stewart (d. 1828), Thomas Brown (d. 1820), and Sir William Hamilton (d. 1856). Reid was the master of this school of thought, Stewart exercised the widest influence on his generation, Hamilton was incomparably the most learned.[1] The Scottish philosophers kept alive an interest in fundamental questions during a period in which clear and original reflection on these questions was almost non-existent. Philosophical activity was at a low ebb; university teaching was futile and men such as Gibbon, Adam Smith, Jeremy Bentham, and Sydney Smith spoke of it with contempt. In a letter to Dugald Stewart dated 1802 Sir James Mackintosh speaks of the want of anything which he could call purely philosophical teaching in England, and a few years later Francis Horner declares that the highest names in speculative pursuits were those of Hobbes and Hartley.[2] The comprehensive curiosity and scholarship of men such as Reid, Adam Smith, Adam Ferguson, Stewart, and, Hamilton retrieved the period from intellectual sterility. Yet the Scottish professors did not rise to the occasion produced by the analytical genius of Hume. Their critical and constructive thought was patently controlled by the determination to brush sceptical conclusions aside and by recourse to popular sentiment. Their persistent failure to perceive the essential ground of Hume's argument and their constant appeal to psychological criteria of truth are symptoms of the remarkable decline of philosophical inquiry that occurred between 1750 and 1850. The advance of materialism, infidelity, and scepticism stirred thought to activity. In Hume's own day any author who came forward with a refutation of the doctrine of the *Treatise on Human Nature* was acclaimed. We have referred to the opinions of James Beattie. A further mention of the celebrated *Essay on the Nature and Immutability of Truth* (1770) will illustrate the sentiments and standards of the times. Beattie follows Reid, whose *Inquiry into the Human Mind* had appeared in 1764, in making the criterion of truth common sense. In the

---

[1] Among the pupils of Dugald Stewart in Edinburgh were Lord Brougham, Lord Palmerston, Lord John Russell, Francis Horner, Lord Lansdowne, Francis Jeffrey, Sir Walter Scott, Sydney Smith, Thomas Brown, Thomas Chalmers, James Mill, and Archibald Alison. See James McCosh, *The Scottish Philosophy*, London, 1875, p. 283. On Sir William Hamilton's immense learning see John Veitch *Memoir of Sir W. Hamilton*, Edinburgh and London, 1869.

[2] McCosh, op. cit., p. 301.

latter portion of the book he criticizes Hume at length. Although
Hume had explained that by ideas he meant the faint images
of impressions in thinking, Beattie takes him to assert that every
idea is a physical replica of an impression. If I have an idea
representing an impression, then when I have an idea of a large
building it must be present in fact. 'The question now is,
where is this thing placed? For a place it must have, and a
pretty large one too.' It seems that 'in no larger vehicle than
a common post-chaise, I can transport from one place to another,
a building equal to the largest Egyptian pyramid, and a moun-
tain as big as Teneriff'.[1] On causation he makes play with the
word contiguous in Hume's definition, ignoring the other factors
in this definition. 'There are now in my view two contiguous
houses, one of which was built last summer, and the other two
years ago. By seeing them constantly together for several
months, I find that the idea of the one determines my mind to
form the idea of the other, and the impression of the one to
form a more lively idea of the other. So that, according to our
author's definition, the one house is the cause, the other is the
effect.'[2] We cannot deny power and efficacy to casual sequences
without being driven to atheism; and this is a sufficient confutation of the theory of the *Treatise*. The sceptical method by
which everything may be made matter for dispute is traced to
the school logic. And in a passage that reveals how much
Hume and his most bitter opponents shared the sentiments of
Locke's outlook Beattie writes: 'Destined for action rather than
for knowledge, and governed more by instinct than by reason,
we can extend our investigating experience with regard to ourselves but a very little way.'[3]

The *Essay on Truth* was loudly applauded. It quickly ran
into several editions and the author received a pension at the
hands of George III. A doctorate was conferred on him by the
University of Oxford and Reynolds executed his portrait.[4]
These manifestations of honour are symptoms of the moral
and religious fears raised by Hume's writings. Others, George

---

[1] *Essays*, 1776, p. 16.   [2] Ib., p. 199.   [3] Ib., p. 259.
[4] The picture represents Dr. Beattie in his robes, clasping the *Essay on
Truth*; beneath appears an angel holding in one hand a pair of scales while with
the other he thrusts down the horrid figures of Sophistry, Scepticism, and
Infidelity. Two of these figures were believed to represent Voltaire and Hume.
A copy of the portrait is prefixed to Forbes' *Life of Beattie*.

Campbell, Alexander Gerard, James Balfour, acquired prestige for their attacks on the great sceptic.

The principal contributions of the Scottish school to the problems by which reflection was now confronted were two. It rejected the orthodox doctrine of ideas that had reigned since the time of Locke and it proclaimed the dependence of knowledge upon self-evident principles. The Scottish philosophers denied the position from which Descartes and Locke had started their explorations, that the immediate objects of cognition are ideas. They pointed out the ambiguous place occupied by ideas, showing that they were at one time taken to be intermediate between the mind and objects, at another to coalesce with the act of perceiving, at another to be the objects of perception. The object perceived must be distinguished from the perceiving of it; ideas as representatives of objects in the mind must be dismissed. Mental states and material qualities have no resemblance to one another. These philosophers moved therefore towards a direct and realist view of knowledge. But their analysis is hesitating and fragmentary. Sensations are described as natural signs that suggest qualities of objects to our minds. Indeed under the usefully vague notion of suggestion (a term also employed by Locke and Berkeley) all the cardinal points in dispute are smuggled in; 'that sensation suggests the notion of present existence, and the belief that what we perceive or feel does now exist; that memory suggests the notion of past existence, and the belief that what we remember did exist in time past; and that our sensations and thoughts do also suggest the notion of a mind, and the belief in its existence and of its relation to our thoughts'. Our belief in causation is also suggested to us by our sensations of change. The metaphysical knots tied by Hume are easily loosened by such procedure. And the doctrine of signs reverts towards the theory of mediate knowledge. The truth is that the Scottish school presume much of the Lockean apparatus. Valuable points are made by Reid: the point, for instance, that simple apprehension or sensation is not the first operation of the understanding, but that our primary apprehension is a complex perception into which judgement implicitly enters; but these critics continue to look upon the processes of abstraction and comparison as secondary and artificial. They display the current propensity to seek reality in what is particular and isolated. Dugald Stewart's position leans towards nominalism and the contents of conceptions are by him restricted to images derived from sensations. He adheres to the psychology of association.[1] And some of the school, for example, James Mylne, were avowed adherents of sensationalism.

But the chief proposal of the Scottish philosophers was to rest belief upon a number of principles of Common Sense, a term that was already in general use in eighteenth-century thought and that looks back to the Stoic common notions of Herbert of Cherbury. 'All knowledge and all science must be built upon principles that are self-evident; and of such principles every man who has common-sense is a competent judge, when he conceives them distinctly.'[2] But the principles offered by Reid and his disciples are widely different in kind. They include belief in the existence of objects as we perceive them to exist, in minds, in the validity of memory, in substances, in causation, and in the testimony of others. They embrace beliefs generally accepted by unsophisticated persons, axioms of logic and self-evident propositions. In proof of these principles the Scottish writers are fond of appealing to evidence from the language of nations and to the uniformity of behaviour among men. Brown undertook a more careful inquiry into the relation of cause and effect than his predecessors, but after rejecting Hume's explanation he falls back on 'an irresistible intuitive belief'.[3] These teachers do not hesitate to prefer the sentiments of the vulgar to the conclusions of the philosophers. At other moments they return nearly to the position of the Cartesians, grounding the veracity of perception upon the goodness of God. But their chief confidence in knowledge rests upon the same irrational basis that had come to the fore in Hutcheson and in Hume; our beliefs stand upon the natural constitution of our nature.

New impulses broke in upon British thought in the lectures of Sir William Hamilton at Edinburgh. Professedly an adherent of the Common-Sense tradition, he transmitted its doctrines with an added weight of learning. The analysis of consciousness

[1] *Elements of the Philosophy of the Human Mind*, 1792. It ought to be added that Stewart's master, Reid, was a moderate Realist.

[2] Reid, *Intellectual Powers*, Essay VI. ii.

[3] T. Brown, *Inquiry into the Relation of Cause and Effect* (1st ed. 1805, enlarged 1818).

discloses ultimate, *a priori*, notions, that are fundamental laws of the mind.[1] In a prolonged examination of the problem of causation he rests the principle upon a necessary condition of human intelligence. He agrees with Reid that consciousness presents us with the conviction of an objective world of things and that philosophy cannot question this conviction; and he follows his predecessors in Scotland in rejecting the assumption that ideas intervene between the mind and the external world. But in many passages of thought he moved beyond the contemporary system. The most powerful source of the revolutionary hints that he uttered was the *Critique of Pure Reason*. Hamilton was the first English philosopher who had carefully and intelligently studied Kant. Earlier discussions of his philosophy, for example by Stewart and by Brown had been quite undiscriminating. Through Hamilton, Kantian conceptions begin obscurely to enter speculation in England and to collide with the habitual current of beliefs. The collision is evident in Hamilton's own mind, for beside the principles inherited from Locke and Reid are inserted views that depart radically from these principles. Two of these innovating suggestions are the stress laid upon the synthetical activity of consciousness and the doctrine of the relative and conditioned character of knowledge. At all levels of knowledge the mind seeks unity; even at the level of simple perception there is a unifying act.[2] The simplest apprehension involves discrimination and contradistinction, in a word judgement; and judgement presupposes synthesis. 'In opposition to the views hitherto promulgated in regard to comparison, I will show that this faculty is at work in every, the simplest, act of mind';[3] and he proceeds to argue that the traditional separation of sense from thought is unsound. These suggestions, for they are never fully worked out by Hamilton, destroy the foundations of the eighteenth-century theory of experience. By declaring the 'law of totality' in opposition to the orthodox law of association he looked beyond his time to the later discovery of German thought by English thinkers.[4] On the second head Hamilton affirmed in certain passages that

[1] *Lectures on Metaphysics*, edited by H. L. Mansel and J. Veitch, Edinburgh and London, 4th ed. 1869, i, p. 270. On this philosopher see *The Philosophy of Sir W. Hamilton* by S. V. Rasmussen, Copenhagen and London, 1926.
[2] *Lectures*, i, p. 67.　　[3] Ib., ii, p. 279.　　[4] Cf. ib., p. 239.

our knowledge is concerned only with phenomena. 'Our whole knowledge of mind and matter is relative, conditional—relatively conditioned.' What a thing is absolutely and in itself—i.e. considered apart from its phenomena, 'is to us zero'; and of the substance of the mind we know nothing.[1] This position appears to repeat the empiricism of Locke and the Newtonians. But there is a fresh note in the phenomenalism. Our knowledge of reality is limited not because it is ultimately derived from impressions and ideas but because it is determined by our faculties. The properties of things known are known with modifications contributed by our organs of sense and our capacities of intelligence. Among such capacities he cites the notion of space. Spatial apprehension is 'a fundamental condition of thought itself'; it is not a generalization from experience, it is native and *a priori*. 'The analysis of Kant, independently of all that has been done by other philosophers, has placed this truth beyond the possibility of doubt, to all those who understand the meaning and condition of the problems.'[2] But the notion of space and other *a priori* notions are the properties of our minds. 'Whatever we know is not known as it is, but only as it seems to us to be.'[3] To think is to condition. Unfortunately this Kantian phenomenalism is present in Hamilton's lectures with contradictory statements, that things are perceived as they are, that primary qualities are real, and that perception is not relative but 'complete'.[4] In these celebrated discourses the oracles of Common Sense and the established forms of empirical theory are traversed by tides of thought from many quarters of the ocean of mind. The amazed listeners at Edinburgh heard references to Proclus and Plotinus, to Boethius and St. Augustine, to Algazel and Durandus, to Jouffroy, Fichte, and Jacobi. No philosophical teacher of his time in England did more to cultivate metaphysical speculation and to widen the perspective of inquirers than Sir William Hamilton.

But the classic scheme, especially in the form transmitted by Hartley and Priestley, persisted throughout these developments. A comprehensive statement of the empirical psychology was formulated by James Mill, in his *Analysis of the Phenomena of*

[1] *Lectures*, i, pp. 137-8.   [2] Ib. ii, p. 113.
[3] Ib. i, p. 146.   [4] Ib. ii, p. 70.

the Human Mind (1829). Here all the old apparatus is fully exhibited and the consequences methodically applied. The chemistry of sensations, simple ideas, and complex ideas, and the mechanical laws of association are rigorously set forth. External objects are clusters of sensations for which names have been devised on grounds of economy in the business of co-operation between men. There are copies of clusters of sensations, such as those given by the sign 'house' and there are clusters of copies of sensations, such as are indicated by the sign 'piety'. The latter are arbitrary signs and ideas corresponding to nothing in the order of nature. Mill pursues this nominalism into the function of adjectives and verbs; they are termed 'marks upon marks', inventions for the purpose of calling attention to features of sensations that are prominent or related to the percipient's activities. Especially interesting is the discussion of the 'fallacy of the copula' for here the empirical standard of truth receives clear definition. The assertion that A is B signifies that a certain name is the mark of the same idea of which another name is also the mark. But the marks properly refer to sensations, and to ideas derived from sensations. When, therefore, the word 'is' is used to associate marks that refer to entities that do not stand for perceptual experiences, it is referring to non-entities. The Platonic ideas and the essences of medieval thought are examples of these non-entities. Similar empirical criteria are pressed against the syllogism, causal prediction, and mathematical reasoning. Geometrical propositions are merely verbal. When we say that the three angles of a triangle are equal to two right angles, we are merely denoting the three angles of a triangle by another name that means more precisely the same phenomenon. Class-names are signs for complex but indistinct ideas compounded of the ideas of a large aggregate of individuals.

External objects are inseparable associations of sensations produced by repeated experiences. Nothing in reality exists besides the blend of sensations, no substance nor cause; and the belief that others perceive the same objects as I do resolves itself ultimately into certain conditional sensations of my own. Memory is dissolved into the play of association, and the recognition of my own identity is shown to be memory of past states of consciousness coupled with an existing state. The irresistible compulsion of association induces the belief in the uniformity of nature. All the 'necessary' propositions and axioms of thought are merely verbal; Mill applies himself to unravelling the concrete associations that are contained in the linguistic abstractions of logic and mathematics. And metaphysical conceptions such as similarity, succession, causality extension, motion, quantity, and quality are shown to be abstract relative terms, that is to say, perceptual associations with the connotations left out. The belief in causation, for example, is thus treated. To have sensations or ideas successively is the same thing as to know them to be successive. Some of the successive ideas appear in constant association, and the antecedents and consequents in these constant sequences we call causes and effects. And besides this, it has been proved by philosophers, that these names mean absolutely nothing.[1] We need not follow the manner in which Mill traces the awareness of a line from sensations of touch and of muscular movements, nor how he applies this experience to the explanation of quantity and extension; nor can we dwell upon his analysis of other metaphysical notions. Mill's book is a literal exposition of the Hartleian theory of thought, a consistent elaboration of the thesis that all the activities of the rational consciousness are resoluble into 'three grand classes of phenomena', sensations, ideas, and trains of ideas.

James Mill's *Analysis of the Human Mind* was reissued in 1869 with notes and comments by two distinguished thinkers of the day, Alexander Bain and John Stuart Mill. These philosophers, writing forty years after the first appearance of the *Analysis*, find many points of detail to criticize. But their general position accords with the doctrine of the book. J. S. Mill was the greatest intellectual leader of reform in political and moral affairs during the nineteenth century in England. 'It is Mill', wrote a contemporary, 'that our young thinkers at the Universities, our young shepherds on the mountains consult, and quote and swear by.'[2] He was the leader of 'the philosophic radicals', disciples of Bentham, whose enormous energy had inspired amendments in every branch of social life. In his writings on metaphysics and on the problems of knowledge

---

[1] *Analysis*, ii, p. 42.
[2] D. Masson, *Recent British Philosophy*, 2nd edition, London, 1867, p. 8.

Mill threw all his weight behind the empirical philosophy. To him this philosophy was the foundation of his liberal creed and he saw the doctrines of Common Sense and of German metaphysics as the citadels of social reaction. Speaking at the end of his life of his *System of Logic*, first published in 1843, he refers to the influence in England of 'the German or *a priori* view of human knowledge and of the knowing faculties'; the *System of Logic*, he says, supplied 'what was much wanted, a text-book of the opposite doctrine—that which derived all knowledge from experience, and all moral and intellectual qualities principally from the direction given to the associations'. And he finds in the notion that truths external to the mind may be known by intuition or consciousness, independently of observation and experience, 'the great intellectual support of false doctrines and bad institutions'. The chief strength of this philosophy lies in the appeal to mathematics and the cognate branches of physical sciences, and to question this evidence is to meet the intuitive theory on ground that it had previously deemed unassailable.[1] In Mill the two schools of thought, the one descending from Descartes through Spinoza, Leibniz to Kant, the other, 'the older and sounder tradition' springing from Bacon, Hobbes, Locke, Berkeley, Hume, and Hartley, are ranged in blunt antagonism to one another; and the English tradition is associated with the cause of liberty and social progress. He perceived in the writings of Sir William Hamilton the main stronghold of 'the metaphysical mode of thought' in this country and he devoted a book to the work of demolishing Hamilton's theories. Whatever subject he is discussing he is quick to detect signs of the *a priori* heresy, even in the utterances of thinkers of his own philosophical party.[2]

The appearance of the *Logic* was a notable event in the history of thought in England. In it Mill took up the inquiries begun by Bacon in 1624. It formulated the rational methods pursued in the experimental activities of science, expounding the logic by which casual relations are established between phenomena. When he treats of the wider connexions of logical theory he

---

[1] *Autobiography* (published shortly after Mill's death in 1873), World's Classics edition, Oxford, p. 190.

[2] See, for example, the passage in *Auguste Comte and Positivism* (1865), p. 72, where he turns aside to deplore 'metaphysical' tendencies in the writings of Herbert Spencer and of G. H. Lewes.

declares with vigour the cardinal maxims of the eighteenth
century. The ultimate premisses of knowledge are our own
bodily sensations and mental feelings. The facts known *per se*
are 'any one's present sensations, or other states of subjective
consciousness'.[1] We are not aware of objects directly but of
the sensations that we receive from objects; the objects are not
perceived but are believed to exist.[2] All of which we are aware
is a thread of sensations, thoughts, emotions, and volitions; of
the nature of body or mind further than the sensations we do
not know anything.[3] In discussing the processes of thought
Mill makes large concessions to nominalism. 'Man' simply
means the whole of the attributes connoted by the word; the
supposed essences of things are names arbitrarily attached to
certain attributes.[4] All reasoning is from particulars to particulars and the general propositions, whether called definitions,
axioms, or laws of nature that are assumed in our inferences
are merely abridged statements of the particular facts that we
think we may proceed on as proved.[5] Accordingly Mill points
out that the deductive reasoning of the syllogism is not a process
of real inference, for its conclusion is involved in its premiss.
The conclusion, Socrates is mortal, is presupposed in the major
premiss, all men are mortal, and we cannot be assured of the
mortality of all men unless we are already assured of the
mortality of every individual man. No reasoning from generals
to particulars can, as such, prove anything; since from a general
principle we cannot infer any particulars but those which the
principle itself assumes as known.[6]

We have seen that Mill perceived that the chief strength of
the deductive or intuitional school of thought lay in the appeal
to the evidence of mathematics and of the cognate branches of
physical science. In the *Logic* he attacks the claim that the
propositions and inferences of mathematics are necessary,
a priori forms of thought. Judged by the only criterion of
truth, the evidence of the senses, the assertions of geometry are
not more than approximately true and the operations of arithmetic rest upon the hypothesis that each unit is the same as

---

[1] *System of Logic*, 7th ed., London, 1868, i. 5, 304.
[2] Ib., p. 58.   [3] Ib., p. 68.
[4] Ib., pp. 121–2. Cf. *Examination of Sir W. Hamilton's Philosophy*, pp. 31 f.
[5] *Logic*, i. 213.   [6] Ib., p. 203.

every other, and this is never accurately true.[1] The whole force of Mill's discussion on mathematics springs from the philosophy of the eighteenth century, the belief that the judgements of science are derived from sensible experience. The certainty and necessity attributed to mathematical truths is an illusion. The metaphysicians refer the belief in their self-evident principles to the inconceivability of their being false. This is the fundamental position of the intuitive school from Descartes to Dr. Whewell, and Mill firmly rejects it. For inconceivability is an affair of accident and is due to long-established and familiar experience. It arises from the power of association over our minds and the constancy of certain sequences in our experience.[2] But there remains the primary postulate of science, that every event must have some cause of which it is the invariable and unconditional consequent. The metaphysicians pronounce the belief to be instinctive. The truth is that we arrive at the belief from simple enumeration, from the generalizations of common experience, such as 'food nourishes', 'fire burns'; and all experience enlarges and confirms the primitive generalizations. The simple generalizations become scientific as the sphere of knowledge widens and as more precise methods are applied, but the law of causation rests on no other proof than the empirical laws obtained from the uniformities of ordinary observation.[3]

These citations are sufficient to illustrate the acceptance of the principles of Hume by the most influential English thinker of the time. But Mill was a man of catholic sympathies, and early in his career he moved not only beyond the creed of Bentham in morals and politics, but also beyond the strict empiricism of his father and of the English tradition. He criticized the sufficiency of association to provide an account of belief, and in working out the theory of inference he found himself compelled at points to abandon the position of empiricism.[4] In the remarkable essay on Coleridge contributed to the *London and Westminster Review* in 1840 he declares his belief that the doctrines of the school of Locke stood in need of an entire renovation. It had penetrated Europe in the form of the shallow ideology of Condillac. The only advance had been

---

[1] Ib., p. 289.   [2] Ib., p. 272.   [3] Ib. ii. 100.
[4] See R. Jackson, *The Deductive Logic of John Stuart Mill*, Oxford, 1941.

made by Hartley and Reid, and the German school had performed a service in recalling men's minds to the difficulties that
empiricists must face. But the great merit of the new mode of
thought to which Coleridge belonged was that it produced a
philosophy of society. Mill hails the *a priori* metaphysicians as
the heirs of Bacon in the field of human culture.[1] And in the
sixth book of his *Logic* he broadens the methods of empiricism
in the search for a science of society. In this interest he exhibits
a fresh influence that had gained ascendancy over English
empirical philosophers, the Positive Philosophy of Auguste
Comte. Comte takes the empirical position as the base for his
extension of the methods of science to all departments of human
knowledge. We have no knowledge but of relative phenomena,
the successions and coexistences of appearances. The theological and metaphysical modes of interpretation have been
superseded by science. The aim of philosophy is to discover
the positive laws of phenomena in all religions of experience,
and to attend especially to generalizations that bear on
social well-being. Sociology is the supreme science. Mill
acknowledges his obligations to Comte in the *Autobiography*
and there were many other thinkers who in several degrees
manifested their indebtedness to the purpose and methods
of the positive philosophy. H. T. Buckle, for instance,
attempted to apply the principles of experimental science to
history, and G. H. Lewes taught countless readers that 'in
the *Cours de Philosophie Positive* we have the grandest, because,
on the whole, the truest system which Philosophy has yet
produced'.

The tale of empirical theory in England, however sweeping,
cannot neglect to mention two other leaders of thought.
Alexander Bain, professor of philosophy at Aberdeen, adhered
in principle to the outlook of his friend Mill, and in *The Senses
and the Intellect* (1855) and in other works he accomplished the
most notable advance in psychology since the time of Hartley.
The accompaniments of mental activity are treated with a
wealth of recent information; the correlates of mental process
are viewed as nerve-currents that display the functions of
recoverability and 'associatiability'; and all the cognitions and
beliefs of man are shown to be represented in the complex

---

[1] *Dissertations and Discussions*, London, 1859, i. 406 f.

organizations of sensory and motor nerve-currents that spring from the rudimentary reflex movements and from the elementary systems of nerves associated with the five senses. This psychology tended strongly to encourage the historic perspective in philosophy, for the basis of the theory of mind and knowledge is association, and the combination of nerve-currents are often substituted for the mental activities. The novel factor in Bain's researches is the principle that belief is essentially related to action. Incipient movements enter into simple ideas, and thinking is restrained speaking or acting.[1] The source of the belief in the external world is to be sought in subjective energy; the notion of the not-self or objective world is a generalization of individual feelings of activity and resistance; belief in the self is a generalization of individual passive sensations. The subjective and objective worlds are constructed of associations of feelings. Another leading thinker, Herbert Spencer, begins his vast edifice, the *Synthetic Philosophy*, with a similar criticism of knowledge. Our understanding cannot penetrate to the inward reality of things. It can treat only of the appearances of things to our senses, and to ask what space, time, matter, motion, and force are in themselves is to seek to pass beyond the relativity with which all our knowledge is imbued. The manifestations of that force which is beyond our capacities to grasp, the Unknowable Reality, are divisible into two great classes called by some impressions and ideas, better termed vivid and faint manifestations, and both of these types are bound together by ties of coexistence and succession. The vivid order of manifestations are original, the faint are copies of the original types; and the continuous series of the latter form the subject or ego, the union of the former comprise the object or non-ego.[2] Relations are of two sorts, relations of sequence and relations of coexistence; they are given directly to consciousness, and by forming abstract conceptions of them we think of time and space. These notions are generated from concrete experiences; in the case of space, from experiences of individual positions ascertained by touch. Similarly, our conception of matter, reduced to its simplest shape, is that of co-existent positions that offer resistance. The idea of extension is

[1] *The Senses and the Intellect*, 4th ed., London, 1894, p. 357.
[2] *First Principles*, 1862, part II. ii. 43, 44.

derived from the consciousness of resistance.[1] Other fundamental assumptions are traced to the same source. They are
derived from impressions. Mind, for instance, is conceivable to
us only as a complex of movements. Spencer accepts the dogma
of association. On the question that was being warmly discussed
whether there are necessary principles known to reason independently of particular experience he offers a curious solution,
according with his biological outlook. He concedes to the
followers of Hamilton the position that there are necessary
principles, such that contradictories are inconceivable, but he
denies that they are prior to human experience. They are an
heritage from the ancestral past and are *a priori* only in the
sense that they have become part of the neurological endowment of the modern individual; a doctrine that was supported by
Bain. The wider aspects of Spencer's evolutionary-naturalism
must be deferred for consideration to the next chapter.

Such, in brief, is the character and course of the main stream
of English philosophical reflection that flows from the later
decades of the seventeenth century to the third quarter of the
nineteenth. A few conspicuous examples among the long
procession of thinkers who maintained the empirical theory of
experience have been recalled. A selective treatment of this
kind is far removed from history, and our review has passed
over many names widely discussed in their generation: Abraham
Tucker and J. F. Ferrier, for instance. We may conclude our
survey of this phase with an utterance to which an exasperated
Hegelian was provoked at the spectacle of the prevailing sentiments of English thought in the year 1865. 'Hume', he wrote,
'is our Politics, Hume is our Trade, Hume is our Philosophy,
Hume is our Religion,—it wants little but Hume were even our
Taste.'[2] That year had seen, in fact, the publication of Mill's
book on Hamilton; a decisive reaffirmation of the empirical
circle of ideas, and an uncompromising rejection of 'metaphysical' knowledge. Here are finally arrayed the set of doctrines pronounced by the great thinkers of the eighteenth
century, the belief in the futility of all speculations respecting
real and absolute being, the view that knowledge is generated

---

[1] *First Principles*, 47, 48. Mill, however, rightly detected *a priori* notions in
Spencer, especially the principle of the inconceivability of the negative.

[2] J. Hutchinson Stirling, *The Secret of Hegel*, London, 1865, vol. i, p. xxiii.

from associations of sensations, that the substantial nature of physical objects and of minds is inexplicable, and that abstract notions are verbal signs. The philosophy of the nineteenth century in England had added little to the ground-plan of the classic system. Mill repeats with slight refinements the old principles and is convinced of their universal competency. It was not until the twentieth century was well advanced that empiricism gave rise to fresh variations and new speculative principles. But let us now turn back to the first period of Newtonianism and observe some wider effects of its reign.

IV

The earlier portion of the period continued to be filled with keen debates on the theological consequences of the new philosophy. The sharp collisions between the old and the recent conceptions of natural theology sprang from conflicting forms of reason. All sides appealed to reason, but the standards of rationality that commended themselves to the several contesting groups differed. Those theologians who relied upon traditional principles of thought differed among themselves, for they referred to a variety of traditional principles; nor was it only those who attempted to base religious beliefs upon empirical theories of experience who were indicted as sceptics. On the contrary those who were deemed the most dangerous and scandalous of the natural theologians founded their arguments on ancient views of reason. The strenuous controversies over natural theology with which the first half of the eighteenth century resounded disclosed the limitations of philosophical criteria assumed by critics and apologists alike, and when the foundations of the old conceptions of reason were shaken by the logic of empiricism, the need for a philosophy of experience that should be adequate to the claims of theology was painfully felt. Theologians snatched at the superficial aid proffered by the school of Common Sense, or the equally superficial support provided by mechanical teleology. With the decline in speculative effort rational theology moved on to a lower intellectual plane. Reason was once more disparaged in favour of faith, and theologians turned from metaphysical discussions to questions of external evidences, such as the position of miracles and prophecy in the system of Christian truth. Yet throughout this period there coursed a vein of spiritual and mystical reflection that prepared men's minds for the religious and theological awakening of the succeeding age.

Let us select some instances of the diverse influences of rational assumptions upon theological principles. The mass of detailed observations that was now rapidly accumulating in all fields of nature brought further into prominence the argument from design. The ancient postulates of Christian theology that furnished the deeper propensities of men's minds directed the interpretation of the new knowledge, even in the realm of mathematical physics. And the promulgation of theories that disputed the scriptural doctrines of creation and providence incited natural philosophers to declare the proofs of these dogmas from the wonders of the world. The most remarkable and the most popular attempt to unite natural and revealed religion on these lines was the book of the great botanist and zoologist, John Ray, *The Wisdom of God in the Creation*, first published in 1691 and subsequently much enlarged. Ray's model is the second part of More's *Antidote against Atheism*, but he displays a vastly wider range of information. No one had advanced knowledge since the appearance of More's book more than Ray, nor could anyone of his time bring to the task of surveying creation such an encyclopaedic grasp of exact science and so judicious a mind.[1] He distinguishes the three theories of the age that threaten religion in the name of natural philosophy. The first is the Aristotelian theory that had disturbed the Oxford theologians of the thirteenth century and had shocked philosophers ever since, that the world had existed from eternity. The old issue had recently been discussed at length by Archbishop Tillotson and by Bishop Wilkins in his book *On the Principles and Duties of Natural Religion*, 1678, and Ray refers his readers to the destruction of Aristotle's position contained in these essays. The second unorthodox hypothesis in contemporary thought is that of the Epicureans, who assert that material atoms and space are the two fundamental principles of things. This philosophy doubtless embraces the theory of Hobbes as well as that of Lucretius, and for confutation of it Ray refers to the writings of Cudworth and of Bishop Stillingfleet in his *Origines Sacrae*. The third danger to religion is the

[1] On Ray see *John Ray*, by C. E. Raven, Cambridge, 1942.

Cartesian hypothesis, which banishes all consideration of final causes from natural philosophy, and supposes the universe to have been formed from the divisions of matter. Again Ray quotes from the *True Intellectual System of the Universe* to show the hollowness of this pretension. And he now points out the advantages of Cudworth's plastic principle in accounting for the vital phenomena. The plastic principle in nature presides over the whole economy of the plant, directing its growth and form and nutrition. 'I therefore incline to Dr. Cudworth's Opinion that God uses for these Effects the subordinate Ministry of some inferior Plastick Nature; as in his Works of Providence he doth of Angels.'[1]

For traces of divine wisdom he explores the visible universe, inspecting in turn the solar system, the four elements, meteors, rain, and wind; and passing into regions in which he was notably expert he describes the species of plants and animals. At every point he draws attention to the remarkable adaptations of bodily structure and of instinctive behaviour with which creatures have been endowed. In the face of this array of evidence the atheist has one subterfuge. It is that 'things made use, and not uses things'. Unless we can show 'that among infinite Trials and Essays at the beginning of things, among millions of Monstrous Shapes and imperfect Formations, a few such animals as now exist could not possibly be produced, these After-considerations are of very little moment'.[2] Is there not an alternative hypothesis that accounts for the marvellous adaptation of animals and plants to their environment, namely, that creatures have been produced by 'millions of trials'? Ray's reply to this objection is largely borrowed from Richard Bentley's Boyle Lectures of 1692.[3] He offers three considerations that defeat the atheist's contention. First, it has been abundantly shown that no motion of the particles of matter could have produced unassisted the organic bodies even of the original monsters. Second, there are many members and powers of animal bodies that are not absolutely necessary to subsistence, but some of them conduce to the happiness of the animal.

---

[1] *The Wisdom of God in Creation*, 3rd ed., London, 1701, p. 56.
[2] Ray, op. cit., p. 368.
[3] R. Bentley, *Matter and Motion cannot think; or a Confutation of Atheism from the Faculties of the Soul*, London, 1692.

Third, some animals have organs appropriate to certain functions but do not use them; for example, the apes have organs of speech and brains. The human use of these organs must depend upon a higher principle. Matter organized could never produce them.[1] The passage illustrates the way in which modern and ancient postulates combined; that a lower principle cannot produce a higher, that the properties of matter, being mathematical, cannot form organisms, that God created all the species of living beings according to the Scriptures. Elements of the ancient metaphysic, securely rooted in Christian theology, persist within the new natural philosophy.

The earlier scientific teleology which harped upon the subtle contrivances and adaptations revealed by the investigation of inanimate matter, of plants, and of the human frame, was given a grander setting by the work of Newton. The *Principia* encouraged theologians and philosophers to perceive in the regularity and harmony of the universal mechanism the evidence of a massive design. The gravitational attraction of the sun and planets, the preservation of the fixed stars in their stations, the interaction of the parts of animal bodies, the marvellous phenomena of sensation and will, all suggest the activity of an incorporeal, intelligent, omnipresent being, who comprehends and directs the universe and all that is in it. In several passages Newton maintained that the origin of the universe and the preservation of its laws required the postulate of divine aid. Writing to Bentley in 1692 he observed that the diurnal rotations of the planets could not be derived from gravity but required a divine arm to impress them.[2] Beside these considerations other theological arguments derived from the new physics were given currency by Newton. He seized upon the theory of the Cambridge Platonists that space manifests divine properties. We have seen that Henry More had met the dangerous tendencies of the Cartesian doctrine of material extension by arguing that space is the expression of immaterial substance or spirit. Newton presupposed absolute space and time as the universal system of reference for the motions of bodies. In discussing these absolutes he associated them with theological conceptions. Space is the 'boundless uniform sensorium' of

---

[1] *Wisdom of God in the Creation*, pp. 369–77.
[2] *Works of Richard Bentley*, edited by A. Dyce, London, 1838, iii. 125.

God. 'He endures for ever, and is everywhere present; and by existing always and everywhere he constitutes duration and space.'[1]

These theological hints were ingeniously elaborated by contemporary thinkers, especially by Richard Bentley. In *Matter and Motion cannot think; or a Confutation of Atheism from the Faculties of the Soul* (1692) the old points made by Cudworth and More against the Hobbists to the effect that matter and motion cannot give rise to feeling and perception are repeated. But the new mathematical theories of the universe are discussed at length in relation to theological belief, and the interpretation put upon them had the approval of Newton. Gravitation is the basis of all mechanism, but it is not itself mechanistic. It flows from the immediate will of God. The laws of attraction cannot be due to chance nor to purely material causes. If we suppose the primitive state of the universe to have been a limited chaos of atoms dispersed throughout space, the result would have been that, under the operation of the unguided laws of attraction, all matter would have assembled into one dense spherical mass. The world, the stars, and the planets that we know could never have come into being. If we assume that the original chaos of atoms was distributed through infinite space, all movement would have been precluded. There would have been a kind of physical equilibrium; the forces of attraction between the particles would have been neutralized; and all bodies would stay fixed in their places. We must conclude that the operation of the laws of gravitation were wisely directed at the creation, and that the divine architect had controlled the movements of matter and constantly supervised its orderly changes. Bentley shows at length that the motion of planets round the sun, the effects of light and heat, and the structure of the human body manifest the evidence of purpose. Similar applications of physics were advanced by a very influential thinker in England, Samuel Clarke. He exerted himself to promote appreciation of Newton's scientific discoveries, translating the *Optics* and publishing detailed criticisms of the Cartesian theories of physics. But the celebrated Boyle Lectures delivered in St. Paul's in 1704 and 1705 open with a passage that transports us to the intellectual world of Anselm and the medieval disciples of Augustine.

[1] *Principia*, iii, prop. 42, General Scholium.

Something now is and it is manifest that something always was, for otherwise things must have arisen from nothing and without cause. But this which has always existed must be an unchangeable being from which all other beings in the universe have been derived, for the supposition that there has been an infinite succession of changeable and dependent beings without any original cause is absurd. The eternal Being must be self-existent, that is to say, it exists of necessity so that its non-existence cannot be supposed without contradiction. So far Clarke proceeds with the classical argument of scholasticism. From this metaphysical position he turns to meet the challenge of the new materialism. Matter cannot possibly be the original and eternal being. For it has been shown that this being must exist necessarily so that it is an express contradiction to suppose it not to exist. But we can without contradiction conceive the material world not to exist, or to exist in a form different from that which it now has; we can suppose more or fewer planets and animals on the earth. The Hobbists say that motion in general is necessary, or that the tendency to move is essential to all matter (Clarke is here referring to the doctrines of John Toland, author of the notorious *Christianity not Mysterious*). In the first place it is ridiculous to deny that any matter can be at rest. And in the second place the tendency to move must be a tendency to move in a definite way, or to move in every way at once. The first tendency presumes some external cause, the second could produce nothing but an eternal rest. Matter in any form cannot be a necessary being. If it includes the power of gravitation then there must be a vacuum (as the incomparable Sir Isaac Newton has abundantly demonstrated), and therefore it is plainly possible for matter not to be. If the power of gravitation is not included in matter, there could never have been any motion, since motion is not necessary of itself. After a brief discussion of the materialism of Spinoza, 'the most celebrated Patron of Atheism in our Time', the author glances at the opinions of these ancient philosophers who taught that the world was not eternal but created in time: and proceeds at length to infer the orthodox positions; the self-existent being must be infinite, omnipresent, one, intelligent, and endowed with liberty and choice. Now, however, he passes from *a priori* arguments to the degrees of perfection in the world, and to the order, beauty, and exquisite fitness of all visible things. His attack on 'the atheists' is, in fact, concerned with their misplaced notions of metaphysical necessity. He points out that the entities taken by his opponents to be absolute realities, namely, matter, motion, or matter in motion, are not self-existent necessary beings but contingent and dependent beings. The atheists are confused and shamed by the discoveries 'which are daily made in Astronomy and Natural Philosophy'. It is 'the Exquisite Regularity of all the Planets Motions, without Epicycles, Stations, Retrogradations, or any other Deviation or Confusion whatsoever', and 'the inexpressible Nicety of the Adjustment of the Primary Velocity and Original Direction of the Annual Motion of the Planets, with their distance from the Central Body and their force of Gravitation towards it' that prove the incomprehensible wisdom of the Creator.[1] The cosmology of Newton has become the grand vindication of natural theology; and that cosmology includes not only the witness of original design, but the evidence of perpetual guidance that exerts itself at every moment in every part of the material universe. In the course of his celebrated correspondence with Leibniz, Clarke protested against the view that the world is a great machine, 'going on without the assistance of a clockmaker'. For this view tended to exclude the continual providence and government of God in the material order.[2]

An important aspect, therefore, of the collaboration between the new physical science and the old theology turned upon the acceptance of a fresh dualism, in the place of the Cartesian dualism of thinking substance and extended substance. The dualism of the Newtonian theologians opposed attraction and matter. Matter is of itself inert, passive, and devoid of internal activity. Upon the atoms of this lifeless matter—'sluggish' is the favourite term—the Creator impresses at each instant a magnetic force in virtue of which all parts of matter compose an orderly system of motions. The principle of attraction is not itself to be explained by corporeal analogies. There are no real forces in bodies. 'We cannot make even one single step in accounting for the phenomena, without admitting the immediate presence and immediate action of an incorporeal agent,

---

[1] Clarke, *A Demonstration of the Being and Attributes of God*, 5th ed., London, 1719, pp. 71, 117.　　[2] *First Correspondence*, Letter 4.

who connects, moves and disposes all things, according to such rules, and for such purposes, as seem good to him.'[1] All the activity in the world and all the admirable conspiring of its parts in the structure of animals and plants express the pervasive force that is actuated by Mind. And without the guiding control of attraction and repulsion matter would be in formless chaos throughout the universe.

Many other thinkers followed Clarke in confident refutation of atheists by vindicating the design of Providence in the universe revealed by natural philosophy. They repeated the arguments demonstrating that the physical system of the universe cannot be described on lines that are purely mechanistic; they reproduced the view that matter requires an immaterial directing agency that complements the mathematical properties of heavenly and terrestrial bodies. Theological proofs drawn from the law of gravitation continued to be included in the catalogue of the admirable devices of nature with which materialists were silenced. William Derham, Rector of Upminster in Essex, was the Boyle lecturer in 1711 and 1712. His discourses imitated the sweeping survey of his friend John Ray in the vastly popular *Wisdom of God in Creation*. The ten books of *Physico-Theology* describe with enthusiastic wonder the properties of air, light, and gravity, the characteristics of the terrestrial globe, its climates, caves, mountains, and volcanoes, the classes of living creatures and their marvellous structures, the body and mind of man, the quadrupeds, the birds, the reptiles, the fishes, the trees and flowers. The new knowledge of his scientific colleagues of the Royal Society is ransacked to provide material for a sustained rhapsody on the architectural skill of the Creator.

'And so when we survey the bare Outlines of this our Globe, when we see so vast a Body, accouter'd with so noble a Furniture of Air, Light and Gravity; with every Thing, in short, that is necessary to the Preservation and Security of the Globe itself, or that conduceth to the Life, Health, and Happiness, to the Propagation and Increase of all the prodigious Variety of Creatures the Globe is stocked with; when we see nothing wanting, nothing redundant or frivolous, nothing botched or ill-made, but that everything, even in the very

---

[1] Berkeley, *Siris, A Chain of Philosophical Reflexions and Inquiries concerning the Virtues of Tar Water*, London, 1744, section 237.

Appendages alone, exactly answereth all its Ends and Occasions: What else can be concluded, but that all was made with manifest design, and that the whole Structure is the work of some intelligent Being; some Artist, of Power and Skill equivalent to such work?'[1]

In another book, *Astro-Theology*, Derham dwells more fully upon the benefits conferred on the system of the spheres by the law of gravity. Gravity prevents the globes from being shattered to pieces by centrifugal force and retains the planets in their orbits.[2]

These allusions to the earlier Boyle lecturers indicate the insistent pressure of the ancient theological assumptions upon the vast discoveries of natural philosophy. They evince the anxiety of Newton and his philosophic interpreters to rebut the continued interest in the mechanical hypothesis of the Cartesians in which the laws of the physical universe could be described without the constant assistance of a superior immaterial agent. The proposal of Descartes to abolish final causes from natural philosophy was still felt as a menace, and the introduction of divine power in relation to the cardinal principle of universal gravitation met the materialists at the critical point of the new cosmology. It became customary for apologists and spiritual philosophers to maintain that gravitation, attraction, elasticity, repulsion, and all the other activities of matter must be ultimately due to powers impressed on matter from outside, and that these powers are immaterial. Almighty God constantly renews and controls the motions of the world.[3]

Descartes, Spinoza, and Hobbes are ritually refuted and the range of modern discoveries that display the infinite skill of the divine constructor are repeatedly adduced. The argument of William Paley in his *Natural Theology*, 1802, is the most celebrated expression of this logic. Drawing largely upon earlier theological naturalists, particularly John Ray and William Derham, he shows in considerable detail the presence, throughout the animal world and in the arrangement of the human face, of 'an artist, master of his work, acquainted with his

[1] W. Derham, *Physico-Theology or a Demonstration of the Being and Attributes of God from His Works of Creation*, 5th ed., London, 1720, p. 36.

[2] *Astro-Theology*, 6th ed., London, 1731, bk. vi.

[3] See, for example, Andrew Baxter, *An Enquiry into the Nature of the Humane Soul wherein the Immateriality of the Soul is evinced from the Principles of Reason and Philosophy*, 2nd ed., London, 1737, i. 27.

materials'. All suggestions that purport to account for the facts except on the hypothesis of a superhuman mechanic who has constructed every item of material nature as a watchmaker constructs a watch, are swept aside. The fruitful theory of plastic nature has given place to an external and mechanical teleology; and recent hypotheses that had appeared relating to the modification of species from simpler forms are easily refuted.

'If it be suggested that this proboscis (the elephant's trunk) may have been produced, in a long course of generations, by the constant endeavour of the elephant to thrust out his nose, (which is the general hypothesis by which it has been lately attempted to account for the forms of animated nature,) I would ask, How was the animal to subsist in the meantime, during the process, *until* this prolongation of snout were completed? What was to become of the individual whilst the species was perfecting?'[1]

Paley's book is the most powerful conjunction of scriptural theology and natural philosophy since the time of Ray. The personal deity of the Bible is seen as the devisor of intricate machines delicately constructed for their purposes. The wider operations of providential guidance traced by the Boyle lecturers in the first period of Newton's reign are not neglected by Paley. He respects the astronomical theology of Bentley and Clarke, and shows how the celestial globes are prevented, under the direction of the Creator, from running together in heaps and hindering one another's motions. 'Attraction itself is controlled and suspended by a superior agent.'

The excellent concord of science and religion on these lines attained its final expression in the Bridgewater Treatises of 1833–6. Their purpose, in fact, was to provide further confirmation of Paley's natural theology. Distinguished members of the Royal Society, Thomas Chalmers, William Prout, William Whewell, Sir Charles Bell, and others, expounded with abundant scientific detail the chemical and physical composition of the environment in which life and mind dwelt, and proved that water, earth, and air must have been intelligently

---

[1] *Works of William Paley D.D. with notes and illustrations by James Paxton*, Oxford, 1838, iv. 231. The new hypothesis had been put forward by Erasmus Darwin in his *Zoonomia*, published in 1794, and at the time when Paley was writing *Natural Theology* it was exciting attention through the early work of Lamarck.

prepared for the advent and sustenance of animals and men. Such considerations brought encouragement to many Christian thinkers in the early years of Queen Victoria's rule. And students in divinity continued to devote themselves to the works of Paley to the end of the nineteenth century, unconscious of the damaging criticisms that had been pointed at the argument from design by Hume and Kant.

During the sway of Newtonianism there were a number of minor and eccentric attacks on the physics of the *Principia* in the interests of a narrowly scriptural position. John Hutchinson, for example, put forward a rambling and abusive refutation of Newton in a *Treatise on Power*,[1] in which the truths revealed to Moses are preferred to the atheistical physics of Newton and Clarke. The Hutchinsonians formed a considerable body, which included several bishops. But we must now notice a more important conflict between orthodox beliefs and rational theology in which both older and newer principles of knowledge were assumed.

V

Above all the discussions of speculative theology sounds the din of the battle with Deism. Already in 1677 Stillingfleet's *Letter to a Deist* manifests the conflict, though the *Letter* is aimed chiefly at Hobbes and Spinoza. The succession of writers who were depreciated by their contemporary opponents as deists formed no coherent party. No common circle of principles can be discerned in the works of Toland, Collins, Woolston, Tindal, Morgan, and Chubb. Some theologians classed as deists professed beliefs that accepted most of the orthodox Christianity of the age; others uttered opinions that verged on complete scepticism and contempt of religious ideas. But even the less extreme critics of orthodox theology, such as Matthew Tindal, the author of *Christianity as Old as Creation* (1730), manifest the extensive suspicion of official religion that prevailed among educated persons. Bishop Butler laments 'the general decay in religion in this nation, which is now observed by everyone, and has been for some time the complaint of all serious persons'. And on another occasion he observes that it was a common belief that Christianity was fictitious, and a subject for mirth

[1] John Hutchinson, *Works*, vol. v, London, 1749.

and ridicule.[1] Many other witnesses bear out the truth of this picture of the contemporary sentiment on religion. The deists energetically express the current contempt of the Church and clergy. But they manifest also the drift of opinion towards natural theology and away from the dogmas of revelation. All the distinguished scholars of the day, Hoadley, Swift, Whiston, Berkeley, Bentley, Conybeare, and Butler, entered the lists against the deists. Anthony Collins's *Discourse on the Grounds and Reasons of the Christian Religion*, 1724, evoked thirty-five replies within two years of its publication; Matthew Tindal's *Christianity as Old as Creation* produced 115 pamphlets and books in answer; Thomas Woolston's *Six Discourses on Miracles*, 1727–30, which treated religious beliefs with the levity of the coffee-house, brought sixty adversaries into the field. Thirty thousand copies of these *Discourses* were quickly sold and whole bales of the book were dispatched to America.

The distinctive note in the writings of the deists is an appeal to reason in religion in contrast to authority. Among the principal freethinkers the chief interpretation given to reason is pre-scientific; it is derived from the Stoic common notions of Lord Herbert of Cherbury, who is frequently quoted by free-thinkers and their opponents. Every man by the light of nature can discover without instruction the main truths of religion, that there is a God, that He is eternal, immutable, and perfect, that He governs the universe, and that He rewards the good and punishes the wicked. These dictates of natural religion are universal and plain to all men; they have been distorted by priestcraft and superstition, by appeals to the miracles and divine revelations of the Scriptures. Natural religion is a law 'not depending on authority and traditions, not darkened by hyper-bolical and figurative expressions, not mutilated by interpolations, corruptions, and imperfect or wrong translations, not capable of being explained away by arbitrary, or split into opposite and contradictory doctrines by various and fanciful interpretations, but written on the heart of every man in capital letters'.[2]

---

[1] *Charge to the Durham Clergy* (1751). Advertisement to *The Analogy of Religion*, 1736. Shaftesbury in his *Characteristics of Men and Manners* wrote of Christian theology with contemptuous irony. Pope told Warburton 'that to his knowledge the *Characteristics* had done more harm to Revealed Religion than all the works of Infidelity put together'.

[2] Philip Skelton, *Deism Revealed*, 2nd ed., London, 1751, i. 35.

The old appeal to innate common principles that had been revived by Charles Blount and Charles Gildon in the previous century in their defence of a system of natural religion was now associated with the new ideals of plainness, simplicity, obviousness. 'The uncorrupted doctrines of Christianity are not above the reach of the vulgar but the gibberish of your divinity schools is.'[1] Religion ought to be universal and clear, whereas no revelation can have either of those properties. Toland associates Herbert's common notions, Cartesian intuitions, and simplicity. 'What is evidently repugnant to clear and distinct ideas, or to common notions, is contrary to Reason: I go on therefore to prove, that the Doctrines of the Gospel, if it be the word of God, cannot be so.' And in a later passage he maintains that Christ rendered the truth 'easy and obvious to the meanest capacities'. The appeal to innate conceptions was a call on doctrines the most opposed to the outlook of the empirical philosophy, and numerous clerical critics of the deists were quick to press the modern account of knowledge against the rational principles of the freethinkers. They denied in the manner of Locke all *a priori* notions, including the universal notions of natural religion. The senses alone supply the materials of knowledge; we possess no other source of notions. The office of reason is not to supply the mind with ideas but to judge of the connexion or disagreement between those already received. The orthodox defenders frequently rely upon the scepticism with which the new philosophy approached metaphysical questions in order to point out the necessity for revelation. 'If few or none can attain to that (true) religion by the mere light of nature, in its present dark and degenerate circumstances, and in the midst of violent appetites, of rooted prejudices, and of sensible objects and ideas only; it will follow, that nothing but revelation will make us perfectly happy.'[2] In short the refutations of the deistic arguments by the bishops and clerics often depend upon the adoption of the empirical apparatus of principles, while it is the supporters of the religion

---

[1] John Toland, *Christianity not Mysterious*, London, 1696, p. 165.

[2] Skelton, op. cit., i. 168. The most candid expression of the old position that we must believe in revealed truth which contradicts our reason appears in *A View of the Internal Evidence of the Christian Religion*, by Soames Jenyns, 1776. The fourteenth-century view was reaffirmed nearly a hundred years later by Mansel in his Bampton lectures of 1859.

of nature and of reason who assume the position of philosophical rationalism. The most celebrated argument against the deists published in the period, Butler's *Analogy of Religion, Natural and Revealed, to the Constitution and Course of Nature*, 1736, was described by Thomas Chalmers as 'an application of the principles of inductive philosophy to revealed religion'. Assuming the existence of God as creator of the world, Butler seeks to discover by a survey of the principles of nature those characters that point in the same direction as the dogmas of revelation. He insists on the limitations of human reason, and in opposition to the demand of the deists for rational demonstration from self-evident principles he proclaims the method of probable reasoning as fitted to the understanding of beings of limited capacities; and he takes the method of arguing by analogy as the chief type of probable reasoning.

On the other hand, despite their Stoic and Cartesian views of natural reason, the deistical writers also refer to the new conceptions of human understanding that had been formulated by Locke and the experimental philosophers. Locke himself was obliged to admit that Toland in *Christianity not Mysterious* had made use of doctrines contained in the *Essay*. The principal point adopted is the consideration that our understanding of divine truths is necessarily restricted by the sensory origin of our thinking, a condition that 'is the undoubted source of all the Absurdities that ever were seriously vented among Christians'. Phenomenalism does not invite us to believe in fables. No Christian doctrine, no more than any ordinary piece of nature, can be reputed a mystery because we have not an adequate or complete idea of whatever belongs to it. 'Nothing is a mystery because we know not its essence, since that is neither knowable in itself nor even thought of by us.'[1] Traces of the Lockean analysis of knowledge are discernible in Collins, Tindal, Morgan, and Chubb. One reference must suffice. Tindal explains what he means by reason. The immediate objects of the rational faculties are ideas, and 'all the ideas we have, or can have, are either by Sensation or Reflection; by the first we have our ideas of what passes or exists without; by the second, of what passes or exists within the Mind; and in the View, or Contemplation of these consists all our knowledge; that being

---

[1] *Christianity not Mysterious*, p. 87.

nothing but the Perception of the Agreement, or Disagreement of our Ideas'.[1] It is true that he proceeds to stress demonstrative knowledge derived from self-evident notions and to depreciate probable reasoning, but he sees nothing incompatible in holding both the empirical theory of the origin of ideas and the belief in self-evident notions by which we discern the immutable relations of things.

The earlier and representative group of deists devoted considerable portions of their writings to the task of exposing the confusions, immorality, and incomprehensibility of the Biblical record and of the orthodox dogmas. Later writers concentrated more upon abuse of the practice and theories of the Church than upon the principles of natural theology. In his cynical *Christianity not founded on Argument*, 1742, the younger Dodwell proclaimed the complete divorce of faith and reason, of religion and philosophy. All attempts to prove the rationality of theological dogmas from the days of the Fathers to those of Tillotson, Clarke, and the Boyle Lectures are useless. The devout Christian must embrace the creed of Tertullian and declare his belief in that which is absurd to his intelligence. The shrillest pitch was attained by the posthumously published letters of Lord Bolingbroke to Pope, in which the author declared that ecclesiastical tradition had been from the first ages for the most part founded in ignorance, superstition, enthusiasm, and fraud; and Christianity as it is usually conceived was the invention of men either very weak, very mad, or very knavish. 'It requires, therefore, no regard nor any inward conformity to it.' The philosophical interest in the deistic arguments collapsed under such frantic methods. At the root of Bolingbroke's outbursts against religious beliefs is a thorough scepticism of human knowledge; for him 'man is a creature placed in the lowest form of intelligent beings', and that such a creature should attempt to unveil the mysteries of Divine Wisdom is 'downright madness'. Deism ended in negation.

We have said that the distinctive mark of the writings of the deists was the appeal to common notions of religion to the dogmas of tradition. The intellectual leaders of the Church often assumed in their treatises a theory of truth that differed little from that of the heretical writers. Prominent moralists of

[1] *Christianity as Old as Creation*, p. 159.

the period referred the authority of ethical ideas to infallible
and universal truths apprehended by men's reason and conscience. Some theologians supported beliefs upon self-evident
and immutable principles, which they preferred to the claims
of tradition and enthusiasm. No author, for example, is more
frequently quoted by the deists than Archbishop Tillotson, and
Collins in the *Discourse on Free Thinking* speaks of him as one
'whom all English freethinkers own as their head'. In his
unceasing fight against atheism and idolatry, in other words,
Hobbism and Roman Catholicism, Tillotson exposes the confusions of ecclesiastical authority and shows the naïvety of
blind submission to the text of the Scriptures. 'Better it were',
he wrote in reference to the sects, 'that there were no Revealed
Religion, and that human nature were left to its own principles
mild and merciful and conducive to the happiness of society,
than to be acted by a religion which inspires men with so wild
a fury.' The utterance was seized upon by Toland in his *Christianity not Mysterious*; little was required to turn this position
into the creed of deism. Many theologians followed the lead of
the archbishop. They agreed with Locke that reason is natural
revelation and that revelation is natural reason enlarged by
God; but they gave more attention to natural religion, resting
upon the uniform conceptions of men, than to dogmatic
theology. The content of divinity is reduced to a series of self-
evident propositions, and religious belief is founded upon the
intuitive knowledge of the nature of things and the fitness of
creation. The deists and their orthodox antagonists moved
within a common philosophy. The biting disputes between the
bishops and the rationalists were often sham fights; and the
attempts to superimpose a defence of the Scriptures upon
the authority of reason were ineffective.

This cool intellectual religion provoked inevitable revulsion.
There were two main currents that loosened the hold of the
religion of reason; and of these one is but superficially our concern. The first is the advance of the empirical view of knowledge of which we have treated in the preceding pages. In
relation to religious philosophy the spread of Locke's outlook
produced interesting consequences. The increasing realization
that reason is nothing but the result of sensation and reflection
led to the conclusion that religious ideas are intimately asso-

ciated with the circumstances in which men find themselves, and that their theology arises largely from the impressions and traditions that beset them. What was being undermined was the age-long belief in the plenary inspiration of the Scriptures.

'If we have never heard nor read of any religion or country besides our own,' observed an anonymous author in 1731, 'if we have not so much as an intimation that there are such and such places in the world besides England and the Church Established, reason, I imagine, would think nothing about it, but content itself with that stock of knowledge it has already attained to without attempting to make discoveries of things that the mind has not the least notion or idea of.'[1]

Experience takes the place of natural reason, and the theologian is invited to apply himself to the influence of custom and education upon the formation of beliefs. In a word there begins to arise a philosophy of history in connexion with theology. In its earlier form, in the hands of writers such as William Berriman,[2] the tendency appears as a 'Gradual Revelation of the Gospel from the Time of Man's Apostasy'; later in the century there is an extraordinary development of historical scholarship manifesting an intense appreciation of the growth of societies and of their ideas. The course of Christianity as a phenomenon of history was treated from varied points of view, and the fashionable abstractions intrude upon the narrative. In Hume's *History* there is implicit the assumption of the unalterable laws of human nature, discoverable by the empirical method; in Gibbon's splendid story there is presupposed the belief in a golden age of reason in the period of the Antonines, and the history of Rome displays the progressive triumph of barbarism and religion. But even here there is search for historical causes side by side with the rationality of the Enlightenment. And in the meantime historical criticism had been applied to the Scriptures. The works of Conyers Middleton on the miracles of the New Testament exemplified the arrival of the new empirical approach to sacred tradition.[3] He sought to show that there

---

[1] Quoted from 'The Religion of Nature considered,' by E. C. Mossner, *Bishop Butler and the Age of Reason*, p. 135. For the effect of the Lockean philosophy on historical writing see R. G. Collingwood, *The Idea of History*, Oxford, 1946, p. 72.   [2] He was Boyle lecturer in 1730–2.

[3] Conyers Middleton, *A Free Inquiry into the Miraculous Powers which are supposed to have subsisted in the Christian Church from the Earliest Ages through Successive Centuries*, London, 1749.

are no authentic cases of miracles after the time of the Apostles, and he traced the credibility in these events in subsequent periods to the intellectual habits of these times. He attacked especially the veracity of the Church Fathers, and, as Hume attests, put all England in a ferment. But he had opened a path of research into the mental outlook of primitive Christianity that was followed by others; Paley's *Evidences of Christianity*, 1794, is the culmination of this trend in the eighteenth century. 'We do not assume the attributes of the Deity, or the existence of a future state, in order to *prove* the reality of miracles. That reality always must be proved by evidence.'[1] The ruling method is no longer the method of demonstration from first principles, but the method of historical inquiry, of probability, and cumulative testimony. The fact that Paley's inferences were different from those of Middleton and opposed to those of Hume does not obscure the similarity of their method. Hume's rules of evidence, that demand 'an opposition of experiments and observations', are in the line of the Baconian and scientific logic of the age, and the reasoning of the Archdeacon of Carlisle is directed by the same propensities. But in his elaborate investigation of the evidence Paley applies the canons of historical criticism far more extensively; behind him lies the new learning that had been brought to bear on the origins of Christianity. The work had been stimulated by the explorations of the deists into Church history; it had gathered force in the writings of Warburton, Lowth, Parvish, and Lardner; and it was soon, in the nineteenth century, to advance far beyond the procedure of Paley. But the failure to appreciate the prior philosophical problem of the possibility of miracles is a gauge of the decline of metaphysical thought since the day of Hume's *Essays*.

The other movement that drew men away from the older intellectual habits in religion was the spreading flood of a fresh enthusiasm. From several sources, but most notably through the inspiring teaching of John Wesley and George Whitefield, there coursed into English life an extraordinary tide of emotional religion. Once more men revolted, as they had revolted in the fourteenth century, against theological metaphysics and clerical formalism; once more, in recoil from a religion of intellectual principles, there was a surging return to the religion

---

[1] W. Paley, *Evidences of Christianity*, 1794, Cambridge, 1850, p. 2.

of the heart. The practical and inward faith of the Moravians and the Methodists loosened the authority of rational religion. For John Wesley faith was not 'a speculative, rational thing, a cold, lifeless assent, a train of ideas in the head', but a rebirth into salvation. The movement that swept the country between 1740 and 1790 had little direct influence upon philosophical theology. Its leaders were content to rest their evangelical gospel upon the doctrine of tradition. But indirectly it exercised through its conception of religious truth two effects upon thought, one restrictive, the other expansive. It strengthened the trend towards implicit and uninquiring faith, towards romanticism in philosophy; it also widened the spiritual vision of the time and prepared the way for a theory of experience in which religious perception should again find place. It broke down by its practical success the profound distaste for the intuitions of emotion that had imprisoned the minds of cultured men. Parallel with the evangelical current and, at times mingling with it, there moved a vein of mystical and allegorical theology in which we meet echoes of the Pseudo-Dionysius, of the Cabbala and of Paracelsus. The principal influence in this revival of mysticism was Jakob Boehme, the remarkable German visionary who had died in 1624. His writings had spread through Europe and had deeply impressed religious minds in England in the seventeenth century. The *Theologia Mystica* (1683) of John Pordage marks, for example, this influence. The scientific master of the age, Newton, had studied Boehme, and had adopted his symbolism in his own writings on the Scriptures. It was, however, largely through the works of William Law that the mystical faith of Boehme entered the religious thought of the eighteenth century. In *A Serious Call to a Devout and Holy Life*, 1729, he revived the old wells of inspiration. Christianity is not a school for the teaching of moral virtue, still less the contemplation of the laws of natural reason. It is a new principle of life, a heavenly illumination. Law had many readers who were profoundly stirred by his message, John Wesley, Samuel Johnson, and William Blake among them, and the lamp he lit shed its beams on fresh vistas of reality. But this mystical and devotional spirit often bore with it a depreciation of reason. Law himself had declared the case against reason in a work published in 1731, and a number

of other spiritual teachers recommended men to ignore human
learning and to hearken to the inward voice of grace, or the
outward symbolism of the inspired Scriptures. In the name of
Christianity the new philosophy and even philosophy itself was
reprobated. John Hutchinson and his followers declared the
theories of Newton to be contrary to the truths of revelation.
Joseph Milner asserted that the views of the philosophers 'have
been found to militate against the vital truths of Christianity
and corrupt the gospel in our times, as much as the cultivation
of the more ancient philosophy corrupted it in early ages'.[1]
More reputable writers, such as John Conybeare in *A Defence
of Revealed Religion*, 1732, and John Leland in his *View of the
Principal Deistical Writers* (3rd edition, 1754–6) depreciated the
capacity of human reason and revived the old thesis that the
Fall had corrupted man's intellect and that revelation alone
supplied the knowledge to which man could not of himself
attain. Mysticism, evangelicism, gnostic readings of the Bible,
mingled with philosophical scepticism; and theologians fell
back upon Scriptural authoritarianism and the argument from
design.

To conclude this brief view of the relations between the
philosophy of naturalism and theology, let us throw a quick
glance forward into the nineteenth century. The new evangelical party that dominated the Church in England during the
early years of the century, the party of Charles Simeon, William
Wilberforce, and Hannah More, displayed little interest in
speculative questions. The stagnant surface of later Georgian
theology was rarely stirred to philosophical reflection. The
leading voices summoned men to divide religious beliefs sharply
from the beliefs of the world, and the theology of the less
influential group of High Churchmen was the theology of the
Caroline divines. The Church is a spiritual organization, providing the channels of grace, and private judgement in religion
is inadmissible. The philosophy of empiricism had ceased to
offer support, and there were few signs of any alternative. The
philosophers, headed by Bentham, George Grote, and James
Mill, rejected the ethics and metaphysics of orthodox theology

---

[1] J. Milner, *History of the Church of Christ*, quoted C. J. Abbey and J. H.
Overton, *The English Church in the Eighteenth Century*, London, 1878, vol. ii,
p. 211.

and recommended to their disciples a vague deism or a negative scepticism. After 1820 there are marks of renewed intellectual life among Churchmen. The most incisive thinker in the new liberal group of ecclesiastics was Richard Whately who called attention to the way in which common metaphysical terms, such as time, cause, eternity, are used in theology without precision of meaning. He also exposed the absurdity of seeking knowledge of the physical order in the Bible. It was no function of religion to anticipate the discoveries of geology and astronomy. But there soon followed an extraordinary renewal of the old ecclesiastical form of religion.

The Tractarian movement was inaugurated in 1833 by John Keble's Assize Sermon at Oxford on National Apostasy, and during the following years it spread widely throughout the country. Oxford was riven with controversy and St. Mary's was thronged to hear the sermons of Newman. The movement was guided by an intense feeling for the Catholic view of the Church. The Church was the unique organ by which divine truth is preserved and transmitted. And the original corpus of doctrine taught in the fourth century and confirmed and extended by the Councils was the truth. The Oxford Movement promoted a notable revival of religious devotion; it encouraged a deep appreciation of ecclesiastical discipline; it reopened the riches of the ancient dogmatic theology; it produced saints. But in relation to the thought of the time it divided the Church from any appreciation of the bearing of modern knowledge upon religion. For the only philosophy with which the great spiritual leaders were closely acquainted was the empirical philosophy, and from the view of reasons asserted there they turned once again to a faith which was 'above reason', based partly on divine authority, partly on a doctrine of spiritual vision. Newman in his sermons at Oxford accepted the teaching of the prevalent philosophy. 'All that we know, strictly speaking, is the existence of the impressions our senses make on us.' Such knowledge can be of little help to us in all that concerns our deepest interest; indeed it only breeds scepticism and despair. There exists another mode of knowledge that precedes and governs logical understanding. This is the 'illative sense' expounded at length in the *Grammar of Assent*. There are a number of truths, that we exist, that some actions are right and

others wrong, that there is an external world which is part of
a system, that there is a Supreme Being, and many other
propositions to which we give unhesitating interior assent.
When compared with the tentative demonstrations of reason
such knowledge is certain. 'In no class of concrete reasonings,
whether in experimental science, historical research, or theology,
is there any ultimate test of truth and error in our inferences
besides the trustworthiness of the Illative Sense that gives them
its sanction.'[1] It is in applying this principle to theology that
Newman is mainly interested. The religious man attains
conviction of the primary truths of theology by a kind of
instinctive perception, not by a formal juxtaposition of propositions. The certainties of faith do not rest on logical grounds,
and Newman frankly recognizes the individual and personal
quality of conviction. The certainty of a belief consists in the
certitude of the mind that contemplates it.

Newman's doctrine of belief is affected by the nominalist and
sensationalist conception of knowledge from which he starts.
His distrust of the traditional notion of reason throws him into
a doctrine of the certainty of subjective assurance. And he can
accordingly embrace the system of revelation 'not as true on
intrinsic grounds, not as probably true, or partially true, but as
absolutely certain knowledge, certain in a sense in which
nothing else can be certain, because it comes from Him who
neither can deceive nor be deceived'.[2] A similar failure to
discover rational claims for religious beliefs on the basis of
current views of experience can be discovered in many other
utterances of the time. A sensation was caused by Mansel's
Bampton Lectures on *The Limits of Religious Thought*. Here
we find an extension of the argument of Butler's *Analogy*,
associated with strains from Sir William Hamilton's philosophy.
Butler had argued that the difficulties in the scheme of Christian
revelation were not greater than those in the scheme of nature.
Mansel attempted to show that the difficulties involved in the
doctrines of religion were parallel to those found by natural
theology. Following Hamilton he showed that all thinking
refers to what is conditioned and relative. Since we cannot form
any notion of an absolute or infinite being we cannot prove or

---

[1] *Grammar of Assent*, 2nd ed., London, 1878, p. 352.
[2] Ib., p. 387.

disprove the dogmas of theology, such as the Trinity. Such principles must be accepted even when they lead to contradictions or even to absurdities. We can investigate the evidences of revelation but we are not at liberty to criticize its contents. 'The doctrine itself must be unconditionally received, not as reasonable, nor as unreasonable, but as scriptural.'[1] The influence of Kant's philosophy is evident in Mansel's argument; he affirms that the highest principles of thought and action are regulative, not speculative. They do not tell us what things are in themselves, but how we must conduct ourselves in relation to them. But there is also present at the root of the discussion the belief that our ideas are only symbols, wholly inadequate in point of knowledge of reality. Reality is essentially impervious to knowledge; all we apprehend is the succession of phenomena. Mansel's position was vigorously attacked by F. D. Maurice and others, it was welcomed by the later generation of scientific 'agnostics'. But many theologians hailed with satisfaction the proposal to put faith beyond the reach of criticism.

One more instance of the bearing of current philosophical principles on theology during this phase may be cited. In J. B. Mozley's Bampton Lectures on miracles (1865) the discussion stands upon the supra-rational nature of theological truth. Christianity is a dispensation undiscoverable by human reason. But what is striking in Mozley's argument is the way in which he adheres to the teaching of Hume. Belief in the order of nature is traced to repetition of physical events. No reason can be given for the belief; Hume has spoken the last word on the question. Now since the belief in the order of nature is an unintelligent impulse of which we can give no rational account, there is no ground for maintaining that miracles, as opposed to the order of nature, are opposed to reason.[2] In later parts of his discourse the writer insists on the traditional argument from design; the proof of a personal deity is inferred from the fact that the physical organization of nature is adapted to the wants of moral beings.[3] And his final consideration is that, since physical laws are suspended every time an animate being moves any part of its body, the suspension of material laws by a spiritual being is entirely possible.

[1] *The Limits of Religious Thought*, London, 1848, p. 180.
[2] J. B. Mozley, *On Miracles*, 2nd ed., London, 1867, p. 48.   [3] Ib., p. 99.

The rejection of metaphysical knowledge and the acceptance of the classical theory of the nature of the knowing mind and its capacity to reach truth left rational theology without a philosophy adequate to its demands. Theologians resorted to defences of supra-rational faith, to ecclesiastical tradition, to miracles, and to crude arguments from design. The latter part of the nineteenth century saw the recovery of philosophical ideas that could provide religion with firmer principles. But meanwhile scientific philosophy had also moved confidently forward to more comprehensive visions of truth, sweeping the traditional theology into the net of cosmic materialism. We have touched on the way in which the old association between metaphysical scepticism and authoritarian faith, a junction that had been a feature of English thought in the fourteenth century, was reaffirmed in the modern epoch. Soon after the year 1860, the system of thought the principles of which had been announced by Newton and Locke at the end of the seventeenth century reached the climax of its course, while a new mode of idealism sprang up in opposition to the classical outlook of English philosophy.

IX

NATURALISM AND IDEALISM

I

IN the latter section of the nineteenth century the vision that had inspired the prophets of the new philosophy in the first steps of its career had drawn perceptibly near. The grand features of a system of truth founded securely on tested observation were confidently discerned. The unifying principles of reality were conceived as generalizations derived from the special generalizations of particular provinces of scientific inquiry. The only philosophical knowledge worthy of the name was science as a whole; philosophy is completely unified science. The plan of the universe was constructed on the broad formulations of physical science. By co-ordinating the general conclusions of the several sciences it was deemed possible to attain a view of the scheme of things as a whole, and it was taught that the general form could be interpreted and justified by following its applications throughout the details of the special departments of knowledge.

This naturalistic panorama of reality was supported on two great pillars. One was the law of the conservation of energy and matter, the other was the theory of the descent of species by natural selection.

The closing years of the eighteenth century and the first half of the nineteenth had witnessed amazing conquests in scientific knowledge. It will be sufficient here to mention a bare few of the masterly experimental and theoretical achievements by which the Newtonian methods had been extended and refined. In 1801 Thomas Young demonstrated practically the wave theory of light and the principle of interference, and some fifteen years later Augustin Fresnel worked out the mathematics of the theory, gathering under one comprehensive view a large mass of observed phenomena. In the meantime the atomic conception of matter, which, as we have seen, had formed a central feature of the revolutionary ideas of nature in the seventeenth century, had received arresting confirmation at the hands of a Manchester teacher, John Dalton. In his

New System of Chemical Philosophy (1808) he pointed out that the chemical elements can be ranged in an order of atomic weight, the unit being an atom of hydrogen. This scheme provided the basis for rapid new departures and Dalton's discovery was applied with extraordinary success to the understanding of the ultimate constituents and relationships of solids, liquids, and gases. An equally striking advance was soon made in the sphere of electrical phenomena. The experiments of the Danish physicist Oersted in 1820 led Ampère to formulate the mathematical analysis of electro-dynamics. Between 1821 and 1831 Michael Faraday, one of the greatest scientific geniuses in our history, conducted a series of brilliant experiments on the phenomena of electro-magnetism and electro-statics. He demonstrated the lines of force of electric currents, thus linking together many disconnected phenomena. These varied discoveries were leading scientific thought to a new and comprehensive conception of matter. Theories concerning properties of light, magnetism, electric currents, and chemical elements were coalescing, both in relation to the doctrine of atomic structure and to the mathematical formulation of the underlying forces of material phenomena. Investigations in the field of thermodynamics strikingly advanced this process. In 1839 John Prescott Joule, a pupil of Dalton, began a chain of experiments in which he investigated the relationship between electrical currents, mechanical force, and heat. The energy produced by electrical and mechanical power was given an accurate definition, namely, the power of performing work, a definition that displays the phenomenalist and anti-metaphysical character of scientific inquiry. As in the seventeenth century, the scientific way of thought was not interested in asking what force is but in discovering what it does and in measuring its effects with mathematical precision. Joule's experiments showed that heat is a form of energy, and that the total energy produced by a mechanical or electrical engine is transformed into an equivalent amount of heat. The same amount of work develops the same amount of heat; the energy is equal and interchangeable. In a lecture delivered in 1847 Joule maintained that not only heat and mechanical energy but also attraction through space and light are mutually convertible, and that in these conversions nothing is ever lost. In the same year the young German authority von Helmholtz applied the formula to the whole range of natural phenomena. He enunciated the principle of the conservation of force. The physical energy in any material system is a quantity that can neither be increased nor diminished by any action between the parts of the system. It can only be transformed into another type of energy. And this principle was applied to the system of the universe. The sum total of all the energy in the universe remains constant. The theory was established by the distinguished achievements of R. J. Clausius in Germany and of William Thomson, afterwards Lord Kelvin, in England, during 1850 and 1851.

Some of the philosophical consequences which were beginning to be drawn by men of science from these developments must be considered in a moment. But during this period of unparalleled activity in the fundamental questions of physics there had been occurring remarkable progress in the study of living beings. In the eighteenth century a number of investigators had explored the physical properties of plants and animals, but the application of the new chemical principles to living organisms now gave a fresh direction to theory. The chemical substances that compose living tissue were isolated and even made artificially by Liebig and his colleagues in Germany from 1830 onwards, and the conception of the cycle of energy between living organisms and their environment was expounded. The maintenance and growth of animals and plants were shown to depend upon a constant exchange of their own substances with the substances of the air and of other factors; upon an intake (in the case of plants) of carbon dioxide and ammonia and a return of these compounds to the air. The cell theory, first proposed by Schleiden in 1838, further promoted a physico-chemical theory of life. The cell from which all living organisms were developed was soon being described as a mass of nucleated protoplasm. The old conviction that the vital processes of vegetables and animals involve principles radically distinct from those found in inorganic matter was beginning to be questioned. In place of a vital or spiritual force that can modify the physical and chemical laws of the body there was substituted a circulation of energy between the organism and its habitat. And influential men of science were asserting that chemical factors were more fundamental in living processes than physiological factors. Speculation in scientific circles played with the hypothesis of La Mettrie who in 1748 had concluded according to the principles of Descartes that man is a machine. There was an increasing disposition to repeat the challenge, 'What will all the weak reeds of divinity, metaphysic, and nonsense of the schools, avail against this firm and solid oak?' Writers echoed the belief of Cabanis that the brain produces thought in the same way as the stomach and intestines operate in digestion. There was indeed sharp conflict between the vitalists and the mechanists and a wrangle arose concerning the possibility of spontaneous generation. But the ideal of mechanistic and materialist interpretation of all phenomena was encouraged by the discoveries of the organic chemists. Huxley's popular lecture *On the Physical Basis of Life*, 1868, summarizes these advances in the analysis of living structure, and points, except for certain characteristic reservations at the end, towards the ideal of comprehensive materialism. He showed an enormous public that the acts of all living things are fundamentally one, and reveal the same underlying structure. And he taught that all vital activity may be said to be the result of the molecular forces of the protoplasm.

The grand generalization of recent natural philosophy, the principles of the transformation and equivalence of all modes of force, was widely felt to possess the most radical significance in relation to the interpretation of reality. The constancy and indestructibility of energy had been demonstrated in the realm of the inorganic world; authoritative voices were applying these laws to organic nature. Men learnt that the matter of the vegetable order was for the most part transmuted gas and that its force was transformed solar energy. They were told that the activity of animals had been proved to be the transferred activity of molecules. They heard that the investigations of physiologists and of psychologists were revealing the neurological basis of mental life. A new Hobbism overshadowed their minds, the product not of tenuous deductions from rational intuitions but of a cumulative mass of precise observations. On most thoughtful persons whose ideas were controlled by the traditional theological assumptions the consciousness of this philosophy weighed like a nightmare; they were jaded and hag-ridden, as a writer in the *Spectator* lamented, by the physical fatalities of modern science. In truth a growing army of intelligent inquirers, detached for the most part from the clerical and classical education of the public schools and universities, eagerly embraced the new materialism. They were ready to accept the 'universal truth' expressed in the doctrine of the axiom of the correlation of forces. The most powerful teacher of the age had made it the cardinal point of his system and had confidently extended it to vital, mental, and social regions. But the representative philosophy of Herbert Spencer, the new apostle of the understanding, as Tyndall named him, must be considered in relation to the other stronghold of the scientific vision of the universe, the theory of evolution.

The question of the descent of species from primitive types had been fermenting since the seventeenth century. It had been mooted by Cudworth, by Hooke, and by John Ray. It had been proposed by the eccentric Monboddo and set forth in considerable detail by Erasmus Darwin. In his *Zoonomia*, 1794, he had suggested the operation of sexual selection and of the struggle for survival in animal forms. Meanwhile the theories of Buffon, of Geoffrey St. Hilaire, and of Lamarck had attracted notice in England. We have seen that Paley refers to these theories with contempt. But Lamarck's theory attracted Sir Charles Lyell who described it in his widely read *Principles of Geology*, first published in 1832. These surmises had not seriously shaken the traditional belief in the special creation of species and in the Biblical view of nature. The gale of criticism that was fanned by the publication in 1844 of *Vestiges of the Natural History of Creation* manifests the persistence of the habitual outlook among men of science as well as among theologians. In this remarkable book the author attacked the postulate of special creation and assembled a quantity of evidence that pointed to the gradual development of organisms during the earlier ages of the earth.[1] He cited the survival of rudimentary organs, the stages of the growth of the embryo, and the geographical distribution of species. He proposed the theory that life had developed from matter without the aid of divine activity. A cry of indignation swept up and the book

[1] The author, whose identity was not revealed until the appearance of the 12th ed. in 1884, was Robert Chambers, an Edinburgh publisher.

was spurned by the scientific leaders who upheld the dogma of the fixity of species, and by the theologians, who assumed without question belief in the Scriptural creation. But the author's ideas, which owed much to Lamarck, were widely discussed and the book ran into many editions. 'You know', gushes Lady Constance in *Tancred*, 'all is development—the principle is perpetually going on. First there was nothing; then there was something; then—I forget the next—I think there were shells; then fishes; then we came—let me see—did we come next? Never mind that; we came at last, and the next change will be something very superior to us, something with wings.'[1]

Some years before Darwin's book appeared Herbert Spencer published an article *On the Development Hypothesis* in which he contended for the belief in a gradual evolution of organisms from early amorphous types, and in his *Principles of Psychology*, 1855, he applied evolutionary laws to the domain of mind. A far-flung philosophy of evolution was further propounded in the essay on *Progress, its Law and Cause*, published in 1857. But the *Origin of Species* placed these speculations on a scientific and inductive foundation. It assembled evidence from many fields, from heredity, breeding, embryology, and geology. The cumulative weight of its arguments appeared to point irresistibly to the main theory, that the diversity of living species had been evolved by natural selection, that is, by the survival of those individuals in a species that have chanced to possess structural variations endowing them with ability to meet the dangers to which their lives were exposed. Offspring tend to resemble their parents and accordingly the favourable variations survived while the remainder were killed off. The scientific strength of the theory lay in its reliance upon observable physical agencies, upon causes the effects of which could be seen to follow according to natural laws. It was unnecessary to assume any metaphysical or vital factor, whether voluntary exertion or implicit purpose. Still less was it possible to find room for the Creator of Genesis or of *Natural Theology*. The action of the Deity was consigned to a remote point of time and

---

[1] A later opinion of scientific doctrine may be added from *Lothair*. 'Instead of Adam, our ancestry is traced to the most grotesque of creatures; thought is phosphorus, the soul complex nerves, and our moral sense a secretion of sugar.'

to the production of a germ capable of development into the simplest type of organism. And conjecture soon leaped beyond this attenuated notion of creation and discerned in matter and energy 'the promise and potency of all terrestrial life'.

The story of the momentary explosion that was fired by the biological hypothesis of Darwin and A. R. Wallace is familiar and has recently been retold.[1] The perennial strife between new knowledge and the established system of theological belief that we have witnessed from the earliest phase of speculation in England broke forth with renewed violence. Press, pulpit, and platform blazed with denunciation and defence. Conservative prelates and conservative men of science, Professor Owen, Professor Sedgwick, and Bishop Wilberforce prominent among them, bitterly attacked the doctrine; other distinguished leaders of opinion, Charles Kingsley, Arthur Stanley, Sir Charles Lyell, accepted it. The greatest of controversialists, Huxley, defended Darwin against criticism from every quarter, and had no difficulty in showing that the theologians were supporting conceptions of nature that were demonstrably unscientific. The clerical writers replied by charging the men of science with infidelity and materialism. The popular clamour concentrated upon the painful disclosure of man's affinity to the monkey. Disraeli's speech at the Oxford diocesan conference of 1864 echoed over the country. 'What is the question', he asked, 'now placed before society with a glib assurance the most astounding? The question is this: Is man an ape or an angel? I, my lord, I am on the side of the angels. I repudiate with indignation the contrary view, which I believe foreign to the conscience of Humanity.'

But this was the froth of the issue. The profound misgivings roused by the doctrine of natural selection were due to its association with the capital principle of the persistence of energy and matter, in fact to its transformation into materialism. And the poignant agitation provoked by the encroaches of scientific principles upon the historic doctrines of revealed and natural theology was aggravated by other disquieting trends of inquiry. Orthodox habits of thought were distressed by a succession of heretical utterances. The steady growth of

[1] In *Science, Religion, and the Future*, by C. E. Raven, Cambridge, 1943, Lecture III.

Biblical criticism was causing unrest and even scepticism, for many found nothing adequate to replace the theory of plenary inspiration. Strauss's *Leben Jesu* provoked consternation in religious circles. It reduced the Gospel story almost to a myth, banished the supernatural, and accredited the Church with the invention of Christian doctrine. W. G. Ward asserted that Strauss's book was selling in his day more than any other publication. Prominent figures such as George Eliot and Charles Hennell declared their adherence to the natural interpretation of Christ. From all sides came criticism of the belief in miracles, part of the central evidence for the truth of Christianity; and books such as W. R. Greg's *The Creed of Christendom* (1851) argued that the doctrines of inspiration and of special revelation were untenable. And F. W. Newman's writings, especially *The Soul, its Sorrows and its Aspirations* (1849) expressed the profound dissatisfaction of many sensitive minds with 'English idolatry' of the Bible. The publication of *Essays and Reviews* in 1860 evoked an uproar. The essayists demanded that the Bible must be interpreted in the same manner as any other book. They pleaded for free investigation, historical, scientific, and philosophical, into the literature and tenets of the faith. One of them, Baden Powell, professor of geometry at Oxford, expressed his belief in 'the grand principles of the self-evolving powers of Nature'; and another dismissed the narrative of Genesis as half-ideal, half-traditional. For these positions the volume was bitterly attacked and the Court of Arches solemnly condemned those who denied that the Scriptures had been composed under the special intervention of Almighty Power. Traditional ideas encountered other shocks such as Bishop Colenso's destructive examination of the Pentateuch and the book of Joshua. A scandalous dispute arose between the author and the bishops. By these events religious England was divided and stirred to its depths. Orthodox conviction met the new conceptions that were invading the structure of theological belief with determined opposition, and scientific rationalists, liberal theologians, and biblical scholars were condemned alike as subverters of morality. This was the period of *Robert Elsmere* and of the wistful doubts of Matthew Arnold, A. H. Clough, George Eliot, and many lesser figures. One who had been a disciple of Darwin and whose reflections were coloured by the philosophy of Herbert Spencer concluded his *A Candid Examination of Theism* with these words:

'So far as I am individually concerned, the result of this analysis has been to show that . . . it equally becomes my obvious duty to stifle all belief of the kind which I conceive to be the noblest, and to discipline my intellect with regard to this matter into an attitude of the purest scepticism. . . . Yet when at times I think, as think at times I must, of the appalling contrast between the hallowed glory of that creed which once was mine, and the lonely mystery of existence as I now find it—at such times I shall ever feel it impossible to avoid the sharpest pang of which my nature is susceptible.'[1]

The men of science had become the prophets of progressive minds. Their pronouncements upon ultimate problems of knowledge and reality became, after 1860, increasingly ascendant and authoritative. A band of natural philosophers, physicists, mathematicians, and biologists, who combined exceptional powers of interpretation with ardent interests in speculative and moral problems, appeared in England, and these men, T. H. Huxley, John Tyndall, W. K. Clifford, and many more, became the popular teachers of the age. Scientific expositions in simple terms attained a sudden and immense vogue; and by 1884 the *Annual Register* reported that writings of any importance were confined to scientific subjects. These subjects were found to 'absorb the intellectual vitality of the writing world with very few exceptions'.[2] The gospel of science was preached with compelling force in a score of books, from Winwood Reade's *Martyrdom of Man*, 1872, to Karl Pearson's *The Grammar of Science*, 1892. Faith in the omnipotence of science, both in the realm of truth and practice, returned with intenser force to the enthusiastic visions of Glanvil's day, and the extravagant fancies of *The Vanity of Dogmatising* became imminent achievements. Scientific thought is not an accompaniment or condition of human progress but human progress itself, declared Clifford. And scientific thought had reached out beyond the departments of physics, biology, and mathematics to grasp all aspects of experience. The principle of evolution was

[1] *A Candid Examination of Theism* by Physicus (G. J. Romanes), 4th ed., London, 1913, p. 114. The book was published in 1878 but written several years before.

[2] Helen M. Lynd, *England in the Eighteen Eighties*, London, 1945, p. 64.

carried over to every region, to ethics, to the theory of government, to society, to economics; and the most popular religious book of the period endeavoured to prove the reign of natural law in the spiritual world. And for the first time since the writings of Hobbes the methods and the ruling ideas of naturalism were fashioned into a vast system of philosophy that embraced all existence from the formation of the nebulous mass of the stars to the final dissipation of universal energy. 'Spencer', observes the historian of recent British philosophy, 'must be ranked among the greatest philosophical architects that history has known.'[1] He amalgamated into one sweeping design the scientific discoveries of the period; he applied the primary doctrines of evolution and of the persistence of force to every manifestation of being and to the universe as a whole. All inquisitive persons in this period read *First Principles* and few took notice of the penetrating criticisms of Martineau and of other thinkers nursed in a very different tradition. The *Synthetic Philosophy* dominated the speculation of the later nineteenth century. It is the representative expression of its naturalism.

II

The conceptions of knowledge upon which this panorama of reality was founded were the classic principles. They were the principles of experiment and observation of phenomena, of mathematical calculation and of search for determined order that had governed natural inquiry since the seventeenth century. Truth was to be looked for among the observable correlations of experience, among what can be physically measured or can be brought within the domain of uniform law, whether special or general. The exact and rigid uniformity of nature in every section, and the interpretation of the unknown and unfamiliar by the operations of the known and the familiar; these were the assumptions and rules of method that had descended from the pioneers of scientific thought. But attached to the technical logic of physical investigation lay the positivist outlook on experience. The great philosophers of Naturalism presumed the doctrines of Berkeley and Hume, complicated by those of Comte and Sir William Hamilton. We know nothing more of existence than the manifestations of phenomena to

[1] R. Metz, *A Hundred Years of British Philosophy*, London, 1938, p. 102.

our senses. Some of these are vivid, some faint. The former precede the latter; recollections and imaginations depend upon perceptions. But the two orders of experience run concurrently in our consciousness, and the double stream of lights, shades, colours, outlines, and their persistence in memory, cohere into groups that are named objects and persons. The faint manifestations can be attended to as a continuous whole and become distinguished as the self; the vivid series forms the not-self, the objective order. What is real is discriminated from what is not real by its persistence through change, and our consciousness of the fundamental notions of knowledge of space and time and matter is composed of relations of sequence and of co-existence; the former relation is the foundation of our apprehension of time, the latter of our knowledge of space. And our conception of matter is derived from the experience of co-existences that offer resistances to our efforts. In such terms Spencer's *First Principles* (1862) repeated the classic epistemology. The universal forms of thought of 'the transcendentalists' are found to be generated by the primary consciousness of faint and vivid impressions of likenesses and differences. Huxley declared himself to be a disciple of Hume, and Clifford grounded his theory of truth upon impressions, which, in the manner of Berkeley, he conceived to be modifications of consciousness. The chieftains of naturalism, indeed, sought to evade the materialism to which they eloquently pointed in their scientific explorations by a resort to the subjectivism of the eighteenth century. Tyndall, for example, held that all our knowledge is constructed from sensations and that these are 'mere variations of our own condition, beyond which, even to the extent of a hair's breadth, we cannot go'.[1] This Berkeleian position provided the scientific philosophers with an escape from realism. Another line of escape was afforded by avowing the standpoint of Locke. We know nothing of matter except as the name for the unknown and hypothetical causes of our sensations, nor of mind save as the series of states of consciousness. Nevertheless Huxley and his friends were fond of assuring their audiences that thoughts are the expression of material molecular changes, and that the physiology of the future will

---

[1] *The Belfast Address* delivered before the British Association, 1874, in *Lectures and Essays*, London, 1906, p. 39.

gradually extend the realm of matter and law until it is co-extensive with knowledge, with feeling, and with action. There will be a banishment from all regions of human thought of what we call spirit and spontaneity.[1] It is difficult to reconcile the confident expectation of the new leaders of thought that nothing in the end will fail to be explained in terms of material and necessary causes with their admission that the proof of materialism 'lies outside the limits of philosophical inquiry'. They spoke for the most part as materialists and when the materialism became too obvious they fell back upon Berkeleianism or upon the scepticism of the empirical philosophy.

Writing in 1882 Henry Sidgwick found empiricism to be the philosophy that students of natural science at the present day had, or tended to have; and also other persons who could not be called students of natural science but whose minds were impressed and dominated by the triumphant march of modern physical investigation.[2] And this empiricism looked back to the position that the human mind knows nothing directly except the modifications of its elementary consciousness. The work of scientific knowledge according to an eloquent advocate of the new framework of belief lies in filling up the gaps in our immediate perceptions, in producing the curves of our fragmentary experience. The mind invents an imaginary substratum in which sensible qualities somehow inhere, whereas there is nothing beyond the coherence of groups of sensations. We cannot peep behind the curtain, for the curtain is the reality; and the endeavour of metaphysicians to look beyond perceptions only plunges us into a region of cobwebs of the brain.[3] The theory of knowledge is the view of Locke and his disciples, coloured by a decided propensity towards mentalism; nothing is immediately and confidently known but particular items of consciousness. Sidgwick was not alone in declaring himself unable to work out a coherent theory of perception and thought on this basis. He and others avowed complete trust in the procedure and results of empirical science but profound distrust in the principles of empirical philosophy.[4]

---

[1] T. H. Huxley, *Lectures and Essays*, London, 1902, p. 55.

[2] *Mind*, vol. vii, p. 533.

[3] Leslie Stephen, *An Agnostic's Apology*, London, 1931, pp. 86 f.

[4] Bain's article in *Mind*, July 1889, is the last expression of the classic theory of knowledge. It is named 'The Empiricist Position'.

But naturalism did not dwell long upon its philosophical assumptions. For its greatest exponent philosophy is completely unified scientific knowledge. *The Synthetic Philosophy*, the volumes of which appeared at intervals from 1862 to 1896, unfolded a co-ordination of the physics, biology, physiology, psychology, and social theory of the day. It achieved Bacon's ideal of 'a true model of the world, such as it is in fact'. The colossal scheme is bound into unity under a single formula that comprehends the two dominant scientific conceptions of the age, the principles of the conservation of energy and the principle of evolution. The universal evolution which is reality consists in an integration of matter and a concomitant dissipation of motion; during which the matter passes from an indefinite, incoherent homogeneity to a definite coherent heterogeneity, and during which the retained motion undergoes a parallel transformation.[1] The rhythm of concentration and of dissolution is illustrated in every region, from the formation of the sun to the commercial organization of modern states. The decline of the Roman Empire and its overthrow by barbarians is associated with the decay of a planet from loss of internal heat and its dissipation into elementary matter by the shock of a comet. The basis of all these applications of the law of evolution is unequivocally mechanical. The universal redistribution of matter and motion is constant according to the ultimate truth that the relations among forces persist. This truth is the source of our consciousness of the uniformity of law. The law of the transformation and equivalence of forces holds throughout the cosmos and is exhibited equally in the slow gyrations of double stars and in the pulsations of the heart. 'The play of forces is essentially the same in principle throughout the whole region explored by our intelligence.' Evolution, at all points, manifests the continuous redistribution of matter and motion. The process moves inevitably under the laws of thermodynamics to some remote state of motionless equilibrium. But Spencer admits that there remains a possibility that energy may be renewed, and that the entire process may recommence. There may have been evolutions that have filled an immeasurable past and evolutions that will fill an immeasurable future.

The daring sweep of *First Principles* captivated the minds of

[1] *First Principles*, 6th ed., London, 1937, p. 358.

men thirsting for scientific truth and in revolt from academic metaphysics and the outworn dogmas of theology. And its patently materialist texture seemed saved from materialism by a device similar to that to which the more popular prophets of naturalism were turning. In the front of his scientific synthesis Spencer erected the doctrine of the Unknowable. His account of it draws upon Sir William Hamilton's theory that our understanding is confined to the relative and the phenomenal. Scientific ideas are symbols of a reality that is inexplicable. To think is to apprehend relations, differences, and likenesses. The Unconditioned is unthinkable. Yet though we cannot attain definite consciousness of the Unconditioned we can have indefinite consciousness of it. The Absolute is not a pure negation; we must suppose a ground of the phenomena that provide the material of our knowledge. This position reconciles religion with science. The vague consciousness of an enduring and incomprehensible Power is the consciousness on which religion dwells.[1]

Such, in brief, was the most embracing vision of scientific truth offered to the eager disciples of the *Saturday Review*, to the students of the Science and Art Department at Marlborough House, to the new public that looked to science for philosophic instruction and to technology for economic salvation. In the *Synthetic Philosophy* are welded together the calculable dynamics that had descended from Newton, the recent refinements and extensions of the Newtonian physics that had culminated in the doctrine of the universal conservation of force, and the more recent theory of Natural Selection by which man's development from primary types of creatures had been brought within the logic of natural law. Reality is an unbroken scheme of material causes. The later stages of the system such as the free commercial states of the nineteenth century are complications of the initial energy of the system. The new scientific philosophy had enlarged the principles of classical physics so as to include the widest applications of the evolutionary hypothesis.

The journals and books of the period were naturally filled with discussion of this outlook on human experience, and much of the debate was acrimonious. The metaphysics of Christian belief that had dominated civilization in England

[1] *First Principles*, parts i, iv, and v.

since the seventh century was threatened with an agnosticism founded on scientific materialism; and the solution of the eighteenth-century divines was rejected by the naturalists. The network of physical agencies was moved not by a divine hand but by itself. All the old arguments were revived by theologians and Christian men of science; the argument from design, from the first cause, from the special qualities of life and mind, from miracles and the tradition of the Church. Nor were other parallels to the fight of More and Glanvil against the materialism of Hobbes lacking in the controversies of this time. Leading defenders of supernatural power turned to the evidences of hypnotism and spiritualist séances.[1] To all these considerations Tyndall, Huxley, and Spencer and their disciples were ready to reply. Yet the meagre solace offered by *First Principles* was seized upon by many writers in the interest of theology and the doctrine of the Unknowable was welcomed even by Bampton Lecturers. 'The omnipotence of something that passes comprehension' was dwelt upon in the same way as the sceptical fideists of the fourteenth century had seized upon ignorance as the ground of faith. Other Christian writers saw little or nothing of the elements of religion in the contemplation of an energy beyond human thought.

The new philosophy of science was subjected to unceasing philosophical attack. Amid the steady stream of articles and books in which the speculations of Spencer, of Huxley, of Tyndall, and of Clifford were examined generally and in detail, the most common line of objections was directed against the materialist assumptions of their theories. How is it possible to explain emotion and thought or even organic activity according to the laws of matter and motion? Memories, habits, and reasoning belong to a region entirely different from mechanical relations. In no sense can the higher forms of life and consciousness be educed out of matter and motion and quantitative force, unless these forms are already latent at the mechanical level. Vast debate ensued upon Tyndall's notorious address at Belfast in which he expressed the belief that life arises from

---

[1] See, for example, Tyndall's article on 'Science and the Spirits', 1864, in *Lectures and Essays*; S. Laing, *Modern Science and Modern Thought*, London, 6th ed., 1888, p. 232; and R. H. Hutton, *Aspects of Religious and Scientific Thought*, London, 1899, p. 161.

material antecedents. The address is interesting in relation to our survey of thought in England, for in its excursions into the history of ideas it brings Democritus and Epicurus to the front and, after a contemptuous passage on Aristotle, passes to the atomic theories of Gassendi. We are within the context of the new philosophy of the seventeenth century and are moving in the aura of Hobbes. And as Cudworth and More attacked the 'democritic atheism' that supposed life and mind to spring from senseless and brutish atoms, so Martineau and John Tulloch and G. H. Lewes argued that Spencer and Tyndall were endowing matter with a capability that their mechanical principles completely denied to it. Either force and primary matter must be something wholly different from that which science declares them to be, or else life and mind cannot be described as complexities of them. Carrying their attack into the discussion of many unguarded passages in the pages of *The Synthetic Philosophy* the critics pointed out that when Spencer comes to treat of the origins of consciousness he includes much more than matter in motion and chemical constituents. He bases his account upon the shocks and impulses of feelings. And his opponents discovered a multitude of other damaging admissions. In relation to the doctrine of the Unknowable, a nest of logical difficulties was exposed; that to pronounce ultimate reality to be unknowable presumes some knowledge of it; that, in fact, Spencer tells us a good deal about it; and that the unknown forces of the first part of the system become the aggregates of matter in motion of the later parts. The great mystery becomes either the movement of evolution and dissipation or a mere blank that has no place in the system. James Martineau had uncovered already some of these difficulties in a brilliant article in the *National Review* in 1859, and he was followed by many other thinkers. But Martineau was the herald of a fresh and powerful interlude in English thought. As in Hobbes' day the opponents of 'atheistic' corporealism had sought in Neo-Platonic idealism a perspective satisfactory alike to the philosophic intellect and to the Christian consciousness, so in the latter section of the nineteenth century English philosophers found in Hegelianism a rational articulation of the universe of things and persons wholly different from the teachings of the scientific agnostics and the disciples of universal law.

III

For in the meantime an extraordinary contrast to the triumphant march of naturalistic speculation had entered the English scene. There had arisen a fresh energy of metaphysical reflection; and the metaphysics exhibited doctrines that were strange to the rational habits of recent generations. The intellectual ruler of the preceding decades had struck instinctively against the 'German or *a priori* view of human knowledge', the 'support of false doctrines and bad institutions'. Mill, as we have seen, perceived this sinister form in the writings of the Scottish school and above all in the metaphysics of Sir William Hamilton. But Mill and Bain had received ill-digested accounts of German idealism. A few slight commentaries on Kant's philosophy had appeared in England, of which the *General and Introductory View of Professor Kant's Principles* by F. A. Nitszch was the first; it was published in 1796. No translation of the *Critique of Pure Reason* was attempted before 1838, nor did any English scholar endeavour to present before the third quarter of the century had passed a systematic interpretation of Kant's analysis of knowledge. Coleridge in the course of his philosophical odyssey through Plotinus, Hartley, and Spinoza came to rest in the neighbourhood of Schelling and Kant. But his utterances are fragmentary. He is chiefly interested in vindicating the moral originality of human will, but in several passages he expounds in his own terms the Kantian distinction between understanding and reason. Reason becomes spiritual vision and the discussion moves towards the mystical teaching of Schelling. Coleridge's theological ideas blew a gust of Augustinianism into the formal groves of English reflection. His influence shines out in the writings of Frederick Denison Maurice, it comes to the surface in the work of Shadworth Hodgson. There is far more of Kant in Sir William Hamilton. Yet even in the *Lectures on Metaphysics* what is chiefly singled out for discussion is confined to phenomena, to what is relative to our faculties. To other cardinal portions of Kant's thought he was unsympathetic. The limited grasp of Kant's philosophy of experience by English scholars may be appreciated by a perusal of the article *Kant* in the contemporary edition of the *Encyclopaedia Britannica* in the course of which the public was informed that the result of the Critical Philosophy was that a whole system of knowledge, underived from experience, was proved to exist in the mind. If Kant said anything in unambiguous language it was precisely the contrary of this. Mansel adapted Kant to his religious agnosticism and in general there is considerable reference to the Critiques among English thinkers before 1860, but no comprehensive investigation of the system. Of Hegel and his relationship to Kant still less has been accomplished. A writer reviewing English philosophy speaks in 1865 of the lack of knowledge of Hegel. He remains unknown save in a specimen phrase or two by reason of his terrible abstruseness. The purveyors of thought between Kant and Hegel, especially Fichte and Schelling, had received more attention.[1] There were indeed several strong minds that had been methodically wrestling with the *Logic* long before 1865; Benjamin Jowett and James Martineau are instances. Jowett's courses at Oxford from 1847 on the history of philosophy became yearly more comprehensive, linking Plato with Hegel and both with theology. It was from him more than from any other man that there welled the stream of the new speculation of the latter portion of the century, for many of the leaders of the movement were his pupils or colleagues at Balliol. But the signal of the discovery of German idealism was the appearance in 1865 of James Hutcheson Stirling's *The Secret of Hegel, being the Hegelian System in Origin, Principle, Form and Matter*. There soon followed a host of articles and books on the Hegelian theme; the essays on and translations of the *Logic* by William Wallace (1874), the books of Edward Caird and Robert Adamson on Kant, Fichte, and Hegel, and the writings of J. P. Mahaffy, Andrew Seth Pringle-Pattison, D. G. Ritchie, and Bernard Bosanquet. The year 1883 saw *Essays in Philosophical Criticism*, by six young Hegelians, and the radical destruction of Mill's empirical logic in F. H. Bradley's *Principles of Logic*; and two years later came the magnificent examination of Kant's philosophy by Caird. The Anglo-Hegelian wave culminated before the close of the century in Bradley's great work on metaphysics, *Appearance and Reality*.

Two closely related impulses may be discerned in this sudden revolution in English thought. From the beginning of the

[1] Masson, *Recent British Philosophy*, 2nd ed., London, 1867, p. 11.

century sensitive minds had been driven towards romantic visions and ideas. They had recoiled from the formalism, the elegant simplicity, the emotional aridity of the previous age. The bright mechanical world of classic literature became profoundly unsatisfying. In all branches of expression men sought freedom, mystery, imagination, and spiritual insight. They turned from order, precision, and correctness to passion and wonder. Art, criticism, and religion responded to the profound craving for 'that which moves with light and life inspired, actual, divine and true'. The great poets of the time, especially Byron and Wordsworth, expressed the stirrings of heart and mind that struck far into all sides of human activity in England. There is no more significant passage in the history of ideas in this period than the pages of Mill's *Autobiography* in which he recalls his sudden revulsion from the creed of Bentham. 'The whole foundation on which my life was constructed fell down'; he perceived that the mental habits that had been inculcated by his father upon the principles of the associationist philosophy had left him stranded without any real desire for the ends to which he had been so carefully fitted. His dejection and despair were relieved by reading a pathetic passage in Marmontel's *Memoirs*, by listening to Weber's *Oberon*, and above all by the rediscovery of Wordsworth's poems. 'In them I seemed to draw from a source of inward joy.' Mill's experience may stand as an epitome of the emotional currents of the age, mounting now in ritualism and sacramentalism, now into *Sartor Resartus*, the *Idylls of the King*, and *Richard Feverel*, now in the paintings of Millais, now in the exploration of darkest Africa. We touch here only on the intellectual aspect of these infinitely varied and conflicting impulses. Mill was not induced by Wordsworth's poems to abandon his philosophic habits, though his masters could not have written the essays on poetry and on Alfred de Vigny. But many young men who had been set to study the *System of Logic* were visited by aspirations and sensibilities that demanded larger horizons. In the writings of Fichte, Schelling, Hegel, and Schopenhauer they apprehended a rational treatment of the intuitions of reality that spoke in English poetry and in the literature of love and worship. They heard of some higher kind of reason into which the affections and the imagination entered; of mind that lives in the world of objects and in the soul; of kinship between the moral purposes of men and the being of Nature; of the fundamental identity of the real and the ideal, fact and value. Martineau, recalling in his old age his youthful discovery of German philosophy, after an earlier pilgrimage through the teaching of the empiricists from Locke to James Mill, describes its effect on him as a new intellectual birth; and the idealist view that he learnt from the study of Hegel in 1848–9 had been opened to him by the poetry of Wordsworth and Coleridge. And a later Hegelian, Bernard Bosanquet, avowed that his generation owed to German idealism 'nothing less than a new contact with spiritual life'.

Naturally it was among the theologians that Hegelianism was most warmly welcomed. The vital task before theology was the task of rehabilitating essential Christian doctrine in the face of positivism and agnosticism. German idealism professed completely to undermine the assumptions upon which scientific naturalism stood. Kant showed that a radical investigation into the postulates of physical science led to the perception that these principles are no foreign necessities to which our thought must be adjusted. They are prescribed by our own nature to experience; we fashion the framework that appears to destroy our freedom and spiritual life. At the centre of the determined interconnexion of phenomenal causes dwells the subject for which the phenomenal world of scientific knowledge exists, and this self is not subject to the categories of science, for it is the source of those categories. The essential character of this primary reality is to be sought in the free self-determining activity of the moral life, and when we inquire into the implications of morality we are led to justify the belief in immortality and in God. But English theologians discovered philosophical arguments for Christian theism in Hegel rather than in Kant. The grand metaphysical doctrine of Hegelianism was the teaching that there is immanent alike in the human mind and in Nature a universal march of reason. Beneath all the limitations and antagonisms of existence there lives a constructive spiritual process. The divisions of the sciences and the scientific method itself are essentially partial aspects of a rational movement that is discerned by philosophical analysis; and the ground-plan of the dialectic by which the searching mind is carried from the primitive abstractions of immediate conscious-

ness to the 'absolute idea', the idea of an embracing spiritual
Being, is unfolded in the *Logic* and the *Phenomenology*. Religious
thinkers in England descried in Hegel on the one hand a penetrating criticism of materialist theory, on the other a sustained
vindication of spiritual faith. Many theologians from the time
of F. D. Maurice turned eagerly to him. And philosophers such
as Stirling, T. H. Green, Wallace, and Caird defended the great
dogmas of religion in Hegelian terms. 'The Hegelian system
supports and gives effect to every claim of this religion', that
is to say, Christianity, declared Stirling; and Edward Caird
wrote that Hegel's *Logic* contained the essential meaning of the
Christian revelation. The pupils of these teachers are found
among the leading churchmen of the following decades. It must
be added, however, that from the days of the first revival of
Hegelianism at Oxford there existed lively suspicion of the
alliance between the new idealism and theology. Mansel, for
example, had voiced his distrust and Mark Pattison uttered
sarcastic remarks about the *a priori* metaphysic of T. H. Green.
A. S. Pringle-Pattison's book on *Hegelianism and Personality*
(1887) is representative of many protests against the attempt
of the Neo-Hegelians to discover an identity between the human
and the divine self-consciousness. The critics also found Hegel
to be ambiguous both on the question of the personality of God
and on the immortality of man. After 1880 we observe a fresh
force in academic thought, the force of Lotze's writings.
Several of the younger school of English idealists attended the
lectures of Lotze at Göttingen and the effect of his views on
all facets of philosophical exploration, on psychology, logic,
epistemology, metaphysics, ethics, and aesthetics appears in
the later expressions of idealism. It is seen in the thought of
Martineau, George Croom Robertson, Charles Upton, Sir Henry
Jones, Pringle-Pattison, and James Ward; it infiltrates into the
Hegelianism of Bradley and Bosanquet. Lotze's influence
persuaded thinkers to return from the position of Hegel to an
outlook nearer to that of Kant. Other German authorities
were read and made their contribution to the ferment of neo-
idealism in Britain. Besides Fichte and Schelling there was
discussion of the work of Herbart, Schopenhauer, and in
theology, of F. C. Bauer. Nevertheless, Hegel dominated the
idealism of the school, and Kant and other German authorities

were viewed as approaches to the *Logic*. Many of the prominent philosophers, T. H. Green and Edward Caird, for example, devoted more attention to the exposition and criticism of Kant than to the interpretation of Hegel. There was good reason for this method. The compelling problems of English thought on ultimate questions arose from the two related schemes of the empirical philosophy and the scientific outlook. The continued authority of an empirical conception of the truth and the striking advance of physical theory invited a return to Kant. For the Critical Philosophy was in the first instance an examination of the nature and validity of the principles assumed in physics. The developments in scientific ideas had been impressive since the time of Kant, as we have noticed; but these developments had not resulted in any fundamental change in principles, they were still Newtonian. And the *Critique of Pure Reason* was also a searching investigation into the account of knowledge expounded by English thinkers from the days of Locke. Kant declared that Hume was the stimulus that led him to his new departure in philosophy. His problems were peculiarly the problems that faced inquiry in England. But in following Kant's penetrating analysis of knowledge the British school read them in the light of the Hegelian system. Writers such as Green and Caird appear to be constantly engaged in refashioning the system in the direction of absolute idealism rather than in explaining directly the architecture of Hegel. This approach to the new idealism by way of a detailed appraisement of Kant called out original efforts of thought. Hegelianism was not transferred bodily to the native soil of Oxford. It was restated and transformed. Neither in Green nor in Bradley do we find a reassertion of Hegel. We find marked independence of his doctrine and decided criticism of some of his characteristic tenets.

Let us attempt a cursory inspection of this powerful current of thought, and endeavour to indicate its affinities with earlier explorations. The gateway to the imposing mansion of British idealism in the nineteenth century is its criticism of the classical doctrine of knowledge. In fact Green's massive discussion of that doctrine in his Introductions to Hume's *Treatise*, published in 1874, was often cited afterwards as the starting-point of the movement. Writing in 1887 Pringle-Pattison declares that 'as regards the critical part of Green's work, there has been of late, I think, a growing admission of its victorious, and, indeed, conclusive character'. Other philosophers unfolded similar refutations of the sensationalist principles, which as we have seen were still living forces in England. The general form of these criticisms was as follows. It will be recalled that the basis of the classic theory was the belief that perception and thought are formed from impressions that are 'entirely loose and separate'. The mind can entertain ideas only when it has previously received the relative impressions, since ideas are the faint images of impressions. There is no visible necessary association between impressions and the simple ideas that arise from them. The coherence of ideas that informs our common beliefs relating to substances or casual connexions or the self is imputed by the prejudices of custom. 'There is nothing in any object considered in itself which can afford us a reason for drawing a conclusion beyond it', says Hume; and all forms of connexion upon which our trust in an objective world, determined by scientific principles, is founded are traced to deep-seated illusions in human nature. The persistent course of this analysis of experience in England has been alluded to in the previous chapter. In its later stages the sceptical aspect of the doctrine falls back and a combination of atomism and phenomenalism becomes the standard of scientific epistemology. We have observed it in Mill and in Spencer, and Huxley wrote a book on Hume in which the great sceptic is transformed into a prophet of scientific method. The idealist critics showed at length that on the principles assumed by the empiricists no perception or thought could possibly exist, and they pointed out that Locke and Hume implicitly recognized the presence of factors that are not sensory particulars. The awareness of a single impression involves a scheme of relations. It must occupy a position in space, and when it is succeeded by another impression the two must be related temporally. A consciousness limited to a momentary impression could not be conscious even of that impression, for the impression is related to a spatial background or frame, and is distinguished from successive impressions. But analysis reveals further principles of connexion and continuity besides those of space and time. Experience presupposes that the elements of perception are organized; all analysis rests upon synthesis. And these uniting forms are not added illegitimately to the sensory items; they are essential features of them, for apart from them the sensory items are sheer abstractions. The chief of these uniting principles are the principle that there is a permanent element in all changes of qualities and the principle that things and events are objectively related. The first corresponds to the ancient notion of substance, the second brings to the fore the belief in causal determination, but the two points are intimately related to one another. The manner in which the idealists proved these two forms of connectedness cannot here be set out in detail. The main procedure was to insist on the intimate association between our ideas and the coexistences and sequences of the objective order. In Caird's words, 'Objects, things, and events —a world of experience—exist for us, and can exist for us, only so far as our sensitive impressions are determined and related to each other according to universal principles.' Apart from these relating elements the world could have no meaning for us. Anything that presents itself to consciousness points beyond the immediate sensory effect to a system of relations.

So far the idealist critics of empiricism were indebted to the considerations adduced by Kant in his first *Critique*. In less technical terms they reproduce the elaborate arguments of the 'transcendental aesthetic' and the 'analogies of experience'. The upshot is a refutation of empiricism in the manner of Kant. The typical English philosophy had conceived the primary material of knowledge to be individual existences. The objects of perception from which thinking starts were collections of particular ideas, and the bonds that unite the collections were attributed to the particulars by the mind. The method of philosophical inquiry was taken over from the natural philosophy of the seventeenth century. It undertook to explore the nature and limits of human knowledge by observing precisely the elementary phenomena of consciousness and by formulating the general laws of their coexistence and succession. The investigation proceeded according to the methods of natural inquiry, and employed mechanical and chemical modes of interpreting knowledge. It sought to explain consciousness by reference to the simplest factors that can be descried. All these assumptions were rejected by the Neo-Kantians. In a

series of articles in the *Contemporary Review* in 1877 and 1878
on *Mr. Herbert Spencer and Mr. G. H. Lewes; Their Application
of the Doctrine of Evolution to Thought*, T. H. Green pointed out
that modern scientific philosophy rested upon the psychology
of Locke and Hume. Only by a direct examination of that
psychology itself can the critic expect to produce the conviction
that the primary question of metaphysics still lies at its
threshold, and is finding in the writings of the men of science
nothing but a tautological or preposterous answer. The primary
question is 'How is knowledge possible?' And the natural
thinkers begin with a doctrine, which, if it means anything,
means that only in a world of consciousness can any material
relation be known, and then proceed to explain consciousness
itself, as one sort of such material relation. 'Only in a world of
consciousness can anything material be known.' This phrase
from Green's article is the guiding thread that leads to the
audacious metaphysical visions of the Hegelian school.

The new students of Kant in England had learnt from him
that the apprehension of the diverse items given in sensory
experience presumes various forms of connexion, and that the
scientific understanding of phenomena also requires these
relations. For Kant there are broadly two factors present in all
perception and thought, the sensory factor and the relational
or *a priori* factor, and he seeks by an original method to isolate
the *a priori* elements, the contributions of 'pure reason'. In
order to vindicate these *a priori* agents in thought he traced
their source to a deeper unity which he named the synthetic
unity of apperception. All the non-sensory modes of connexion
that are implied in our thinking presume the awareness of the
multifarious items given to the senses as parts of a single and
continuous experience, for otherwise experience would be
fundamentally broken and incoherent. The relations of time,
space, inherence, cause, reciprocity are special forms of a pervasive synthesis that supports rational experience. We could
not, for instance, distinguish even particular items unless we
were also aware of the context or series in which the items appear;
and generalizing such considerations, Kant asserts that there
must be a universal system of unity in diversity in order that the
diversity may be comprehended in a single act of thought.
In important passages he argued that the unity-in-diversity,

that is the postulate of knowledge, is, when applied to the world as a whole, an activity of mind; but he conceives this comprehensive synthesis as a logical presupposition, a purely formal implication of all rational reflection. He distinguishes it firmly from the individual and personal consciousness of men. It is the common element in all consciousness, by which consciousness is what it is; the form by which spatial and temporal data are apprehended as elements in a whole that points beyond the data. On the other hand, he declared that this formal and complex unity must be presumed to exist in the objective universe and in nature. His central doctrine was that the self-identity through difference of the transcendent consciousness and the systematic order of the objective realm are two aspects of the same universal synthesis.

The crucial step taken by Hegelians such as Green and Caird was to transform Kant's formal unity of experience into a substantial and metaphysical unity, and in taking this step they followed the criticism and completion of Kant's work offered in the philosophies of Fichte and Hegel. In showing that the objective world has no meaning except for a 'self' that transcends individual selves the *Critique of Pure Reason* had, in their view, indicated the conclusion that objects must be understood as elements in a process of existence that reveals itself as a spiritual process. There must be a unity beyond the difference of object and subject. Self-consciousness depends upon the objective order and the objective order depends upon the synthetic activity of mind; and the recognition of a uniting process that comprehends both sides of the whole resolves the dualism that dominates the Kantian scheme.[1] Our human and defective knowledge is a consciousness of union with, and at the same time separation from, a perfect intelligence for which the process of development is completed.

Green's famous enunciation of the principle may summarily be put as follows. Reality is essentially a system of relations. The notions of what is real and objective have no meaning save for a consciousness that presents its experience to itself as determined by relations, and real arrangements of relations are distinguished from unreal by reference to standards of per-

---

[1] See, for instance, Caird, *The Critical Philosophy of Kant*, Glasgow, 1889, vol. i, p. 404 f.

manence, coherence, and necessity. The presupposition of all inquiry is that there exists an unalterable order of relations, a complete system. Now we can understand the nature of relations only on the analogy of our own consciousness. We know of no other medium by which the unification of the manifold items of perception can take place except a thinking and self-distinguishing consciousness. This function of consciousness cannot itself be a succession of perceptions for it is the condition of there being a succession of perceptions. The source of the necessary regularity of phenomena that makes an intelligible experience must be a consciousness that is not involved in the temporal and spatial order of nature since that order depends on such consciousness. There must be an eternal consciousness that communicates unity and coherence to the universe. This absolute spiritual principle is manifested in all particular existences and eminently in human beings under the limitations of their physical and psychological organization. 'We must hold then that there is a consciousness for which the relations of fact, that form the object of our gradually attained knowledge, already and eternally exist; and that the growing knowledge of the individual is a progress towards this consciousness.'[1] In the language of Nettleship we are potentially the consciousness which has the universe for its object.

Other thinkers expressed the thesis of idealism in different terms, but the cardinal doctrine was that all things and beings constitute a system of relations which finds its unity in the absolute mind. The philosophy of the Hegelians was embraced, as we have noticed, with enthusiasm by many thinkers in the regions of art, morality, and religion. It brought the great realities with which these living experiences treat into the centre of the stage and it confounded the soulless abstractions of naturalist theory. It reanimated the sense of the whole, and without prejudice to the infinite play of diversity. It united man to God in a more intimate union than any philosophy in England had succeeded in attaining since the Platonism of the seventeenth century. These romantic and theological claims were opposed by a stream of critical discussion. The scientific leaders of thought naturally rejected idealism with scorn. They ridiculed the *a priori* methods of the metaphysicians, pointed

---

[1] Green, *Prolegomena to Ethics*, 5th ed., Oxford, 1906, p. 80.

out the scientific misunderstandings of Kant and Hegel,[1] and reiterated their sceptical position that the substance of matter and spirit must remain unknown. But serious attacks developed also within the circle of academic and idealist thinkers. The most pronounced of these attacks was contained in Pringle-Pattison's *Hegelianism and Personality*, 1887. Green is criticized for his concentration upon the eternal self in dissociation from the world, and the critic quotes the observation of A. J. Balfour that 'it is as correct to say that nature makes mind as that mind makes nature; that the World created God as that God created the World'.[2] But the writer's chief contention is that the Hegelian school had abolished the indefeasible reality of personality. The radical error is the identification of the human and divine self-consciousness. Each self is a unique existence and while it is in familiar relation with other selves it is essentially distinct and independent of others. Religion lends no countenance to the representation of the human soul as a mere mode of the divine; and the doctrine that individuals are aspects of the universal being revives the extreme realism of the earlier scholastics.[3] This protest against the all-absorbing Idea in Hegel and equally against Neo-Hegelianism that 'erects into a god the mere form of self-consciousness in general', was taken up by a number of younger thinkers, such as Hastings Rashdall and W. R. Sorley; and it won the approval of the veteran Martineau and his disciples. Yet these idealists acknowledged the highest obligations to Hegel and declared his doctrine that self-consciousness is the ultimate principle of explanation to be an imperishable gift to thought.

There is another facet of the Hegelian outlook on the world that must be mentioned, since it forms an important point of division between the earlier and later stages of the movement in England. By the great pioneers such as Caird the spiritual reality that comprises being and thought was viewed as a process. It is a universal dialectic through which reality moves in a logical order dictated by the nature of reason. At naïve levels thought conceives a limited and one-sided interpretation

---

[1] See, for instance, Clifford's criticism of Kant's Newtonian conception of space, in the lecture *On the Aims and Instruments of Scientific Thought*, 1872.

[2] A. J. Balfour, *Mind*, ix. 80.

[3] *Hegelianism and Personality*, Edinburgh, 1888, p. 229.

of reality, such as animism or crude materialism. The imperfection of the account drives thought into asserting the opposite theory. This opposing conception is seen in course of time to be no less one-sided than the earlier view, and thought is carried on to a more adequate set of principles that embrace both of the earlier partial positions. But the new and richer standpoint turns out to be insufficient and the same process of statement, counter-statement, and amalgamation is repeated at higher stages. Now, as we have noticed, Hegel held that thought in its search for truth penetrates into the heart of what is real; in a word it creates reality. The categories of reason shape the contents of the world of objects which thus become a living and dynamic rhythm of logical conflict and reconciliation; and the dialectical succession can be traced in nature and in history. 'The truth therefore, is', wrote Caird, 'that definiteness, finitude, or determination, as such, though they have an affirmative or positive meaning, also contain or involve in themselves their own negation. There is a community or unity between them and their opposites, which overreaches their differences or opposition, though it does not by any means exclude that difference or opposition in its proper place, and within its proper limits.'[1] The insistence of science upon 'facts' and upon mechanism is justified within the contexts of scientific thinking, but for the comprehensive and concrete inquiry of philosophy these notions are seen to be abstract and subordinate. The antitheses of the moral and religious consciousness, the opposition between the divine and the human and between literal ideas of right and wrong, direct thought to the unity that gives meaning to the differences. In his works on the evolution of religion Caird traced the moments of the idea of God in history in the light of the Hegelian dialectic, and his concern with the universal marks of differentiation and integration drew him into a superficial sympathy with the evolutionary formula of Spencer. Under the same Hegelian influence Green looked upon the course of ideas as a manifestation of the dialectical movement. The empirical doctrines of the eighteenth century are necessary stages in the advance of thought, inviting the opposite bias in the work of Kant. For the earlier generation of idealists the Absolute is not a state of motionless being, but

[1] Caird, *Hegel*, Edinburgh, 1909. The book was published in 1883.

a living activity, not a mere resting identity, but an eternal movement, an ἐνέργεια ἀκινησίας.

In the minds of the later thinkers the dialectical march of rational being recedes into the background. The Absolute becomes a changeless harmony. Thought cannot be the essence of the universe for it is intrinsically relational and fragmentary. In thinking we are dependent upon particular connexions, most of which are empirical and given from outside.[1] And having denied the conformity of reason and reality Bradley and Bosanquet go on to reject all ascription of change and activity to the Absolute. 'For nothing perfect, nothing genuinely real can move. The Absolute has no seasons, but all at once bears its leaves, fruit and blossoms.'[2] But the extraordinary organization of scepticism, empiricism, and Hegelianism, embodied in *Appearance and Reality* (1893), cannot be dealt with in a few sentences. The most exciting and disturbing philosophical pronouncement of the closing years of the century, it departed in many respects far from the orthodox types of idealism.

Evolutionary naturalism was the philosophy of the recent developments in physical theory and in biology. But it was also the child of the Newtonian picture of the world and was nourished by the experimental views of knowledge. The idealist movement in England was not an outgrowth of indigenous tradition. Its guiding principles were imported from Germany and its main doctrine ran counter to the methods and ideas by which general experience had been long interpreted. In this revolution of intellectual habits there was little reference to the types of idealism that had been impressively propounded in the seventeenth century by Cudworth and Norris. And there was scarcely any consciousness of connexion between German idealism and the species of Augustinian Realism that had formed the philosophical structure of Christian belief in the days of Anselm and of Grosseteste. The men who proclaimed the new idealism in the sixties and seventies of the nineteenth century did not look beyond the treatises of Kant and his successors in Germany. Jowett encouraged young men at Oxford to relate Hegel to Plato, but few associated him with the Neo-Platonism of the schoolmen or of the renaissance divines. Yet Hegelianism

---

[1] F. H. Bradley, *Appearance and Reality*, 2nd ed., London, 1908, p. 477.
[2] Op. cit., p. 500.

marks the re-entry into English thought of the logical impulses and shapes of earlier phases of speculation. Several of the distinctive principles of Anglo-Hegelianism recall the notes of medieval Augustinianism. The conception of the universal self that occupies the centre of T. H. Green's philosophy is attained by reasoning that revives the procedure of extreme Realism. Individuals and particulars are vehicles of the all-embracing universal being, the identical essence appearing in different things and events. The divine substance includes all individual substances; all life is its life manifested in the infinite variety of creatures. The protests of critics such as Pringle-Pattison and the personal idealists against the pantheistic tendencies of Hegelianism echo the remonstrances of the disciples of Abaelard in England against the engulfing Realism of the Parisian masters. And a closer parallel is provided by the later struggle of orthodox thought against Averroism, against the doctrine that there is one immaterial intellect that embraces all human intellects. Objective idealism hovers between ultra-realism and moderate or Aristotelian realism, and its logic is similar. And it attacked empiricism on the lines by which Anselm, Roger Bacon, and Duns Scotus had attacked nominalism and conceptualism. There are striking resemblances between the measured progress of the Hegelian dialectic and the scholastic hierarchy of being, controlled not by its primordial factors, but by the divine reality. The ultimate metaphysical principles are viewed in both systems as a genesis of consciousness through a number of stages from immediate perception to the apprehensions of *intellectus*. And the absolute life is conceived as Being, that which alone truly is. But strict Hegelianism was utterly divided from scholastic theology, for which God was transcendent, creative, and self-complete.

Thus at the opening of the twentieth century two main systems of rational belief divided the interests of thoughtful men. One, popular, defiantly secular, the philosophy of physicists, technicians, and leaders of labour, had its roots in the experimental naturalism that had dominated English reflection for two centuries. The ultimate constituents of the world are matter and motion; they are the primary factors not only of the material universe but also of the mental empire; minds are secondary and episodic events in the order of things.

Materialism was evaded by timely resorts to agnosticism and phenomenalism. We do not know what matter and mind really are; all 'metempirical knowledge', as G. H. Lewes named it, is impossible. Metempirical knowledge includes theology, and the disciples of Huxley join hands with the sceptical followers of Dean Mansel. Positivist philosophy invited the students of evening classes in London and Manchester to get rid of all belief outside the scope of scientific inquiry. Meanwhile the minds of undergraduates at the universities were occupied with a very different universe. The academic thinkers cut at the roots and branches of positivism with weapons borrowed from Kant. We can begin to construct the castle of truth only by a fresh investigation of the nature of knowledge, and the investigation reveals the fundamental association of subject and object in experience. Experience is not erected upon a disconnected multiplicity of sensations. It implies from birth certain fixed arrangements, and these make a common world, and point to a universal organic unity with which our individual experiences are continuous. Our reason is confronted and determined by universal reason. The new idealists, like the Cambridge masters of the seventeenth century, enlarged the conception of reason, and their analysis of knowledge led to comprehensive revaluations of human pursuits, moral, social, religious, and artistic. In such works as Bradley's *Ethical Studies* (1876), Edward Caird's *Essays on Literature and Philosophy* (1892), and John Caird's book on the *Philosophy of Religion* (1880), the highly technical discussions of the Anglo-Hegelians penetrated the interests and emotions of cultured men. And since theological prepossessions still moved the inward reflections of educated Englishmen it was especially in the region of theology that idealism made its wider appeal. It appears in a wide variety of discussions on spiritual themes, of which Bishop Frederick Temple's Bampton lectures on the relation between religion and science and Sir Henry Jones's book on *Idealism as a Practical Creed* may be cited as earlier and later instances.

At the turn of the century idealism stood triumphant over its rival. A crushing blow was delivered by James Ward's article on psychology in the *Encyclopaedia Britannica* (1886) which cut the ground from under the associationist doctrine of Mill and Bain. And the same philosopher in his *Naturalism and Agnosti-*

cism (1899) exposed in detail the confusions of the mechanical theory in Spencer's philosophy in evolution, and Huxley's doctrine of physical epiphenomena. The argument culminates in a declaration that experience is richer than science, for whose sake 'the historical is ignored, the metaphysical eliminated, substances and cause become fetishes, God a superfluous hypothesis, and mind an enigma'.[1] The realm of nature is an abstract aspect of the realms of Ends. But Ward's later version blossomed from the Kantian and Hegelian stem. Before its sudden decline after the First Great War Hegelianism was transformed into systems that diverged far from its German source and from the idealism of the preceding generation of English Hegelians. The great expositions of Bradley and of Bosanquet and the completely independent speculations of McTaggart bear only loose affiliations to the teaching of the *Logic* and the *Phenomenology*. And by the time McTaggart's extraordinary work on *The Nature of Existence* had appeared, a powerful tendency towards positions fundamentally opposed to idealism had already become manifest. The rhythm of reason, after its short-lived sweep from empiricism and naturalism, began to move back to the tradition that had ruled English thought since the days of Boyle and Locke. It reverted more closely to the temper of Hume, though it displayed new refinements in philosophical method destructive not only of the stories and foundations of idealism but also of the bases of the world-views founded on mechanistic and evolutionary science. Nevertheless, in the accent that it laid upon scientific methods of inquiry it was in general sympathy with the classic procedure of the eighteenth century, and like the long line of Locke's disciples it devoted much of its attention to the problems of perception and elementary knowledge. It decried metaphysics and speculation, and its minutely analytical and critical process (which led to highly varied conclusions) was inimical to all demands for a rational system of experience.

Here we must break off our cursory view of twelve centuries of philosophical thought in England. The movement of ideas

[1] Ward, *Naturalism and Agnosticism*, 4th ed., London, 1915, p. 573.

during the period of the Great World Wars in the early portion of the twentieth century is too recent to be comprehended within the wide perspective of our survey. The issue of the new developments of empiricism and the precise investigations into perception and language; the effect of revolutionary notions of physics upon fundamental conceptions; the consequence of the embracing systems of metaphysics that were constructed by English philosophers at this period; these must await the appreciation of an observer of the twenty-first century. We must cut short our rapid inspection of the long career of reflection in England at a vital point when thought was turning, after the brief interlude of Hegelian idealism, to fresh and penetrating criticisms of beliefs and to novel syntheses. The purpose of this survey has been to exhibit the continuity of inquiry on first principles from the earliest age, and to distinguish some of the cardinal changes in the forms of intelligibility that have occurred during our history. We have observed certain idioms of understanding that have been lifted into prominence at stages of our national progress, schemes of conceptions relating to the material universe and to the mind of man. And we have glanced at the conditions of knowledge that supported these philosophies.

The story opened in the wild dawn of Catholic culture in the island. We entered English thought by the gates of the Saxon schools at Canterbury and York, in which was transmitted from the south of Europe the rhetorical and ecclesiastical learning of the previous epoch. Already there were present elements that continued for many centuries to shape the character of thought. The rhetorical precepts of the monastic schools penetrated the intellectual habits of the Middle Ages; nor is it possible to estimate the revolution of ideas in the seventeenth century without relating it to the fashion of oratorical logic that flourished in the preceding period. The Scriptural exegeses of Bede introduced us to qualities of inquiry that influenced the discussions of scholars up to the eighteenth century. But the analogical and tropological modes of reasoning were associated with the system of theological beliefs that provided thoughtful men in all but the latest moments of speculation with the most impressive material for their investigations. Until the seventeenth century the reality that was first imposed upon the mind of the inquirer was the scheme of revealed truth. During the earlier phases of thought the principal task was that of justifying the truths of faith and of adapting the developments of knowledge to the religious principles of Catholicism. There were two broad conceptions that were imposed on thought by Christian belief. On the one hand, Christian belief was based on the Hebraic notion of a single absolute Being radically distinct from the universe which is His creation; on the other, God was held to be immanent in history and in man. By uniting these opposing conceptions the central course of philosophical theology was able to evade the negative theology of oriental religion and the self-sufficient humanism of Stoic theory. In the earlier phase it was the former element of the theological tradition that occupied rational exploration. The type of reasoning that guided reflection descended from Plato, Plotinus, and Augustine to Anselm. It proceeds from faith and ascends to the realism of timeless Ideas by the dialectical path. Self-evident intelligible principles are the criteria of reality; and the intelligible realities discerned by the *intellectus* are united in the mind of God who creates the world and the heavens in thinking them. In this philosophy references to empirical phenomena are meagre. The existence of truth leads necessarily to the existence of the eternal and divine truth already apprehended by faith; and truth is moral as well as intellectual. Anselm's logic of eternal truth continued to be echoed throughout English philosophy. Augustinian realism and the demonstrative proofs of religious truth were prominent notes of Oxford thought in the thirteenth and fourteenth centuries; they were powerfully revived in the seventeenth. They were recalled to life under fresh terms in the nineteenth.

The complementary impulse of Christian theology was partly fulfilled in the thirteenth century after the renaissance of the twelfth. Aristotelian science promoted an interest in the sensible order of existence. The classification, analysis, and co-ordination of contingent reality was pursued in every department, and Oxford philosophers explored the nature of mind, the interaction of reason and experience, and the principles of proof according to Aristotelian teaching. But the vitality of thought in this brilliant period was enhanced by the rich diversity of doctrines that pressed for recognition. There were rival inter-

pretations of Aristotle's doctrines, and in their Arabian shape
they aroused deep misgiving on the part of theologians who
were attached to the older system of metaphysics. Numerous compromises at all points of inquiry were proposed by
English masters. A striking mark of thought in England was
the persistence of Augustinian views. The age that followed
witnessed a violent revolt from this tradition. A movement of
logical analysis and criticism assaulted the established newer
positions. The objectivity of universal concepts, the theory of
abstraction, the traditional doctrine of matter, the immaterial
nature of the soul were shown to be irrational or incapable of
proof. The most disruptive consequences of this critical phase
of our thought flowed from the rejection of the rational arguments in support of faith. The disjunction between the system
of faith and human reason pronounced by the Scotists and
Ockhamists encouraged a growth of simple piety and mystical
theology that passed far into succeeding periods. The unphilo-
sophic and practical type of religion descended to the sects of
the Reformation period. On the other hand, the breach with
reason promoted the insistence on religious discipline and
authority that was a feature of the fifteenth century. The new
logic concentrated upon the science of significant language and
discouraged the ancient metaphysical inquiries. There are
interesting parallels between the historical circumstances, the
scepticism and empiricism, the investigations into linguistic
forms of English philosophers of the twentieth century and the
terminists of the fourteenth and fifteenth. And the association
between philosophical scepticism and implicit faith reappears
at several later moments of our theological history.

Our survey has dwelt lightly upon the long transition from
the older phases of thought to the new. The universities preserved the natural philosophy, the logic, and the first philosophy
of Aristotle; and doctrines of Thomism and Scotism were
discussed and reduced to codes without bringing to light any
fresh conceptions. English thinkers were not prominent in the
investigations that were leading nominalists abroad to fruitful
theories of natural process. The religious upheavals of the
sixteenth century occasioned a ferment of disputation, but the
novel theological doctrines that entered England from the Low
Countries and from Switzerland did not produce any signal

change in philosophical understanding. The frame of conceptions remained what they had been in the thirteenth century, and the first notable expression of the philosophy of the independent Church, the work of Richard Hooker in 1594, draws deeply upon scholastic principles. It is possible to detect amid the debates on the doctrine of the Eucharist at the crisis of the Reformation instances of revolt from the classical theory of knowledge, and the extreme reformers often associate themselves with the empirical criteria of the Ockhamists. But in the reign of Elizabeth academic thinkers and poets assumed the cosmology and the metaphysics of the Middle Ages.

Nevertheless, the abounding secular energy of the sixteenth century was discovering fresh visions in every quarter of the mental universe. It seized on Greek biology and medicine, Italian Neo-Platonism, the occult systems of the hermetic books, Stoicism, Epicureanism, and Scepticism. By the year 1600 many sensitive observers saw the foundations of the intelligible world that had been their home dissolving beneath them. The new phase of thought entered amid Jacobean gloom. Men despaired of learning and fled for safety to the discipline of a stoical religion or to a philosophy of instinctive truth. The new way had been tentatively explored by earlier inquirers in England, but it was the unparalleled ambition of Francis Bacon 'to try the whole thing anew upon a better plan, and to commence a total reconstruction of sciences, arts and all human knowledge, raised upon proper foundations'. The better plan was to turn from fundamental questions of metaphysics and theology to the face of external nature and to seek there not magical powers but material fruits that would confer manifold benefits upon men. Human power and human knowledge were to meet in one; for it was from ignorance of causes that operations had failed. The new phase was the product of the secularization of life, of Elizabethan passion for the empire of men in this world; it was also the offspring of the Protestant spirit which sought to unite knowledge with action. But the concern for practical ends brought the sense of a strange order in natural things, an order of relations determined independently of human interests, rigid and indifferent, necessary and uniform. For natural processes can become the instruments of man's desires only when they are calculable. In the pursuit of this type of knowledge the groups who met at Oxford and in London after Bacon's death separated themselves fundamentally from the scholastic and the renaissance conceptions of material phenomena. The ancient belief in qualitative changes and grades of being, the doctrines of opposite characters and of form and matter, are replaced by the conception of uniform necessary connexion. Natural philosophy reverts after nearly two thousand years nearer to the outlook of the school of Plato, touched on at the beginning of our survey. All natural processes become arrangements of a number of simple entities, the relationships of which can be mathematically measured. This turning from philosophy to sciences, from being to becoming, from universal conceptions to sensory particulars, imposed a new logic on thought, which rapidly grew to be the standard of reason in all spheres of inquiry. In England the Baconian element in scientific thinking prevailed, and the philosophers and theologians of the Royal Society were acutely sensible of the threat to moral and religious ideas that lurked in the vast mechanical vision of Descartes and that were openly avowed by Vanini and Hobbes. The leaders of a new philosophy insisted on confining knowledge to that which falls within the range of empirical verification. This empiricism is prominent in the triumphant synthesis of Newton and in the philosophical exposition of the scientific view of reason by Locke. There was a brief revival of Neo-Platonism and of Augustinian idealism, but the main trend of thought moved with the philosophy that 'traced all those sublime thoughts that tower above the clouds, and reach as high as heaven itself', to outward and inward sensations.

The problems of philosophical thinking during the eighteenth and nineteenth centuries in England were provided by the assumptions impressed upon rational belief by Newtonian physics and its later refinements. The main assumption was that reality was fundamentally twofold. It was objective and subjective. The objective was the universe described by science, the system of spatio-temporal relations, self-contained and independent of the minds that contemplate it. The subjective side of reality consisted of individual minds, the chief content of which were ideas or sensations. These were derived from the mind's own resources upon stimulus from the objective world, and they included qualities that common sense ascribes to objects, colours, sounds, tastes, odours. The crucial question accordingly became 'How is knowledge possible?' For the correspondence between the objective world presented by science and the subjective order of mind confined to its own ideas was indirect and problematical. Thought was confronted with two realms, the realm of physical bodies from which the mind is wholly excluded, and a realm of perceptions from which the physical realm is shut out. Concentration upon the nature of perceiving and reasoning brought much valuable analysis in the psychology of these functions. The investigation proceeded upon the prevailing models of chemical and physical inquiry. It sought for primary data of experience as science sought for the elements and atoms, and it formulated the laws of physical and chemical behaviour. But in its speculations concerning the warrant and range of human knowledge, the radical division of reality and the contracted province of inquiry assumed at the outset united with the experimental logic to promote a pheno-menalist, a relativist, and a positivist view of things. And the phenomenalism verges upon scepticism. Since the ultimate components of knowledge are transient and unrelated states of individual consciousness, the permanence and unity of the material world is arrived at by logical construction or associa-tion. We know nothing beyond appearances; the essential natures of mental and material substances must be unknown, and the causal connexions and the uniformity of nature are inexplicable. Representative English thinkers of this phase, Locke, Hume, Reid, Brown, Hamilton, Mill, Spencer, declare the native limitations of knowledge; the boundaries of possible sense-experience cannot bring insight into necessary truths. All truths are contingent. The postulates of scientific philo-sophy invited critical inquiry to doubt science itself, and the grandest synthesis of knowledge of this section of our history, that of Herbert Spencer, stood on the belief in a transcendent reality that must always be unknown. 'The antithesis of subject and object, never to be transcended while consciousness lasts, renders impossible all knowledge of that ultimate reality in which subject and object are united.'[1]

[1] Spencer, *Principles of Psychology*, London, 1872, vol. i, p. 272.

In the eighteenth century the subjective part of the dichotomy was explored by philosophers. Little that was new was added by the philosophers of the nineteenth century until the arrival of German idealism. It was in the objective division of truth that the later period made impressive advances. Two embracing principles, the theory of the transference and equivalence of all types of energy, and the doctrine of the natural descent of species were made the foundation of a fresh Hobbesian materialism. The new philosophy of the seventeenth century had once more culminated in the conception of reality as a completely unified physics of motion and matter, in which minds, societies, and spiritual values were regarded as by-products of the vast mechanical order. During the earlier period theologians and religious naturalists had drawn upon the evidence of adaptation and design in the world for proof of divine intention. And the law of gravitational attraction was shown to imply the wise direction of Providence. In the later portion of this phase of thought the abolition of the final or purposive note from nature, upon which the English critics of Descartes had fastened, appeared to be established by the teaching of Darwin; and many thoughtful men frankly discarded the ancient dramatic philosophy of Christian thought and embraced the creed of evolutionary materialism. In spite of efforts by scientific moralists on the one hand and by literal theologians on the other, the religious and the scientific creeds remained apart from one another.

The profound demand for a rational interpretation of experience that would respond to the impulse of religion and offer support to the Christian creed was met by the strong advance of German idealism. The Hegelian thinkers rejected the postulates of the classical English philosophy that was still being maintained in their day. They denied the antithesis between reality and the work of the mind, between the matter and the form of knowledge. And they declared that knowledge of particular and changing items required a permanent and continuous consciousness by relation to which the items are apprehended. Reality is the perfect unity in variety, the indwelling self-consciousness of nature that is confusedly present to thought from the beginning to the end of its quest. The story of speculation returns, with salient differences, to the dialectical way.

Our sketch has borne us from the cloister-thinking of the Saxon age to the secular naturalism of the modern epoch. The scientific scheme of ideas, when it is related to the older phases of thought, is recent. It is barely two and a half centuries old; and its first Newtonian form underwent far-reaching transformation soon after the point at which our survey closes. It has long been fashionable to restrict attention to the classic period of scientific philosophy, and to exclude from the tale of thought in England the thousand years of discussion that preceded the publication of the *Novum Organum*. We perceive the tradition of English philosophy with contracted and parochial vision when we limit our gaze to the period of Bacon and Locke; when we ignore the whole speculation of the Renaissance and of the medieval schools. We cannot understand the modern revolution in rational beliefs without acquaintance with the scholastic principles from which they sprang. And throughout the earlier cycles of thought England bred groups of scholars who made notable contributions to the metaphysic and natural philosophy of the West. I have sought in this brief outline to throw a bridge between the new outlook and the older theories of reality, to trace some of the chief stages of discussion in this country, and to recall the names of some of the thinkers who explored the perennial problems of experience. Many philosophers who were eminent in their day have been passed over, many phases of thought have been ignored. But a more detailed account of reflection in England must at least show the historic continuity of the modern epoch with the greater expanses of the past. It must look back to the inquiries of Hooker and Pecock, to the treatises of Bradwardine, Peckham, and Grosseteste, to the *Metalogicon* of John Salisbury, to the disciples of Anselm, and to the *Commentaries* of the Venerable Bede.

INDEX OF NAMES

PRINTED IN GREAT BRITAIN
AT THE UNIVERSITY PRESS, OXFORD
BY CHARLES BATEY, PRINTER TO THE UNIVERSITY

Date Due

JUN 3 0 '55		
OCT 2 5 1958		
MAY 2 5 1959		
JUN 1 9 1959		
DEPARTMENT		
FEB 5 '62		
MY 31 '62		
JA 1 0 '63		
MY 2 '63		
DE 1 0 '65		
FEB 2 1966 DEPT.		
DE 8 '66		
FE 6 '67		
JA 3 '68		
Ⓖ	PRINTED	IN U. S. A.	